# Signs
# of the
# SPIRIT

*world council of churches*

# Signs
# of the
# SPIRIT

official
report
seventh assembly

Canberra, Australia, 7-20 February 1991

*edited by michael kinnamon*

WCC Publications, Geneva
Wm. B. Eerdmans, Grand Rapids

The report of the assembly is also available in French, German and Spanish, with a personal introduction by the editor of that language edition.

Cover design: Edwin Hassink

Cover photo: WCC/Peter Williams
All photos by Peter Williams unless otherwise identified

ISBN 2-8254-1000-4 (WCC)
ISBN 0-8028-0628-7 (Eerdmans)

Printed in Switzerland

Now there are varieties of gifts, but the same Spirit; (...) To one is given through the Spirit the utterance of wisdom, and to another the utterance of knowledge according to the same Spirit, to another faith by the same Spirit, to another gifts of healing by the one Spirit, to another the working of miracles, to another prophecy, to another the discernment of spirits, to another various kinds of tongues, to another the interpretation of tongues. All these are activated by one and the same Spirit, who allots to each one individually just as the Spirit chooses. For just as the body is one and has many members, and all the members of the body, though many, are one body, so it is with Christ. For in the one Spirit we were all baptized into one body—Jews or Greeks, slaves or free—and we were all made to drink of one Spirit.

1 Cor. 12:4, 8-13 (NRSV)

It is not in [our] power to banish sin and death from the earth, to create the unity of the Holy Catholic Church, to conquer the hosts of Satan. But it is within the power of God.... As those who wait in confidence and joy for their deliverance, let us give ourselves to those tasks which lie to our hands, and so set up signs....

Amsterdam Assembly, 1948

Let anyone who has an ear listen to what the Spirit is saying to the churches.

Rev. 2:7

O, Giver of life,
who brought all things into being,
sustain and replenish your whole creation
that it may reflect your glory.

Come, Holy Spirit,
fill all life with your radiance.

O, Spirit of Truth,
who convinces the world of sin,
consume, as a mighty fire,
the powers of evil that bind your people
and set us free to walk in your light.

Come, Holy Spirit,
and illumine our hearts and minds.

O, Spirit of unity,
judge, restore and call us again.
Bestow on us the gifts
that build us up into your people.

Come, Holy Spirit,
and light the flame of love
on the altar of our hearts.

O, Holy Spirit,
transform and sanctify us,
that we and all people
may have life in all its fullness.

Come, Holy Spirit,
renew the whole creation.

Litany used at the Canberra assembly

# Contents

# *Preface*

Assemblies of the World Council of Churches are crucial events for the ecumenical movement. Our growing together is marked by such names as Amsterdam, New Delhi, Uppsala, Vancouver, each one signalling new emphases and challenges in our attempts to follow the leading of God's Spirit towards deeper unity and more faithful mission.

I am pleased to commend the official report of the WCC's seventh assembly which was held 7-20 February 1991 in the capital city of Australia, Canberra. Each assembly leaves a legacy of reports and addresses that deserve serious study in the churches. But an assembly can never be reduced to such documentation. That is why this volume also includes a personal overview by our editor as well as lively accounts of the major plenary debates. Taken together, these materials provide a comprehensive record of "Canberra".

At this point, one can only speculate on what will be remembered from the seventh assembly. Its theme, "Come, Holy Spirit — Renew the Whole Creation", was not only the first assemby theme to focus on the activity of the Spirit but also the first to take the form of a prayer. The Australian setting called the churches' attention to an often-neglected part of the world. At Canberra the church in China rejoined the global fellowship, and startling developments in South Africa and Europe were celebrated and discussed. And, of course, Canberra will be remembered as gathering under the shadow of war.

This assembly also placed enormous challenges on the agenda of the WCC and its member churches. The question of the gospel's relation to culture was raised more directly and pointedly than ever before. While the need for inculturation is widely accepted, the forms it must take and the limits that must be set continue to be controversial. And questions of "participation" — of women, youth, laity, and the differently-abled —

cry out for further attention. So do questions raised about the limits of participation.

Our thanks go to Michael Kinnamon, a former member of the WCC staff, for his work in editing this official report in English. We are also grateful to the editors of the other language editions, Walter Müller-Römheld (German), Marthe Westphal (French), and Hugo Ortega (Spanish).

I hope that this volume will be given careful consideration as a guide to future ecumenical work. It is also my sincere wish, however, that this report, and the assembly it records, will be seen as a witness to the One God of all creation, Father, Son and Holy Spirit.

May we all be enabled to look for and to appropriate the signs of the Spirit in our churches and our life together as a fellowship of churches.

EMILIO CASTRO
General Secretary
World Council of Churches

# *Come, Holy Spirit:*
# *The Assembly Message*

The World Council of Churches is a "fellowship of churches which confess the Lord Jesus Christ as God and Saviour according to the scriptures and therefore seek to fulfill together their common calling to the glory of the one God, Father, Son and Holy Spirit". We have gathered together as the seventh assembly of the World Council of Churches. Meeting in Canberra, Australia, from 7 to 20 February 1991, we send greetings to all churches, Christians and peoples.

We were welcomed by the Aboriginal people of the land. Their understanding of land as being integral to their very life has had an impact on our thinking. We were also welcomed by the churches, the government and the people of Australia. We express our deep gratitude to all of them for their hospitality, and for the assistance they extended to us in a great variety of ways.

The theme of this assembly is the invocation "Come, Holy Spirit — Renew the Whole Creation". In worship, reflection and life together, we sought to understand the hopes and challenges of our times through the four related prayers:

Giver of Life — Sustain your Creation!
Spirit of Truth — Set us Free!
Spirit of Unity — Reconcile your People!
Holy Spirit — Transform and Sanctify Us!

We rejoice in the diversity of cultures, races and traditions represented at the assembly, and we give thanks to God for the many expressions of the Christian faith and for the growing sense of unity amidst this diversity. We praise God for the many local developments in ecumenism.

At this assembly we have been stirred by the manifold forms of prayer, spirituality, theology and Christian commitment to which we have been exposed; we wish to share this enrichment with our churches and with people everywhere. The participation of women has been a reality at the assembly, and we commend once again the Ecumenical Decade of the Churches in Solidarity with Women. We recognize the crucial importance of the ecumenical youth movement and look forward to the global ecumenical gathering of youth and students in 1992. We are grateful for the witness made by differently-abled persons and urge the churches to provide for their full and active participation in the churches' life and mission.

The presence of representatives of other world religions as guests at the assembly reminds us of the need to respect the image of God in all people, to accept one another as neighbours and to affirm our common responsibility with them for all of God's creation, including humanity.

We meet at a time of growing threats to creation and human life. At this time when our fragile environment is in crisis, we recognize anew that human beings are not the lords of creation but part of an integrated and interdependent whole, and we resolve once again to work for the sustainability of all creation. Amid the oppression to which many indigenous peoples, minorities and peoples of colour are subjected, we pledge support for and solidarity with marginalized people everywhere. In the face of the growing gap between rich and poor, we commit ourselves to work for justice for all.

At a time of conflicts in various parts of the world, and particularly in the Gulf, we appeal for an immediate end to hostilities, and for a just resolution of conflicts in all countries of the world.

Many divisions still prevail in our world. Some are economic and political. People, particularly many women, children, youth and the differently-abled, experience brokenness of relationships and are subjected to various kinds of injustices. The Holy Spirit draws churches into relationships of love and commitment. The Holy Spirit calls the churches to an increased commitment to the search for visible unity and more effective mission. We urge the churches to heed the call of the Spirit, to seek new and reconciled relationships between peoples, and to use the gifts of all their members.

We ourselves, the churches in council, still experience brokenness. Reconciliation between churches remains incomplete. However, in the ecumenical movement, we have been enabled to come out of isolation into a committed fellowship: we experience a growing responsibility for each other, in joy and in pain, and under the guidance of the Holy Spirit we seek ways to be more accountable to one another and to our Lord who prayed that we "may be one" (John 17:20). But we also recognize that the fullness of reconciliation is a gift of God and that we can appropriate it only insofar as the Holy Spirit transforms and sanctifies us.

God and humankind are reconciled by the costly sacrifice we see in the cross of Christ. Our appropriation of reconciliation and our acceptance of the ministry of reconciliation (2 Cor. 5:18) are also costly. Through our acceptance of the ministry of reconciliation, we become a missionary people, not in that sense of dominating over peoples and nations which has all too often characterized missionary work, but in the sense of sharing God's own mission of bringing all humanity into communion with God through Christ in the power of the Spirit, sharing our faith and our resources with all people.

We pray that the Spirit of God may lead Christians to a renewed vision of God's rule, so that we may be empowered to assume the stewardship of "the mystery of the gospel" (Eph. 6:19). We pray that we may be enabled to bear the "fruit of the Spirit" and thus witness to God's rule of love and truth, righteousness and justice and freedom, reconciliation and peace.

We are convinced that to repent, to be forgiven by God and to forgive one another are essential elements in such a renewed vision of God's rule on earth as in heaven. Responding to the rapid and radical changes taking place in many parts of the world, we commit ourselves to sustained action that will express the new perspectives which we have gained in our ecumenical journey and during our time together, on issues such as world debt, militarism, the ecosystem and racism.

We believe that the Holy Spirit brings hope even amidst all that seems to militate against hope, and gives strength to resolve the conflicts which divide human communities. Repentance must begin with ourselves, for even in this assembly we have become aware of our own failures in understanding, sensitivity and love. As we commit ourselves to continuing repentance, so we call all people to share in that commitment and to pray for the renewing power of the Holy Spirit to renew in us, personally and corporately, the image of God.

As we continue on our journey to the unity of the church and of humankind under God's rule, we pray, with people around the world:

Come, Holy Spirit,

Come, teacher of the humble, judge of the arrogant.

Come, hope of the poor, refreshment of the weary...

rescuer of the shipwrecked.
Come, most splendid adornment of all living beings,
the sole salvation of all who are mortal.
Come, Holy Spirit, have mercy on us,
imbue our lowliness with your power.
Meet our weakness with the fullness of your grace.
Come, Holy Spirit — Renew the Whole Creation.

# 1. Canberra 1991:
# A Personal Overview
# and Introduction

Canberra, in the language of the Aboriginal people of Australia, means "meeting place". From 7 to 20 February 1991, Canberra was indeed a global meeting place as representatives of over 300 churches, from more than 100 countries, gathered for the World Council of Churches' seventh assembly. This assembly, like its predecessors, bore witness through an astonishing array of languages and cultures to the churches' common confession of the Triune God and to their commitment to "stay together" despite all that would pull them apart.

Several images come quickly to mind when I think of the setting for the seventh assembly. I recall, for example, the blue kangaroo footprints painted on the sidewalks of downtown Canberra to mark the two-kilometre route between the Australian National University, where most of the participants lived, and the National Convention Centre, where plenary sessions were held. I think also of the canvas shoulder bags that grew heavier by the day thanks to the work of numerous drafting committees. Decorating the bags was the assembly logo depicting a dove or a flame, biblical symbols of the Holy Spirit, but also leaving the impression of movement as the winds of the Spirit fill the sails of the ecumenical ship.

Another image is of paper fans contributed by Korean participants — a much appreciated gift considering the heat of the Australian summer. One journalist remarked that the un-airconditioned plenary hall, filled with waving fans, looked like "a field of butterflies".

And then there were the pieces of art: the "circle painting" by Aboriginal artist Miriam Rose Ungunmerr, representing people from the corners of the world bonded by the sacrificial love of the cross, which hung near the platform in the worship tent; the huge painting in colours of the Australian landscape, by Australian painter John Coburn, which served as backdrop in the plenary hall... One of my favourite images is of two "cloth mosaics" made up of more than 1,000 patches sewn, woven or painted by parish groups from churches belonging to the Australian Council of Churches. Designs on the patches grew out of local Bible study dealing with the assembly's theme: "Come, Holy Spirit — Renew the Whole Creation".

Just as it helps to have mental images of the setting, so it may be useful to have in mind certain dominant issues when reading the materials that follow. Many issues stand out: the question of intercommunion or eucharistic hospitality, raised powerfully by the WCC general secretary Emilio Castro in his report to the assembly; new developments in South Africa and Europe; the return to the WCC fellowship of the Protestant Church in China; ecological destruction; the financial situation of the WCC. In my opinion, however, four issues or concerns claimed special attention:

— the rights of indigenous peoples, especially the Aboriginal people of Australia;
— the churches' response to the war in the Persian Gulf;
— the relationship between gospel and culture;
— the tension between demands for "participation", especially of those formerly excluded from decision-making, and existing patterns of leadership in the churches.

The debates over these and other issues ranged from exciting to frustrating — at times even chaotic. It remains to be seen whether they may be regarded as signs of the unpredictable Spirit of God at work among the churches.

## 1.1. THE TASK

Official delegates of the WCC's member churches have met in assembly once every six to eight years since the World Council was inaugurated at Amsterdam in 1948. An assembly is the highest governing and decision-making body of the WCC. As such, it is responsible for assessing work done by the Council since the previous assembly, providing policy guidelines for the coming years, and electing members of the WCC's presidium and central committee.

Assemblies, however, are also occasions for celebration and witness. By the very act of coming together, the churches reaffirm the covenant they have made with one another. Through worship together, they show forth their common confession of the Triune God. In public statements together, they bring this confession to bear on pressing political and social issues of the day.

In all of these ways, assemblies are intended to help the World Council of Churches fulfill several functions and goals. These are summarized in the following litany of common commitment used during the opening plenary session at Canberra:

Leader: We are constituted to call the churches to the goal of visible unity in one faith and in one eucharistic fellowship, expressed in worship and in common life in Christ.

People: We commit ourselves to one another, and to the goal of unity that God wills for us.

Leader: We are called to facilitate the common witness of the churches in each place and in all places, to support the churches in their witness, to foster the renewal of the churches in unity, worship, mission and service.

People: We commit ourselves to support one another, and to seek to fulfill our common calling.

Leader: We have come together into this fellowship to express the common concern of the churches in the service of human need, the breaking down of barriers between peoples, and the promotion of one human family in justice and peace.

People: We commit ourselves to stand together, and to grow together in God's service in the world.

## 1.2. THE PARTICIPANTS

Another image: delegates in cassocks and T-shirts, clerical collars and saris, Western-style suits and African *agbádás boubous* engaged in animated conversation during the breaks for coffee and tea. It is almost impossible to describe the human diversity at Canberra. The following statistical profile, while important, only hints at the richness of such a gathering.

Participants in the seventh assembly included:
— 852 voting delegates chosen by member churches to speak and vote on their behalf;

— 5 presidents of the WCC, elected by the Vancouver assembly in 1983, and 22 members of the outgoing central committee (in addition to those serving as delegates);
— 21 delegated representatives from associate member churches (generally churches too small to meet full membership requirements);
— 74 delegated representatives of those councils of churches which are associated with the WCC and of its Commission on World Mission and Evangelism, of world ecumenical organizations that collaborate with the WCC, and of various Christian world communions;
— 73 advisers invited by the WCC executive or central committee because of their particular experience or expertise;
— 23 delegated observers from the Roman Catholic Church and other non-member churches with which the WCC has a working relationship;
— 45 specially invited guests;
— 138 observers representing councils of churches, ecumenical or international organizations, churches or other religious bodies;
— 172 stewards, young people serving as volunteers to assist the assembly in its work, from 84 countries;
— 182 members of the WCC staff;
— 151 coopted staff, including more than 80 interpreters and translators;
— 417 accredited members of the press.

When the approximately 1,100 accredited visitors, 774 day visitors, and numerous local volunteers are taken into account, over 4,000 persons a day participated one way or another in the assembly at Canberra.

The "guest" category included ten persons from faiths other than Christianity. Prof. Is-Haq Oloyede, a Muslim from Nigeria, offered greetings to the assembly on their behalf. These persons, said WCC president Lois Wilson in a brief response, "are more than guests. They are companions on the way as we seek a more authentic human existence."

*The delegates*

The number of delegates available to each member church is determined by the WCC's central committee. Nine hundred and forty-six delegate slots were announced before the assembly; many could not come, due at least in part to the war in the Gulf.

The central committee had also established goals for delegates to Canberra — 40 percent women, 20 percent youth and 50 percent laypersons. The actual percentages, however, were 35 percent women (compared to 31 percent at Vancouver in 1983), 46 percent lay (the same as Vancouver), and 11 percent youth. Of the delegates to Vancouver, 13 percent were youth, but that was based on an age limit of 30. Since then, the central committee has set 27 as the limit for the youth category. If the old limit had been in effect, 17 percent of the delegates to Canberra would have been considered as youth.

The Credentials Committee reported to the assembly that 84 churches with more than one delegate did not conform to the central committee guidelines. Youth participants were particularly outspoken in their disappointment. The "message" from the pre-assembly youth event (see section 7.4) says that "... we are often deprived of freedom by our churches which render us voiceless, powerless and marginalized in the name of 'experience' and 'knowledge'". Differently-abled persons also spoke out in plenary about the barriers to their full participation at Canberra and called upon the WCC to recognize them in official criteria for the selection of future assembly delegations.

In terms of regional distribution, delegates to Canberra came from Africa (132), Asia (141), the Caribbean (13), Europe (301), Latin America (26), the Middle East (67), North America (144), and the Pacific (28). Confessionally, there were 98 Anglicans, 36 Baptists, 12 Disciples, 125 Lutherans, 96 Methodists, 12 Moravians, 130 Eastern Orthodox, 47 Oriental Orthodox, 170 Reformed and 84 from United churches. Smaller numbers came from Brethren, Friends, Hussite, Mar Thoma, Mennonite, Old Catholic, Assyrian Orthodox, Pentecostal, and various independent churches.

Special mention should be made of those delegates and other participants who identified themselves as "evangelicals". "We felt welcomed in the dialogue," they wrote in an open letter; but, "despite such a sincere commitment to take more seriously that major segment of the worldwide church which those with evangelical perspectives represent, evangelicals remain under-represented at Canberra..." The full text of their letter is found in section 7.8 of this report.

*China welcomed*

Between Vancouver and Canberra, 31 denominations became full or associate members of the WCC. Six of these, including the Dutch Reformed Mission Church in South Africa, were officially received into membership during the opening plenary.

The most dramatic addition, however, came at the beginning of the assembly's final week when the China Christian Council (CCC), the "post-denominational" Protestant church in the People's Republic, was unanimously accepted as the 317th member of the WCC. In remarks to the assembly, Bishop K.H. Ting, president of the CCC, stated that "our membership will in no way impair the independence and integrity of any church outside mainland China" — an apparent reference to the Presbyterian Church in Taiwan (PCT). During the acceptance ceremony, Rev. C.M. Kao, widely-respected leader of the PCT, came forward to welcome and embrace Bishop Ting. It was one of those special moments when the churches, through the WCC, give evidence of the Spirit's work of reconciliation across the divisions of the world.

*The cloud of witnesses*

Greetings and messages of inspiration were received from numerous church leaders and international organizations. Three that received particular attention (and are included in this volume, 7.2) were from the Ecumenical Patriarch Dimitrios I, Patriarch Alexy II of Moscow and All Russia, and Pope John Paul II. The WCC has a close working relationship with the Roman Catholic Church. The papal statement called particular attention to the document *Baptism, Eucharist and Ministry*, produced by the WCC's Faith and Order Commission which includes a number of Roman Catholic scholars. Such work, wrote the pope, is "surely a sign of the Holy Spirit drawing us closer to the unity which Christ wishes for his disciples".

The absence of other friends was noted with sorrow, and gratitude for their service. Since Vancouver, several former leaders of the WCC and the entire ecumenical movement had died, including the Council's first two general secretaries, Willem A. Visser 't Hooft and Eugene Carson Blake.[1] Dr Visser 't Hooft is widely regarded as the outstanding figure of the modern ecumenical movement. He was largely instrumental in shaping the structure and vision of the WCC and served as its first general secretary from 1948 to 1966. His successor, Dr Blake, guided the Council during the turbulent period of 1966-72. Their passing symbolizes the major transition in ecumenical leadership evident throughout the assembly. Others remembered included Dr Charles Ranson, the last general secretary of the International Missionary Council; former WCC presidents, Dr Martin Niemöller, Archbishop Michael Ramsey, Dr John Coventry Smith, Dr Cynthia Wedel, Bishop Alphaeus Zulu and General

---

[1] See "Willem A. Visser 't Hooft, Eugene Carson Blake", *The Ecumenical Review*, Vol. 38, No. 2, 1986.

T.B. Simatupang; former deputy or assistant general secretaries Dr Robert Mackie, Bishop Stephen Neill, Dr Norman Goodall and Mr Victor E.W. Hayward; former vice-moderator Metropolitan Meliton of Chalcedon; former staff directors Prof. Nils Ehrenström, Prof. Nikos Nissiotis and Prof. Hans-Heinrich Wolf; and Dr Kathleen Bliss, a leading ecumenist right from the start.

## 1.3. THE WORLD CONTEXT

It is hard to argue with the assessment of Australian prime minister Bob Hawke, that no previous World Council assembly "has been held at a more historic moment in the unfolding of world events than this assembly in Canberra". WCC general secretary Emilio Castro spoke in his address (4.3) of "the acceleration of history". "Four years ago, when the theme for this assembly was chosen, we could hardly have imagined the kind of far-reaching changes that have since then overtaken us. Ideologies have collapsed and barriers broken down. Winds of change have swept over Eastern Europe and South Africa. But the end of the Cold War has not ushered in a new era of peace."

The war in the Gulf was barely three weeks old when the assembly was convened on 7 February. Several church leaders had recommended that the assembly be postponed due to the crisis, and this option was kept under consideration until the final days before the assembly opened. Others contended, however, that this was precisely the time when the world church needed to meet and speak a word of peace and hope.

The war did not, as many had feared, overshadow all else on the agenda; but it did provide a constant, sobering backdrop to the gathering. Following the afternoon plenary on Saturday, 9 February, assembly participants and local supporters held a silent march through downtown streets to the worship tent on the university campus. The procession was led by children carrying a large ball painted to look like the earth. Other marchers carried signs saying "Spirit of Peace — Reconcile Your People". Most participants observed a fast from lunch on Saturday until after the celebration of the Lima liturgy on Sunday morning, and many took part, during the block of time allocated to their region, in an all-night prayer vigil for peace.

The assembly's attitude towards the war was clear from the opening address by prime minister Hawke. The delegates sat quietly while Mr Hawke spoke of Australia's support for allied military operations; but they gave sustained applause to WCC president, Metropolitan Paulos Mar Gregorios of India, when he suggested in a response to the prime minister that, while nobody questioned the need for Iraq to leave Kuwait, "many people hold grave doubts about the means taken to make Iraq do that".

The major debate on the war came in response to the report of the Public Issues Committee and is described in section 5.1 of this volume. There were, however, other opportunities to hear the mind of the participants.

At a special hearing on the war, Lebanese Archbishop Aram Keshi-shian clearly spoke for the vast majority when he stated that the war "is neither holy nor just". Vocal opposition to the demand for an immediate and unconditional cease fire came chiefly from members of the Church of England delegation. "Do we want", asked Bishop Tom Butler, "to feel good or do good?" Calling for an unconditional cease fire may feel good, but it will leave serious issues unresolved. More constructive would be support for UN resolutions linking a cease fire to Iraqi withdrawal. Other speakers warned that the conflict threatened to inflame Christian-Muslim tensions in various parts of the world and to divert precious resources from the poor. The most frequently quoted line at Canberra came from an earlier interview with the general secretary of the Middle East Council of Churches, Mr Gabriel Habib. Asked which side of the war God is on, Mr Habib answered: "God is on the side of those who are suffering."

## 1.4. THE AUSTRALIAN CONTEXT

The Canberra assembly was shaped not only by the times in which it was held but also by the place. Participants got a dramatic, colourful glimpse of Australian history and contemporary society through a special evening programme entitled "Gathering Under the Southern Cross". An estimated 10,000 people watched the presentation of music, drama and video in a park in the centre of Canberra. The production took fifteen months of planning and six months of rehearsals by more than 1,000 actors and singers.

Delegates got a more first-hand exposure through parish visits scheduled for the assembly's final weekend. Many visited congregations in the Canberra area, but others travelled by planes, buses and cars to such places as Bendigo, Westernport and Wagga Wagga — all in the southeastern corner of the world's sixth largest nation.

Aboriginal people comprise only one to two percent of the Australian population (approximately 17 million), but their concerns and culture received considerable attention from the WCC. The report from pre-assembly visits to two Aboriginal communities described conditions as "not just horrific but genocidal". The WCC teams spoke of a people demoralized by political exclusion, a demoralization evidenced by alcohol abuse, a high rate of police detention, high drop-out rates in schools, the loss of language and culture, and inadequate opportunities for employment and training.

A major theme was sounded during the opening plenary. Anglican Bishop Arthur Malcolm, himself an Aborigine, welcomed the delegates and then urged them to "share the dreamings of my people in obtaining respect for them and for getting some type of repayments for use of their land". This issue was picked up the following week in a plenary on "Land Rights and Identity". That presentation used slides, video and Aboriginal speakers to emphasize that the colonial notion of Australia as *terra nullius* ("land belonging to no one") was patently wrong. Up to 700 tribes — with developed systems of religious, political and economic life — lived throughout the continent when the British arrived in 1788.

The plenary ended with another of those miraculous, unexpected moments of reconciliation which, if matched by action, may be a sign of the Spirit. The Aboriginal band, Yothu Yindi, had just finished playing on a stage filled with representatives of indigenous peoples from around the world when Gregor Henderson, general secretary of the Uniting Church in Australia, came to the front. "Aboriginal sisters and brothers," he called out, "will you allow us non-Aboriginal Australians to join you in the journey to bring about a new, just Australia — please?" His request was met with applause and many persons came forward.

I have heard several participants say that their most vivid memories from Canberra involve demonstrations of Aboriginal culture: painted dancers, circle paintings, the didgeridoo (a long pipe blown at the beginning of each morning's worship), smoke from burning gum leaves through which worshippers passed at the opening service (a traditional Aboriginal rite of cleansing). But I suspect that participants will also long recall the moving apology made by a local organizer of the peace march.

There was a misunderstanding over whether the children or a group of Aboriginal people were to lead the procession. When the Aboriginal group was asked to give way, they moved completely to the rear — angry and humiliated. The next morning's apology was a powerful reminder that two centuries of oppression and mistrust are not easily overcome, even through carefully planned efforts at solidarity.

## 1.5. THE THEME

For the first time the theme of a WCC assembly focused on the third person of the Trinity, and for the first time the theme took the form of a prayer: "Come, Holy Spirit — Renew the Whole Creation". The participants at Canberra seemed to find such a theme particularly appropriate for our times. Various materials prepared in advance of the assembly[2] spoke of renewed longing for spiritual values, especially in the West where it is increasingly clear that material well-being alone does not constitute life in all its fullness. There is also growing awareness, however, that the whole of creation is threatened by the poverty, injustice, war and pollution that mark so much of life on our planet. And there is an increasing realization that *our* attempts to fix things are, by themselves, woefully inadequate. God alone is the source of creation. God alone is the source of our unity as Christians. It is to God, ever present through the Spirit, that we must turn in prayer if we would be renewed.

Several of these ideas were developed by Patriarch Parthenios of Alexandria in a paper (see 2.2) presented to the Canberra participants by an Orthodox colleague during the assembly's second day (Patriarch Parthenios was unable to attend the assembly because of the war in the Gulf). "There is no church, no creature, no human person", wrote the patriarch, "apart from the Spirit." One sign of the Spirit's activity is the

---

[2] Among the preparatory materials were several publications, including a book of six Bible studies on the theme and sub-themes; *Energy for Life* by Krister Stendhal, also on the theme; *Let the Spirit Speak to the Churches*, which was meant as a guide for the study of the theme and the issues; a book on the Australian religious experience entitled *Land of the Spirit?*; a selection of articles from the July 1989, April 1990 and July-October 1990 issues of *The Ecumenical Review* which were all devoted to theological reflections on the Canberra theme, under the title *To the Wind of God's Spirit*; and six "audiovisual prayers" on the theme in which music and images join with words.

search for unity that draws the churches together in the WCC. "May we realize the pain of our separation. It wounds Christ. We hinder the Holy Spirit's action and prevent his working with us. In the struggle for union there is room for neither neutrality nor standing aside." Finally, however, "our goal is the unity of the world. Such unity", he concluded, "is not alien to the work of the Holy Spirit and the church. The Spirit blows where he wills, and we have no right to restrict his movement and his breathing, to bind him with fences and barbed wire."

The theme, however, also raises a number of questions on which Christians have long disagreed, including "How do we discern the true activity of the Holy Spirit in the midst of 'the spirits' of the world?" This question became a focus of debate at Canberra thanks to an electrifying presentation on the theme by Prof. Chung Hyun Kyung of the Presbyterian Church in South Korea (see 2.3). Her entrance into the Convention Centre's Royal Theatre, following the reading of the Patriarch's address, was accompanied by sixteen Korean and two Aboriginal dancers, complete with gongs, bells, drums, clap sticks and candles. The address itself began with an invocation of the spirits of an eclectic collection of martyrs, from Hagar to the students in Tiananmen Square, from "the spirit of Earth, Air, and Water" to "our brother Jesus, tortured and killed on the cross". After setting fire to this list and letting the ashes drift to the ceiling, Prof. Chung spoke of Korea as a land of "spirits full of *Han*". *Han* refers to the "grudge", the anguished cry, of those who have died with their misery unappeased. "These Han-ridden spirits in our people's history have been agents through whom the Holy Spirit has spoken of her compassion and wisdom for life. Without hearing the cries of these spirits," she continued, "we cannot hear the voice of the Holy Spirit. I hope the presence of all our ancestors' spirits here with us shall not make you uncomfortable. For us they are the icons of the Holy Spirit..."

Reactions to the address were, to say the least, mixed. "There was passionate applause", said one delegate, "but there was also passionate silence." A word frequently heard during the next few days was "syncretism". "You can't just take something that isn't Christian", said Dr Constance Tarasar of the Orthodox Church in America, "and name it Christian." Statements by Orthodox and evangelical participants in particular stressed the need for serious ecumenical study in order to develop criteria for determining the limits of theological diversity in this radically pluralistic age. "We must guard", said the Orthodox statement (see 7.7), "against a tendency to substitute a "private" spirit, the spirit of the world or other spirits for the Holy Spirit who proceeds from the Father and rests in the Son. Our tradition is rich in respect for local and national cultures, but we find it impossible to invoke the spirits of "earth, air, water and sea creatures".

Prof. Chung responded to the swirl of controversy by challenging her critics to a public debate. A debate as such never took place, but a special plenary session was called to deal with the topic of the gospel and inculturation. Nearly twenty speakers took their three minutes at the microphone. Some contended that the Holy Spirit always points to Jesus Christ and that the church's role is to Christianize the cultures in which it is placed. Others called for an acceptance of "new theologies" which sought to make the gospel relevant to various cultures. The final word was Prof. Chung's. Beneath all the talk of syncretism, she said, is the question of power. Western, male theologians have set the limits of the Spirit's work. "We have been listening to your intellectualism for 2,000 years... please listen to us." "Third-world theologies are", she maintained, "the new paradigm, the new wine that can't be put in your wineskins.... yes, we are dangerous, but it is through such danger that the Holy Spirit can renew the church."

This debate will surely be with the WCC for years to come as it struggles, in the words of a mandate from the Vancouver assembly, to develop a "vital and coherent theology" capable of creatively integrating more "classical" and more "contextual" approaches.

## 1.6. THE PROGRAMME

The assembly did its work in three primary ways:

1. The whole body gathered regularly in *plenary sessions* in order to hear presentations on the theme and various issues facing the churches and in order to deal with reports and other items of business.

2. All official participants were assigned to one of four *sections*, each section focused on one of the sub-themes of the assembly:
— Section I:   Giver of Life — Sustain your Creation!
— Section II:  Spirit of Truth — Set us Free!
— Section III: Spirit of Unity — Reconcile your People!
— Section IV:  Holy Spirit — Transform and Sanctify Us!

At previous assemblies, "sections" or "issue groups" gave attention to current concerns on the ecumenical agenda. Their deliberations were set within the general framework of the assembly's theme, but did not necessarily bear a direct relationship to it. At Canberra, however, special effort was made to integrate pressing issues of the day with reflections on the theme and sub-themes through the work of the sections. What, for example, does a focus on the reconciling activity of the Holy Spirit say to us about the unity we seek? What does our confession of the Spirit as "the giver of life" say to us in the face of threats to creation in this era?

Each section was further divided into sub-sections of approximately thirty persons. It was in these groups that the most intensive discussions, as well as Bible study, took place. Statements drafted by the sub-sections formed the basis of section reports that were received by the assembly during its final week (see 3.2-3.5).

3. The assembly elected some 200 delegates to serve on nine *committees*:

— Business Committee: functioned as the steering committee for the work of the assembly as a whole;
— Nominations Committee: proposed persons for election as presidents and as members of the central committee;
— Credentials Committee: recommended action on questions related to the accreditation of delegates;
— Programme Policy Committee: recommended policy guidelines for shaping the programme of the WCC in the coming years (see 4.5);
— Public Issues Committee: produced draft statements on major issues of international concern (see 5.2-5.9);
— Message Committee: prepared the text of the assembly's official message;
— Report Committee: prepared a report on the work of the assembly, in particular synthesizing the work of the sections (see 6.2);
— Reference Committee: recommended action on the reports of the moderator and general secretary, on relationships with member churches and various ecumenical partners, and on other matters referred to it for consideration (see 4.4);
— Finance Committee: considered the WCC's general financial situation and recommended actions for dealing with it (see 4.6).

*Week I (Thursday 7 February-Sunday 10 February)*
It is, of course, impossible to divide the work of such a complex gathering into neat compartments. Still, it may help to sense the "flow" of the assembly by noting that its programme (see 7.1) falls roughly into three parts.

In addition to worship, the first four days were marked by opening ceremonies, presentations dealing with the theme and sub-themes (see 3.1), including the report of the general secretary (see 4.3), and special activities related to the war (most notably, the peace march and vigil described above).

Two dramatic presentations were also part of the assembly's first weekend. "The Spirit Speaks to the Churches" included sketches of Christians attempting to discern the guidance of the Holy Spirit in their lives. Should Christians stay and witness in the Middle East despite enormous risk? How should the church in Australia respond to AIDS? What is the role of the church today in the former German Democratic Republic?

The second presentation, this one in the worship tent, focused on themes raised by the WCC's programme "Justice, Peace and the Integrity of Creation" (JPIC) and was led — through drama, dance and song — by children from Canberra. The images were gripping: children playing while wearing masks to filter out pollution in Czechoslovakia, children "playing" at real combat in the Middle East.

*Week II (Monday 11 February-Sunday 17 February)*

During the second week, the assembly settled into a rhythm of section and sub-section work in the mornings and programme-oriented plenaries in the afternoons. Plenaries included "Covenanting for Life" on the challenge to the churches posed by JPIC, "Without a Vision People Will Perish" on progress towards visible church unity, "Land Rights and Identity" on the struggle of the Aboriginal people in Australia, "Churches in Solidarity with Women" on issues related to the Ecumenical Decade of the Churches in Solidarity with Women initiated by the WCC in 1988, and "Sharing Our Life — Towards New Community".

The plenary on sharing is a good example of the attempt, made in each of these presentations, to put a human face on WCC themes and programmes. Between Vancouver and Canberra, three world meetings sponsored by the WCC explored different facets of the ecumenical concern for mission and service.[3] This plenary attempted to highlight and integrate the work of these conferences by way of representative stories.

---

[3] "Diakonia 2000: Called to Be Neighbours" (Larnaca 1986), "Sharing Life in a World Community" (El Escorial 1987), and "Your Will Be Done — Mission in Christ's Way" (San Antonio 1989).

One video story told of rubbish collectors in Brazil who organized themselves into a basic Christian community. In another segment, South African Christians described a 1988 church-initiated boycott of white-manipulated elections. One participant warned that "apartheid, sick as it is, is still alive". A third story, this one again on video, told of a small congregation in the USA whose members offered sanctuary to Central Americans fleeing persecution, even at the cost of their own imprisonment. A fourth described efforts at "mutual accountability" between a donor agency, Norwegian Church Aid, and its ecumenical partners in Asia, Africa and Latin America.

Signs of reconciliation continued to appear. Delegates from the US and Middle Eastern churches forged an "ecumenical coalition of compassion" to supply aid to the young and the elderly in Iraq and Israeli occupied territories. Representatives of the delegations from North and South Korea stood hand in hand before the assembly as a demonstration of their solidarity and common longing for reunification.

*Week III (Monday 18 February-Wednesday 20 February)*
The final week was devoted almost entirely to plenary business sessions where delegates could hear and act on reports from the four sections and the various committees. As it turned out, however, two items dominated these final days (making it impossible to give sufficient attention to much of the other work): the proposed statement on the Gulf war (see 5.1 and 5.2) and the difficult process of nominating and electing persons to serve as presidents of the WCC and as members of its central committee.

Since there are only 150 places on the central committee, some churches, countries, or ethnic groups are bound to lack direct representation — and to feel disappointed. The disappointment grew, however, when the Nominations Committee's slate failed to meet stated minimum goals for the percentage of women (40 percent) and youth (20 percent). The Committee noted publicly that some delegations were simply unwilling to accept youth or women as their representatives. Indeed, it was angrily reported that some persons included on early Nominations Committee lists had been under heavy pressure to step aside.

At the plenary on 18 February, proposals were made to replace ten names on the Committee's slate. All ten were rejected. There was considerable support for including C.M. Kao of Taiwan and K.H. Ting of China on the central committee but, after much discussion and confusion, these proposals were also defeated. The delegates did vote to ask the new central committee to find an appropriate way for representatives of the China Christian Council and the Presbyterian Church in Taiwan to participate in its meetings.

After the slate was finally accepted, youth delegates and stewards brought forth a banner proclaiming that the marginalization of youth is "ecumenical suicide". Ten percent of the previous central committee were youth. Only 8 percent of the newly-elected committee are under 27.

On the assembly's final day, delegates looked briefly at a "discussion paper" prepared by youth participants. A proposal to include youth advisers in central committee meetings was adopted and other proposals, dealing with youth participation in future assemblies, were referred to the new central committee.

The election of the new presidium proved equally painful. An early Nominations Committee document spoke of WCC presidents as "eminent persons of seniority and considerable experience". The "seniority" criterion was challenged, however, and the assembly decided that one of the presidents should be under 30. There were already guidelines specifying that two of the seven presidents should be Orthodox and that at least three should be women, in addition to expectations of regional and confessional balance — and the task proved impossible. When the slate of nominees was returned two days before the close of the assembly, it listed six persons, only two of whom were women and none of whom was from Latin America, the Caribbean, or sub-Saharan Africa.

The election was deferred amid numerous points of order. The beleaguered Committee was instructed to bring back a list of seven names, including three women and one African. But the African delegates had already decided on a nominee, and he was a male. In the end, the only way to escape the impasse was by asking the new central committee to approve an expansion of the presidium to eight.

## 1.7. THE WORSHIP

Vancouver has often been called "the praying assembly" because of the outstanding quality of its liturgical life. Canberra attempted to learn from and build upon its predecessor. Like Vancouver, the worship materials drew on an incredible variety of cultures and confessions and were meticulously prepared in four languages. Also like Vancouver, worship at Canberra took place in an enormous tent, capable of seating 3,500 worshippers. This "canvas cathedral" was filled with symbols of the Spirit, including a large, flame-shaped candle with seven wicks — one for each WCC assembly.

Music played a crucial role in worship at this assembly, as it had in Vancouver. An exceptional group of worship animators from Sweden, Taiwan, Brazil, South Africa, Ghana, Indonesia and Yugoslavia/USA, along with an 80-voice choir from the Canberra area (the majority of them Roman Catholics), enabled the congregation to sing with real "spirit", even when the tunes and tongues were unfamiliar.

Three major services punctuated the assembly. Sir Paul Reeves, former Anglican archbishop and now representative of the Anglican communion to the United Nations, was the preacher at the opening worship. "Who are we gathered at this assembly?" he asked. "We are people of hope who are part of God's creation which still contains promise even though it lacks peace." Speaking as a Maori, the indigenous people of New Zealand, Bishop Reeves maintained that Christians cannot separate God's promise of redemption from our human responsibility to cherish the earth.

Preaching at the closing worship was Dr Birgitta Larsson (director of the Church of Sweden Mission). The pain we have experienced at this assembly, she suggested, is the pain of birth as the Holy Spirit has brought forth new things from our sharing life with one another. The question now is: What do we do with what has been born? How do we translate the challenges of Canberra into our local situations? This service, like the opening one, ended on a note of joyous celebration as the overflow congregation sang the South African hymn "We Are Marching in the Light of God", complete with clapping and dancing.

In between was a eucharist service using the "Lima liturgy" prepared by members of the WCC's Faith and Order Commission on the basis of the widely-studied document *Baptism, Eucharist and Ministry*. There were also special eucharistic celebrations led by Oriental Orthodox and Eastern Orthodox participants.

Each day of the assembly included morning prayers (attended by most participants), a mid-day preaching service, and evening prayers. One of the morning services was conducted entirely by children from the assembly children's camp. Scripture truly came alive as children played the roles of foot, ear, eye and head, bound together in the body of Christ. A "message" from the children's camp included this request: "When you tell the story of this assembly, tell the children in your churches that we were a part of it." Indeed, they were an important and valued part.

## 1.8. SURROUNDING EVENTS AND PROGRAMMES

More than 300 women, and a similar number of youth, gathered in Canberra for two conferences in the days leading up to the start of the assembly. The events were designed to explore assembly-related issues of particular importance to these groups, to acquaint participants with how an assembly functions, and to foster a sense of solidarity and community. The message from the pre-assembly women's meeting (see 7.3) called attention to the fact that women, youth and children are often the primary victims of war and economic disparity. The youth message (7.4) expressed alarm "at the extent of environmental degradation of the world which we are inheriting".

On the grounds of the university were tents devoted to the concerns of three particular groups: the churches in the Pacific, the Aboriginal people of Australia, and women. The tents provided space for informal sharing as well as for educational programmes and events. Each of these three groups also sponsored a special evening programme during the course of the assembly.

The visitors' programme seemed to receive high marks from those who took part. The 1,100 accredited visitors, along with hundreds of daily visitors, participated in the worship life of the assembly and in its plenary sessions. A special programme of Bible studies and discussion of topics related to the assembly's sub-themes was arranged for those times when other assembly participants were meeting in sections.

Mention should also be made of the small bands of placard-carrying protesters whose presence added to the striking diversity so characteristic of any WCC assembly. Groups of anti-Catholic Protestants and True Orthodox Christians kept watch outside the worship tent whenever the assembly gathered for major liturgical celebrations.

## 1.9. BEHIND THE SCENES

No picture of such an event would be complete without at least a glimpse behind the scenes at some of the activities that made it work.

Assembly preparations in Australia were carried out by two groups, a Canberra committee (with twenty-five task forces of local volunteers) and a national committee formed under the auspices of the Australian Council of Churches. Nearly 700 congregations joined what was called "the assembly line", supporting the assembly through Bible study, prayer, and financial gifts.

A special feature of this type of international conference is, of course, the need for translation of written materials and simultaneous interpretation of presentations and discussions. More than 80 interpreters and translators took part in the Canberra assembly. During plenary sessions, participants could dial their headphones to English, French, German, Spanish, Russian, Greek or Indonesian. At times it could all get quite complicated. If, for example, a delegate spoke in Russian, the Indonesian interpreters would listen to the English interpretation before giving theirs in Indonesian. It was also true, however, that this assembly witnessed, to an unusual degree, what one interpreter called "the imperialism of the English language".

Stewards were another indispensable part of the assembly — carrying messages, handing out materials, duplicating reports, and generally performing the tasks that make an assembly possible. The stewards' programme, organized by the WCC Sub-unit on Youth, also had an educational purpose. Stewards had an opportunity to grasp the ecumenical vision of the global church as well as to contribute through their presence and insights to a significant moment in the life of the ecumenical movement.

Finally, mention should be made of the assembly's excellent daily newspaper, *Assembly Line*, through which participants (especially those able to read English) gained an overview of this multi-faceted gathering.

## 1.10. THE CHALLENGE OF CANBERRA

It seems far too early to "evaluate" so complex an event as the seventh assembly. The assembly's ultimate value may well be determined by the sustained programmes, bonds, or efforts at renewal that develop as a result of these fourteen days. It may not be too early, however, to identify some of the challenges that Canberra poses for the WCC, the churches and the ecumenical movement.

One challenge mentioned earlier arises from the tension between demands for broad "participation" in the work of the WCC and present patterns of leadership and accountability in the churches. There is much to celebrate in the diversity of delegates who gathered in the Australian capital. The Council is surely enriched by the voices of women, youth, laity and others who historically have been marginal to the churches' decision-making processes. The problem is that many of the churches have not themselves implemented inclusive models of leadership — which means that their assembly delegations, if they meet WCC guide-lines for inclusivity, often include persons who are unable to speak with authority for or to their churches.

It is really impossible to participate in a World Council assembly without being deeply influenced by what John Bluck, in a final plenary on communicating Canberra, called "the never-to-be-repeated chemistry of people and place". It is not at all clear, however, that the results of Canberra will go beyond the delegates to affect the lives of the member churches.

The dilemmas are compounded when the delegates are also unfamiliar with the issues and procedures of international ecumenism. At Canberra, some 80 percent of the delegates had not been to a previous WCC assembly and nearly 60 percent had never attended a WCC event of any sort. Is it realistic to expect such a body, no matter how intelligent or committed the participants may individually be, to assess the Council's work and chart its future course?

The plenaries at Canberra, as at Vancouver, provided noteworthy opportunities for the churches to tell of how the Spirit of God is working through and among them. Many participants may have rejoiced that there were few major addresses on issues of the day or theological expositions of the scope and role of WCC programmes themselves. But the lack of substantial theological input — coupled with the shortage of experienced leadership, the dearth of ecumenical memory, and the tyranny of time — meant that the documents "commended to the churches for study and appropriate action" are of less than the highest quality. And the credibility of the Council suffers accordingly.

All of this points to challenges that must be faced. The churches are challenged to become more inclusive in their own leadership and to prepare their delegates as thoroughly as possible for the work to be done. The WCC is challenged to rethink what it means for an assembly to act as the Council's supreme legislative and governing body. Expectations of what an assembly may reasonably accomplish may need to be revised. Revision may also be needed for the process of nominations, a process that had the effect at Canberra of pitting categories against competence, and women and youth against regional representation — and, thus, of deepening our divisions.

Worship is usually mentioned as a highlight of Canberra — and deservedly so. Through prayer and song, participants experienced not only the rich diversity of the church of Christ but also something of that vision of the reign of God that holds us together. The challenge here however is to integrate prayer and public statement, liturgy and decision-making. At the seventh assembly, the two frequently seemed divorced by more than location. Many participants spoke of Canberra as two assemblies — one a "festival of faith" that was generally quite fine, the other an exercise in conciliar governance that was at times quite disturbing.

We move now to a different area of challenge. One strength of Canberra, of WCC assemblies in general, is well captured in the following sentence from *The New York Times*: "... the World Council of Churches remains the only place where a patriarch from one of the first great centres of Christianity and a feminist liberation theologian from a church less than a century old could not only be joint keynote speakers but also embrace the hope that, however long it takes, their successors will some day be united..."

The challenge of Canberra is for the World Council to provide a framework wherein such amazing diversity can move beyond encounter to genuine understanding and (dare we hope?) mutual growth in Christ. One of the major mandates from Vancouver was for the WCC to develop a "vital and coherent theology" capable of creatively integrating the contextual and the classical, the theoretical and the practical, the concern for continuity and the concern for relevance. But as Dr Heinz Joachim Held noted in his report as moderator of the central committee (see 4.2), "... despite all the efforts so far made, the task we were set still remains ahead of us". This challenge was renewed at Canberra especially by Orthodox and evangelical participants. "At present," said the evangelical statement (see 7.8), "there is insufficient clarity regarding the relationship between the confession of the Lord Jesus Christ as God and Saviour according to the scripture, the person and work of the Holy Spirit, and legitimate concerns which are part of the WCC agenda... The challenge is to develop a theology forged in the midst of obedient action for the sake of the gospel, so as to bring together the apostolic faith and the suffering of the oppressed..."

Finally, and perhaps most fundamentally, Canberra represents a challenge for the ecumenical movement to recover a common vision capable of holding together a wide array of disparate priorities. There was a tendency at Canberra to think in terms of particular agendas rather than common goals and affirmations — to concentrate, as one delegate put it, on what divides us rather than on what unites us — which meant that, at times, the assembly resembled a political convention with various constituency groups competing for the attention and favour of the majority. There was little apparent trust that one who is not from "our group" can represent "our interests" — which accounts, at least in part, for the Nominations Committee's headaches.

"And yet it moves." The very fact that the assembly was held at such a moment in world history may well be the strongest indication of the Spirit's presence and prodding. For all of their diversity, the churches obviously share a sense of belonging to a fellowship that is important for their faithfulness, mission, and self-understanding. And through their gathering in Canberra they were able to show signs of God's reconciling work among them. While bombs and rockets rained in the Middle East, participants in the seventh assembly envisioned and prayed for a truly new world order, one shaped by the realities of the Triune God.

"Come, Holy Spirit — Renew the Whole Creation."

MICHAEL KINNAMON

# 2. The Theme: "Come, Holy Spirit — Renew the Whole Creation"

## 2.1. INTRODUCTION

The theme was the focus of plenary sessions on the assembly's second day, 8 February. Before the speakers were introduced, participants sang "Come down, O love divine/seek thou this soul of mine,/and visit it with thine own ardour glowing;/O Comforter, draw near,/within my heart appear,/and kindle it, thy holy flame bestowing."

The first presentation had been prepared by His Beatitude Parthenios III, the Greek Orthodox Patriarch of Alexandria and All Africa. Unfortunately, the patriarch was unable to attend the assembly because of pastoral duties related to the war in the Persian Gulf. His address was read by an Orthodox colleague, Grand Protopresbyter Georges Tsetsis. This address was followed directly by that of Dr Chung Hyun Kyung, professor at Ewha Women's University in Seoul, South Korea.

There was no immediate opportunity for discussion of the presentations in plenary. Such discussion took place in the sub-sections and in the specially-called plenary session on "the gospel and inculturation" described in section 1.5.

## 2.2. THE HOLY SPIRIT

*Parthenios,*
*Patriarch of Alexandria and All Africa*

The World Council of Churches acts in the name of the Father and of the Son and of the Holy Spirit. Our Council is making ecclesiastical history. Each of its assemblies, meetings of Christians "with one accord in one place", marks its progress under the Triune God "in this world" for the church of God, which is also his people.

The themes of the assemblies of the World Council of Churches have until now been related to the Son of God, the Christ, the second person of the Holy Trinity. In our assembly here in the continent of Australia we have decided that our theme is to be the Holy Spirit, the third person of the Holy Trinity.

The central committee decided on this theme with blessed assurance and holy audacity. I say this because we are continuing our journey towards church unity, the unity of all, and we want to move into the mystery of God. The way is not easy. The Holy Trinity is a mystery, the Holy Spirit is a mystery, and the church itself is a mystery.

The Holy Spirit is a favourite theme for the church and its history. Many believe that traditionally and historically it is Orthodoxy that lives and moves and has its being in the Holy Spirit and is "pneumatological". I believe, however, that all the churches live and move in the Holy Spirit. There is no church, no creature, no human person apart from the Spirit. Wittingly or unwittingly, we follow the way of the Holy Trinity, we live in it, and it is our faith and our hope. In the New Testament we often come across the expression: "in the Holy Spirit". This preposition "in" is of great significance. Herein lies the mystery. When we speak about the Holy Spirit, we are speaking about the Holy Trinity. There is no Holy Spirit apart from the Holy Trinity. We live in the Father, in the Son and in the Holy Spirit. We do not separate them. Our God is one. In our creed they are ever one, undivided, indivisible, unchanging, of one substance.

We strive to pray, to listen to, to feel the holy mystery, the mystery of God. Our desire is to worship the Father, the Son and the Holy Spirit, to proclaim to our churches, with the one, holy, catholic and apostolic church, the sublime, ineffable, arcane, unutterable, incomprehensible mystery of God, of whom St John the apostle says in his first epistle:

> Something which has existed since the beginning, that we have heard, and we have seen with own eyes; that we have watched and touched with our hands: the Word who is life — this is our subject (1 John 1:1).

Please understand that it is with diffidence that I speak to you at this moment. It is not possible for us, human beings that we are, to understand the Holy Trinity, to comprehend God, Father, Son and Spirit, one God. As the patriarch of Alexandria, St Athanasius the Great, said: "A God who is understood is no God." Our starting point is "ignorance", the impossibility of knowledge. The church fathers said of the mystery of God: "Go no further, say no more."

The mystery is the theology of the Trinity, Christology, Pneumatology and Ecclesiology. You cannot catch hold of it with human words, you cannot demonstrate it with human arguments of any kind, the intellect or the wisdom "of this world". Speaking of this search for knowledge the apostle Paul says that only "foolishness" can understand the mystery. It is something beyond knowledge. "It was to shame the wise that God chose what is foolish by human reckoning" (1 Cor. 1:27); Christ chose "little children" and bids us become as children so that we may possess him and be made sharers in his kingdom (Matt. 18:3).

The Holy Spirit is the Paraclete, who proceeds from the Father and is sent by the Son. Christ sent the Spirit to his disciples, as he said himself, to show them his love, to assure them that on the way they would not be alone.

The church, his people, all we who truly believe, also lives in the Spirit. The Holy Spirit dwells in us, encompasses us, embraces all things. We call upon the Holy Spirit to renew creation, the world and the earth. With him we would strive for the salvation and redemption of all. Because we are his disciples, it is fitting that we should be his friends, since we are his church, his people.

We are in fact "in a realistic way" spiritual, because we belong to the Holy Spirit. Just as we are Christians because we belong to Christ's church. Therefore the church is the great event and not something static. It moves, surpasses all things and is the life of the world and of humanity. On its journey the church takes on its eschatological identity. It lives out its history in the mystery of the Holy Spirit and is moving towards the last things.

The church's great feast is Pentecost. It is its birthday, on which it begins its journey, the "extension of the Passover" to the kingdom of heaven, inspired by the Holy Spirit. The church has no existence without Pentecost, without the Holy Spirit. We live by the Holy Spirit, we, the people of God who gives us the life of Christ so that we may go to his Father.

There is no other way; this is the only, the eternal way, which Christ gave us in his church: the way of the Paraclete. Our life becomes so to speak "paracletic", and it is felt by all who strive for love, freedom and justice, the Holy Spirit's gifts to the church, which bestow joy and beauty. Christ's life was also "paracletic", with the Holy Spirit present and active in his incarnation, sacrifice and crucifixion, his resurrection, in his church, in his eucharist, in his seven sacraments, in our life which is his life.

In the holy eucharist, which we celebrate daily and which is fellowship (koinonia) in the Holy Spirit and Christ's offering but also our own communion, offering and thanksgiving, our everlasting food and prayer through the Holy Spirit, we experience our God in his church and his Pentecost.

Therefore in our eucharist, our liturgy, we, his people, in our invocation (epiclesis), in our own prayer, beseech the Holy Spirit to come and change the bread and wine into the body and blood of Christ, so that the Son of God, Christ, may dwell in us and that we, human beings, may become the tabernacle of God's dwelling. We become a new creation, are renewed in God's image, united with the Father, Son and Holy Spirit, the Holy Trinity. We are, more, an ecclesial communion, men and women united among ourselves, of one flesh, of one blood, of one essence, people together, united in the one body of Christ.

This is the mystery of the Holy Spirit, given to us, to humanity, to the whole creation. The holy eucharist, the other sacraments of the church effected by the Holy Spirit, even its symbols, are themselves a manifestation, showing forth, revelation and operation of the Holy Spirit for the blessing of humanity and nature. A wind, a breath that "bloweth where it listeth", a dove, a roaring sound, fire, a tongue of fire, these are the Holy Spirit. The chrism, the water, baptism, the bishop's hand, holy order, the marriage crowns, that great mystery of Christ and the church, the oil of holy unction, confession, repentance, the forgiveness of sins: all are in the church by the operation of the Holy Spirit. And all have their beginning in the church on its birthday of Pentecost.

Every sacrament is a sacrament of Pentecost, a descent, a coming down and inspiration, an indwelling of the Holy Spirit. All things are sanctified by the Holy Spirit, from the beginning of creation, when he hovered over the abyss, and now in nature, in heaven and on earth, in humanity, in all beings, in every living soul.

From Pentecost the new creation, the new life, has its beginning, and all things are made new, here and now and always. What we are experiencing is the words of St John's Apocalypse: "The one who guarantees these revelations repeats his promise: I shall indeed be with you soon. Amen; come, Lord", the Alpha and the Omega, the first and the last.

In our Orthodox church on Pentecost Sunday and Whitmonday the hymns and chants are a doxology to the third person of the Holy Trinity. We say of this day that all is wondrous. The words, readings and lessons are strange. They are all words of the Holy Spirit, who is without beginning, of the Spirit of life, the life-giver, enlightener and source of goodness. On this day there is one single worship of the Holy Trinity, Father, Son and Holy Spirit, the Spirit who is God and makes us gods, who is the fire that purifies us, who speaks within us and enriches us with his gifts.

On the day of Pentecost all we see and hear is wondrous. By the Holy Spirit we are taught to theologize, to make our faith come alive. We are alive in this Spirit of fear and wisdom, who is prince and sovereign, who grants rest to our fathers, mothers, sisters and brothers, to all souls.

All is the gift of the Holy Spirit. He lays down the law of the church. He is of one substance, seated on one throne with the Father and the Son. He is Paraclete. The consubstantial Trinity, Father, Son and Holy Spirit, is one power, one substance, one Godhead. We read of him and find him in the Old and New Testaments, and we see him "as in a glass darkly". This is the faith which our Council's message issued at Pentecost 1990 intended to underline. It was a statement inspired by the message which the apostle John gives in his first epistle, regarding the mystery that had been concealed: "that life was made visible: we saw it and we are giving our testimony, telling you of the eternal life which was with the Father and has been made visible to us. What we have seen and heard we are telling you, so that you too may be in union with us, as we are in union with the Father and with his Son Jesus Christ" (1 John 1:2-3).

This is the intercessory, supplicatory and eucharistic experience of the one, holy, catholic and apostolic church. It is also the way of the sister churches, of our World Council, for the entire world, the universe and creation, always and everywhere.

This subject is endless, it is inexhaustible and everlasting.

The only thing I can and would say, in all humility, is that we need this life of the Holy Spirit in the church and in the world, so that we may live it in the strengthening of the same Paraclete. This so that we may capture something of his nature and wisdom, his glory and saving truth, so that we may bear our witness and perform our ministry to every human being and to all creation, seen and unseen, with the internal personal relationships of the Holy Trinity as our model. So we believe "in the Holy Spirit, the Lord, the giver of life, who proceeds from the Father, who with the Father and the Son is worshipped and glorified, who has spoken through the prophets", and so our prayer, the new prayer of us all, is "Come, Holy Spirit, renew the whole creation".

*Hagios ho theos* Holy God, who has created all things through the Son by the working together of the Holy Spirit. *Hagios ischuros* Holy strong one, Christ, through whom we have come to know the Father. *Hagios athanatos*, Holy immortal [is] the all-holy Spirit, who proceeds from the Father and rests in the Son.

On Whitmonday, the feast of the Holy Spirit, we celebrate, according to our calendar, this all-holy, life-giving and all-powerful Spirit, the one God in Trinity, one in honour, one in substance, one in glory with the Father and the Son.

The Father is light, the Word light, the Holy Spirit light.

Our daily prayer, which we learn as little children and say, often without understanding the language of the age in which it was composed, is the prayer to the Holy Spirit:

"Heavenly King, Paraclete, Spirit of truth, who art present everywhere and fillest all things, Treasury of goodness and Giver of life, come, dwell in us and cleanse us from all stain, and, of thy mercy, save our souls. Amen."

All of this is familiar to all, having been said a thousand times over. It is a feature of our daily intercourse. It is the creed of our churches, our life, the long-expected, final and everlasting hope of our people, yesterday, today and tomorrow, our future and last end, our salvation and redemption, for the salvation of the world, the liberation of humanity from error, wickedness and sin, for our unity, rebirth, renewal, regeneration and resurrection, for peace, for beauty in the world and universe, for the victory that has triumphed, does triumph and will triumph over this world, for the kingdom of heaven, for the second coming in the last times and days.

I must mention one thing more. It is a reality we Christians very often forget. It is there however, alive and present everywhere. It is another mystery. I am thinking if the mystery of evil, of the devil, Satan, the "spiritual hosts of wickedness in the heavenly places" (Eph. 6:12). I shall add nothing to that. In the wilderness Jesus was tempted by the spirit of evil, the tempter. That same spirit tempts us also. It tempts the church, the people of God. Only the Holy Spirit can save us. Holy Spirit, "deliver us from evil!"

And now, let us speak of our own life, we who are gathered here as representatives of our churches, of this here and now, this present time. Let us confess, let us bear each other's hardships with Christ, whose yoke is easy and whose burden is light, united as brothers and sisters, we children of God who seek the union of the churches and the unity of humanity.

Without fear or passion may we take the way of truth, may we confess our errors and our sins; may we forgive one another. May we not continually rehearse the same old clichés, reckoning that we are the carriers and bearers, each one separately and all together, of our own history and tradition which is "of this world", with all our habits and practices, which have solid worth and excellence but are also overlaid with errors and, above all, with sins. Would that we might forget the ugly and evil things. May we not repeat them nor mention them again. Let us blot them out.

May we realize the pain of our separation. It wounds Christ. We hinder the Holy Spirit's action and prevent his working with us. In the struggle for union there is room for neither neutrality nor standing aside. Let there be no refusal. May we learn to have confidence in one another, to deepen our love and understanding of one another.

It is well, I think, that we should study together, with the guiding light of the Holy Spirit, St John's Apocalypse, "the revelation given by God to Jesus Christ" (Rev. 1:1) written by the disciple-apostle whom he loved. We are churches. Listen, then, to "what the Spirit is saying to the churches" (Rev. 2:7).

Let all of us, representatives of 310 churches, large or small in number, study what the Spirit is saying to the angels of the churches in Asia Minor: Ephesus, Smyrna, Pergamum, Thyatira, Sardis, Philadelphia and Laodicea. In some of the words addressed to these churches of the little flock we are able to recognize ourselves. What is written is for us too, and we should have our ears open to hear.

To the church in Ephesus: "I know all about you, how hard you work and how much you put up with... Nevertheless I have this complaint to make; you have less love now than you used to... do as you used to at first" (Rev. 2:1-7).

To the church in Smyrna: "I know the trials you have had, and how poor you are — though you are rich — ... Even if you have to die, keep faithful" (Rev. 2:8-11).

To the church in Pergamum: "You still hold firmly to my name, and did not disown your faith in me... Nevertheless I have one or two complaints to make:... among you, too, there are some as bad who accept what the Nicolaitans teach... You must repent" (Rev. 2:12-17).

To the church in Thyatira: "I know your faith and devotion and how much you put up with... Nevertheless, I have a complaint to make: you are encouraging the woman Jezebel who claims to be a prophetess, and by her teaching she is luring my servants away... hold firmly on to what you already have until I come" (Rev. 2:18-28).

To the church in Sardis: "I know all about you: how you are reputed to be alive and yet are dead... do you remember how eager you were when you first heard the message? Hold on to that. Repent... There are a few in Sardis... who have kept their robes from being dirtied, and they are fit to come with me" (Rev. 3:1-6).

To the church in Philadelphia: "I know all about you;... though you are not very strong, you have kept my commandments and not disowned my name... hold firmly to what you already have, and let nobody take your prize away from you" (Rev. 3:7-13).

To the church in Laodicea: "I know all about you: how you are neither cold nor hot... since you are only lukewarm, I will spit you out of my mouth... so repent... Look, I am standing at the door, knocking. If one of you hears me calling and opens the door, I will come in to share his meal" (Rev. 3:14-22).

On our journey of unity, witness and service, by word and deed, we shall show forth, in love and truth, what the Holy Spirit is saying to us. If only we would listen to him. There is no other way. Only this one.

May our striving for unity continue, so that we may fulfill God's will, in accordance with Christ's prayer "that they all may be one". Let our prayer be addressed to the Holy Spirit, that he may lead us to the unity which is our Council's main concern.

I have been in the World Council of Churches since 1954. I owe the Council much. I have met and got to know many brothers and sisters. Some are in God's nearer presence, and some are here. I remember all of them with love. I have learned much from all of them, men and women. May we remain ever faithful on our road to unity. Unity is not a vision yet unseen, nor just an unrealizable dream. It exists in God the Father, God the Christ and God the Holy Spirit. It exists invisibly in the Holy Trinity and in the church. Our search is for visible unity. It is a holy task. It is the daily striving of the churches. When unity will be accomplished is of no importance. What is important is faithfulness to this endeavour, ministry and witness for unity. Full unity will be accomplished in the fullness of God's own time.

Father, Son and Holy Spirit are working for this unity of ours. Christ prays for it to his Father. It is for this that the Holy Spirit lives in the church. It is one single unity with the Holy Trinity, for in the Holy Trinity all are made one. This is what Christ said: "That they all may be one, as we are one." Let us not forget this "as we are".

We shall continue this journey. We must not interrupt it. Unity may happen even tomorrow, or maybe later. The way we work for our visible unity is none other than cooperation with the will of the Holy Spirit.

The Orthodox church has been in the World Council of Churches from the beginning. It will always remain a member of it. The membership of the Council is increasing steadily. This working together for unity on the part of us all, ancient, more recent and younger churches, takes much love, and it must always be fraternal cooperation.

This unity is not one of those matters that can be settled by votes and counting heads. Each member has its own history, some going back over many centuries, some only just of yesterday. May one member help another and respect the other; may we learn to be humble, for unity demands much humility, forgiveness and repentance. It requires boldness and confidence, but good sense as well.

Our ministry and witness for unity begins with mission and evangelism in the name of Christ. The church is located everywhere in the world, embracing all humanity. There are members of the church, and its ministers and witnesses throughout the world, the whole *oikoumene*. Our mission to the world is an unhurried mission, without fanaticism and without proselytism at the expense of other religions and among ourselves. May our journey have as its basic rule the freedom of every religion and every conscience, and the freedom of the human spirit.

Our witness is one of mission and dialogue. All tongues, nations, races, sexes, all kindreds, tribes and peoples *are God's*. They should be free. We must strive for their freedom. This is our ministry in the Holy Spirit, always and everywhere. Our dialogue with other religions and ideologies has the same basis. Our goal is the unity of the world. Such unity is not alien to the work of the Holy Spirit and the church. The Spirit blows where he wills, and we have no right, nor is it an act of love, to restrict his movement and his breathing, to bind him with fetters and barbed wire.

Christ proclaimed that there is neither Jew nor Greek, barbarian, Scythian, slave or free, male or female. Discerning how the Holy Spirit is moving is an act of devotion calling for love, freedom and truth, accompanied by prayer.

Peace, justice and the integrity of our created world are all one. We have to keep our world "very good", as God created it, for over it hovers the Holy Spirit. May we not pollute, contaminate and defile nature and humanity. May we always love humanity and creation. May there be no slaves, may all be free. May we be just, may none be treated unjustly. May there be no famine. May we support youth and old age. May there be no illiterate, uneducated, poor, refugees, migrants, forgotten ones, abandoned or lonely people. May we declare war on war. May we fight for peace, "the peace of God, which passes all understanding" (Phil. 4:7).

We are all united on this march. Our Council rightly defined this journey as for all people, so that it may promote both the union of the churches and the unity of the world and wholeness of creation. Certainly we have to confess that our Council often procrastinates and hesitates, and sometimes is lacking in boldness. We have to tell the truth. I want to stress that we should never procrastinate or hesitate on the subject of freedom of religion, freedom of the church and freedom of humanity. There is no room here for either compromise or procrastination.

In all these things the Holy Spirit is friend and provider. Without him we can do nothing.

One more thing, and with this I shall end. Let us not forget that the Spirit is holy and the church is holy, because the Spirit dwells in it.

We are used to thinking about the church's unity, catholicity and apostolicity. But we forget about its holiness. We forget that we have to become holy, as far as we can, since we enjoy the comfort of the holy Spirit and the help of Christ's church. "Be ye holy," says the scripture, perfect, as God alone is, from beginning to end, eternally holy and perfect. Without holiness nothing comes to fruition. Everything, and especially the union of our churches, needs holiness, repentance, forgiveness, prayer, love and truth.

So on the day of Pentecost in the Orthodox church we kneel to pray for mercy, from God first, then from men and women. May we become men and women of God. May we experience the transfiguration and the true revelation.

Christ made God known to us. The Holy Spirit makes humanity known to God.

The Blessed Virgin, the theotokos and Mother of Christ our God, and all holy men and women, known and unknown, whose lives are seen or "hidden", transform human life, for all of us, and help us in our striving after holiness, by the will of the Father, the sacrifice of the Son of Man and the comfort of the Holy Spirit, for the restoration of all things at the last. There are not many of us Christians in this world. Let us at least become the leaven (1 Cor. 5:6), "the remnant, chosen by grace" (Rom. 11:5).

With all these things we shall wrestle during these days, united in our love for one another. Our prayer will be:

> Come, Holy Spirit, renew the whole creation.
> Giver of life, sustain your creation.
> Spirit of truth, set us free.
> Spirit of unity, reconcile your people.
> Holy Spirit, transform and sanctify us. Amen.

## 2.3. "COME, HOLY SPIRIT — RENEW THE WHOLE CREATION"

*Chung Hyun Kyung*
*Professor of Theology, Ewha Women's University, Seoul*

### Invocation

My dear sisters and brothers, welcome to this land of the Spirit. We are gathered here together today to be empowered by the Holy Spirit for our work of renewing the whole creation. Let us prepare the way of the Holy Spirit by emptying ourselves. Indigenous people of Australia take their shoes off on holy ground. When an Australian Aboriginal woman, Anne Pattel-Gray, came to my church in Korea to preach she took off her shoes, honouring our holy ground. Returning her respect for my people and land, I want to take off my shoes, honouring her and her people's holy ground. For many Asian and Pacific people, taking off our shoes is the first act of humbling ourselves to encounter the Spirit of God. Also in our Christian tradition God called Moses to take his shoes off in front of the burning bush to enter the holy ground — so he did. Do you think you can do that too? I would like to invite all of you to get on the holy ground with me by taking off your shoes while we are dancing to prepare the way of the Spirit. With humble heart and body, let us listen to the cries of creation and the cries of the Spirit within it.

Come. The spirit of Hagar, Egyptian, black slave woman exploited and abandoned by Abraham and Sarah, the ancestors of our faith (Gen. 21:15-21).

Come. The spirit of Uriah, loyal soldier sent and killed in the battlefield by the great king David out of the king's greed for his wife, Bathsheba (2 Sam. 11:1-27).

Come. The spirit of Jephthah's daugher, the victim of her father's faith, offered as a burnt offering to God because he had won the war (Judg. 11:29-40).

Come. The spirit of male babies killed by the soldiers of king Herod upon Jesus' birth.

Come. The spirit of Joan of Arc, and of the many other women burnt at the "witch trials" throughout the medieval era.

Come. The spirit of the people who died during the crusades.

Come. The spirit of indigenous people of the earth, victims of genocide during the time of colonialism and the period of the great Christian mission to the pagan world.

Come. The spirit of Jewish people killed in the gas chambers during the holocaust.

Come. The spirit of people killed in Hiroshima and Nagasaki by atomic bombs.

Come. The spirit of Korean women in the Japanese "prostitution army"[1] during the second world war, used and torn by violence-hungry soldiers.

Come. The spirit of Vietnamese people killed by napalm, Agent Orange, or hunger on the drifting boats.

Come. The spirit of Mahatma Gandhi, Steve Biko, Martin Luther King Jr, Malcolm X, Victor Jara, Oscar Romero and many unnamed women freedom fighters who died in the struggle for liberation of their people.

Come. The spirit of people killed in Bhopal and Chernobyl, and the spirit of jelly babies from the Pacific nuclear test zone.

Come. The spirit of people smashed by tanks in Kwangju, Tiananmen Square and Lithuania.

Come. The spirit of the Amazon rain forest now being murdered every day.

Come. The spirit of earth, air and water, raped, tortured and exploited by human greed for money.

Come. The spirit of soldiers, civilians and sea creatures now dying in the bloody war in the Gulf.

Come. The spirit of the Liberator, our brother Jesus, tortured and killed on the cross.

## In the land of the Spirit with these spirits full of Han

I come from Korea, the land of spirits full of *Han*. *Han* is anger. *Han* is resentment. *Han* is bitterness. *Han* is grief. *Han* is broken-heartedness and the raw energy for struggle for liberation. In my tradition people who were killed or died unjustly became wandering spirits, the *Han*-ridden spirits. They are all over the place seeking the chance to make the wrong right. Therefore the living people's responsibility is to listen to the voices of the *Han*-ridden spirits and to participate in the spirits' work of making right whatever is wrong. These *Han*-ridden spirits in our people's history have been agents through whom the Holy Spirit has spoken her compassion and wisdom for life. Without hearing the cries of these spirits we cannot hear the voice of the Holy Spirit. I hope the presence of all our ancestors' spirits here with us shall not make you uncomfortable. For us they are the icons of the Holy Spirit who became tangible and visible to us. Because of them we can feel, touch and taste the concrete bodily historical presence of the Holy Spirit in our midst. From my people's land of *Han*-filled spirits I come to join with you in another land of spirits full of *Han*, full of the spirits of the indigenous people, victims of genocide. Here, in Australia, we are gathered together from every part of our mother earth to pray for the coming of the Holy Spirit to renew the whole creation. Indeed it is a happy occasion, a big family gathering. I wish I could celebrate our coming together with you all, but my heart is overwhelmed with sadness due to the ongoing war in the Persian Gulf.

> A voice is heard in Ramah,
> lamentation and bitter weeping.
> Rachael is weeping for her children;
> she refuses to be comforted for her children
> because they are no more (Jer 31:15).

This is a time to weep. Rachael's bitter weeping for her lost children is so loud. The cries of mothers, wives and sisters who lost their beloved in the war break our heart. Now we need a wailing wall in order to weep with them. "... the whole creation has been groaning in travail" (Rom. 8:22), surrounded by the smell of death. In the midst of this senseless destruction of life with billion-dollar war machines, we call upon the Spirit who "intercedes for us with sighs too deep for words" (Rom. 8:26). We pray to the Spirit asking her help desperately: "Come, Holy Spirit — Renew the Whole Creation."

But what do we mean by this prayer? "Oh God! We messed up again. Come and fix all our problems." Are we saying "Come Holy Spirit, come and stop the Gulf war and repair the ecological catastrophe", or are we saying "O God, we know you are the strongest warrior, so powerful... we are sure your armament is stronger than Saddam or Bush"? If that is our prayer, I fear we may be returning to an infantile faith. Isn't this our temptation, to remain in our passivity, using prayer as an excuse not to struggle in solidarity with all forms of life? After many years of such infantile prayers, I know there is no magic solution to human sinfulness and for healing our wounds. I also know that I no longer believe in an omnipotent, macho, warrior God who rescues all good guys and punishes all bad guys. Rather, I rely on the compassionate God who weeps with us for life in the midst of the cruel destruction of life.

The spirit of this compassionate God has been always with us from the time of creation. God gave birth to us and the whole universe with her life-giving breath *(ruach)*, the wind of life. This wind of life, this life-giving power of God is the spirit which enabled people to come out of Egypt, resurrected Christ from death and started the church as a liberative community. We also experience the life-giving Spirit of God in our people's struggle for liberation, their cry for life and the beauty and gift of nature. The Spirit of God has been teaching us through the "survival wisdom" of the poor, the screams of the *Han*-ridden spirits of our people and the blessings and curses of nature. Only when we can hear this cry for life and can see the signs of liberation are we able to recognize the Holy Spirit's activity in the midst of suffering creation.

## From the spirit of Babel to the Spirit of Pentecost

However, what we see around us at this time are the signs of death. We feel suffocated by the wind of death. What makes us separated from this life-giving breath of God? I want to call it the unholy spirit of Babel (Gen. 11:1-9). It is a spirit of so-called upward mobility, acquisitiveness and division. The story of Babel is the story of human greed without limit. This tower of greed made all people divided. They talk to each other, but no longer understand each other. They have lost the ability to *feel with* each other, imprisoned by their own greed at the expense of others. Our brother Jesus once called this greedy acquisitiveness "mammon". He said: "No one can serve two masters... you cannot serve God and mammon" (Matt. 6:24). Mammon, carrying great wealth on its back, exploits, breaks and kills people in order to possess more wealth. This madness for possession divides human communities and finally destroys our fragile earth. This is the evil spirit which produces a missile worth more than a million dollars, nuclear bombs and chemical weapons to keep its peace without justice.

This mammon which divides people is active not just in the Gulf but everywhere. It is in the division of north and south Korea; apartheid in South Africa; genocide of indigenous people in Australia, the Americas and many other parts of the world; devaluation of women and children, people of colour and differently-abled people; first-world dominated, ugly Uruguay Round talks and finally the eco-cide of our earth. This is the same evil spirit which crucified Jesus.

However, the spirit of mammon could not overcome the spirit of our compassionate God. God did not abandon us to despair. God did not allow us to indulge in self-pity as helpless victims. God called us to come out of our prison of despair, cynicism and oppression. God empowered us to choose life. When God's Spirit was upon the people on the day of Pentecost, God confronted their broken hearts and called them into discipleship. Their nightmare of witnessing Jesus' death turned into an apocalyptic vision of a new world. Mary's and Rachael's bitter weeping for their dead children turned into the foundation for building a new community for life. When the life-giving power of the Spirit poured onto the faithful, they saw the vision of a new world:

> where their sons and daughters shall prophesy
> and their young men shall see visions
> and their old men shall dream dreams
> and their women and men slaves shall prophesy (Acts 2:17-18).

The rush of wild wind and fire for life from God called them out from the culture of silence, violence and death, and called them into speech, the language of their own. They no longer need to communicate with the language of their colonizers, rulers and imperialists. They can hear the good news in their own native languages. The common language they lost at the greedy tower of Babel was restored in a radically new way at Pentecost. Now they can hear each other and understand one another, not with the mono-language of the Roman empire, but with the diversities of languages of their own. It was a language of liberation, connection and unification from below. The wild wind of God breaks down the Babel tower and all the divisions it produced within us, among us and around us. This wild wind of life calls us to be passionate lovers and workers for a new creation.

### Call for metanoia: towards a "political economy of life"

Then what should we do when the spirit calls us? The first thing we should do is repent. While I was preparing for this reflection in Korea, I had a chance to spend some time with Christian grassroots women activists in Korea. I asked them if there was anything they wanted me to say to the Christians from around the world gathered in Canberra with the theme "Come, Holy Spirit — Renew the Whole Creation". They told me: "Tell them they don't have to spend too much energy to call the Spirit because the Spirit is already here with us. Don't bother her by calling her all the time. She is busy working hard with us. The only problem is we do not have eyes to see and ears to hear the Spirit, as we are occupied with our greed. So tell them 'repent!'"[2] So, sisters and brothers, I give you a "not-so-pleasant" greeting from my sisters, "Repent!" Indeed *repentance* is the first step in any truthful prayer. What should we repent about? Many things, but first of all we should repent for our hidden love for mammon and our secret desire for the Babel tower. To prepare the way of the Spirit, we need to be set free from the spell of mammon by emptying ourselves. In Asia the practice of "voluntary poverty" has been the basis of religious life. When we become free from our own greed by practising "voluntary poverty" in every area of our life, we will achieve the moral power to fight against "forced poverty" in all its forms.

Genuine repentance, metanoia, also means a radical change of direction in our individual and communal life. In order to feel the Holy Spirit, we have to turn ourselves to the direction of the wind of life, the direction the Holy Spirit blows. Which direction is she blowing? It is the direction leading to creating, liberating and sustaining life in its most concrete, tangible and mundane forms. The Holy Spirit empowers us to move in this direction in our struggle for wholeness. This is the Holy Spirit's "political economy of life".[3] This is the political economy not based on the power of domination by capital, weapon or manipulation. This political economy is based on the life-giving power of mutuality, inter-dependence and harmony. If the former is the "political economy of death", the latter is the "political economy of life".

In order to be an active agent for the Spirit's "political economy of life" I envision three most urgent changes we should actualize if we are to have a chance to survive on this dying planet.

The first is the change from *anthropocentrism* to *life-centrism*. One of the most crucial agendas for our generation is to learn how to live with the earth, promoting harmony, sustainability and diversity. Traditional Christian creation theology and Western thinking put the human, especially men, at the centre of the created world, and men have had the power to control and dominate the creation. Modern science and development models are based on this assumption. We should remember, however, that this kind of thinking is alien to many Asian people and the indigenous peoples of the world. For us the earth is the source of life and nature is "sacred, purposeful and full of meaning".[4] Human beings are a very small part of nature, not above it. For example, for Filipinos the earth is their mother. They call her *Ina*, which means "mother" in Tagalog. *Ina* is a great goddess from whom all life comes. As you respect your mother, you should respect the earth. Isn't it true also that in the Christian tradition we affirm that we all come from the earth? God made us from the dust of the earth.

If we compress the earth's whole history into twenty-four hours, "organic life would begin only at 5 p.m... mammals would emerge at 11.30 p.m ... and from amongst them at only seconds before midnight, our species".[5] We are the late-comers on this earth. The earth is not dead. It is "alive" with creative energy. The earth is "God-breathed", and a "God-infused" place.[6] Human beings have exploited and raped the earth for a long time, now is the time that nature and earth are beginning to take revenge on us. They do not give us clean water, air and food any longer since we have sinned against them so extensively.

In the theological world, liberation theologies express the yearning for human wholeness. They echo voices from many oppressed people such as the poor, black, women, indigenous, *dalit* people. They re-read the Bible and reinterpret Christian tradition and theology from their experience of oppression and liberation. This is perhaps the time we have to re-read the Bible from the perspective of birds, water, air, trees and mountains, the most wretched of the earth in our time. Learning to think like a mountain, changing our centre from human beings to all living beings, has become our "responsibility" in order to survive.

The second major change required is the change from the habit of *dualism* to the habit of *interconnection*. In many parts of the world the ways of human life are organized by the assumption of dualism. Our body and our spirit, our emotion and our mind, our world and God, immanence and transcendence, women and men, the black and the white, the poor and the rich, the endless list of division in polarity results in a "split culture",[7] where the latter element of polarity is more valuable and important than the former one. Split culture breeds people of "split personality". In this culture "we are divided against ourselves".[8] We forget that we all come from the same source of life, God, and all the webs of our lives are interconnected. "In the beginning" there was a relationship.[9] God's yearning for relationship with cosmos led to the creation of the whole universe. When God created the universe God liked it and felt it was beautiful. It was beautiful because it was in "right relationship",[10] no exploitation, no division. It had its own integrity, all beings in the universe danced with the rhythm of God, not against it. However, when the dualistic habit came into the world in the name of science, philosophy and religion, we began to objectify "others" as separate from ourselves. In dualistic thinking others are the objects one can control as one likes. This is the basis of all military action. They shoot the enemy (people) and when the target (people) are destroyed they say they "feel bloody good".[11] There is no balance, mutuality and inter-dependence in this objectification. There is also no ability to *feel with* others in this thinking. There is only a wall of separation between enemies.

In traditional North East Asian thinking we call life energy *ki*.[12] For us *ki* is the breath and wind of life. *Ki* thrives in the harmonious interconnec-tions among sky, earth and people. When there is any division or separation, *ki* (life energy) cannot flow and this leads to the destruction and illness of all living beings. Therefore for us renewal means to break the wall of separation and division so that *ki* can breathe and flow in harmony. If we are to survive we must learn to live with not dividing dualism but integrating the interconnectedness of all beings.

The third change I envision for metanoia is change from the "culture of death" to the "culture of life". What is happening right now in the Persian Gulf shows the best example of the "culture of death". The way the conflict is solved is through killing the enemy. By eliminating the conflicting part they think they will achieve peace. Peace achieved by this kind of violence, however, will only lead the world into greater oppression. No cause can justify the innocent shedding of blood in a war. Who goes to the war and whose blood is shed, in any case? Mostly young people from poor families. Many of them are people of colour. Why do they go to war? For the economic and political interest of the few in power, who are mostly older people, and not to further their own interests.

War is the consequence of the patriarchal culture of "power-over". In the patriarchal culture of hierarchy, winning for the dominant group's interest is more important than saving life. Throughout human history, women have been crying over the death, in war, of their beloved brothers, husbands and sons. Women know that patriarchy means death. When their men shed blood, women shed tears. Their powerful tears have been the redemptive, life-giving energy for the tearless men's history. Indeed weeping has been "the first prophetic action"[13] in human history. Only when we have an ability to *suffer with* others *(compassion)* can we transform the "culture of death" to the "culture of life".

Korean church women declared that they would carry on the movement for "life-promoting culture". They also work for the "year of jubilee" declared by the Korean National Council of Churches. The "year of jubilee" for us is the year 1995 which is the fiftieth year of our division into north and south Korea. This division, brought about by the world power struggle between East and West, has been the source of death for Korean people. The truce line between the north and south suffocated our *ki* (life energy) and put us under the constant oppression of the national security law and the threat of war. In the jubilee year we want unification of our people. We want to recover our ability to *feel with* and to *suffer with* our North Korean sisters and brothers through our intertwining of "culture of life" and "jubilee" movements to bring about unification. The movement for justice, peace and a healthy ecology all over the world is a movement for life. Without justice, peace and the integrity of creation, there is no "culture of life".

## Break down the wall with wisdom and compassion

I want to close my reflection on the Holy Spirit by sharing with you my image of the Holy Spirit from my cultural background. This image embodies for me the three changes of direction I have described as necessary for metanoia: life-centrism, the habit of interconnection and the culture of life. The image does not come from my academic training as a systematic theologian but from my gut feeling, deep in my people's collective unconsciousness that comes from thousands of years of spirituality.

For me the image of the Holy Spirit comes from the image of *Kwan In*. She is venerated as the goddess of compassion and wisdom by East Asian women's popular religiosity. She is a *bodhisattva*, enlightened being. She can go into nirvana any time she wants to, but refuses to go into nirvana by herself. Her compassion for all suffering beings makes her stay in this world enabling other living beings to achieve enlightenment. Her compassionate wisdom heals all forms of life and empowers them to swim to the shore of nirvana. She waits and waits until the whole universe, people, trees, birds, mountains, air, water, become enlightened. They can then go to nirvana together where they can live collectively in eternal wisdom and compassion. Perhaps this might also be a feminine image of the Christ who is the first-born among us, one who goes before and brings others with her.

Dear sisters and brothers, with the energy of the Holy Spirit let us tear apart all walls of division and the "culture of death" which separate us. And let us participate in the Holy Spirit's political economy of life fighting for our life on this earth in solidarity with all living beings, and building communities for justice, peace and the integrity of creation. Wild wind of the Holy Spirit, blow to us. Let us welcome her, letting ourselves go in her wild rhythm of life. Come Holy Spirit, Renew the Whole Creation. Amen!

NOTES

[1] During the second world war, Japan recruited poor, rural Korean women (by force) in the name of "army labour forces". Instead of working in the factories these women were forced to be official prostitutes for Japanese soldiers. Most of them died of venereal diseases or were killed during the war. For more information on these women, see my article, "*Han-pu-ri*: Doing Theology from Korean Women's Perspective", *The Ecumenical Review*, Vol. 40, No. 1, January 1988.

[2] These words came from my discussion on the Holy Spirit with my sisters in the Korean Association of Christian Women for Democracy. I especially want to express my appreciation to Sohn Ewn Wha, Myung No Sun, Kho Ae Shin and Kim Jung Soo for their insights.

[3] For the term "political economy of life" I am indebted to Korean minjung theologian Suh Kwang Sun.

[4] Kwok Pui Lan, unpublished Bible study delivered at the world convocation on "Justice, Peace and the Integrity of Creation" in Seoul, Korea, 8 March 1990.

[5] Joanna Macy, *Thinking Like a Mountain*, p.42.

[6] Jay McDaniel, *The Ecumenical Review*, Vol. 2, No. 2, April 1990, p.167.

[7] Susan Griffin, "Split Culture", in Judith Plant ed., *Healing the Wounds: The Promise of Ecofeminism*, Philadelphia, New Society Publishers, 1989.

[8] *Ibid.*, p.7.

[9] See Dorothy Sölle, *To Work and To Love: A Theology of Creation*, Philadelphia, Fortress Press, 1984, for a creation theology based on mutual relationship between God and us.

[10] See Carter Heyward, *Our Passion for Justice*, New York, Pilgrim, 1984, for her concept of justice as "right relationship".

[11] This is what a pilot of the allied forces said after bombing Iraq. I saw it in an Australian daily newspaper, 20 January 1991.

[12] For this understanding of *ki* I am indebted to Korean minjung theologian and New Testament scholar Ahn Byung Mu. I learned about the similar nature of *ki* and *ruach* from Dr Ahn's lecture on "*ki* and the Holy Spirit" presented at the theological preparation meeting for the seventh assembly of the WCC, organized by the Korean National Council of Churches.

[13] See Walter Brueggeman, *The Prophetic Imagination*, Philadelphia, Fortress Press, 1978.

*Left: Grand Protopresbyter Georges Tsetsis, who read the presentation by Patriarch Parthenios. Right: Prof. Chung Hyun Kyung.*

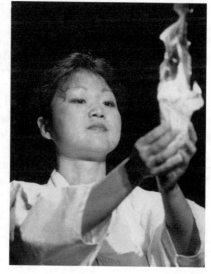

# 3. The Sub-themes

## 3.1. INTRODUCTION

How do human beings talk about the activity of the Holy Spirit? Scripture and the Tradition of the church speak of the Spirit's work in a variety of ways, four of which were lifted up as sub-themes for the seventh assembly.

The Spirit, for example, is intimately linked in scripture with creation. In the beginning "the Spirit of God was moving over the face of the waters" (Gen. 1:2). The same Hebrew word is used in Genesis 2 when God breathed into humans the breath (or spirit) of life. This biblical witness to the life-giving work of the Spirit is behind the familiar confession of the Nicene Creed: "I believe in the Holy Spirit, the Lord the giver of life." It is also the basis of the first sub-theme: "Giver of Life — Sustain your Creation!"

Another emphasis is found in John's Gospel where the Spirit is identified as the one who reveals, exposes, convicts, and leads believers "into all truth" (John 16:13). This points towards the second sub-theme: "Spirit of Truth — Set us Free!"

The central event connected with the Holy Spirit in scripture is the descent of the Spirit upon the disciples at Pentecost (Acts 2). Here the focus is on unity and community. This understanding is further developed in the letters of Paul where the apostle speaks of the gifts of the Spirit which bind and build people together into a community of reconciliation. Thus we have the third sub-theme: "Spirit of Unity — Reconcile your People!"

Within the history of the church considerable attention has been paid to the tranforming and sanctifying activity of the Spirit, the one through whom we experience newness of life. It is on this that the fourth sub-theme focuses: "Holy Spirit — Transform and Sanctify Us!"

These four sub-themes (actually formulated as prayers) were explored in plenary through a "round-table discussion" on the assembly's second day. Veteran ecumenist, Dr Pauline Webb (Methodist, United Kingdom), served as animator, with brief presentations made by four "panelists": Rev. David McDonald (United, Canada), member of the House of Commons in the Canadian parliament; Dr Philip Potter (Methodist, Caribbean), former general secretary of the WCC; Dr Mary Tanner (Anglican, England), ecumenical officer for the Church of England; and Metropolitan John of Pergamon (Eastern Orthodox, Turkey), professor at the University of Thessaloniki and at London University. We include here major portions of three of the presentations.

"... Truth in the New Testament is no abstract word. The Greek word for it means not hidden or closed, not covered up, that which is made open, made visible, uncovered, disclosed — that which becomes transparent.

"In Hebrew truth is *emeth, amunah* — Amen, meaning faith and faithfulness, trust and trustworthiness, reliability, commitment.

"It is in this sense that Jesus said 'the world cannot receive the spirit of truth because it neither sees nor knows him'. This is the tragic bondage of the world which thrives on hiding, covering up, closing reality, a world in which trust, reliability and mutual commitment are in such short supply.

"It is in contrast to this that Jesus said to his disciples in John 8:31-32: 'If you continue in my word, you are truly my disciples and you will know the truth and the truth will make you free.' The prayer to the Spirit is to enable us so to appropriate by faith the message of Christ that our lives will become open, trustworthy, trust-creating, reliable and free — and therefore liberated. Our liberated existence will be marked by transparency and trusting, trustful, reliable commitment to people and causes.

"It is in the light of this radical call to faith and freedom that we are invited in this assembly to wrestle with some of the most vital questions of our existence today as human beings, as communities, nations, races, sexes, and as those who communicate with one another.

"What, then, are some of the specific tasks before us in the assembly and in the coming years?

"1. Our economic systems, capitalism and the monetary and financial systems which undergird it, have become more and more hidden, covered up, faceless and especially unaccountable. We have talked a great deal about justice and a free and open market, but when we try to understand the structures of political economy they escape our grasp. In fact there is no international authority to which these structures are accountable. The existing systems set in place at Bretton Woods after the second world war, such as the World Bank, the IMF, GATT, as well as the mysterious workings of stock exchanges, are either dominated by a very few industrialized countries or in their transnational manifestations are free from any responsible control in any meaningful democratic way.

"In our world in which so many economic and political systems are in crisis, now is the time to bring a Christian understanding and judgment to bear on them for the sake of any meaningful existence as a human family.

"2. The whole system of national security, interstate conflicts, the arms race, and open conflicts have their roots in attitudes of universal mistrust based on the determination to hide, cover up our intentions from each other. Nor are we willing to entrust conflictual situations to the one body we have which has the potentialities for promoting open discussion of trust and of collective security — the UN and its many agencies. Our assembly, I hope, will reaffirm the support we gave in 1948 to the UN and do so in ways which will mobilize our member churches to challenge the member states to enable the UN to be the guardian and hope of our rights and obligations and our well-being as a human race.

"3. In an age of enormous development of the communication media, we need to join the WACC in advocating a more comprehensive and acceptable world information and communication order, which can ensure that people everywhere are well informed of what is happening in their world and, through a dialogue of cultures, be mutually enriched for a more human community of caring and sharing.

"4. We must allow the Spirit of truth who is the Spirit of community and communion to enable both sexes and all races and cultures to be liberated, and to exercise the diversity of their gifts in the unity of love, joy, peace, mutual goodness and respect."

PHILIP POTTER

"A major challenge to sub-theme 3 will be to give some account of visible, reconciled living which will defy the overworked, stale jargon that has lost, it seems, all power to convince us. We desperately need a 'mobilizing' portrait of visible, reconciled life that will hold together an absolute commitment to the unity and renewal of the church and an absolute commitment to the reconciliation of God's world and show us the inseparable relation between them. We shall be an inward-looking, selfish, self-interested group of people if our search for the unity of the church is separated from the search for justice and peace: but will we not become simply another secular movement or political party if we divorce the mending of the world from the unity and reconciliation of Christians in one body of Christ?

"But can we find a 'mobilizing' vision that will convince us:

— that we are required to confess our faith together in words — for truth does matter — but in words that pass into lives of serving Christ in the hungry and poor;

— that we are to be formed and sustained in one sacramental life of grace, entered by baptism and celebrated at a single, simple round table where all are welcome and from which all are sent out in the power of the Holy Spirit to work for justice and peace;

— that we are to be served, not lorded over, by a single ministry which nurtures the gifts the Holy Spirit gives us for serving God's hurting world;

— that we are to be bonded together by structures of grace which will enable us to decide and speak together and through which we are most effectively the people of God for the world?

"We have been singularly unsuccesful in providing a captivating picture of renewed and reconciled life in the church.

"And if this portrait of visible unity is to convince us it must astonish us with its diversity. We are not looking for a super church which will knock us into submissive uniformity. It must say, 'be Aboriginal Christians with God and each other in authentic Aboriginal ways'; 'be Indian Christians with God and each other in authentic Indian ways'; 'be African Christians with God and each other in authentic African ways'; 'do not deny your identity and do not stifle the uniqueness the Spirit gives!' There are tolerable limits to diversity. But we can be confident that authentic diversity will flourish on the basis of a rediscovered unanimity in faith, baptism, eucharist, ministry and bonded common and caring life.

"And if the portrait is to convince, it must make quite clear that in the communion of the church the personal and relational is always prior to the institutional. It must be so, for our unity is grounded in the personal and relational life of God. Without the institutional, the personal and relational is hampered. Equally, we cannot grow in institutional unity unless this springs out of a growth in personal communion and community living. So we must learn to love and to know one another.

"And if the portrait is to convince, it must make quite clear that difference of opinion, disagreements, creative tensions, yes, even conflicts, are always going to be a part of common Christian living. The truth of God is wondrously complex, delicately balanced, infinitely subtle; it cannot be trapped in human moulds. Because there will be differences as we seek to perceive truth we must be ready to bear and stick with the unavoidable pain of difference. Sharp things that divide us can paradoxically turn out as gifts, not only because they open up deep theological issues, but because they touch deep levels of pain and passion, which test what it means that we are called to love our enemies. The world in all of its divisions of political parties and creeds is not used to such a possibility as this; that those on opposing sides should stay together, should bear one another's burdens and enter one another's sufferings. If we can live together in the communion of the church, bearing the cost of difference, we shall get hold at a deeper level of a communion with a God who suffers and we shall be rewarded with an experience of reconciliation and unity grounded in the unity of God the Holy Trinity, at whose heart is forever a cross. Somewhere in here is the key to the cost of reconciled living: for there is no reconciliation without the cross. If we can model this, then both in our being and by our doing we shall be 'sign' to the world of the life and values of God's kingdom and 'sacrament' for the world."

MARY TANNER

"There are two ways of asking the Holy Spirit to be involved in any process of transformation leading to holiness. One is to ask the Spirit to *assist* with our efforts. This is the way of ethics: *we* do the planning, *we* make the effort, and the Spirit is asked to help. The other way is to leave everything to the Spirit. We do nothing but pray, and leave everything to the Spirit. Both of these extremes are wrong, but of these two the first one is probably the one we have to watch out for more carefully at this time of widespread rationalism and planning.

"The Spirit seems to have an obsession with freedom. He blows where He wills, and does not like to be told what to do. We must certainly try, and we must definitely do our best. But when we pray for the Spirit to come we must be prepared for the unexpected. Our computers may well prove to be wrong or even useless...

"Holiness means setting apart someone or something for God. The ethos of holiness requires an attitude towards all that exists (our bodies, our minds, the material world, etc.) as if it by nature belonged to God. We cannot own ourselves, our bodies, our lives, our natural resources, etc. — they belong to God. We are in the world as the priests of creation endowed with the privilege of referring back creation to its Creator.

"This eucharistic ethos is the first thing that we need today at a time of severe ecological crisis. This is a spirituality that flourished among the desert Fathers, but has been forgotten in the meantime. It has to be recovered urgently, now that we need to be redeemed from an anthropomonistic attitude to existence....

"Finally, holiness means liberation or rather freedom. 'Where the Spirit of the Lord is there is freedom' (2 Cor. 3:17). Liberation is *from* someone or something; freedom is *for* someone or something. Both aspects are associated with the work of the Spirit, who is freedom. These take various forms:

a) liberation from the past (forgiveness through repentance (metanoia));
b) liberation from passions of ego-centricity (= *ascesis*, healing one's self);
c) liberation from injustice, exploitation, poverty and all social evil;
d) liberation — yes! — even from decay and death (something we speak so little about);
e) freedom to love, even one's enemies; to allow for personal, cultural and other differences and identities to exist and to create; to give one's life for others as our Lord gave it on the cross.

"We must work for a spirituality that will make sense for all human beings in all walks of life. Yet we must guard ourselves against an easy spiritualism. We often speak too easily and too quickly of the presence and the activity of the Holy Spirit in what we do. We must humbly submit what we are and what we do to his purifying judgment, waiting for him to reveal the truth. There is always the danger to *confuse* the Spirit of God with our own psychological experiences or certainties. The Spirit is God, He is Lord, He cannot be contained by our own feelings. The best we can do is to worship him as Lord, to pray to him to dwell among us, and to await patiently upon him in all that we do."

JOHN OF PERGAMON

All official participants at Canberra were assigned to one of the four "sections", and each section focused on one of the sub-themes. The reports from these sections were eventually summarized and incorporated into the "Report of the Seventh Assembly" (see 6.2) which was presented in plenary for formal adoption. The section reports, printed below, were also presented in plenary during the assembly's final week but not for adoption or amendment. Instead, the assembly was asked to approve the

substance of the reports and to commend them to the churches for study
and action. Since amendment was not allowed, comments made at the
plenary discussions have been summarized and included as appendices to
the section reports.

The reports were presented by Ms Ruth Abraham (Lutheran,
Ethiopia), Dr Margot Kaessmann (United, Germany), Dr Turid Karlsen
Seim (Lutheran, Norway), and Prof. Kwesi Dickson (Methodist, Ghana).
They appear here as they were prepared by the sections in Canberra.

# 3.2. REPORT OF SECTION I:
# "GIVER OF LIFE — SUSTAIN YOUR CREATION!"

## Prologue

The work of section I, "Giver of Life — Sustain your Creation!", was
enriched by the use of several background materials which delegates wish
to mention. These included the official *Resources for Sections* book, as
well as *Orthodoxy and the Ecological Crisis*, prepared by the Ecumenical
Patriarchate, and the report on "The Churches' Role in Protecting the
Earth's Atmosphere" from a recent meeting of several churches and
ecumenical organizations held in Gwatt, Switzerland.

In particular, the section delegates wish to underscore the contribution
of the pre-assembly consultation on sub-theme 1 held in Kuala Lumpur,
Malaysia, in May 1990. This report served as a most valuable resource
and reference for the work of the section.

## I. Theology of creation: challenge for our time

A. INTRODUCTION

1. The boundless mystery of the universe, the abundance, beauty and
grandeur of creation and of this precious planet manifest the glory of God.
We confess the Triune God as the source of all life. The Holy Spirit, to
whom we pray in the prayer-theme of this assembly, manifests God's
energy for life present in all things and reminds us of the total dependence
of all things on God. Through Jesus Christ all things have been made, and
in him God's creation comes to its fulfilment. Through Christ's cross and
resurrection we are assured that the entire creation is made new. All

things have been reconciled to God in Jesus Christ and through the Spirit we begin to experience God's future.

2. The divine presence of the Spirit in creation binds us as human beings together with all created life. We are accountable before God in and to the community of life, an accountability which has been imaged in various ways: as servants, stewards and trustees, as tillers and keepers, as priests of creation, as nurturers, as co-creators. This requires attitudes of compassion and humility, respect and reverence.

3. Yet, while the earth was created by God out of nothing in a pure and simple act of love, and the Spirit has never abandoned the creation or ceased sustaining it, the earth on which we live is in peril. Creation protests its treatment by human beings. It groans and travails in all its parts (Rom. 8:22). Ecological equilibrium has been severely broken. Through misinterpretation of our faith and through collective and individual misbehaviour we as Christians have participated in the process of destruction, rather than participating in the repentance that God requires.

4. In the Bible danger and destruction are understood as the signs of the time which call for repentance and renewal of the relationship with God and the whole creation. The stark sign of our time is a planet in peril at our hands. The invitation is to return to God and call upon the Spirit to reorient our lives accordingly. At this assembly, we commit ourselves anew to living as a community which cares for creation.

5. Responsibility requires that we recognize the character of the crisis in our midst. In the present international scene we confront two major problems: (a) the worldwide social justice crisis; and (b) the global ecological and environmental crisis. Pursuing justice requires us to learn new ways of paying attention to all creation — the land, water, air, all people, plant life and other living creatures. A new vision will integrate our interdependent ecological, social, economic, political and spiritual needs. We want to say as forcefully as we can that social justice for all people and eco-justice for all creation must go together. Social justice cannot happen apart from a healthy environment, and a sustainable and sustaining environment will not come about without greater social justice. Justice is truly indivisible, not only as a matter of theological conviction but in practice. The biblical concept of justice recognizes the need for healthy relationships in creation as a whole. This way of viewing justice helps us understand the linkage between poverty, powerlessness, social conflict and environmental degradation.

6. Yet we live in a moment of extreme jeopardy. For the first time, cumulative human activity threatens destruction not only of local and

regional eco-systems but the planetary ecology as a whole. The warming of the earth's atmosphere poses grave danger to the capacity of human and other life to survive and flourish. We are further threatened by the cumulative effect of other factors, including destruction of the earth's protective ozone shield, land degradation through deforestation, erosion, desertification, salinization, commercial exploitation, militarization and wars, water pollution, air pollution, species extinction and more. All of creation seems broken, wounded and hurt. It is shocking and frightening for us that the human species on this earth, which came on the scene somewhere around 80,000 years ago in the 4.5 billion-year-long history of this earth, has been able to threaten the very foundations of life on our planet in only about 200 years of industrialization. This crisis has deep roots in human greed, exploitation and economic systems which deny the elemental truth that any and every economic and social system is always a sub-system of the eco-system and is totally dependent on it. The industrial/post-industrial economic systems treat nature simply as "natural resources" and abuse it for profit.

7. The destruction of the environment cries out for urgent repentance and conversion. We are beckoned to rediscover a biblical vision and a new understanding of ourselves and God's creation. The only future foreshadowed by the present crises, both social and ecological, is massive suffering, both human and other than human. "Giver of Life — Sustain your Creation!" is our prayer; we should pray it without ceasing.

B. Towards a deepened understanding of creation

8. In exploring our prayer-theme, "Giver of Life — Sustain your Creation!", we have discovered common perspectives along the following lines.

9. The scriptures, both Old and New Testaments, reveal the essential truths about creation and our relationship to it as human beings. God is the Creator of all that exists, the creation (Gen. 1:1ff.), and has declared that "it was very good" (Gen. 1:31; 1 Tim. 4:4). God's Spirit continually sustains and renews the earth (Ps. 104:30). The scriptures teach that human beings were created by God from the earth. In addition, God gave them the breath of life (Gen. 2:7) and created them in the divine image and likeness (Gen. 1:26-27). A special aspect of the image of God in human beings is to reflect God's providence for the created world, to care for it and to serve as its protector. Thus, humanity is both part of the created world and charged to be God's steward of the created world.

Human beings are charged to "keep" the earth and "serve it" (Gen. 2:15), in an attitude of that blessed meekness which will inherit the earth.

10. The biblical creation stories affirm that humanity is an integral part of the creation, but has a special responsibility for it. This relationship between the Creator, creation and humanity is often expressed in covenants, beginning with the covenant made with Noah, and renewed with the people of God. Human sin has broken the covenant and subjected the creation to distortion, disruption and disintegration — "to futility" (Rom. 8:20). Our economies and greed have brought it to the brink of destruction.

11. However, the Bible reminds us that the redemptive work of Jesus Christ was renewal not only of human life, but of the whole cosmos. Thus we have hope that the covenant promises for the earth's wholeness can find fulfilment. In Christ, "the creation itself will be set free from its bondage to decay and will obtain the freedom of the glory of the children of God" (Rom. 8:21).

12. In the whole of the Christian life, we take up the created things of this world and offer them to God for sanctification and transfiguration so that they might manifest the kingdom, where God's will is done and the creation glorifies God for ever. The sacraments of Christian worship use the elements of the created world to manifest the Triune God present among and in us. This sacramental Christian perspective influences our approach to the creation in general. We must never forget that "the earth is the Lord's and all that is in it, the world, and those who live in it" (Ps. 24:1).

13. Exploring the prayer "Giver of Life — Sustain your Creation!" also exposed great theological failures of the past. Many streams of the tradition have misunderstood dominion (Gen. 1:28) as exploitation and God's transcendence as absence. The more theology stressed only God's absolute trancendence and distance from the material sphere, the more the earth was viewed as a mere object of human exploitation and "unspiritual" reality. Nature has been subjected to human ownership and unqualified manipulation. The divine image and likeness have been perverted into arrogant, ruthless rulership with little regard for the earth and fellow human beings. Dualistic thinking about spirit and matter, male and female, and the relationship among races has resulted in structures and patterns of domination and exploitation that parallel the domination of nature. While we repudiate these consequences, we have to confess that they belong to life-styles and power structures which have received theological support and sanction.

14. Reviving the biblical concept of service and stewardship, of the coexistence and interdependence of all parts of cosmic life, and of collective accountability (Matt. 25:21), we need to listen to various traditions and streams of thinking within and outside Christianity.

a) Women worldwide have told of the parallel ways in which they and the land have been imaged and treated, and the work of the Spirit in healing the wounds of both. Women's experience is indispensable to understanding the relationships of humans and the earth, and to healing it. In similar ways, those who till the land and nurture the earth have rich insights to be shared.

b) The poor teach all of us things we must know for an adequate theology of creation. They invariably suffer first and most from a degraded environment. In a world intricately interconnected, their struggles are thus a critical practical starting point for restoration and well-being.

c) Learning from the Old Testament and from the Jewish perception of our relation to creation is crucial to a new ecological sensitivity. Precious insights can be learned also from dialogue with other faiths, and with the heritage of indigenous peoples and non-Western cultures, especially those who have retained their spirituality of the land and the sacredness of all life.

d) The knowledge and insight of scientists is also indispensable. Scientists are the keepers of the most powerful tools for the empirical understanding of nature and of nature's fragility in the face of human onslaught. Our sense of the mystery of life and our awe and wonder at the Creator's handiwork are deepened from the discoveries of science.

e) The differently-abled among us have not been sufficiently heard to date. Without doubt, they have much to teach all of us for creation theology.

C. CONCLUSION

15. We believe this exploration of creation theology should continue. We as the WCC recommend undertaking a major worldwide study of our understanding of creation and its biblical foundations.

16. We affirm our commitment to the healing of creation and restoration of relationships that build harmony, wholeness and the kingdom of God. We believe strongly that the WCC, member churches and all Christians should seek justice, peace and the renewal of all creation. This challenges churches to study the situation and consider radical social change. We call for a reordering of personal and corporate life-styles,

relationships and the overall economic system. At Canberra we were able to re-examine, deepen, enhance, change and develop our view of creation as Christians. In this effort we have prayed for guidance by the Holy Spirit, remembering that we are called not to trust every spirit, but to be led into truth. We are grateful for the opportunity of Christian fellowship and sense of community that we experienced here.

## II. Towards an ethic of economy and ecology

A. VISION

17. Our vision is of people of different faiths beginning to learn from each other's spirituality and inspiration while developing practical examples in commitment to community and sharing. Our vision is of those with enough material goods beginning to live with less while replacing their idolatry of consumerism with a new spirituality, and of those with economic and political power making decisions based on the needs of all creation, leading to a fuller life for all. Our vision is one in which the local communities of this planet are empowered to resist the many threats to our survival. Only by acknowledging the fundamental worth of all creation can we hope to reverse the direction of destructive, human-created processes. Only from the grassroots can people be persuaded to follow the gospel while resisting the pressures of greed and covetousness that pervade human life. We envision a world in which the needs of all creation are integrated with the workings of governments and international business, where importing and exporting do not spell hunger and environmental degradation for the poor. In such a world bio-regions are more important than national boundaries. Our vision is that the industrialized countries develop new patterns of energy-consumption in order to slow down considerably the dangerous process of global warming. In our new vision, the resources of the various sciences, technological research and economic analysis will be in the service of all of creation. New concepts of economic development coming from intellectual work will respect the integrity of all life-forms. The goal of technology will be to work with nature and its mysteries and not to master it.

18. For Jews and Christians together the institutions of the sabbath, the sabbatical year and the jubilee year provide a clear vision on economic and ecological reconciliation, social restoration and personal renewal. Sabbath reminds us that time, the realm of being, is not just a commodity, but has a quality of holiness, which resists our impulse to control,

command and oppress. In the concepts of the sabbatical and jubilee year, economic effectiveness in the use of scarce resources is joined to environmental stewardship, law to mercy, economic order to social justice. It is not production and consumption that sustain our earth but rather the ecological systems that have to support human life. There exists an intimate and unbreakable relationship between economy and ecology as the churches' process on justice, peace and integrity of creation has amply demonstrated. Should we not contemplate and revitalize the biblical concept of sabbath, sabbatical and jubilee year to substitute a global liberation of creation within fifty years for the gloomy future now predicted by ecologists from all over the world?

## B. OBSTACLES

19. One of the major obstacles to a realization of the biblical vision for the fulfilment of creation lies in ideologies which separate subject from object, mind from matter, nature from culture. Political economic thinking still sees progress as production and consumption of more and more goods while development is equated with growth. But the planet is finite and its capacity to sustain growth already is seriously affected.

20. A second constraint lies in the division of the world into industrialized and non-industrialized nations. The isolation of wealth from the needs of the poor has resulted in a North-South confrontation which is causing more and more polarization and conflict. Exploitation of nations by nations, of people by companies, of those who have no more to offer than the work of their hands by others who have access to economic resources, affects creation utterly negatively. The food we eat while our neighbour is hungry and the wealth we enjoy at the expense of others separate us from the realm of life while destroying the integrity of our souls. It is, in the words of Pope John Paul II, *the structures of sin* that have to be destroyed. Any policy or action that threatens the sustainability of creation, by whatever means — exploitation of environment or people, industrial pollution, agricultural over-production, scientific development or wasteful consumerism — needs to be questioned. No longer can we ignore the burdens of a debt that could never be repaid. The excessive and persistent debt that afflicts many poorer nations leaves them with little alternative but to degrade creation and with it also societies and cultures. This problem is magnified by the perpetuation of so many regimes that do not base their policies and behaviour on the rights of the poor or on human obligations towards nature, and which are not subject to democratic control. The same applies to other institutions including global corpora-

tions. Such institutions increase the monetary wealth of some through the loss of natural wealth for all. In efforts to increase the gross *national* product, the gross *natural* product is diminished.

21. Neither can we close our eyes to the potential misuse of biotechnologies in which the moral and spiritual dimensions of life are ignored. No longer can we ignore the root causes of population growth which lie, more than in anything else, in the poverty and the lack of social security still prevailing in two-thirds of our world.

22. In the end the main obstacle to the realization of our vision lies in our own hearts, in our fear of change, in our lukewarmness, in our lack of spirituality, in apathy and uncritical conformity to the status quo, in our lack of trust in God. We desperately need the dynamic power of the Spirit that integrates our faith with our daily lives, our worship with our action, and our justification with our sanctification.

## C. STRATEGIES

23. The free-market economy provides a mechanism for rapid response to those needs which can be expressed in terms of money and which are backed by a money income. Essential as such systems of markets and prices may be, they do not possess any inherent morality. The shameful arms trade which is one of the root causes of the Gulf war, as well as of poverty, hunger and malnutrition in many regions, provides a clear illustration of the immorality of business in our world today. While innumerable people were starving, valuable resources were spent on military equipment. Now the states which supplied the arms to Iraq have deemed it necessary to form a coalition to destroy the military hardware they themselves delivered. As another painful example of victims of militarization we mention the people in the Pacific who suffer and die because of nuclear testing and the dumping of nuclear waste. As Christians we feel shame regarding the immoral arms trade and the militarization of our world.

24. The world ecumenical movement has a long history of moral criticism of the economic order. Points of critique included the lack of economic democracy, social injustice, and the stimulation of human greed. Although in some parts of the world it has been possible to correct gross inequality and complete unaccountability of those holding economic power, there still persists a flagrant international inequality in the distribution of income, knowledge, power and wealth while acquisitive materialism has developed into the dominant ideology of our day. There is a constant urge to move up in the hierarchy of possessors of goods.

25. To the still valid critique of the economic order that was expressed by previous ecumenical gatherings, we have added the totally irresponsible exploitation of the created world, resulting in a horrific degradation of the planet earth.

26. Noting that reform of the economic order in the past never came automatically, but always through contradiction, opposition and social struggle, we are aware that now more than ever the market economy is in need of reform. We have discussed the following instruments to overcome the basic constraints of our time to a realization of social justice and ecologically responsible human behaviour.

*1. Local self-empowerment*

27. Around the world we see that small groups of people of all races and classes, filled with courage and hope, can make a difference. Their action takes two forms. First, they organize themselves in order to resist. They resist the global corporations with their policies for "development" from above. Their action is based on the strong belief that what is not good for marginalized people is not good for society.

28. Secondly, these small local communities try to live against the trends of an acquisitive society in which individual greed and social and ecological exploitation predominate. In some places where colonization and marginalization of people have devastated the lives of communities, those forms of local direct action often bring a new quality of life based not primarily on acquiring goods but rather on living in right relation with all of creation.

29. With sadness we must admit that the efforts of local communities to resist and to change the trends do not always end in positive outcomes. But where they do, these experiences can inspire and stimulate the self-empowerment of other local groups. Hence we commend the *monitoring of positive change* based on such questions as the decision-making process, means of financial control and the way in which people were empowered by the decisions made.

30. It is important to note that experiences of local communities in their direct action should not only inspire other marginalized groups. It is particularly the *life-styles* of those in more privileged positions that need encouragement towards a radical change. Many constructive suggestions regarding such a change have already been made and only need to be followed.

## 2. Reform of the international economic order

31. In discussing empowerment of local people, we should not lose sight of how the world community must be accountable to the whole creation and responsible for the economic and ecological choices to which the world trade system leads. In the realization of economic, social and cultural rights (the so-called second generation of human rights) we have only just started our efforts. It is an illusion to think that the United Nations covenant outlining these rights could be implemented while the exploitation of nations by other nations continues. Particularly the churches in industrialized countries must put great pressure on their governments to establish just patterns of trade and to share their resources with the poorer nations. Initiatives should be taken to overcome the international debt crisis. Control of the immense power of the global corporations still presents the largest challenge at international levels of decision-making.

## 3. Rethinking economics

32. With modern communications, prices can be known immediately all around the world. However, knowing the price of something does not mean we know its value. To think that price equals value is a conventional economic fallacy. Price is only one specific way of looking at value: the value in exchange. In a market economy price is based on demand and supply, which are both being calculated on a very narrow, short-term basis. Immaterial needs get no price; hence these needs are often increased instead of being satisfied through consumption. Waste, in which all material production ends, is usually disregarded. And since the poor have little money, their needs get excluded. In measuring supply, the market responds only to those costs which can be expressed in money. Moreover, it is an advantage to producers to leave out those costs which they do not pay for themselves, such as environmental degradation and human disease that may result. As a consequence, a good deal of environmental damage is being caused without entering "into the books".

33. What we need, therefore, is first of all a new concept of value, based not on money and exchange but rather on *sustainability* and *use*. Humankind has failed to distinguish between growth and development. While advocating "sustainable development" many people and groups in fact often have found themselves promoting "growth". Growth for growth's sake — the continued addition to what already is present — is the strategy of the cancer cell. Growth for growth's sake is increase in size without control, without limit, in disregard for the system that

sustains it. It ultimately results in degradation and death. Development on the other hand — like the strategy of the embryo — is getting the right things in the right places in the right amounts at the right times with the right relationships. Development, while supported both by growth and *reduction* of its parts, results in a self-sustaining whole. Development of the earth by human beings, if accomplished in a manner similar to development of the human body, maintains a balance among all parts of the whole. What is "just" and "right", then, must be found in social, biological and physical relationships involving humanity and earth. True development, as opposed to simple growth, focuses on the eco-system level.

34. It is necessary, then, to correct prices in such a way that they take into account the need to maintain the ecological functions which nature is offering humankind. For example, those living in wealthy nations would have to pay far more for the use of exhaustible energy resources. It should be noted that particularly energy prices, prices of raw materials and agricultural prices are already subject to effective manipulation. The means of public manipulation of prices should be used to reflect both ecological requirements and the need for distributive justice. The churches in the European Community, for example, should press for a radical change in the Community's agricultural policy, detrimental as this policy presently is to both the environment and African, Asian and Latin American farmers. The practice of the USA to dump their agricultural surplus in developing countries should also be vigorously opposed.

## 4. The United Nations human rights framework

35. The world is well aware of the existence of the Universal Declaration of Human Rights. Although the judicial mechanisms for the implementation of these rights are still very weak, their formulation does serve as a moral standard for the way in which governments and other institutions as well as individuals should treat their fellow human beings.

36. Children form a full and integral part of humankind. We have to recognize their rights and our human obligations towards the world they will inherit. There is an urgent need to pursue the implementation of the UN Convention on the Rights of the Child. As Christians we also emphasize our obligations towards future generations and our duty to respect life already in its process of formation.

37. In working towards a universal declaration of human obligations towards nature, we wish to combine our efforts with other NGOs as well as governments and the United Nations. In June 1992 the second United

Nations Conference on Environment and Development will take place in Brazil. In particular, it will present a plan for an "earth charter". Such a document would comprise an international agreement regarding the obligations of governments to respect the inherent value of the global environment and the obligations towards future generations. In the process leading to this charter, we feel the following points should be stressed:

a) The chapter on governmental obligations should be supplemented with a section on obligations of industrial and agricultural producers of goods and services, with special reference to global corporations, as well as a section on the responsibilities of consumers with regard to the environmental effects of their behaviour.

b) Judicial mechanisms for the implementation of the charter should be established at an international level, at continental levels, as well as at national and regional levels. When states commit ecological crimes these should be brought to international attention, concern and action.

c) In order to utilize the value of the charter as a moral code of conduct, an international organization might be founded, comparable to Amnesty International, whose purpose would be to expose any violations of the charter while mobilizing international shame. We should also like to stress the importance of collective consumers' actions as a way of enforcing ecologically justified behaviour for producers. Countervailing consumers' action might also be a means of combatting the power of advertising in its appeal to human greed.

## 5. *Democracy and good government*

38. With the collapse of the centralized command economies, it would be a fallacy to think the problem of a just and responsible society had found its solution in the combination of a free-market economy with parliamentary democracy. Of the many reforms necessary in national political and economic systems, we mention the struggle for more participation in political and economic decision-making and the need for good government.

39. Without political and economic democracy there will be no respect for creation. If the people who live closest to the earth cannot participate in the power structures of society, how can we expect ecologically responsible decisions?

40. Democracy should go together with good government. This requires a system of administration that is both functioning properly and good for its own people. Unfortunately in many parts of our world we are

still confronted with bad government, in two senses of the word: incapability and corruption.

41. The limits to bureaucratic control have become clearly visible. Legislation can reach its aims only if it has a place in a wide process of social change while being applied through an adequately functioning legal system. In many countries much more could be done to promote the effectiveness and democratic character of governmental control.

42. Governments should do everything to encourage ecologically responsible economic behaviour. Ecological crimes should be investigated, prosecuted, and punished. The apparent impunity of ecologically criminal acts in many parts of the world is a matter of great concern.

### 6. Conscientization, education and spirituality

43. We need a spirituality that connects our lives to past, present and future, and to God who sustains it all. With a spirituality based on global interdependence we can recognize the unity of all creation. With a spirituality based on empowered local communities we can have courage and hope to take direct action in the face of overwhelming obstacles that seek to tell us we cannot make a difference. With a spirituality that is as prevalent as today's mass media, we can protest against the influences that seek to define all of us as exploiting, acquisitive, human-centred creatures. A sustainable spirituality will give us the strength to make the changes necessary to save life on our planet as we know it. Only a concern for the well-being of the planet will bring the nations of the world into a global community based on peace. Only the recognition on a worldwide scale of the oneness of creation can provide the critical global consciousness necessary to chart a new course for a sustainable future.

44. Through such a spirituality we can educate ourselves, each other and our children in the new ecological values and responsibilities. This education will have to take place at many levels: families, school, the church, places of work, etc. The universal declaration of human obligations towards nature might serve as a basis for public education.

45. The learning process is not just a matter of books. Learning comes through watching and thinking and making the most of every given opportunity that comes our way.

46. There is an urgent need today for a new type of mission, not into foreign lands but into "foreign" structures. By this term we mean economic, social and political structures which do not at all conform to Christian moral standards. Naturally, we are aware of the corrupting tendencies of power which often transform anyone who participates in

power structures into part of the problem rather than of the solution. It is for this reason that the churches have to make a great and continuous effort in morally equipping their people for their missionary work in the foreign structures of our time.

### III. The church: covenanting for the life of all creation

47. The crisis presented by the brokenness of the whole community of life challenges the churches to renew their commitment to justice, peace and the integrity of creation. Churches have the responsibility to translate this commitment in concrete and practical terms.

48. But first we need to confess that we — as a community drawn together by the Holy Spirit — have failed to recognize and therefore fulfill our human responsibility towards creation. Christian teaching and practice, based on misinterpretation of scripture, have reinforced systems and structures of power that deny life. These should be examined and clarified.

49. The church is a sign of "new creation" in Christ, redeemed from brokenness to wholeness, from death to life. As a redeemed community, the church has a crucial role in the renewal of creation. It is the church's prophetic task and the church is called upon to respond with faith, courage and hope.

50. The power of the Holy Spirit enables the church to be a life-giving, healing and sustaining community where the wounded and the broken derive wholeness and renewal. This empowerment provides opportunities to explore just and sustainable social and economic arrangements and to discover creative, contextually relevant ways to fulfill this responsibility.

51. A critical examination of the church's faith, polity and structures may be necessary if the spiritual and organizational resources of the church should meet human and ecological needs. This implies a redirection of church policies, priorities and programmes.

52. The understanding of creation theology and of an ethic of economy and ecology should be reflected in the life and work of the church, through its study of the Bible, its teachings, hymns, liturgies, prayers, the institution of the sacraments and through its witness.

53. The task of renewal requires a continuing discernment of God's creative activity in the world, Christ's redemptive act, and the empowerment of the Holy Spirit that enables us to be faithful.

54. To this end we call upon the WCC member churches all over the world to take urgent action as follows:

*Life and worship*

55. Reflect on and review our own internal structures, doctrines, policies and practices which affect the environment and influence our behaviour towards the creation.

56. Encourage churches and local congregations to manifest this commitment through worship, particularly in the celebration of the sacraments. For instance, baptism and the eucharist, as a celebration of God's redeeming activity, bring together the elements of the created world. This sacramental perspective should influence our attitude towards creation.

57. Assist people at the congregational level to make choices within their reach, to change life-styles, and to offer alternative patterns of living such as the Gandhian approach. Another recommendation would be to help reduce use of energy and finding alternative forms of energy, recycling waste, etc. in industrialized societies. The Gwatt report on "The Churches' Role in Protecting the Earth's Atmosphere" (1991, p.25) provides further concrete possibilities for action.

*Education*

58. Reflect concern for the creation in the ecumenical calendar. The WCC should initiate a global decade for justice, peace and the integrity of creation, observed through an annual ten-day celebration, a time of prayer, reflection and action by all member churches.

59. Develop a new understanding of creation theology for all aspects of our churches' life which:
— addresses the tensions within the churches' order, i.e. gender, age, race, class, differences in physical abilities, etc.;
— draws upon the special gifts and learns from the value systems of those suffering from oppression;
— resists, through courage, power, commitment and reflection in the Holy Spirit, those forces and pressures which are harmful to people and destruction of nature;
— supports those that are already engaged in the process of renewal of the creation;
— draws upon our own cultures, traditions and local situations;
— pursues questions of the gospel's relationship to cultures.

60. Develop and implement educational programmes (information, education and communication), both in churches and in other communities, on issues related to environmental and ecological concerns. This should include the matter of responsible stewardship of human

fertility and should lead to an appreciation of and reverence for creation.

61. Study, reflect upon and address with sensitivity, ethical issues concerning bio-technology (including genetic engineering), prolonging of life, euthanasia, surrogate motherhood, etc.

*Advocacy*

62. Continue the Justice, Peace and the Integrity of Creation process as a framework for study and action on these issues. This should be part of a global ecumenical movement towards reordering our personal and corporate life-styles, our relationships with nature and the ecological reorientation of our overall economic system. For continuing the JPIC process in these ways the WCC should be a centre of exchange in which initiatives and contributions of member churches are shared and brought together.

63. Send a delegation composed of church representatives from the eight regions of the world to attend the United Nations Conference on Environment and Development (UNCED), to be held in June 1992 in Rio de Janeiro, Brazil. It is the first time since 1972 that such a world conference is being held to discuss, on a global level, the burning environmental issues of today, including the preparation of a convention on protection of global climate, and the link between environment and international trade. Work together with world religions in designing a common process towards UNCED, and in drawing up a universal declaration of human obligations towards nature. Such a universal declaration would acknowledge that human beings are part of creation as a whole and that we have an obligation to be instruments of God's design for creation.

64. Act together in defence of life. Facilitate and encourage the participation of people against the powers of oppression and destruction. Build a network of churches and Christians to facilitate exchange, cooperation, and appropriate collective action in the fields of ecology and economy.

65. Renew study of the international economic order including the need for new conceptual models based on cooperation, not on competition. Pursue initiatives to relieve those countries which continue to suffer from their critically heavy debt burdens. Highlight the plight of poor women and children who are always hit the hardest.

66. Urge the concerned member churches in the South and in the North to address and develop coordinated action on problems of sex tourism, nuclear testing, toxic-waste dumping, global warming, fishing, mining, etc.; to make their members aware of the dire consequences of

these practices; to dialogue with their governments and concerned corporations to stop such actions; and to influence appropriate legislation for the protection of the environment and of human life.

67. Campaign against the militarization of regions (such as the Pacific) for the protection of human life and for the preservation of the environment. On the international level, campaign for the abolition of the institution of war.

*Redirection of programmes*

68. Develop programmes to combat environmental degradation which include concerns about creation, economy and development, and establish plans of action at the regional and global levels.

69. Address the issue of science and technology in order to work towards the development of technology which is suitable and appropriate to the needs of the majority of the people, particularly of poor women and children, the carriers of wood and water all over the world.

70. Give continued attention to the relationship of faith, science and technology, exploring possibilities for continuing consultation involving scientists, theologians and others.

The following recommendations concerning particular regions were also made:

71. The Pacific Conference of Churches (PCC) is urged:

a) to include on the agenda of the next PCC assembly, discussion of a training programme dealing with the ecumenical vision of a new understanding of creation;

b) to pay special attention to the environmental concerns of smaller island churches, e.g. Marshalls and Carolines;

c) to assure the proportional representation of women and youth at the PCC level, so that their views and concerns on the care for creation may be adequately reflected.

72. The Canadian and US member churches are urged:

a) to jointly focus attention on common environmental agenda and mutual concerns, e.g. acid rain, concerns of indigenous peoples, sustainability in agriculture, etc.;

b) to work with other living faiths in addressing environmental concerns in the region.

73. The European member churches are urged:

a) to call upon the WCC to endorse the report of the ecumenical consultation of churches on "The Churches' Role in Protecting the Earth's Atmosphere" (Gwatt, Switzerland, 1991), as a basis for

<u>Signs of the Spirit</u>
<u>Official Report,</u>
<u>WCC Seventh Assembly</u>

Page 260: The title should read
          "New WCC presidents"

Page 324: Delete line 3

opening a dialogue with the Commission of the European Community
on global environmental and ecological issues;
b)  to listen to the voices of African, Asian and Pacific churches regarding the poisonous effects of nuclear waste disposal in their countries, and to take action to dispose of this waste within Europe;
c)  to affirm the need to take joint action to address the environmental concerns in the whole of Europe.

\*    \*    \*

## PLENARY DISCUSSION

*Bishop Anastasios of Androussa* (Eastern Orthodox, Greece): Para. 17: It is preferable to say that our vision remains the biblical vision, though we can also learn from the religious experience of humanity. Para. 57: Reference should be made to the rich ascetic tradition of the Eastern churches, a tradition valuable not only for monks but also lay people.

*Dr Emmanuel Klapsis* (Eastern Orthodox, USA): The report needs more emphasis on the problem of individualism. It should also stress that only God can turn the JPIC vision into reality, overcoming the sin to which all human initiatives are subject.

*Frau Ursula Urban* (United, Germany): The JPIC process must continue. Para. 62: The WCC should set up an office with adequate staff to coordinate work on JPIC.

*Prof. Vlasios Pheidas* (Eastern Orthodox, Greece): There is no ecclesiological perspective in the introductory section. The intimate link between church, Spirit and Christ is missing.

*Bishop Herbert Chilstrom* (Lutheran, USA): Para. 19: Even if we fulfilled all mandates outlined in this report, we would still be living with brokenness. Our fulfilment is beyond the present order of creation.

*Bischof Sigisbert Kraft* (Old Catholic, Germany): Mention should be made of ecclesiological damage resulting from the war in the Gulf. It is a sin against the Holy Spirit.

*Dr Matthias Sens* (United, Germany): The report refers to the duality of justice and integrity of creation, but peace is not taken fully into account. The Gulf war shows that the three must be held together.

*Bischof Walter Klaiber* (Methodist, Germany): Para. 16: We are called to ease sufferings, but only God can overcome them. Our hope must be seen in eschatological perspective.

*Dr Constance Parvey* (Lutheran, USA): Para. 47: The crisis mentioned is also a challenge to us and a call to overcome our brokenness in unity.

*Dr Mary Tanner* (Anglican, England): The report lacks an eschatological dimension and an emphasis on the search for the visible unity of the church. Without the latter, JPIC and church unity will not be brought together.

*Metropolitan Chrysostomos of Peristerion* (Eastern Orthodox, Greece): Para. 14: Must stress our responsibility to Christianize other traditions. Throughout, the perspective is more anthropocentric than Christocentric or theocentric. The emphasis should be on humans as co-creators to whom God has given specific responsibilities for creation.

*Prof. Angus Holland* (Presbyterian, South Africa): Para. 20: "Consumerism" can mean "the interests of consumers". What is meant here is excessive consumption.

*Ms Pauline Edgar* (Friends, USA): Para. 67: Opposition to militarism needs a theological basis. Reference should also be made in the report to over-population.

*Mme Cécile Souchon* (Reformed, France): We must unite our efforts on behalf of creation with those of people of other faiths.

*Dr Thomas Dipko* (United, USA): Churches in the North Atlantic have appropriated materialism and other ideologies of their culture. This is syncretism and should be condemned.

*Dr Hans-Gernot Jung* (United, Germany): JPIC is a spiritual process of repentance and conversion. Confession of Jesus Christ must be at the heart of the process.

*Archimandrite Theofilos Giannopoulos* (Eastern Orthodox, Jerusalem): A theology of creation must stress that Christ is the new person through whom creation was delivered for anthropotis.

## 3.3. REPORT OF SECTION II:
## "SPIRIT OF TRUTH — SET US FREE!"

### I. Theological perspective

1. "For freedom Christ has set us free,... For you are called to freedom, brothers and sisters..." (Gal. 5:1,13).

The *freedom* we enjoy as a gift of the Spirit is a personal word. It is a word that frees from the power of sin, death and evil. But freedom is more than a personal word, it is not merely internal, individualistic, "spiritual", other-worldly freedom. It is a freedom we are also called to experience in a material, this-worldly and communal sense. We, as people who experience the freedom of the Spirit, are called to break down the barriers which make people un-free. This Spirit of freedom lays upon us the task which Jesus himself accepted as a consequence of the Spirit coming upon him.

We, as people who have received the gift of freedom and who have received this calling to be free, cannot cease to struggle for the release of those who are captive to sin and to unjust social and economic systems. We cannot cease to address physical ill-health or spiritual blindness in our world. We are called to be in solidarity with the oppressed in their struggle for liberation. Thus, by the force of the Holy Spirit, Christian churches give witness of the gospel of Jesus Christ almost everywhere in the world — North and South, East and West — in spite of the diversities which characterize our societies (Eph. 4:1-6). The churches live the *gift* of unity and are *called* to practise their freedom transcending human barriers. In this sense, this worldwide fellowship of churches manifests the life of the Spirit by sharing among ourselves our expectations and anxieties, our visions and struggles (1 Cor. 12:26). Therefore, churches seek each other and care for each other, sharing our vocation to be free in the fulfilment of God's mission.

2. "When the Spirit of truth comes, he will guide you into all truth" (John 16:13a).

The Spirit of truth re-establishes and restores the integrity of the human person and human communities. As Christians and as churches, we constantly experience the danger of becoming captives to the systems and structures of the world. They are the principalities and authorities, "the cosmic forces of darkness, the spiritual forces of evil" (Eph. 6:12), which induce all human beings to be tempted to do injustice to others. By the spirit we know the truth, and the truth makes us free (John 8:32).

Therefore, we are no longer captives of systems which oppress and enslave. We are free to give witness of the justice of the kingdom of God, *resisting* unjust dominations, be they economic or political, cultural or social, of gender or race. Furthermore, we are all free to strive for the building up of just societies, both domestic and international. The force of the Spirit moves us to have an ecumenical concern in the struggle for justice and peace.

3. "... For in hope we are saved. Now hope that is seen is no hope. For who hopes for what is seen? But if we hope for what we do not see, we wait for it with patience" (Rom. 8:22-25). We who live in the Spirit are living by *hope*. In spite of the seemingly gloomy picture of the world, we are not moved to despair. We believe that the force of the Spirit of truth is at work in history, opening new paths to humanity. The future, which the powers of this world strive to shape and close over and over again, is permanently opened by the force of the Spirit. Christians and churches who receive this gift and are called to live in it, have to witness this reality, affirmed in our faith.

## II. Issues and recommendations

ISSUE ONE: THE CHALLENGE TO BE FREE IN ORDER TO STRUGGLE

Both as individuals and as churches we have often forgotten our communal vocation and task to render an authentic witness to the gospel. This is true, in particular, wherever the work of the Holy Spirit has been limited to an exclusively internal and personal experience. It is important, therefore, to be reminded that the Spirit of truth, in bearing witness to Jesus Christ, will convince the world about sin, righteousness and judgment (John 16:8). Wherever the Spirit is at work, people are being drawn into painful and costly but, at the same time, liberating processes of conversion.

The Spirit frees us from captivities of mind and body, making us members of God's family, engaging us to struggle individually and collectively against the power structures of this world which claim absolute obedience. Even in the midst of poverty and suffering, violence and marginalization, the Spirit opens our eyes to confront the contradictions within reality and thus engages us in the struggle for full liberation. It is the Spirit of truth who unmasks the myths which are being used to legitimize oppressive power structures.

While obliging us to face the contradictions and engaging us in the struggle, the same Spirit releases the energies that are being held down by conformity and passivity, by silent submission and brutal oppression.

Both as individuals and as churches, we must recognize our responsibilities for the divisions in the church and in the world and follow the path of repentance. The biblical terms for repentance, *te' shuvah* and *metanoia*, mean a radical change of mind and transformation. Repentance is the way leading to reconciliation, sanctification and salvation in Christ.

Our unity must be based on the realization that "so many of us as were baptized into Jesus Christ were baptized into his death" (Rom. 6:3). Our commitment as Christians is to see Christ in the other person for whom Christ died. Through the help of the Holy Spirit, we must share the suffering of others.

The collective, corporal or communal indicates a unique, direct, personal relationship with the Holy Spirit and opens new dimensions in our struggle for wholeness. The wholeness must include the differently-abled and people of all ages who bring special gifts to the community. This internal liberation by the Spirit empowers us to understand the world from the perspective of the vulnerable. We are empowered for our option for the poor.

*Recommendations*
1. The WCC should encourage spirituality and unity among member churches in addition to cooperating with people of other faiths in our common struggle for liberation. Spirituality in unity should be held together with issues of justice, peace and integrity of creation in the programmes of the WCC. This means also hearing the voices of the pentecostal churches.
2. The WCC should establish a laity department which will, through its programmes, empower people for leadership and ecumenism.
3. The WCC and its member churches should:
   a) engage in dialogue with those in power at all levels — whether local or international — on the issues of justice, peace and the integrity of creation (JPIC);
   b) support Christians engaged in working on JPIC;
   c) build communities of justice recognizing the role of monastic and faith communities.
4. We recommend that the churches be aware of the gifts of the differently-abled who are often forced to the fringes of our societies and churches. Their full participation must be ensured.
5. We encourage Christ's people to emulate the spirit and example of our Lord Jesus Christ (Phil. 2:6-11). In obedience to Jesus Christ we are

called to re-examine and repent of attitudes, practices and structures which reduce or prevent the liberating influence of the Spirit.

6. We urge the Christian community to seek out and engage those within and without the churches who are struggling to be free from oppression, despair and destruction.

ISSUE TWO: THE CHALLENGE TO EVOLVE A SUSTAINABLE VALUE SYSTEM

Through the six preceding assemblies, the World Council of Churches has called the attention of its member churches and the public at large to serious contradictions and imbalances prevailing in the world economic system. Established structures continue to prevent the economic growth and social justice of the poor and exploited peoples and nations. It is necessary to build a new international economic order. Since the first assembly, the WCC has repeatedly emphasized that there is an urgent need to review the existing world economic order and, in particular, the economic mechanisms that were created at Bretton Woods, USA, in 1944-45 — the International Monetary Fund (IMF), the International Bank for Reconstruction and Development (IBRD, most commonly known as the World Bank) and the later General Agreement on Tariffs and Trade (GATT) — which are dominated by powerful industrialized countries and are unaccountable to any international authority in which all nations are involved. Such a review should lead to more accountable and just economic and monetary structures within the jurisdiction of the United Nations and of the International Court of Justice.

Furthermore, the conciliar process aimed at Justice, Peace and the Integrity of Creation confirmed the assessment that prevailing models of economic growth and world trade, as they are controlled globally by transnational corporations, do not create conditions for a sustainable society. Rather, they destroy the ecological systems of the world through environmental destruction and the excessive exploitation of the resources of poor nations and indigenous lands, provoking massive migrations as well as causing wars through human greed to control natural resources.

In this economic system, a disproportionate burden is placed on women, particularly on poor, peasant, working and indigenous women.

Markets have existed and do exist in all societies and cultures. In most cases a market is a lively and human place. However, modern international markets have been perverted by interests and powers which have gained control of the market mechanisms causing injustice and unsustainability. The values that prevail in this market penetrate into all societies creating the impression that a global market system is being shaped as a totality. However, many are excluded from this system. There are also many who pay high social costs in order to keep the system functioning in their countries. For such people, the demands of the market are unbearable. Low salaries and unemployment force many men and women, excluded from the benefits of the "legitimate" market, to seek survival through "underground economies" of which the drug trade and arms trade are main manifestations. While we see in these desperate situations creative efforts to develop models for alternative economies, the so-called "wealth of nations" is merely the wealth of a minority in the world. In order for the "free market" to function effectively, basic human rights are being violated and the plight of the poor grows worse every day.

The structure of the present economic order and the shape of the international markets are closely linked to the ongoing debt crisis. Its development since the end of the 1970s has meant the impoverishment of the most indebted nations of Africa, Asia, the Caribbean, Latin America and the Pacific. In spite of efforts to follow the economic readjustments prescribed by the IMF and the World Bank, their economies do not improve. In order to pay the service of the debt, salaries lose their real value, and the necessary investments needed to preserve the quality of public utilities are not made. This, in turn, means that the quality of people's lives, especially of the poor, is deteriorating. At the same time, the debt crisis is already threatening the prospects of the former "socialist" nations of Eastern Europe and introducing tensions, financial instability and economic recession in North America, Western Europe and Japan. Furthermore, the corruption which unfortunately exists at some levels of government in some countries has compounded the problems of the poor.

What can the WCC and the churches do? The problems are so serious that the temptation to give up our prophetic responsibilities is sometimes very strong. But the gift of freedom, the force of the Holy Spirit that allows us to live in hope is once again calling the WCC and its member churches to share their energies and resources with the victims of this system, whose critical reformulation must be one of our priorities.

As Christians we seek a world of social and economic justice. This includes the empowerment of the victims of injustice and their inclusion in decision-making, respect and care for those who are vulnerable, oppressed and dispossessed, as well as the nurture of the environment. The networks of concern that churches and Christian communities can build together and with other organizations can play a positive role in this process.

After the economic system of the so-called "socialist" countries plunged into deep crisis, many hopes were expressed about the system of the free-market economy. But it appeared that the free-market economy is also unable to adjust to the new world economic order without new social and ecological institutions.

In some instances, it will be necessary to reinforce the authority of intergovernmental organizations which can speak on behalf of the majority of people such as the United Nations Organizations and the International Court of Justice. In other cases, churches must remind all the authorities of the nation states that they are called to serve people's needs and expectations, rather than attend to the economic readjustments required by those who manage the "free-market system". Furthermore, churches must recognize the increasing importance of the "civil societies", those non-governmental public organizations which express the interests and concerns of the people. It is in the "civil societies" that the energy of people aimed at greater emancipation and justice emerges. Churches belong to this "civil society" in the large majority of nations. They must put part of their resources towards the growth, development, empowerment and consolidation of these societies. This will reinforce possibilities for the exercise of democracy and fairness in socio-economic and political relationships.

Furthermore, taking into consideration the global character of the world's economy at present, as well as the role played by international networks such as Amnesty International and Greenpeace in fostering the cause of human rights and ecological preservation, the WCC and its member churches should join forces with such organizations at the domestic and international levels in order to monitor, from the people's perspective, economic developments as they emerge.

Part of our task is the education of people to raise their consciousness about the world economic and political situation in order to provide them with the tools to practise freedom and justice. As part of this process, in Germany, Switzerland, the Philippines, Brazil and some other countries, churches have taken initiatives to support the victims of the international debt crisis in accord with various positions enunciated by the WCC on different occasions (for example, at the central committee meeting in Buenos Aires in 1985). These initiatives should be followed by other churches.

*Recommendations*

1. The WCC welcomes the initiatives taken by the Swiss Protestant Church Federation, the National Council of Christian Churches in Brazil, the Evangelical Church in Germany and other ecclesiastical as well as ecumenical bodies, which have requested the WCC to start a study and action programme around the international debt crisis.

2. The WCC and its member churches should support the "Foreign Debt and the Drug Trade: Declaration of Kingston" that reiterates the immorality and illegitimacy of the external debt imposed as "tribute" that burdens the major sector of the people of the world.

3. The WCC and its member churches should follow critically the notions of the UN and the International Court of Justice in order to monitor more effectively current economic developments.

4. The WCC and its member churches are called to draw world attention to the plight and victimization of millions of youth and women who are denied employment and the possibilty of a life of dignity by the unjust international economic system.

5. The WCC and its member churches should give support to networks of organizations of the "civil society", both at the national and international levels, aiming at the progress of social and economic justice.

6. The WCC and its member churches should join with and provide resources for efforts to organize people's energies for the affirmation of sustainable value systems.

7. The WCC is called to serve as a catalyst for churches and groups in search of sustainable value systems and to facilitate their work through networking and other appropriate means.

ISSUE THREE: THE CHALLENGE TO WORK FOR RACIAL JUSTICE

Racism is one of the terrible sins of humankind. It is not only personal prejudice, but is embodied in the structures and institutions of society. When members of one race or group seek to dominate those of another, they are not truly free but are enslaved by their own fear and desire for control. Being oppressed and being an oppressor are both spiritually disabling. We affirm the need for individual repentance of this sin, and also for concrete changes in structural and institutional racism.

Wars, famine, drought and other disasters have created a growing population of refugees, displaced persons and asylum-seekers who must find new homes. They often face racism in the form of unfair immigration and employment practices. Immigration policies, especially in the emerging new Europe, must be carefully monitored. Our member churches all over the world must be alert to the potential dangers of increased racial tension as the result of the current massive migrations of people. This is especially true where European migrants are encouraged to emigrate to countries where there is already a large, underemployed population.

Women experience the worst consequences of racial, caste and economic violence. Displaced women and children experience double discrimination under racism since they are particularly vulnerable to exploitation. Women are often driven to prostitution in order to support their families, and children are abandoned on the streets to fend for themselves. During the Ecumenical Decade of the Churches in Solidarity with Women, we call on the churches to lift up the concerns of the women suffering under racism and caste-ism specifically and plan intentional programmes to enhance the participation and contribution of these marginalized groups.

We note the discrimination against the dalits in India who are struggling for dignity, equality, freedom and humane living conditions, both at the church and government levels.

Ethnicity, as it is emerging in Europe, is another major challenge to the churches. Often ethnic groups are defined by their religion as well as by their language and origin. Many of them are deprived of their basic human rights. Christendom runs the risk of being a divisive rather than a unifying force within the new political realities that are emerging. That makes it more urgent to be aware of our calling to unity as well as to continue our dialogue with the Roman Catholic Church. It should be of great concern to churches and Christians that anti-semitism, believed to have been overcome for good, is again surging in several European countries.

We recognize that there are disturbing undercurrents of racism in the present conflicts in the Middle East between Christians and members of other faiths. We also recognize the disproportionately high numbers of young black and hispanic Americans who are under arms in the Gulf region. There are similar undercurrents of racism in many other regions of conflict in the world, particularly in Central America.

At this assembly meeting in Australia, we are particularly conscious of the struggles of our Aboriginal brothers and sisters for a recognition of their history, their culture, their spirituality and their land rights. We recognize the resistance of many indigenous people against extermination and the denigration of their culture and the continued appropriation and exploitation of their traditional homelands. We are with them in their struggles. We are also aware of issues of indigenous rights in the

Americas and elsewhere in the world. In particular, we call on the various levels of governments of the United States, Canada, and Central and Latin America to address the pressing issues facing *their* indigenous people with fairness and equity. We call on the churches of the United States and Canada to repent of their complicity in the exploitation of the indigenous peoples in the past and to work towards reconciliation and mutual liberation through concrete action.

The 12th of October 1492 marked the beginning of 500 years of racial oppression and environmental destruction in the Americas. It also marked the starting point of the decimation of Africa through the slave trade which was an integral part of the exploitation of the Americas' lands and resources. This process enriched and made powerful European nations and churches and funded the colonization of other parts of the world by the same nations and churches.

We urge churches around the world to use the occasion of the 500th anniversary of the arrival of Columbus in the Americas to hold up to the world the oppression of the indigenous peoples on that continent. It is also an appropriate time to remember Africans and Asians of the diaspora, and the mestizos and mulattos created by the conquerors and conquered in North, Central and South America, and the Caribbean. We further urge that it be a time for sober reflection, reparation and commitment to combat the bitter legacies of imperialism and colonialism, including racism. Of particular concern must be the racism practised in the Dominican Republic where the 1992 celebrations are scheduled to begin in the Americas. There the only people officially identified as Black are the oppressed (and enslaved) Haitian sugar workers, most of whom live in the "batayes" in inhumane conditions, while all other Blacks are categorized as Indians.

We recognize that many came and continue to come to North and South America as refugees from political, religious and economic repression in other places in the world. While these people and their descendants should join with others in acknowledging the negative aspects of colonization, there is also legitimate reason for them to give thanks for the new freedoms they have found in many nations.

Caste-ism and other racism within the church must be fought. We must be constantly mindful that racism is deeply rooted in the hearts of many who consider themselves to be Christian all over the world. They need to hear the liberating voice of the Spirit calling them to embrace their sisters and brothers in love and in the spirit of justice.

*Recommendations*

1. We support affirmation III of the WCC convocation on "Justice, Peace and the Integrity of Creation" held in Seoul in 1990, and we affirm the fourth concretization of the Act of Covenant of this conference.

2. There should be a staff person in the WCC drawn from an indigenous community, whose special concern will be the issues surrounding indigenous peoples. Further, adequate representations of indigenous peoples should be ensured in the central committee, in all commissions and working groups of the WCC.

3. We affirm the work of the WCC on racism and we urge that it continue to be a priority issue in all WCC programmes and recommend that the programme be strengthened by ensuring adequate women staff and funding for it.

4. We recommend that the programme of Women under Racism be fully incorporated in the Decade of the Churches in Solidarity with Women and that an international gathering of women under racism and caste-ism be organized as a major contribution to the Decade.

5. We recommend that the Programme to Combat Racism (PCR) take responsibility for issues of ethnicity as well as racism.

6. We recommend that racism and its impact become a subject of theological education in seminaries as well as in the WCC's PETE-Bossey Programme. Churches should be encouraged to implement Christian education programmes which teach people to fight against racism.

7. We recommend that in view of the activities in connection with the 500th anniversary of Columbus's arrival in America, the WCC:
   a) begin a dialogue with the Roman Catholic Church as well as other churches in Europe, the Caribbean and Latin America with a view to acknowledging our complicity in the evils of colonization;
   b) call upon the churches to repudiate the 1992 celebrations of 500 years of colonization, and instead lend their support to the activities of the indigenous peoples surrounding that event;
   c) invite all churches, including the Roman Catholic Church, to confession and repentance for the subjugation and exploitation of the indigenous peoples. We recommend that ethnicity as it exists in some parts of Africa and Asia be addressed by the WCC as an urgent socio-political problem.

8. We recommend that member churches be encouraged to study and implement suggested actions regarding racism from the Darwin decla-

ration (PCR consultation, Darwin, 1989) and the report from the 1989 world mission conference in San Antonio.

ISSUE FOUR: THE CHALLENGE OF COMMUNICATION FOR LIBERATION

Communication is prophetic. We need to communicate to serve the cause of justice, peace and the integrity of creation. Communication, in the light of the Spirit, supports and sustains the building of a community of justice, and equips us to challenge the powers that are opposed to the Spirit of truth.

We are enjoined by Christ to love one another. When we communicate with one another, we must do so in love. We must speak to where our sisters or brothers are. We must listen to hear what is truly being said to us, not what we want to hear. Interpersonal communication is a two-way process. In this way, all members of the community can fully exercise their human rights and participate in decisions that are made.

Print and electronic media can wield such power. Means of communication are powerful tools of hidden control. Often, as in the present military situation in the Gulf, governments, even the governments of the Northern democracies, control what the media can communicate. The truth is not told and we cannot exercise free judgment. More insidiously, where the market controls what is said in the media, the dominant culture controls, by popular demand, what is written or produced by the media. We must seek ways to educate our people to be discerning listeners, viewers and readers in the context of education for the laity.

The mass media are a means of cultural imperialism where the lifestyle of the North Atlantic countries and Japan is seen to be the only one possible. Wherever possible, indigenous radio and television should be developed. People's participation is a precondition for communication for liberation and the fulfilment of human rights. We must ask questions about whose information is passed on to whom. Should communication technologies give a voice to the voiceless?

In all countries, churches should monitor the influence of the media, vigorously express their opposition when what is communicated distorts the truth, reinforces negative stereotypes or sanctions violent behaviour, and seek ways to influence the media. Individual Christians who work in the communication system are urged to exercise their Christian witness in the work place.

It is costly to produce programming of any quality, and our power to influence government and commercial media will continue to be limited. Therefore, we must find ways to ensure that our member churches have access to non-censored information so that we can act. Only when we are informed fairly about the situation can we be free to respond to our sisters and brothers in need. Our member churches must ensure that the messages are passed down to the members in ways that are accessible and understandable to them. We must continue to tell the stories of the people. Here interpersonal communication and the mass media intersect. Our concern should be to help our people in their prophetic mission.

Churches must draw attention to the fact that communication suffers as people become mere consumers of all forms of media that increasingly promote violence, pornography and obscenity. Communication for liberation is distorted when the media make people objects of propaganda. The media add to the militarization of the culture. Children especially are the victims of media that advertise violence. Communication and thus relationships between human beings are destroyed by uncritical consumption of the media.

*Recommendations*
1. The WCC should renew the call for "A New World Information and Communication Order", and enable its member churches to participate in its creation.
2. The WCC and the World Association for Christian Communication should assist churches and communities in their struggle for the communication of the truth.
3. Churches, where possible, should take advantage of means of mass communication.
4. Churches must enable the powerless to express their demands for justice and freedom in their own way, by providing support for universal primary education.
5. Churches must speak out prophetically for the rights of the powerless, regardless of whether the source of oppression be the church, state, or any other institution.
6. Churches should help develop alternate means of communication such as theatre, special liturgies and local, indigenous newspapers and radio.
7. Churches should ensure that their representatives to ecumenical meetings include the disadvantaged.
8. Churches should organize boycotts of the products of those who sponsor programmes that promote violence, sexism, racism, pornography and obscenity.

9. Churches should promote media awareness training at all levels particularly through lay training centres.

ISSUE FIVE: THE CHALLENGE FOR LASTING PEACE AND MEANINGFUL SECURITY

*Introduction*

In over one hundred wars since 1945, a number of common patterns can be observed. The wars are almost always in countries of the South and usually against racially-oppressed groups. Women, youth and children suffer the most. An excessive proportion of those participating in the fighting are also from oppressed groups and young people. This reflects failure to provide alternate economic and educational opportunities for their future.

The root causes of war include greed, materialism and consumerism which lead to the accumulation of wealth and power in the hands of the few and oppression for the majority.

*Regional dimensions of lasting peace and meaningful security*

The search for lasting peace and meaningful security presents different challenges in the various regions of the world.

In *Africa* attention is focused on the massive poverty and dislocation exacerbated by regional and civil wars — often fed by outside intervention or neglected by world opinion. For example, in Ethiopia, the Sudan and Somalia and in Liberia, Angola and Mozambique, there is mass starvation as the wars continue, heightening poverty and human misery as well as perpetuating serious environmental degradation.

In *Asia* issues such as the presence of foreign bases, militarization, the suppression of peoples' movements and of democratic opposition require continued attention. The continuing civil conflict in Sri Lanka and the struggles for self-determination in Cambodia and Taiwan continue to merit world attention.

The *Caribbean* suffers from its proximity to the USA — the hemispheric super-power with its economic domination and frequent military interventions, and colonial control of Puerto Rico which is used as a military enclave. The region is a victim of low-intensity conflict which causes destabilization and economic dependency. In *Central America*, low-intensity conflict, the war against the poor and the assault on democratic movements is a continuing pattern.

In *Europe*, there are still people suffering from political, social and religious instability, e.g. Albania, the Ukraine, Romania and Czechoslovakia. Even after the Cold War, the vast number of weapons in place indicates that the legacy of the East-West divide has still not been overcome. There is an urgent need for nuclear and conventional disarmament. It is an alarming new sign that NATO is now considering out-of-area operations. In addition, many new conflicts have emerged as the straightjacket of the Cold War has been relaxed.

*Latin America* has largely been freed from the military dictatorships of the 1970s and early 1980s but cannot provide meaningful economic security for its people because of the crushing burden of the debt crisis. A number of countries suffer from serious political instability.

The *Middle East* urgently requires an immediate cease-fire and the establishment of a stable, politically-negotiated, comprehensive security framework in which the rights of all people are preserved. This is the urgent priority for the region. The Gulf war has dramatized the fragility of this region. In particular the rights and security of the Palestinian people need to be affirmed in the context of a comprehensive Middle East peace process. This process could be promoted by holding an international conference in which all the problems (Cyprus, Lebanon, Palestine, Israel and the Gulf) could be dealt with.

The urgent issue for *North America* is whether the USA can abandon its super-power role in favour of a domestic defence policy which is not dominant and interventionist. Poverty and racism are rife.

The *Pacific* looks for international support for the legitimate struggle for independence in the remaining colonies in the Pacific and in opposition to French nuclear-bomb testing and US missiles and SDI (Star Wars) tests in the Marshall Islands.

*Instruments for lasting peace and meaningful security*

1. The Amsterdam assembly of 1948 affirmed that "war is contrary to the will of God". Sharing this conviction, we urge the United Nations to work towards a universal convention which would ban war as a means of conflict resolution.

2. Our commitment to the United Nations (UN) and the strengthening of its peace-making and conflict-resolution role need to be reinforced. The jurisdiction of international law and the International Court of Justice must be universally accepted. Existing international agreements should be respected. All UN Security Council resolutions should be implemented.

3. States should not establish military bases nor send troops into other countries. Where these already exist, they should be withdrawn.

4. Peoples' movements engaged in the struggle for human dignity and liberation should be supported, and understanding of peoples' security should replace national security doctrines and low-intensity conflicts.

5. Conflict resolution and major aid efforts are required in Ethiopia, the Sudan, Somalia, and other areas of regional conflict. Renewed pressure for negotiated settlements between governments and liberation movements in El Salvador and Guatemala is required.

6. Zones of peace should be created and developed (e.g. the Indian Ocean, the Pacific, the Caribbean).

7. Regional security structures should be strengthened. Churches should urge their governments to implement the Helsinki agreement in Europe and encourage them to develop the Conference on Security and Co-operation in Europe into an effective instrument for safeguarding democracy, human rights and the peaceful resolution of conflicts. Effective steps for nuclear and conventional disarmament as well as measures for confidence-building should be taken.

8. Military budgets should be reduced to release funds for development and ecological protection. Development assistance should not include a military component.

9. Deterrence by weapons of mass destruction should be rejected. Nuclear weapons should be radically reduced and eliminated as quickly as possible. In the meantime, intrusive verification measures should be allowed by all governments. Therefore, defensive, non-threatening security systems and civilian-based defence should be developed.

10. Immediate and effective steps should be taken to end hunger and starvation — and waste in other regions.

Further detailed recommendations based on the section of the Seoul JPIC covenant on demilitarization have been referred to the Programme Policy Committee. They concern registering and restricting arms transfers, conscientious objection and war taxes, denuclearization of the world's navies, elimination of chemical and biological weapons, and support for the Non-Proliferation Treaty and a comprehensive test-ban treaty.

*Commitment of the churches*

The churches should commit themselves to the affirmations of the Seoul convocation. Justice, Peace and the Integrity of Creation should continue to provide the orienting framework for church commitment to peace and justice. The Seoul covenant, with its stress on protection of the environment, alleviation of debts, demilitarization of international relations and the rejection of racism, provides four interlocking elements for social involvement.

### Recommendations to the churches

1. Regional solidarity in the peace work of the churches must be strengthened. The member churches and the WCC should establish ecumenical ministries for JPIC and shalom services as proposed by the Swedish Ecumenical Council and others.
2. The preferential option for the poor should be the guiding principle of the churches' efforts in the defence of life and opposition to governmental economic and military policies which create or exacerbate conflicts.
3. Lay training, leadership formation and ecumenical learning must be strengthened as a key instrument to promote many WCC priorities, especially JPIC.
4. Programmes of peace education should begin at an early age and continue throughout life.
5. Help should be provided to the churches through appropriate channels for understanding more deeply the connection between violence, institutionalized racism and the oppression of women. Three of the strongest roots of violence are oppression through race, sex and class.
6. Churches must reject the manufacturing of enemy images (particularly relating to Islam at present).
7. Churches must always serve as an example of peace-making, not least by making peace between themselves.
8. Churches must resist the use of religion to cause or exacerbate conflict. They must  initiate the call for a new international treaty prohibiting the testing of weapons delivery systems, including the SDI programmes.

### Recommendations for the WCC

1. The JPIC emphasis must be strengthened as a focus of WCC work.
2. The advocacy role of the WCC at the UN should be reinforced.
3. The WCC should establish the structural possibility of acting as an intermediary between churches in conflict with each other. The WCC hould take an active, reconciling role in situations where religion is a factor in conflict.
4. The WCC should pay greater attention to intra-state conflicts and press the UN and other relevant bodies also to do so. The WCC

should create an early warning system for the prevention of conflicts or their detection in an early stage before large-scale violence is used.
5. The WCC must educate the churches in understanding the connection between violence, institutional racism and the oppression of women.
6. The WCC should support regional "peace networks" and monitor their coordination through an "exchange centre" in Geneva.

ISSUE SIX: JUSTICE FOR WOMEN

*Women in society*

The Christian community affirms that God has called women and men to live in relationship with each other, with one another, with creation and with God. We recognize that there are major cultural differences in such relationships around the world. There are also differences between generations within the same society. Over against these cultural and generational differences, however, we affirm that "in Christ there is neither male nor female" (Gal. 3:28). We must strive to free ourselves from the scourge of bias based on gender. Within our Christian families, we must strive for equality of relationship and mutual respect, a sharing of tasks and the acknowledgment that human sexuality is a gift of God.

We reject all systems and relationships built on domination and subjugation that shape economic, social, political, cultural and ecclesial structures in which men wield power. These affect both men and women since neither is free when the other is oppressed.

We are concerned about economic injustices to which women are subjected and the feminization of poverty. The major factor that contributes to it is the unjust global economic system exacerbated by the current recession and increasing burden on debtor nations, which places impossible demands on marginalized sections of society — particularly on women. Women's work is often unpaid and systematically under-valued and they have limited access to the centres of economic and political power. This restricts their choices in work and in education. Added to this, they experience sexual harassment and other forms of intimidation in their places of work.

The church has a responsibility to ensure that adequate health care is available to all women. New reproductive technologies and other family planning programmes that affect women and their rights raise serious ethical issues that the churches must help to resolve.

All forms of violence that women experience in society, even in the privacy of their homes, need to be dealt with through adequate legal safeguards and in the churches' ministry. In nations where human rights are violated, women face particular problems — such as the torture of women prisoners. Women in many parts of the world have been affirming and applying the power of non-violent forms of resistance within people's movements. This must be honoured and supported by the churches.

Men and women in many cultures traditionally feel compelled to solve disputes by confrontation rather than by conciliation. When exercised by men, confrontation often leads to violence against women and children in the home. Confrontation also often leads to armed combat. The churches should take the lead in examining and affirming cultures based on conciliatory models of caring and sharing.

*Women in the church*

In many of our churches, we need to come to an understanding of the male-dominated systems and how they operate — how they affect both men and women. In those systems men take power, define what power is and who is to participate in it. They are systems from which both men and women suffer since neither is free.

Sometimes language is used as a tool of domination. We propose to recover holistic language that can be used, where appropriate, in the liturgies of the churches. It is vital to educate people and clarify misunderstandings regarding the role and place of women in church and society in order to promote unity among men and women.

We affirm the role played by countless women throughout the world in the service of the church. We urge that contributions made by women in staff and volunteer positions be valued for what they are — the loving service to God — equal to, though different from, other contributions.

In some confessions, the equality of women is seen in terms of women's ordination. We affirm the struggle of our sisters in their search for ordination, but we recognize that ordination does not mean that in these confessions women are no longer marginalized. Churches that are not discussing the ordination of women must be respected. It must be realized that women and men within those traditions are also dealing with the women's issue on the ministries and mission of women in church and society.

The church must be a caring community that, through patience and faithfulness, values and supports *all* its members. In Christ's church, all should be free to celebrate their life in him equally.

*Recommendations*
1. We call upon the WCC, within the framework of the Ecumenical Decade of the Churches in Solidarity with Women, to convene a study conference of leaders within the churches on the roles of and relationships between women and men in our communities.
2. We urge our member churches to use inclusive language and female imagery to express the faith.
3. We encourage the WCC to continue and strengthen its study of marriage and family, with special attention to new, emerging family patterns.
4. We ask that the WCC undertake a study of the implications of the new reproductive technologies for women and for society as a whole.
5. We ask that special attention be paid to health issues as they relate to women and children. We are particularly concerned about the production of banned birth control pills and the dumping of toxic wastes of all kinds.
6. We must continue to support literacy programmes for women and promote women's education at all levels, including theological training and leadership training.
7. We recommend the establishment, where they do not exist, of ecumenical regional networks for women through which women's unique gifts can be shared.
8. While respecting theological perspectives that do not accept the ordination of women in some traditions, we affirm that women's participation in the ordained ministries should remain on the ecumenical agenda.
9. We ask the WCC to organize a special study commission which will do research on the existing differences in teaching and tradition regarding women between the Orthodox and Protestant churches, as well as the Roman Catholic Church.

## III. Common themes

We brought to this assembly the presuppositions of our cultures and traditions. We have found that, through the working of the Holy Spirit, we have come to hear more clearly what others have been saying. This has been made evident by the way that, in our work together, several common themes have emerged.

## *1. Human rights*

The underlying theme of this section is expressed in the comprehensive deliberations that took place on human rights. Human rights, or the violation of them, is a fundamental element in each of the issues discussed in this section: the rights of women and children, the rights of minorities, peace with justice, economic justice and racism.

The advocacy of and struggle for human rights should be central in the churches. We urge that the defence and promotion of human rights be understood as central to the gospel, and their promotion a responsible and ethical engagement by Christians in social life.

The Universal Declaration of Human Rights and the more recent declaration for the rights of the child provide us with instruments of appropriate vision. What is needed is to promote these instruments through human rights education and through campaigning for their ratification and implementation.

## *2. The role of the United Nations*

During the last forty years the UN has played a very important role in understanding and promoting peace and justice among the nations of this world. It was created immediately after the end of the second world war and therefore it belongs to the group of institutions shaped in the context of a world order controlled by the super-powers of the liberal and the communist blocs. With recent events, this order came to an end. There is a concern about how far the UN's structures and style of operation reflect this change of situation. The Security Council is, indeed, one of these structures which should be revised in order to make it more democratic and open to the expectations of the less powerful nations. Furthermore, with the fading fortunes of the USSR as a super-power, it only leaves the USA and its allies to maintain a stranglehold on the UN. We therefore urge an international process to evaluate the role and effectiveness of the UN with a view to restructuring and reshaping it. We recognize that the UN and its agencies are valuable instruments for the maintenance of peace and security as well as for interstate cooperation in world affairs. Nevertheless, its structures must reflect the present historical trends and its authority should reflect the concerns of all nations.

## *3. Dialogue, gospel and culture*

Many Christians, especially in Africa and Asia, feel threatened by Islamization and the introduction of the Sharia law. The WCC must take this issue very seriously in its dialogue with people of other faiths.

The prominence of Aboriginal issues at this assembly and the debate about syncretism have, as in Vancouver, drawn our attention to the relationship between gospel and cultures.

In Latin America the commemoration of the 500th anniversary of the arrival of the conquistadores and the beginning of Christian mission in that part of the world is also creating a debate about gospel and cultures. As the WCC reflects more and more the diversity and cultural riches of the ecumenical family, this issue has to receive prominence.

*4. Community*

The relationship between peoples is often distorted by ideologies, racism, enemy images, sexism, etc. Listening to the teachings of Jesus, Christians know that they have to overcome those barriers that also divide them. As a sharing and healing community, Christians must become a prophetic voice in a world that is torn apart.

*5. Power*

Powerful institutions claim to be engaging in rational activity, and this justification appeals to those whom the institutions benefit. But for those whom they oppress, the outcome is a chaos of irrationality. We need a greater understanding of the human effects of the exercise of secular power.

Power is not a limited commodity. Power must be redefined and shared in a new way. We understand power as an enabling force which will allow us to transform relationships so that domination can be overcome.

But the power of the Holy Spirit is a potent force. It enables us to shape life. Through the Spirit's power the churches are part of the positive force for good.

\*  \*  \*

## PLENARY DISCUSSION

*Dr Lois Wilson* (United, Canada): The report should speak of sexual harassment of women in the churches as well as in society.

*Bishop Anastasios* (Eastern Orthodox, Greece): "Theological perspective" section: Christological and ecclesiological perspectives are dangerously absent. Our criterion for discerning the spirits is Christ. More biblical and theological reflections are needed on the question of truth. The main work of the Spirit is to guide us into all truth, giving us personal, existential knowledge of the truth in Christ. It is also necessary to stress the relation of the Spirit of truth with the church. The coming of the Spirit at Pentecost transformed individuals into an apostolic community responsible for continuing the work of Christ, for making known the truth of God. Finally, the freedom we have is not only from something but for somebody. Only in Christ are we truly free.

*Dr Milton Itar Efthimiou* (Eastern Orthodox, USA): Issue 6: We should not substitute inclusive language for the time-tested language of the Bible or the fathers. Female imagery has been prevalent within the Orthodox tradition (e.g., in iconography), but the Trinity cannot be subjected to female language.

*Pastor Jorge Domingues* (Methodist, Brazil): The concerns of youth are missing in the recommendations. The WCC should support youth participation in the decision-making bodies of the churches.

*Dr Emmanuel Klapsis* (Eastern Orthodox, USA): The Spirit seems to drop out of consideration after the first section. The Spirit creates community and challenges the churches to liberate themselves from the sin of diversity. The report also fails to mention the freedom from death which leads to martyrdom.

*Prof. John Romanides* (Eastern Orthodox, Greece): All who received glorification have experienced Pentecost. This is important for women who, together with the prophets, are the foundation of the church in Ephesians. The ordination of women, however, is another matter. Issue 3: Reference is made to the Roman Catholic Church's role in the exploitation of Latin America. This is also true of Reformation churches in other parts of the world.

*Ms Christine Grumm* (Lutheran, USA): In difficult economic circumstances it is often the positions held by women that are cut. This must not be true for the WCC. How much support do women staff get in the World Council? The system is designed and dominated by men.

*Bishop Zacharias Mar Theophilos* (Mar Thoma, India): Issue 3: A simple note in the reports on the dalits, the poorest of the poor in India, is not enough. We must express our solidarity with them and our support for their struggle.

*Mrs Rachel Mathew* (Mar Thoma, India): Issue 6: Ordination should be recognized as a calling and not as an issue of equality.

*Rev. Puafitu Faa'alo* (Reformed, Tuvalu): Issue 5: The omission of any reference to Irian Jaya and East Timor shows the incapacity of the WCC to deal with sensitive issues of peace and justice.

*Rev. Mary-Gene Boteler* (Presbyterian, USA): Issue 6: The report addresses the issue of violence against women but makes no recommendations. Such violence is on the rise; women need places of sanctuary, even at a WCC assembly.

*Prof. Adebisi Sowunmi* (Anglican, Nigeria): Issue 3: The Programme to Combat Racism should take responsibility for issues of ethnicity and Islamization as well as racism and should address these as urgent socio-political problems.

*Ms Ellen Kirby* (Methodist, USA): Issue 2: The WCC should take advantage of the study already done by five churches regarding the international debt crisis and play a strong role in coordinating action towards solutions of this very serious problem. Issue 5: It is imperative that the WCC give top priority to full-time representatives at the United Nations.

*Ms Stephanie Lynn* (United, Canada): Issue 3: Freedom, contrary to what is implied in this report, cannot be achieved by taking away the freedom of others.

*Ms Annathaie Abayasekera* (Anglican, Sri Lanka): Reference should be made to the problems faced by people from the South who are migrant workers or refugees in countries that belong to the European Community.

*Prof. Angus Holland* (Presbyterian, South Africa): The text from John 8 — "You shall know the truth and the truth shall make you free" — is unique in the Hebrew tradition in its affirmation that it is the truth that binds one to the truth lest freedom become anarchy.

*Prof. Peter Widmann* (Lutheran, Denmark): The report lacks concrete analysis and fails to make necessary distinctions, especially between what God does and what we do. As a result, we confuse our good intentions with the work of God.

*Archbishop Aram Keshishian* (Oriental Orthodox, Lebanon): In many WCC programmes, there is a competition between global and contextual definitions of justice. This assembly has shown how our concepts are locally conditioned; JPIC may help us move towards a global understanding.

*Mrs Prakai Nontawasee* (United, Thailand): Issue 4: Reference should be made to the evil impact on Asian societies, especially on women and children, of the "flesh-trade" (prostitution) and the tourist industry.

*Prof. Bastiaan De Gaay Fortman* (Reformed, Netherlands): The report offers clear theological definitions of what is meant by "the freedom of the Spirit". It must mean the freedom to follow Jesus as Lord.

*Dr George McGonigle* (Anglican, USA): The report includes recommendations to add to the number of WCC staff, something that is not likely to happen in the present financial situation. References to the unjust economic system failed to acknowledge that such systems were also found within nations.

*Landesbischof Horst Hirschler* (Lutheran, Germany): We must emphasize the first sentence that Christ sets us free. We are not sisters and brothers because we have the same interests or views but because Christ is our common Lord.

*Rt Hon. David Bleakley* (Anglican, Ireland): The WCC needs a "programme to combat war-ism".

*Archdean George Austin* (Anglican, England): Issue 4: The call for a new information order is part of discredited UNESCO proposals. It would not lead to liberation but to a new form of slavery.

# 3.4.   REPORT OF SECTION III:
## "SPIRIT OF UNITY — RECONCILE YOUR PEOPLE!"

**Introduction**

The seventh assembly has a special logo which we have all seen on banners, T-shirts and books. Within this one logo are combined a number of the symbols of the Holy Spirit — the dove, tongues of fire, and a boat with its sails filled with the wind of the Spirit. It all depends on the angle from which one looks at the drawing.

In section III as we reflected on the life of the church we came to realize that Christians see truth in different ways and yet at the same time all are united in the power of the Holy Spirit. This rich diversity of insights and practices is a gift of the Holy Spirit. Sadly this is not recognized even in the life of the church, and all too often diversity is a cause of division.

Christians are divided from each other by history, doctrine, culture, class, gender and wealth. New Christian movements such as the pentecostal and charismatic movements add to the diversity. Christians need to recognize that only in a sinful world does diversity become divergent while in Christ diversity is held together in unity. We are already united by our common baptism as the basis of koinonia, guided by the Holy Spirit. What we work towards is unity of faith, life and witness.

In this process it will be especially important to face up to the divisions which prevent us from sharing the eucharist together and those which make it impossible for churches to recognize the ministry of others.

Christians are even more deeply divided from people of other faiths and ideologies even though we share a common humanity and face common challenges and tasks. There are also deep divisions within and between other living religions and ideologies. From the depth and pain of our divisions we cry "Spirit of unity, reconcile your people!"

Reconciliation has to take place in a historical context. Reconciliation works when there is honest recognition of the actual sin committed against your neighbour and when practical restitution has been made for it. In other words those who have been guilty of oppression and injustice must show genuine and costly repentance (metanoia). Forgiveness is pre-eminently mediated through the victim in the historical context. This process of repentance and reconciliation may well be a long one. We must open ourselves to the Holy Spirit who works among us and also in the world — leading the whole of humanity into the community (koinonia) which is both a present and eschatological reality.

## A. Spirit of unity

### 1. Ecumenical perspectives on ecclesiology

The reflection of numerous churches about their own identity as well as many ecumenical developments — for example the response of churches to the *Baptism, Eucharist and Ministry* (BEM) document — call for comprehensive discussion on the nature and mission of the church. The idea of koinonia can be a most helpful perspective in this work. As expressed in the book *Resources for Sections:* "Koinonia in the Holy Spirit is based on sharing in the life of the Trinitarian God and is expressed by sharing life within the community. (It) becomes possible through reconciliation with God and with one another in the power of the Holy Spirit". This reconciliation can come about only if, recognizing the baptism that binds us together, we also recognize other factors relating to ecclesiology which need further ecumenical study:

a) *Unity and diversity:* Diversity has always been an essential in the life of the Christian koinonia. It is an expression of the church's catholicity. But there are also certain limits, namely the confession of

Jesus Christ as God and Saviour according to the scriptures, who is the same yesterday, today and for ever. Diversity that builds up the body is life-giving; diversity that divides and excludes cannot be accepted.

b) *Church and culture:* The gospel from which the church is born finds its historical expression in many cultures. Such incarnation calls the churches to serious dialogue with the respective cultures. In the search for a contextual application of the gospel, it is important that national and ethnic identities be respected and that the unity of the church be preserved. In the light of the gospel, all cultures need to be transformed and renewed.

c) *Authority:* The whole question of authority needs further ecumenical study. Aspects include diverse structures of teaching with authority in the churches and common structures of decision-making as an element of visible unity.

d) *Roman Catholic Church:* We affirm the value and participation of Roman Catholic observers and advisers at this assembly and especially their contribution in the area of Faith and Order. We encourage the continuation and development of existing dialogue as appropriate in the spirit of our prayer to the Spirit of unity.

## 2. Koinonia and unity

The 1987 central committee of the WCC asked Faith and Order to prepare a draft statement on "The Unity We Seek" to be submitted to the assembly in Canberra. The statement, "The Unity of the Church as Koinonia: Gift and Calling", was discussed by the section and appropriately amended, and later adopted by the assembly. The full text is included in the Report of the Reference Committee (4.4).

## 3. Community of women and men

A renewed and transformed community of women and men calls for a non-oppressive understanding of power grounded in relationships of love, repentance and forgiveness, modelled on the life and ministry of Jesus and exemplified for us on the cross. A truly renewed community will value the gifts of every group of people. This community, united by baptism, shares differently but equally in the gifts of the Holy Spirit. Churches today are being enriched by many new and renewed ministries of women, both among those churches that ordain women and those that do not. Yet, serious differences continue to exist between the churches on this issue. Because these different positions appear to "raise obstacles to mutual recognition of ministries" and thus may be a hindrance to unity, it is important that an ecumenical study on this issue be undertaken as part of the work of Faith and Order.

RECOMMENDATIONS

1. That a study on ecumenical perspectives of ecclesiology be undertaken in the WCC with a view to re-enforcing our work towards the unity of the church. This study should be closely related to the ongoing Faith and Order studies on the common confession of the apostolic faith and to other work in the WCC, especially to the ecclesiological implications of the Justice, Peace and the Integrity of Creation (JPIC) process. The provisional theme of the 1993 Faith and Order world conference "Towards Communion in Faith, Life and Witness" also points in the same direction. The member churches of the WCC are invited to participate in and support the preparation of this conference.

2. That the Faith and Order study document "Church and World" be studied in the churches as a help for convergence in their ecclesiological thinking, and particularly to highlight the inter-relation between the nature of the church as a communion of the Holy Spirit and its mission as an instrument of God's saving and transforming purpose.

3. That the assembly express its gratitude to the churches for their active participation in the BEM process, in which considerable convergence in the understanding and practice of baptism, eucharist and ministry has already been achieved.

4. That a special fund for the Community of Women and Men be set up to stimulate further reflection and action locally on relevant issues.

5. That the WCC continue to focus on women through the Decade of the Churches in Solidarity with Women.

6. That the WCC inaugurate a programme of ecumenical training to enable the churches to equip women and men, lay and ordained, for partnership in ministry in local congregations.

7. That member churches monitor their educational programmes and resources to incorporate insights into faith, worship and mission through the Community of Women and Men.

8. That the WCC continue to seek ways of ensuring that the rich variety of gifts and leadership and participation among women are channelled appropriately into its assemblies, commissions and committees. A detailed statistical analysis of delegations to assemblies might encourage this.

## B. Mission in the power of the Spirit — the ministry of reconciliation and sharing

The reconciled community that we seek can only be found through Jesus who laid down his life for his friends and forgave those who nailed him to the cross. The suffering of the victims of division is intertwined with the cross. There is a solidarity in suffering on the part of those who share in the pain and suffering of Christ through which they are also united with the pain of all humankind. The reconciliation brought about by the cross is the basis of the mission of the church.

A reconciled and renewed creation is the goal of the mission of the church. The vision of God uniting all things in Christ is the driving force of its life and sharing. Sharing also means that we work concretely to overcome economic disparities and social antagonisms between classes, castes, races, sexes and cultures. The diversity of cultures is of immediate relevance to the church's ministry of reconciliation and sharing for it affects both the relationships within churches and also the relationship with people of other faiths.

### 1. Wholeness of mission

We affirm that we are called to share the gospel among all peoples locally and globally and we recognize that the Holy Spirit leads different people and churches into mission in different ways. Our mission needs to be in Christ's way, in full obedience to the will of God as it was analyzed at the world mission conference in San Antonio. Wholeness of mission demands a will to break down the barriers locally and globally. We affirm JPIC as a mission imperative that promotes interconnectedness and mutual commitment.

While the unity of the church and wholeness of its mission are inseparable, we do not need to achieve visible unity of the churches before we address the needs of the world together. Indeed such common endeavour in the world may further the unity of the church. Each church acting in mission is acting on behalf of the whole body of Christ. At the same time we affirm local ecumenical endeavours where people of various churches engage in mission together. The possibility of such ecumenical endeavours could be greatly increased as the churches grow towards consensus on issues such as baptism, eucharist and ministry which at present impair their communion. We need to remember our original understanding of mission which is preaching, teaching and healing. This involves the whole people of God in sharing, serving and renewal in a spirit of love and respect. Mission is both local and global and we must be sensitive to each situation and the ways to address each situation.

It has been customary to speak of "sending churches" in some parts of the world. Where aggressive "sending" has been done by churches, particularly from the West to the South, the phrase is problematic. If we continue to use the term we should emphasize that *Christ* sends through the church in the power of the Holy Spirit. Structural changes are required where "sending" perpetuates denominational engagement in mission and separated churches.

Our brother and sister Christians in many parts of the world suffer pain, persecution and oppression. Many are exploited to satisfy the desire of people in the North and the West. The church must be in solidarity with these victims in their suffering. Christians in these prosperous areas must have the humility to learn from those oppressed sisters and brothers. Thus there can be a real sharing and a partnership in mission even in the midst of economic injustice and political hostility and this is a witness by the church to the gospel of reconciliation.

Evangelism is a vital part of mission and is the responsibility of all members of the church and not of some particular individuals. Here again the churches of the North and West have much to learn from Christians in Latin America and Africa.

Proselytism among the churches was identified by the section as both a scandal and a challenge. The WCC defined and repudiated proselytism in 1960. More work needs to be done on this to avoid increasing bitter relations between the churches and the tendency to advance the concerns of one group at the expense of another.

Religious fanaticism and the alliance of religion with forces of injustice and oppression have often torn human society apart and today threaten the very possibility of a world at peace. The danger is within all religions. Our conviction that Jesus Christ through the action of the Holy Spirit is "God's saving presence for all" is not hesitant or partial and we seek to live in respect and understanding with people of other living faiths.

## 2. The community of sharing

We affirm that all sharing begins with the recognition that what we call "ours" is given by God in love, that we have a duty to serve as stewards of those gifts, and that sharing is shown forth when the church manifests itself as one body, the body of which Jesus is the head and all the faithful are members. Sharing depends upon creating opportunities for offering up and receiving emptiness and suffering as well as fullness and joy.

The church's mission is reconciling all humankind with God and with each other. Sharing means giving and receiving by all to one another to effect reconciliation and to promote growing together. In response to the cries of the poor and marginalized in the world, sharing means committing ourselves as churches to the sharing of power and resources so that all may fully participate in mission.

Sharing happens at all levels: individually, locally, nationally, and internationally. We should not just share with those whom we like and with whom we have good relationships. We are compelled to share with those from whom we differ and whom we have neglected and ignored because of their sex, race, caste, etc. This is the way to bring about lasting reconciliation.

We must begin immediately to enable further the community in sharing by endorsing the "Guidelines for Sharing" (El Escorial, 1987) and by urging the churches to implement these guidelines. We recognize that there have been impediments to sharing in the process so far and we must all work to remove and overcome them. The community in sharing must not bar people for reasons of sex, age, caste, ethnicity, or economic, political, physical or mental capacity.

We confess our own lack of recognition and acceptance of the gifts of others. We recognize that all individuals and communities have gifts to share and that all must be encouraged to offer these gifts if we are to become the truly inclusive community.

We strive for a community in which sharing will be carried out within the framework of the covenant agreements of the JPIC and gospel imperatives such as those found in the Beatitudes in Matthew 5.

### 3. Community of cultures

Culture can be defined as a system or framework of meaning, behaviour and symbols and the way in which we orient our lives within it. In the interaction between the gospel and culture, the gospel may challenge various elements of that culture and there is also the possibility of a culture questioning a particular understanding of the gospel.

There is a need for some churches to repent of the ways in which the gospel was brought to particular cultures. Through the healing power of forgiveness, God's creative spirit can then enable them to renew their old structures in order to promote justice, peace, and the integrity of creation.

Christians are called to be sensitive to the fact today that they live in pluralistic communities with all the attendant problems of racism, tribalism, sexism, age-ism that are exacerbated by economic and social injustices which further polarize people. Young and old are often lured by false claims of community which are put forth by TV and advertisers: these tend to further factionalize us and make us confused, afraid, and disoriented and then drive us into drugs and harmful sub-cultures. We need to ask: how far does the church create tension and how far does the church promote reconciliation? We need to discern what parts of the culture help communicate the gospel and what parts are outside the gospel. We also need to study colonialism and neo-colonialism in relation to missionary activity to be more aware of the tendency to present the gospel from the perspective of the dominant cultures.

RECOMMENDATIONS

1. That sharing be fostered through experimentation by member churches in different contexts assisted by the WCC and its guidelines for sharing, and that the results of this experimentation including reporting in story form be offered as a resource for others.
2. That the WCC identify and promote models to enable the churches to share in mission in the next century.
3. That member churches be encouraged to convene regional and local consultations to identify gifts and needs and to propose action.
4. That the resource-sharing process be termed "community *in* sharing" in order to give better expression to our understanding of the church in mission.
5. That the WCC assist the member churches in establishing priorities for sharing which recognize the special gifts of marginalized groups, e.g. women, young people, indigenous people and the differently-abled.
6. That the WCC identify the special gifts of member churches and stand ready to call on them to share these gifts on behalf of the whole body at times of special need (e.g. the historic peace churches in times of war).
7. That the WCC be socially responsible in its investment policies.
8. That member churches be encouraged to develop partnerships with churches from other cultures, north and south, east and west, to promote koinonia and healing.

9.  That the WCC promote a process of analysis and study about Christian
    faith, cultural domination and their incidence in the missionary con-
    ception.

## C. Spirit of unity and the encounter with peoples of other faiths and ideologies

### 1. *Reconciliation with people of other faiths*

The Holy Spirit is at work in ways that pass human understanding: the
freedom of the Spirit may challenge and surprise us as we enter into
dialogue with people of other faiths. The gospel of Jesus Christ has taught
us the signs and fruit of the Holy Spirit — joy, peace, patience and
faithfulness (Gal. 5). Dialogue challenges us to discern the fruits of the
Spirit in the way God deals with all humanity.

The Bible testifies to God as sovereign of all nations and peoples as
the one whose love and compassion include all humankind. We see in the
covenant with Noah a covenant with all creation. We recognize God's
covenant with Abraham and Israel. In the history of this covenant we are
granted to come to know God through Jesus Christ. We also recognize
that other people testify to knowing God through other ways. We witness
to the truth that salvation is in Christ and we also remain open to other
people's witness to truth as they have experienced it.

Today in many parts of the world religion is used as a force of division
and conflict. That religious language and symbols have been used to
exacerbate conflicts makes us more urgently aware of our need for
dialogue as a means of reconciliation. There are many barriers to this
reconciliation, however. Too frequently we are ignorant of one another
and unwittingly bear false witness or become intolerant. Political and
economic realities as well as the inequality of minority religious communities often inhibit dialogue. Yet the difficulty of dialogue must not
deter us from recognizing the urgency of dialogue in situations throughout
the world where religious communities are divided by fear and mistrust.

The need for reconciliation and building mutual trust leads us to move
beyond meetings, exchanges and formal encounters to what we might call
a "culture of dialogue". This culture of dialogue begins at the local level
with our daily living and relationship to people of other faiths and leads to
common action towards a common future, especially around concerns of
justice and peace, given the overwhelming problems of our interdependent world. We have heard many stories of reconciliation and growth in
mutual understanding which have occurred in places of shared encounter.

In situations where dialogue at a local level is difficult, relationships at a regional or international level can play a role in building bridges and enabling dialogue to begin.

The first step in dialogue is to know the other as a person. In mutual encounter, people come to know and trust one another, telling their stories of faith and sharing their concerns and service to the world. Both the telling and the hearing of faith are crucial in discerning God's will. Dialogue can help people and communities to understand one another's stories. Part of dialogue is standing together under God and leaving space for us to be touched by the Holy Spirit. We enter into dialogue with the other asking God to be present among us. Empowered by the Holy Spirit, we build bridges of trust.

Dialogue is an authentic form of Christian witness, and an encounter of commitments. As Christians we affirm the Holy Spirit counselling us to keep faith in the revealed Christ and to encounter the other's faith. Dialogue is an authentic ministry to which many are today being called and which we affirm is urgently needed. Interfaith dialogue has proved difficult for some churches and Christians because of our continuing problems in understanding religious plurality and God's relationship to people of other religious traditions. It is important to continue to explore this issue in ways that open up our churches to the challenges of living in a world of many faiths.

## 2. Dialogue with ideologies

Churches today find themselves in acute confusion about the role of ideologies in society. Until recently one could speak of prevailing, dominant ideologies, but the obvious failure of communism as a state ideology has created a new situation. It challenges the churches in a fresh way to discriminate between constructive and destructive elements in any ideology and to clearly express the criteria of truth and justice as a basis for critical dialogue with the adherents of such ideologies.

Ideological conflicts arise when an ideology demands absolute loyalty, ignoring the essential ingredient of accountability. This has affected most strongly churches in a Marxist-dominated society. For a long time Marxism was seen as a possible partner in dialogue with Christianity. Now we are confronted with the collapse of this system. There is no reason for the triumphalism of the free-market system given its negative effects. The churches have no pretension to construct an alternative social and economic system. The JPIC process can provide important criteria for every social and economic order and inspire new concepts.

Ideological trends can be found in fundamentalism and nationalism. We must learn to distinguish between convictions that affirm our identity and fundamentalism, whether Christian or not, which becomes an intolerant ideology, closed to other approaches and realities. Nationalism and ethnicity are becoming new phenomena intended to be unifying factors in the struggle for cultural, religious and political self-determination, but which sometimes become dominant ideologies that exclusively interpret history and are not open to the reality of people's experience. These ideological expressions become difficult when faith components are used as an instrument to justify exclusive approaches. Churches as communities of reconciliation need to take into account that we have inherited an understanding of missiology and evangelism rooted in exclusive values and dressed with Western patterns. This reality does not always facilitate dialogue and a comprehensive approach to reality. In this moment when plurality is affirmed in many contexts, mission and evangelism must pay attention to those trends, and churches need to be spaces of encounter of people, visions and even of ideologies.

There are also "hidden ideologies" which are not institutionalized or publicly supported. Nevertheless they are very influential and deeply rooted in social consciousness. This seems to be especially a problem for Western societies which think that they have overcome ideologies altogether. Hidden ideologies include: (1) patriarchy which is rooted in, and in turn strengthens, a system of religious beliefs shared by many of the world's religions; (2) economic materialism which reduces value-judgments to the calculation of costs and benefits and thus disregards the dignity of human persons and the integrity of creation; (3) achievement-oriented individualism which places personal achievement above efforts aimed at the well-being of society; (4) pluralism, resulting from uncritical affirmation of secularization making the Divine less than creation; (5) modernization which aggressively breaks up the liberative cultural values of the two-thirds world, affecting in particular the lives of young people.

The tasks of the community of faith are: (1) to name the hidden ideologies and to expose the contradictions between the ideological claims and the realities of people's lives; (2) to enter into critical dialogue with the exponents of such ideologies on the basis of the biblical criteria of God's preferential option for the marginalized and for the well-being of creation. It is the power of truth as encounter with reality which brings these hidden ideologies to accountability.

RECOMMENDATIONS
1. That the WCC immediately seek to bring leaders of the Christian, Muslim and Jewish communities together to explore ways of working together for peace and justice in the present context of the Middle East crisis.
2. That the WCC encourage member churches to convene interfaith dialogue meetings for youth.

## D. Pentecostal and charismatic movements

*1. Charismatic movements (within our historic churches)*

In this century the world has witnessed the rise and growth of movements which emphasize the Holy Spirit and the gifts of the Holy Spirit. While these movements and churches are by no means uniform, they are commonly known as charismatic or pentecostal.

Insofar as they emphasize the charisms of the Spirit described in the New Testament and represent a rediscovery of the ministry of healing, they are valid expressions of Christian living. They also represent a commitment to strong faith and fellowship, increased spontaneity, openness and freedom among worshippers, all of these leading to greater participation in the life of the churches.

These movements can contribute to Christian division when a particular experience of the Spirit is introduced as normative for all Christians. Over-emphasis on the Holy Spirit as working independently of the Father and the Son can also be divisive.

*2. Our relation with charismatic and pentecostal churches*

The development of the pentecostal movement has profoundly influenced the life and worship of many churches related to the WCC. But the relationship between pentecostals and Christians of other traditions sometimes suffers from mutual misunderstanding. Pentecostals have sometimes felt excluded and have been accused of emotionalism, over-enthusiasm, sectarianism, and lack of social concern. Within the pentecostal movement there is much diversity. Some pentecostals have rejected the traditional churches. Some have rejected the ecumenical movement as a human attempt to produce Christian unity, or because of genuine theological differences on the part of its members concerning the nature of the Christian faith and how to express it in the modern world. But others have sought fellowship with Christians outside their boundaries, particularly with evangelicals. They have begun to take interest in questions of visible church unity; traditional churches have in turn become more open to the spiritual and theological insights that pentecostals bring. In Latin America, for example, pentecostals (now the numerically dominant form of Protestantism in the area) take part in the Latin American Council of Churches. Similar dialogue has been taking place in other areas as well. These hopeful signs bode well for the future efforts to bring the churches closer together.

RECOMMENDATIONS

1. That churches endeavour to rediscover the New Testament teaching that each Christian has at least one gift of the Holy Spirit for the building up of the church.

2. That churches endeavour to deepen their teaching on the Trinity, on pneumatology (the work and gifts of the Holy Spirit), and on the charisms described in the New Testament.

3. That the WCC recognize the congregations of pentecostal churches as part of the historical development of the Christian church and its rich diversity.

4. That the WCC seek to uphold the validity of the pentecostal experience for those whose lives are touched by this movement, while taking care not to give the impression that pentecostal belief and practice are prerequisites for genuine Christian experience.

5. That the WCC help to foster the relationship between the ecumenical and pentecostal movements.

6. That a study project be undertaken to help clarify and understand the great diversity in the pentecostal movement.

7. That dialogue between Latin American, African and Asian pentecostals — many of whom are open to the ecumenical movement — and North American and European pentecostals — many of whom are suspicious of ecumenism — be encouraged by the WCC.

8. That the WCC invite pentecostals to share in its programmes.

9. That a number of pentecostal theologians be invited to join the Faith and Order Commission, giving due recognition to the regional, ethnic and gender diversities that exist in the pentecostal movement.

10. That worship at assemblies and other WCC meetings seek to reflect authentic expressions of our different traditions. There should be occasions when worship is conducted by pentecostals.

# E. Issues from the regions

The ecumenical issue of koinonia and unity takes diverse forms in the regions of the world, with varying emphases. On the basis of the regional discussions of section III, the following were identified as major issues relating to koinonia and unity:

1. A major issue in several regions is the reconciliation of Christians and Muslims. In that context, the search is for mutual recognition, living together, sharing of the culture of life and avoidance of the culture of death, promotion of religious freedom, and dialogue which is to be seen as a two-way process, an "encounter of commitment" with a view to knowing and being known. That search for reconciliation should be put in the context of mission and evangelism.

It should be noted that such dialogue is regarded as especially difficult by many Christians in Africa who are suffering discrimination and persecution as a result of the political and economic power of Islam. These Christians need the concrete support of the whole church as they live and bear witness in their situations of pain, and the WCC should ensure that such support is given.

2. A second issue is unity in diversity, and the criteria for possible limits to cultural and confessional diversity. In this regard, attention needs to be paid to the encounter between so-called classical theology and other contextual theologies, as well as with women's voices in theology.

3. A third issue is the place of spirituality in the search for koinonia and unity. There can be no reconciliation without repentance and mutual forgiveness. In the same vein, worship should also reflect regional/denominational flavour.

4. Another concern is the implementation of the JPIC insights as a way of achieving reconciliation between communities.

5. Meeting in Australia, we are reminded of the plight of Aboriginal peoples and minorities here and in other parts of the world. Reconciliation in these circumstances demands recognition of their identity as human beings created in the image and likeness of God; repentance, and restitution made for atrocities committed against them; and a resolve not to develop them in the image of the dominant culture.

6. Language is an important tool for forging reconciliation and unity. In this regard it was suggested that the language of "first" and "third" worlds should be expunged and replaced with the name of the region.

7. The importance of study for forging unity cannot be over-emphasized. One aspect of this would be ecumenical learning. But

equally important is a study of fundamentalism with a view to understanding clearly what it represents for mutual dialogue.

## F. Proposal from the youth

The life of the church is enriched by young people and children who, by their presence in worship and all other aspects of church life, equip the church in meeting the needs and challenges of contemporary society. We urge our member churches to encourage and equip their young people to play as active a part as possible in their total life and witness. Only when the church recognizes the distinctive roles and gifts of *all* her members will she reflect the type of community that God intends. We urge the WCC to continue in its support and recognition of youth.

## Conclusion

In our study we came to see that it takes all sorts and conditions of humanity to build koinonia and community. But koinonia and unity are not human creations. Above all, they are the gift of the Triune God, Father, Son and Holy Spirit.

\* \* \*

## PLENARY DISCUSSION

*Mr Tolly Estes* (Anglican, USA): The WCC has sought to include indigenous people in this assembly, but they also need to be included in the whole process of theology.

*Mrs Birgitta Rantakari* (Lutheran, Finland): In this assembly, expressions and signs of division have at times been more visible than our unity. We seem more interested in asserting our diversities than our essential unity. The report lacks passionate commitment to work for visible unity.

*Rev. Angelique Walker-Smith* (Baptist, USA): The WCC must encourage member churches to reflect critically on the role of culture in their life so that the relevance of the gospel in specific contexts might be better understood, the witness of the church clarified, and dialogue among the churches increased. This might be done through the creation of a commission on gospel and culture.

*Rev. Walter Taylor* (Disciples, USA): There must be a Christological grounding to all of our talk about forgiveness and reconciliation. At the same time, our confession of Christ must be set in a Trinitarian framework in order to avoid Christomonism.

*Ms Helgma Tuomi* (Lutheran, Finland): Our delegation welcomes the continuing work on JPIC. The present task is to integrate the goals and projects of JPIC into the churches.

*Rev. David Coffey* (Baptist, Great Britain): The positive recommendations with regard to Pentecostals should be extended to include evangelicals.

*Dr Robert Reber* (Methodist, USA): The churches today face no more critical challenge than the need for interfaith dialogue. We live increasingly in communities that are religiously pluralistic. We must commit ourselves to dialogue and trust in the guidance of the Spirit.

## 3.5. REPORT OF SECTION IV: "HOLY SPIRIT — TRANSFORM AND SANCTIFY US!"

### 1. Understanding spirituality

1. "Do not be conform to the standards of this world, but let God transform you..." (Rom. 12:2). God calls people to be transformed and sanctified. God's grace is given to penetrate our lives and structures so that we may serve humanity and all creation, and in all things glorify God, Father, Son and Holy Spirit.

2. It has been said that spirituality is so to organize life as to allow the Holy Spirit room to act. Spirituality has thus a practical dimension. It has to do with setting the priorities, calendars and rhythms of life. Schedules and structures, culture, tradition and personality affect how communities and persons express their spirituality. Different experiences of God's presence through the Holy Spirit in word, church and life also determine our understanding.

3. There is a deep human longing for fulfilment, a spiritual hunger to become what we were intended to be through creation, already are in Christ and are yet to be. We were made in the image of God; we are growing in the likeness of Christ.

4. The whole creation, in bondage through human sin, "waits with eager longing for the revealing of the children of God" (Rom. 8:19). Things are not right or complete as they are. Enslaved humankind with all creation awaits the freedom which is given through the Holy Spirit.

5. Spirituality is rooted in baptism, whereby we are grafted into the death and resurrection of Christ, inaugurated into a life of discipleship, become members of his body and receive the gifts of the Holy Spirit to lead a life consecrated to the service of God and God's children.

6. Spirituality is the celebration of God's gifts, life in abundance, hope in Jesus Christ the crucified and risen Lord, and transformation through the Holy Spirit. Spirituality is also the constant, often painful, wrestling with living in the light in spite of darkness and doubts. Spirituality is to take up the cross for the sake of the world, to share the agony of all, and to seek the face of God in the depths of human misery.

7. Spirituality — in its manifold forms — is about receiving energy for life, being cleansed, inspired and set free, in every way being conformed to Christ.

8. An ecumenical spirituality for our times should be incarnational, here and now, life-giving, rooted in the scriptures and nourished by prayer; it should be communitarian and celebrating, centred around the eucharist, expressed in service and witness, trusting and confident. It will inevitably lead to suffering; it is open to the wider oikoumene, joyful and hopeful. Its source and guide is the action of the Holy Spirit. It is lived and sought in community and for others. It is an ongoing process of formation and discipleship.

## 2. The mystery of the Holy Spirit

9. The Holy Spirit cannot be understood apart from the life of the Holy Trinity. Proceeding from the Father, the Holy Spirit points to Jesus of Nazareth as the Christ, the Messiah, the Saviour of the world. The Spirit is the Power of God, energizing the people of God, corporately and individually, to fulfill their ministry. The Holy Spirit is "holy" by virtue of the very nature of the Holy Trinity. It is distinct from other "spirits", benign or demonic (1 John 4).

10. The Holy Spirit is gloriously free and unbound (John 3), freeing and unbinding God's people from the structures and strictures of this world (Rom. 12). The challenge to God's people is to discover, accept and live in this freedom. To live in the Holy Spirit is to yield one's life to God, to take spiritual risks; in short, to live by faith.

11. It is by the power of the Holy Spirit that God raised Jesus from the dead. The promise is that by the same power we shall be raised to be with him in glory (Eph. 2:6).

## 3. The church as sacrament and sign

12. Since Pentecost, a visible Christian community of repentant and redeemed believers has been constituted by the work of the Holy Spirit, in order to become the fullness of the body of Christ in history, a sign and sacrament of the kingdom of God among the nations.

13. We believe in the holy church. The church is holy and is becoming holy by the work of the Holy Spirit. The church, in spite of its historical limitations, is a place where sanctification and transfiguration occur. Throughout the centuries, Christians have sought ways to bring the fellowship of the church closer to the ideal of the fellowship of the kingdom that Christ proclaimed.

14. One of the common theological grounds of the ecumenical community is the Trinitarian understanding of God. The communion of the Holy Trinity is also a paradigm of the people of God — the church. It is the Holy Spirit who draws the church to model its life on the relationship of the Trinity and draws the people of God into the communion of the Holy Trinity.

15. There are various forms of Christian communities such as house churches, small prayer groups, base Christian communities, which complement parish life by focusing on particular aspects of the kingdom, such as a simpler life-style, concern for identity or political justice.

16. The church's holiness is a holiness for the whole world, a holiness experienced as reconciliation, peace and justice, which are to be realized in the community.

## 4. Responding to the Holy Spirit

17. Our approach to God the Holy Spirit must be in humility and penitence. The life of the church has not always exhibited the marks of the Holy Spirit. Sinfulness is evident at every level of life. As we come in penitence, the Holy Spirit enables us to empty ourselves *(kenosis)* to receive forgiveness and the grace *(charis)* to live for the sake of others.

18. The church needs to repent of racism, sexism, caste-ism or any other form of discrimination and oppression in which it has been involved. The churches and the ecumenical community should therefore actively continue to develop programmes to identify and combat all forms of dehumanization in church and society. At the same time we need to strive for a renewal of our congregational life, and to live out the new community for which we call.

19. The church is called to mission and evangelism. The proclamation of the gospel is impelled and empowered by the Holy Spirit. A true

sharing in mission and evangelism remains open to the contribution of other churches, and is quite different from the denial of their life, truth and faith which characterizes a destructive proselytism.

20. Nations in the North now receive many immigrants and refugees of different faiths and cultures. Such nations need the help of churches in the south in relating to these persons, whether they practise a living faith or have no faith. New religions and alternative forms of spirituality present a further challenge in our time.

21. The Genesis affirmation of God's resting on the seventh day has built the principle of rest into the very structure of the cosmos. The sabbath became an invaluable contribution from the Jewish faith. Liturgical times, rites and rhythms provide a frame and support for many kinds of Christian spirituality. The history of faith comes alive, new generations make their pilgrimage with the people of God through the ages.

22. The sabbath principle serves as a protection against unlimited activity and unrelenting desire for profit. The sabbath year, once in fifty years, was intended to break the spiral by which the rich became richer and the poor poorer (Lev. 25:8-17). It is relevant to apply this in the debt-ridden parts of the international community. The burden of debts should be lifted and the world economic order revised in favour of the poor.

23. Churches need to recover the notion of "sacred time", both to honour God and for the well-being of all people. God's time, the kairos, enters the chronos of the mundane world and enables new visions and fresh opportunities.

24. Women have been workers for, and witnesses to, spirituality from the time of the earliest church. Through the ages women have played a vital role in the rich tradition of the saints as models and teachers of Christian spirituality. Women's responses to the Holy Spirit in our time constitute a great gift to the churches.

25. People of faith witness to hope in Jesus Christ. In a world where misery and despair mark the lives of uncountable masses, many Christians raise signs of hope by humble perseverance in their work and witness for justice. We remember these witnesses, together with saints and martyrs throughout the ages, with thanksgiving. Their example kindles the Christian life of many; they belong to the great "cloud of witnesses" surrounding us and keeping company with us.

26. The Holy Spirit renews hope and upholds hope beyond hope. As social and political visions crumble and unbridled exploitation prevails, the discipline of those who identify with the course of liberation could weaken. The field could be left to anarchy, with aimless violence being

born out of desperation. Hope is a precious and vulnerable gift. There is an authentic spirituality maturing in the midst of struggle, nourished by the One who gave himself up for the freedom of others.

## 5. The Holy Spirit calls and moves us towards unity

27. Throughout history and especially during this century, the Holy Spirit has drawn the churches out of isolation and division. The Holy Spirit is calling us to acknowledge the unity that exists among us and to overcome confessional and other barriers in order to be able to share our energies, gifts and ministries on a common spiritual journey towards visible unity.

28. The ecumenical journey has been marked by significant points of growth on the way. Churches have moved from a situation of confrontation and co-existence, through comparison and cooperation to acknowledge their complementarity on the way to communion and visible unity.

29. Throughout the world, churches find themselves at different points on the way towards manifesting visible unity "so that the world might believe". Through councils of churches at national, regional and international levels, churches have been helped to initiate dialogue with each other and to take the risk of being vulnerable to each other so that a new creation might emerge.

30. As the churches move towards each other on the ecumenical pilgrimage, the Holy Spirit calls us to repentance and engagement in a process of forgiveness. Churches have anathematized each other, and have contributed to polarization leading some to define themselves in opposition to others. The churches need to repent of their stances and actions in respect to each other, and to take responsibility for the positions which they adopt and for their theologies. Without repentance and forgiveness no new creation as reconciled communities can emerge. The Holy Spirit has been evident in enabling the churches to repent, forgive, reconcile their histories and come to union in God through Christ.

31. There are many examples of this. The Eastern Orthodox and Oriental Orthodox churches are in process of expressing their repentance and forgiveness to each other and may celebrate Orthodox unity in a rite which will publicly declare mutual recognition and the creation of a situation of communion. A similar process has brought the Reformed and Mennonite communities towards mutual acceptance.

32. The Spirit draws people across denominational boundaries. Various interdenominational groups and renewal movements challenge the churches to a greater openness and towards the breaking of denomina-

tional barriers. Since the Holy Spirit is the Spirit of unity, Christians are called to exercise vigilance so that new divisions do not emerge to cause pain and tension among God's people.

33. It is evident that the Holy Spirit has been active in strengthening the relationships between the Roman Catholic Church and the various national and regional councils of churches. The Basel assembly (1989) organized by a regional council of churches and the regional episcopal conference might provide a useful model of cooperation.

34. The churches have in the past committed themselves to act together in all those areas where deep differences do not compel them to act separately (Lund 1952). However they have failed to fulfill this commitment, and need to acknowledge this with penitence. They need integrity in word and action. Recently, similar commitments have been made at Seoul (Justice, Peace and the Integrity of Creation) and with respect to the Decade of the Churches in Solidarity with Women. These must be taken seriously, be formative for the life of all the churches and remain at the centre of the ecumenical agenda.

35. Sanctification entails continuous commitment to the life of a visible community and seeking to overcome the stumbling blocks to full unity. Common prayer for unity, intercessions, united witness, community life, and recognition of the pieties of others are all part of ecumenism today.

## 6. The Holy Spirit in the world

36. The Holy Spirit, the Giver of life, continues to breathe life into all creation. As all life emanates from God and ultimately will return to God (Ps. 104), the ethos of holiness requires holding an attitude towards all that exists as if it by nature belonged to God. We do not own ourselves, our bodies, our lives, the air and the soil. All is given by God.

37. Though inseparably belonging to creation, we are in the world as stewards and priests of creation. We are endowed with the privilege and responsibility of referring creation back to its Creator. The church is now challenged to define the relationship of humanity to the rest of creation in dialogue with science. Anthropomonism (the idea that human beings are the only concern of God) denies the integrity of creation. Sacralizing nature may lead towards pantheism and the denial of the uniqueness of men and women, created in the image of God.

38. The Holy Spirit is at work among all peoples and faiths, and throughout the universe. With the sovereign freedom which belongs to God the Wind blows wherever it wants. Recognizing this, the church

rejoices in being nourished by the ministry of the Holy Spirit through the word and sacraments, thereby participating in salvation.

39. Spirits must be discerned. Not every spirit is of the Holy Spirit. The primary criterion for discerning the Holy Spirit is that the Holy Spirit is the Spirit of Christ; it points to the cross and resurrection and witnesses to the Lordship of Christ. The fruits of the Spirit, among them love, joy and peace, offer another criterion to be applied (Gal. 5:22). We believe that these criteria should also operate when we encounter the profound spirituality of other religions.

## 7. The transforming role of the people of God

40. The church is the entire people (laos) of God empowered by the Holy Spirit. As the laity of the church — whether women, men or young people — live in the world, they are agents of the Holy Spirit for transforming society. Through the church they receive strength, direction and identity. In fulfilling their mission they need all the enabling, encouragement and support the church can give. In many instances, however, they are offering their ministry in the world without full support and cooperation from their churches. They need to be recognized as giving a powerful witness and as serving at the forefront of the church's mission.

41. For many, the family — in one form or another — provides the appropriate space and ethos for spiritual formation, prayer and spirituality. Family units are threatened in many ways today and need the support and nurture of the whole community of the church. We need to explore diverse models and structures of family spirituality, spiritual formation and prayer life.

## 8. The inclusive community

42. The church is called to demonstrate God's inclusive love. God loved the world and all people (John 3:16). In some situations, such as a Pacific island village or a rural small town, inclusivity is natural; the fellowship of a local congregation is the fellowship of the sociological community. The challenge may come when an outsider tries to join the community and congregation.

43. In other cultures the human factors of language, race, sex, caste, or economic status may seem insurmountable barriers to those seeking to join the Christian community — or to the community's striving to be inclusive towards the society.

44. Inclusivity has to do with power and powerlessness. It needs to be defined by those who are or who feel excluded; the sharing of pain is the beginning of forming an inclusive community. To be inclusive we need to cultivate an attitude of intensive listening: to hear and heed the voice of the Holy Spirit who so often speaks through the person "on the other side of the road" (Luke 10).

45. Inclusivity means equality, full participation and respect for all — children, young people, women, differently-abled, people of other ethnic or educational backgrounds, people of different spiritual understandings, and all who are — or feel themselves — marginalized. This assembly has experienced this challenge as we have met with Aboriginal brothers and sisters.

46. The Spirit challenges us to an active inclusivity. This means a relentless struggle, in which we side with minorities and oppressed peoples. We cannot wait for others to come to us, we must reach out to them in love, we must "walk the second mile" and go more than half way (Matt. 5). We must act in faith, trusting in the guidance and help of the Holy Spirit (Eph. 2:8).

## 9. Making peace

47. Another manifestation of spirituality is a peace-oriented life-style, exploring the power of active non-violence for the transformation of society. Power operates in all areas of life — in both church and society. The exercise of power within the church should always attempt to reflect and promote Christian love (John 14 and 15). The church's critique of worldly power (the dominant mode in political and economic structures) must always point towards love as the better way, even though it may not be understood (Phil. 4). But Spirit-led peace-making and peace-living generates the joy and contentment of the blessed of God (Matt. 5). The challenge is to translate this from personal and interpersonal living into the life of our congregations, the community at large and into economic and political structures.

## 10. For the life of the world

48. Eucharistic spirituality lived by a local Christian community is in itself the most valuable diaconal service that can be given and a missionary witness of immeasurable significance.

49. No congregation lives for itself. As Jesus gave himself up for the life of the world, so the church is called to surrender power, resources and interests to God in serving society, world and creation.

50. The prayers of the worshipping community join the voice of the voiceless. Both repentance and thanksgiving are expressed also on behalf of those who are absent. Bread and wine and water brought before God with thanksgiving represent all creation. The sharing of peace at the eucharist commits the community to work for peace. The partaking of communion symbolizes justice and love. Our dependence on the fruits of the earth for our physical and spiritual life makes every eucharistic celebration a call to preserve the integrity of creation. Through all this the Spirit keeps flowing, renewing the face of the earth.

51. Spirituality expresses itself in the liturgical life of the people of God. Worship takes a variety of forms in different churches. Sharing experiences and insights of worship is enriching for the whole body of Christ. The fundamental nature of the Christian life is to gather around word and sacrament in fellowship and prayer (Acts 2:42). The experience of worship is both the stimulus for and the result of the inner relationship with the Spirit. It involves life, gives life, and is a means for evangelism and grassroots ecumenism. Every worshipping community should be a model for an inclusive community. Worship space needs to be designed so that all people are able to participate fully. A lively ministry of hospitality, welcoming all in the name of the Lord, is most important. The plea of young people for forms of worship and celebration which fit their culture must be taken seriously.

52. The Holy Spirit frees people to committed stewardship in relation to creation, church and community. In a world which values things more than relationships, and where wealth and health are seen as more important than service in love, the Holy Spirit calls us to different values. All life is to be lived for God. We should be ready to give up personal security for the sake of the gospel.

53. The Holy Spirit challenges God's people to holy living, personally and corporately. Personal sanctification and corporate transformation belong together. At all times life is to be lived under and by the power of the Spirit. This may become most manifest at times of tragedy, loss or joy in personal or corporate life.

## 11. Moving with the Spirit

54. Renewal brings out the truth which was already and always given by the Spirit. Sometimes this truth will have fallen into disuse; sometimes it may have been deliberately repressed. We recover it and implement it with joy and thanksgiving.

55. We give thanks for the spiritual renewal that has been evident in the life of the worldwide church. This renewal needs to be continued and stimulated by mutual sharing with those inside and outside our churches, and through the ecumenical movement.

56. The Holy Spirit accompanies us on our ecumenical journey; keeps alive the vision that all things in heaven and on earth will be united in Christ; encourages, corrects, challenges and moves us forward until we come to our true unity and glory in God through Christ. Come, Holy Spirit, come!

## Recommendations

57. (1) As churches draw closer to each other on the ecumenical pilgrimage, they are increasingly recognizing the place of Christian life-style, spiritual discipline, holiness, a spirituality of active non-violence, personal and common prayer, worship, art and icons. We therefore call on the World Council of Churches to explore the various forms and expressions of ecumenical spirituality, and to consider holding a world-wide consultation on this theme.

58. (2) The central role of worship in the Christian life was strongly emphasized during the discussions in this section. Worship in its richness has a variety of dimensions and implications: it relates to evangelism, spirituality, social justice, human values, integrity of creation, unity and peace, even as it celebrates salvation. This concern for the centrality of worship should therefore be further developed within the World Council of Churches. The sharing of liturgical material, music, prayers and forms of worship should be developed as a means of helping local congregations to renewal and participation in the spiritual life of the oikoumene. A new ecumenical hymnbook, including prayers and liturgies, is called for.

59. (3) The World Council of Churches recognizes the role of the laity, and especially young people, and the significance of lay, renewal, charismatic and pentecostal movements within the churches. All these challenge the churches to a greater openness. These movements should be seen as agents in mission and service. The World Council of Churches should also continue to develop dialogue with movements, organizations and Christian communities that are at present outside the structural life of the WCC.

60. (4) As churches develop worship and theology reflecting their cultural context, questions arise concerning the relationship between church and culture. The section urges the World Council of Churches to develop programmes to support all member churches as they wrestle

with issues of inculturation and seek to preserve the integrity of the gospel.

61. (5) As inclusivity has been a major theme of discussion, the section expresses deep concern that the World Council of Churches maintain and strengthen programmes to combat racism and other forms of social, economic, political and religious oppression, and that the special programme for differently-abled persons be continued.

\* \* \*

## PLENARY DISCUSSION

*Dr Larry Pickens* (Methodist, USA): The Holy Spirit calls us not only to forgiveness but to struggle as well. Racism, sexism and exploitation are unforgivable and require challenge and struggle. Pain and tension cannot be avoided in the face of injustice. There should also be a focus on the presence, status and role of children in the oikoumene: children are threatened by war, violence and exploitation.

*Pfarrer Dietrich Werner* (Lutheran, Germany): There is an urgent need for mutual learning between the churches of the North and South, East and West concerning the missionary renewal of the life-style of local congregations. A major study on missionary renewal and ecumenical commitment of local Christian congregations should be undertaken in the coming period.

*Rev. Gordon Straw* (Lutheran, USA): When we talk of dialogue between churches and people who have contact with the land you must talk to the indigenous people. The history of Western culture has divorced us from the interconnectedness of the creation. Because of our belief that all life is sacred we are often accused of pantheism.

*Bischof Sigisbert Kraft* (Old Catholic, Germany): Our responsibility in creation is not only given in the eucharist but also in baptism. The water of baptism binds us to responsibility in the creation as a whole. It is not a matter left to our choice as to whether or not we want to get involved.

*Frau Ursula Urban* (United, Germany): Ninety-nine percent of people of God are lay even if this is not clear in the assembly. God lives through the lay people and the WCC should be grateful for that fact.

*Rev. Nikolaos Stefanides* (Evangelical, Greece): The Greek Orthodox Church (98 percent of the population) does not recognize the Greek

Evangelical Church. In this assembly they may see us as brothers and sisters, in Greece they see us as heretics.

*Pastor Franco Giampiccoli* (Waldensian, Italy): Proselytism is not clearly defined. In 1960 the WCC rejected proselytism and condemned it as a form of conquering that takes advantage of unstable situations (fear, illness, hunger, etc.). But it was not made clear that we should accept those who have different ways of worshipping.

*Mrs Maureen Goodman* (Brahma Kumaris World Spiritual University, England): This is a very generous and open-minded statement, particularly as it talks of equality with reference to people of different spiritual understandings and other beliefs. The other crisis we are in now is the reflection of a very deep spiritual crisis. Spiritual values cannot be emphasized enough.

*Ms Jutta Gerschau* (United, Germany): Spirituality has to be lived and worked through in one's own context. Spirituality is often seen as separate from practicality. This should not be so.

*Prof. Vlasios Pheidas* (Eastern, Orthodox, Greece): The Evangelical Church in Greece and the Greek Orthodox Church have contact with each other and have always had good relationships. But there is proselytism which causes some problems.

*Pasteur Isabelle Marc* (Reformed, France): A new hymnbook would be of great help to us. We ask the WCC to publish this in the languages that have been used here.

*Pastor Juan Pedro Schaad* (Evangelical, Paraguay): Thousands of lay persons have been rediscovering the Bible in worship. There is a lack of reference to this in the document. Here it is forgotten that the word of God has a central role. It has helped lay people to combat oppression and go out together in the life of the world.

# 4. The Work of the WCC: Past and Future

## 4.1. INTRODUCTION

A central purpose of any World Council assembly is to assess work done by the WCC since its last assembly and to offer directions for its work in the coming years. At Canberra, delegates had several resources to help them accomplish these responsibilities, including the official report of the central committee, *Vancouver to Canberra*, and the report of the moderator of the central committee, Dr Heinz Joachim Held. The reports of the general secretary, Dr Castro, and of the moderator of the finance committee of the retiring central committee, Dr J. Oscar McCloud, helped complete the picture of WCC activities since Vancouver.

In his report, Dr McCloud noted that "despite the faithful and increased giving to its work [by member churches and traditional donor agencies], the WCC is, on the whole, not 'better off' than seven years ago". Four factors contribute to this situation: "The cost of living in Switzerland has risen more sharply than in the previous period... The exchange values of most income currencies have further declined against the Swiss franc. A global economic slowdown has begun which means most donors cannot increase contributions as much each year as they could in the late 1970s. And the undesignated income to meet the programme demands and programme initiatives is an even smaller percentage of total Council revenues."

The WCC, said Dr McCloud, is not in a "crisis" of the sort faced by the Nairobi assembly in 1975; but "the underlying fragility of the Council's situation has become increasingly evident. The reality is that the WCC cannot continue to do effectively all that it has been doing in the style and manner of the past. Nor can the Council undertake new initiatives even from this assembly without discontinuing some of the present activities." The number of staff must also be reduced.

There were two primary ways for the assembly to respond to these reports: (1) through plenary discussion of the presentations by the general secretary and moderator; and (2) through the work of the Reference Committee, the Committee on Programme Policy, and the Finance Committee.

## Discussion of the reports of the general secretary and moderator

A wide range of issues was raised during a plenary set aside for this discussion on Monday, 11 February.

The Rev. José Carlos Barbosa dos Santos (Roman Catholic, Brazil), speaking from a wheelchair, urged greater representation of differently-abled ("disabled") persons in the work of the WCC. Ms Ruth Pullam (United, Canada) urged that steps be taken to increase the impact of the Ecumenical Decade of the Churches in Solidarity with Women. Ms Mari Kinnunen (Lutheran, Finland) expressed appreciation that the moderator had added a reference to a proposed international youth gathering (Brazil, 1992) to the oral presentation of his report; but she also voiced concern that the Youth sub-unit not be diminished in the future work of the Council.

Prof. Bastiaan de Gaay Fortman (Reformed, Netherlands) argued that statements are not necessarily the best way to respond to public issues. Dr Konrad Raiser (United, Germany) stressed that the mandate from Vancouver to develop a "vital and coherent theology" has not been completed. He also expressed disappointment that the churches have not responded to the challenges posed by the Seoul conference on "Justice, Peace and the Integrity of Creation".

Archbishop Aram Keshishian (Oriental Orthodox, Lebanon) warned against a tendency in the life of the Council to focus on the self-understanding of the WCC rather than on the unity of the church. Ms Jean Mayland (Anglican, England) called attention to an omission in the moderator's report: the question of the WCC's relationship with the Roman Catholic Church. "I hope", she said, "that we will invest more time and thought in this relationship in the next seven years." Prof. Ya Mpiku Mbelolo (Reformed, Zaire) called for the creation of a commission for cultural education in order to deepen the churches' understanding of the various cultural contexts of the global Christian community.

Metropolitan Kalinik of Vratsa (Eastern Orthodox, Bulgaria) spoke of threats to ecumenism arising in the wake of changes in Eastern Europe, including proselytism, fundamentalism, and the increased strength of Islam. Prof. Abraham Karickam (Mar Thoma, India) voiced impatience with assembly theological discussion on the Holy Spirit while outside "the whole world is burning".

Perhaps the most dramatic intervention came from Archbishop Kirill of Smolensk (Eastern Orthodox, USSR). It is quite clear, he contended that "liberal, radical and contextual theologies have a dominant place" in the WCC. As a result of such developments as the ordination of women and a "tendency to syncretism", we are witnessing new divisions in the church. The WCC is acquiescing to majorities instead of holding to the apostolic faith. He called for a "radical U-turn" before ecumenical hopes are exhausted.

In his response the general secretary stressed that the WCC has never advocated the ordination of women as such, but has invited the churches to explore the place of women in church and society. We must be patient, he argued, as we raise these "irritating questions" with each other. Dr Castro also rejected any notion of syncretism, noting that other religions have no interest in blending with Christianity. Christian theologians, however, have "a right and duty" to stretch the boundaries of the church's thinking as they seek to relate the Christian message to their cultural contexts.

## Presentation of committee reports

The Reference Committee's mandate was to review and make recommendations regarding the reports of the moderator and the general secretary, as well as the Council's relationships with member churches, various ecumenical organizations, Christian world communions, and other ecumenical partners, including the Roman Catholic Church. At Canberra, the Reference Committee was also asked to consider a document on "The Unity of the Church as Koinonia: Gift and Calling", prepared by the WCC's Faith and Order Commission and amended by Section III.

The Committee's report was presented to the assembly on Tuesday, 19 February, by the Committee's co-moderators, Ms Vasiti Raiwalui (Methodist, Fiji) and Metropolitan Bartholomeos of Chalcedon (Eastern Orthodox, Turkey), and by Dr Konrad Raiser (United, Germany). Various recommendations scattered throughout the report were adopted by the assembly, including four "guiding principles" concerning the relationship between the WCC and regional ecumenical organizations. A strong plea was heard from Oberkirchenrat Walter Arnold (Lutheran, Germany) for the WCC to take the concerns of evangelicals more directly into account.

Most of the debate over the report of the Reference Committee focused on two items: the Faith and Order statement on "The Unity of the Church as Koinonia" and recommendations regarding the Joint Working Group between the Roman Catholic Church and the WCC. After several amendments to the unity statement were approved by the assembly, the delegates voted to adopt the statement and to send it to "the churches". The major challenge to the text as a whole was that the statement does not adequately celebrate racial, ethnic, cultural and theological diversity in the church.

A number of issues were touched upon during the discussion of the Joint Working Group (JWG), including tensions between the Roman Catholic Church and Orthodox churches, especially in Eastern Europe, the apparent shift in emphasis from multilateral to bilateral dialogue, and the sense that ecumenical progress is occurring more at the "grassroots" than at the international level. Objection was raised regarding the recommendation to reduce the size of the JWG but, finally, all six recommendations were adopted. A recommendation from the floor, calling for a more formal relationship between the JWG and regional and national councils, was also approved. Following the vote, Archbishop Alan Clark, Roman Catholic co-moderator of the JWG, spoke briefly to the assembly.

The report of the Committee on Programme Policy was presented on Tuesday, 19 February, by co-moderators, Pastora Nélida Ritchie (Methodist, Argentina) and Dr Soritua Nababan (Reformed, Indonesia). In the discussion that followed, the JPIC programme received strong support. The WCC was encouraged to help integrate the goals of JPIC into the work of the denominations and to serve as a link between the various JPIC-related initiatives undertaken in the member churches. It was also stressed that the programme policy report must be read alongside that of the Finance Committee, given present financial difficulties. The Council, it was argued, needs to learn how to set priorities more effectively for its future work.

A number of editorial changes and more substantive amendments were proposed. Members of the Committee met during the evening to consider the proposals and reported in the plenary the next morning (20 February) that all had been accepted. The report was subsequently adopted as amended.

# 4.2. REPORT OF THE MODERATOR

## *Heinz Joachim Held*

1. My task in this report is to present a review of the work done by the World Council of Churches since the last assembly in Vancouver. In view of the short time at my disposal this cannot be more than a brief survey, highlighting points which I see as important.

For much of the work, and especially for fuller details, you should refer to the official report presented to you by the central committee in the book *Vancouver to Canberra*. The central committee's written report of its work and my oral report here will be discussed in the next plenary session together with the general secretary's report, and should also be discussed in the sections and sub-sections.

2. The written report on the work provides a comprehensive account of the vast range of programme work, studies, consultations, visits and publications which have filled the life and work of the World Council of Churches on the road from Vancouver in 1983 to Canberra in 1991. It is impressive indeed to see all that has been done in these years and I take this opportunity to express our heartfelt thanks — first to the members of our staff in the Ecumenical Centre in Geneva under the leadership of our general secretary, Emilio Castro, who as always have continued to do the work entrusted to them with great devotion and competence at all levels. But our thanks must also go to the members of programme committees and working groups which have planned and guided this work in detail; and to our member churches from which the Geneva staff and the members of the programme committees come. In this way we have been able to learn from the experience of the member churches and be assured of their confidence, financial support and constant prayers. I think, too, of the many donor organizations within and outside our churches which have given such generous financial help to our programmes. But above all we must express our gratitude to the Triune God who has brought us together in the World Council, who makes hearts and hands willing for giving and doing and on whose blessing alone all success depends.

## The Vancouver programme guidelines

3. The sixth assembly placed the future programme work of the World Council under a vision of growth — "the vision of growing more

and more into Jesus Christ, the Life of the World".[1] Corresponding guidelines were thus set for the WCC's activities in the years ahead:

Growing towards unity

Growing towards justice and peace

Growing towards vital and coherent theology

Growing towards new dimensions of the churches' self-understanding

Growing towards a community of confessing and learning

I should like to take these guidelines as the framework of my report today and refer at the same time to some important priorities in the work of the last seven years.

## A vision of growth

4. Let us pause for a moment to think about the "vision of growth". Growth assumes the gift of life. But life is a mystery, a gift which we can only receive, preserve and cherish. So we are bound to give account to one another of our work in the past seven years and consider how far it has indeed served goals such as growth towards unity and towards justice and peace. If we really take to heart this vision of growing more and more into Jesus Christ, the Life of the World, we are speaking of a mysterious process of a properly sacramental nature, a spiritual process. For growing in grace into a living relationship with Jesus Christ can only happen through the action of the Holy Spirit. It will be clear then that in choosing a prayer for the coming of the Holy Spirit as the main theme of this assembly our intention has been to take up and develop the concerns of the last assembly.

However, growth is always unfinished, never completed. The process of spiritual growing and maturing into Jesus Christ, the life of the world, will go on beyond the period from Vancouver to Canberra. So it seems that all the programme guidelines fixed for the future work by the sixth assembly will in fact still hold good for the years ahead.

5. The last assembly seemed to feel the same, for it confirmed the programme thrusts outlined by the previous assembly in Nairobi in 1975 and developed them in its own way. These were: the quest for a truly ecumenical fellowship; the search for an authentic incarnation of our faith (through common witness to the gospel of Jesus Christ in word and in action); the struggle for true humanity. I remind you of these for two reasons: for one thing, because we must always be aware of the fundamental continuity between this and the previous assemblies; and for another because, as we think about the guidelines of Nairobi 1975 and Vancouver 1983, we must realize that

growing more and more into Jesus Christ, the Life of the World, is a permanent, ongoing task.

## Towards unity

6. Vancouver said: "The search for concrete steps towards the goal of *visible unity* must remain a priority in the years ahead. A new dynamic has developed in this area which should be sustained and promoted."[2] In this connection, specific reference was made to the reception process of the Lima convergence texts on *Baptism, Eucharist and Ministry* which was in its early stages seven years ago. During these years it has been going ahead in the churches and its effects have even made themselves felt in the life of local congregations. In a statement to the churches the Commission on Faith and Order noted at its meeting in Budapest in August 1989 that the evaluation of the official responses received from some 185 churches had revealed "a broad convergence on basic Christian affirmations". It has shown "sometimes surprising agreements". It proves that the churches had been stimulated to "discussion of their own traditions and practices; [that] they show a willingness to change perceptions of other communions' beliefs, worship and practices".[3] This seems to me to be no mean achievement. Clearly something has been set in motion here which serves the growth towards the unity of the faith, a community of worship and service, across all remaining differences and divisions. These certainly must not be overlooked, and must call for continuing in-depth work. No doubt this is a very slow and painstaking process calling for great patience. Nonetheless, the Lima process in and between our churches remains a noteworthy and astonishing fact. It is no small achievement that the churches, far beyond the more immediate membership of the World Council, have been drawn into a movement of convergence and are giving account of their convictions to one another in a binding, long-term multilateral process of theological conversations; and that they are prepared to bring their own theological and church traditions into the discussion and to listen and learn from one another and seek a way forward to full fellowship with one another in faith and in worship.

7. I can only mention in passing here the other projects undertaken or continued by the Commission on Faith and Order on the instructions of the last assembly. I think in particular of the study document "Confessing the One Faith" which on the basis of the Nicene-Constantinopolitan Creed aims to arrive at a common expression of the old apostolic faith for the churches in the world of today. It would be an excellent thing if these

important texts could go through the same kind of study and reception process in our churches as did the Lima convergence texts. By way of this reception process, the churches have embarked on a road on which all involved have expressed their will for binding fellowship with one another but which has shown us the many difficulties in the way of quick progress towards achieving that fellowship.

## Visits and meetings

8. Clarification of controversial theological and ecclesiological questions is, of course, not the only means by which we can foster growth towards unity. Another important aspect in this is the exchange of visits among the churches and the visits made to them by representatives of the World Council. The Vancouver assembly rightly noted that "the growth and vitality of the ecumenical movement depend on the encounter and trust between people more than on institutional links".[4]

In order to strengthen links with the churches the central committee held three of its six meetings between Vancouver and Canberra away from Geneva, at the invitation of its member churches: 1985 in Buenos Aires, Argentina; 1988 in Hanover, Federal Republic of Germany; 1989 in Moscow, Soviet Union. The executive committee likewise met in March 1986 in Kinshasa, Zaire, and in September 1986 in Reykjavik, Iceland; in September 1987 in Atlanta, Georgia, USA; in March 1988 in Istanbul, Turkey; and in September 1990 in Oslo, Norway.

The same purpose was served by the many consultations and conferences held by the WCC with its member churches and the visits made to them by its officers, presidents and staff members. I cannot even begin to enumerate them here.

9. It turned out to be impossible to realize the hope that after the Vancouver assembly a "regular process of ecumenical visits between member churches" could be arranged.[5] Nonetheless, every opportunity was taken, for instance in conjunction with meetings and consultations, to make visits and hold meetings with the churches and church institutions in the area. The Vancouver assembly's recommendation that a staff post be established in the General Secretariat with responsibility for coordinating and monitoring this process of ecumenical visits was thus not implemented. However, in its recent discussions about the restructuring of the Council's programme work, the central committee was very much aware that the fostering of relations with member churches should in future receive special attention in its own right. Our general secretary has

taken this special responsibility upon himself in these past years and discharged it to the best of his ability.

## Common worship

10. Another way in which we experience growth towards unity — and by no means the least important — is in the common services of worship held at ecumenical gatherings and meetings at all levels of church life. In this respect our last assembly in Vancouver was an unforgettable experience. Many participants discovered in a very special way the gathering and unifying force of worship and prayer. So it is not surprising that the common worship at our meetings has been so carefully and lovingly prepared and conducted, as it was for instance at the conference on world mission in San Antonio, Texas, in 1989, and at the world convocation on "Justice, Peace and the Integrity of Creation" in Seoul, Korea, in 1990. I have the impression that we can see here the gradual emergence of common ways and forms of praying based on elements of our different church traditions, which we hope will enable us one day to experience and express more forcefully our God-given spiritual unity than we feel free to do at present.

## Praying for one another

11. In this connection I would like also to mention the common service of prayer for one another to which our churches have been more committed in recent years than they were in the past, whether with the help of the Ecumenical Prayer Cycle, which was published in a new edition in 1989, or through special days of prayer when churches living and witnessing in difficult situations have asked for the prayers of their sister churches throughout the world: for instance, for an end to apartheid in South Africa in 1986; for freedom and independence in Namibia in 1987; for the reunification of Korea in 1989; and for justice and peace in the Middle East in 1990. The call to prayer for peace and justice in that region has become all the more urgent with the outbreak of war in the Persian Gulf.

All in all, the ecumenical movement of the past decades has created many links among the churches, cutting right across confessions and continents. These links have often also been between one local congregation and another. They have led to exchange of visits, regular intercession and tokens of solidarity across all political and social boundaries.

If prayer really possesses a unifying power and if it can help loosen some of our rigid positions, we must continue to devote equal if not greater attention and energy to this part of our priestly service as God's people on earth, not least by taking up the theme of this assembly, which is a prayer for the coming of the reconciling, renewing and unifying divine power of the Holy Spirit.

## Sharing with one another

12. Under the heading of growth towards unity we must also include the programme for the Ecumenical Sharing of Resources. After lengthy preparations this programme, at the consultation towards the end of October 1987 in El Escorial, Spain, addressed a demanding challenge to our churches and diaconal agencies in the form of its "Guidelines for Sharing". These try to take seriously the fact that "one Lord, one faith, one baptism" (Eph. 4:5) also calls us to a fellowship of sharing, of receiving and giving, in the spiritual and the material sense, following the example in the account of the life of the first local church in Jerusalem after Pentecost, in the Book of Acts (2:42-47) — an example which points the way for all the churches. We readjac in the "Guidelines": "The new life given by the Holy Spirit in Christ creates us as a new people — members of one body, bearing one another's burdens and sharing together in God's gift of life for all."[6] No doubt in practice we still have rather a long way to go before we form a "healing and sharing community within the WCC and the member churches",[7] as Vancouver put it. Discussion of this commitment on the basis of faith has scarcely begun in our member churches and in the World Council itself, even though here and there steps have been taken in that direction. This points to another way in which we can grow towards unity. While we do not yet have full communion in the apostolic faith and in the sacramental life of the church, we are able meanwhile to express the mutual fellowship we confess, for which we work and pray and which is promised to us in all its fullness, through a constantly developing fellowship of mutual sharing, and the reciprocal giving and receiving of spiritual and material goods and gifts.

## Justice and peace

13. "Growth towards full ecclesial, spiritual and political commitment to this expression [of justice, peace and respect for the integrity of all creation] by all member churches, in all their dimensions, should be one of the purposes of all programmes of the WCC" — so said Vancouver.[8] This too sets a goal that goes far beyond the period from Vancouver to Canberra. But it is clear that it summarizes one of the

overall concerns of our Council in a clear concept and that it is affirmed by all its programme sub-units. For instance, the world consultation on interchurch aid, refugee and world service, held in Larnaca, Cyprus, in November 1986 on the theme "Called to be Neighbours — Diakonia 2000", developed an understanding of interchurch aid which is deliberately and determinedly linked with the struggle against all forms of injustice, poverty and oppression. The Larnaca declaration pledges "from this day forward, to work for justice and peace through our diakonia".[9] This is a new and different understanding of interchurch aid and diakonia that goes far beyond the traditional understanding and practice of diakonia in our churches.

14. Besides its well-known commitment to the fight against the injustice of the system of apartheid in South Africa, the Programme to Combat Racism has in recent years become increasingly involved in the struggle for the recognition of the rights of other oppressed population groups. It held its commission meeting in 1989 in Madras, India, with the express intention of having conversations with Dalit representatives and gathering information about their situation and looking for ways to support them in their struggle for the recognition of their human dignity, for social equality and political liberation. A programme in support of the Dalits is now in fact to be implemented.

Also in 1989 the Programme to Combat Racism organized an international consultation in Darwin, Australia, attended by representatives of indigenous peoples from all over the world, where the main issue was their struggle for their right to land and, hence, their survival. Significantly enough, the theme of this consultation was "Land is Our Life: Integrity of Creation, Justice and Peace". The Darwin declaration adopted at the end of the meeting speaks of the centuries of disregard for the basic rights of the indigenous peoples and with a sense of urgency declares "that a state of emergency exists in regard to the survival and status of indigenous peoples worldwide". The churches are reminded that they bear a share of the responsibility for this situation and are called upon to "confess to having been part of the problem and to rise to become part of the solution in keeping with the principles of the gospel".[10]

## Integrity of creation

15. The assembly in Vancouver, as it were officially, added the third element, the integrity of creation, to the World Council's traditional commitment to justice and peace.

Ecumenical interest in this question is not however wholly new. At the fifth assembly in Nairobi in 1975 the Australian scientist, Charles Birch, gave an impressive address in which for the first time the attention of the wider ecumenical public was drawn to the danger to the creation caused by human behaviour. He referred to the connection between human justice and the replenishing of the earth and between human injustice and the deterioration of the environment. He called for a radical change in our human behaviour towards the natural world. In line with this the Vancouver programme guidelines also asked for "a caring attitude to nature".[11]

This threefold formula for an ethic of life in terms of justice, peace and the integrity of creation has meanwhile established itself and the indissoluble connection of these three themes is generally acknowledged. Here the conviction grows increasingly stronger that the integrity of creation is basic to a life of justice and peace. But we must become fully aware that the integrity of creation is not only an imperative if we are physically to survive, but also an ethical act which is theological in quality, through which we give practical expression to our faith in the Triune God who is the source of all life and the Creator of the world. Just as according to God's will there should, as the first assembly in Amsterdam stated, be no war, and just as discrimination, exploitation and marginalizing of human beings by other human beings is a sin in the deepest theological meaning of the word, so too, in the last analysis, disrespect for creation and the destruction of creation can only be described as an act of godlessness. This fact gives a new relevance to the injunction of the last assembly to engage member churches in a conciliar process of mutual *commitment (covenant) to justice, peace and the integrity of creation*. It is not merely an urgency forced upon us by outward circumstances but carries with it a significant theological emphasis the source of which is our confession of faith.

16. It is therefore logical, even if perhaps unusual in many of our traditions, that at the world convocation for "Justice, Peace and the Integrity of Creation" in Seoul at the beginning of March last year, ten basic affirmations of our faith were worked out and approved on the themes that were to be discussed. They link the confession of faith with the commitment to corresponding action and attitudes in everyday life. In the first instance the "acts of covenanting" arising out of this represented only a personal affirmation of commitment by the participants. But they are aimed at something more — they are aimed at mutual commitment by the churches. Here a path is being followed which perhaps still gives rise

to many questions of detail but is intended to express aptly the unity of faith and life, theological conviction and moral action.

## Mutual commitment

17. But this is precisely what characterizes the "conciliar process" for Justice, Peace and the Integrity of Creation which the last assembly gave us as a task for the road we have to travel. It really is a new impetus and for all its troubles and inadequacies it counts as one of the outstanding landmarks on the road of the WCC from Vancouver to Canberra. For reasons of our own understanding of dogma and church law many of us have difficulties with the expression "conciliar process". We should pay heed to these scruples. But the meaning it has always been given may best be described as "growing into mutual commitment" for justice, peace and the integrity of creation — and not indeed as a task which we are given as churches to deal with as seems best to us, but as one which we must regard as part of our ecumenical calling which we "seek to fulfill together... to the glory of God, the Father, the Son and the Holy Spirit", in the words of the basis of our constitution. Moreover, one of the express aims of the World Council is "the promotion of one human family in justice and peace". This task has been seen from the start as a mutual commitment of the churches, as one can see from the message of the first assembly in Amsterdam in 1948. There it was said:

> We have to learn afresh together to speak boldly in Christ's name both to those in power and to the people, to oppose terror, cruelty and race discrimination, to stand by the outcast, the prisoner and the refugee. We have to make of the church in every place a voice for those who have no voice, and a home where every man will be at home... We have to ask God to teach us together to say "No" and to say "Yes" in truth. "No", to all that flouts the love of Christ, to every system, every programme and every person that treats any man as though he were an irresponsible thing or a means of profit, to the defenders of injustice in the name of order, to those who sow the seeds of war or urge war as inevitable; "Yes", to all that conforms to the love of Christ, to all who seek for justice, to the peacemakers, to all who hope, fight and suffer for the cause of man, to all who — even without knowing it — look for new heavens and a new earth wherein dwelleth righteousness...

## Work after Seoul

18. The world convocation in Seoul in March 1990 was, for the time being, a climax. But it marks only an initial stage, not the end of the conciliar process of the growing together of churches and Christians into

mutual commitment for justice, peace and the integrity of creation. What should happen now? At its last meeting in March 1990 the central committee, in a preliminary evaluation, confirmed "the long-term commitment of the WCC to the JPIC process up to and beyond the Canberra assembly".[12]

It suggested two ways of doing this. On the one hand, care must be taken that the focus on justice, peace and the integrity of creation is incorporated in our programme work in an organic and binding way. Then the churches must consider the final document of the assembly for its acceptability and practicability. Fundamentally there would have to be an official process of work and reception in our member churches and other communities, in which these texts could also be related more precisely to the concrete problems on the spot and in the individual regions. In this way a growing convergence in convictions and modes of action could be facilitated in this field of justice, peace and the integrity of creation.

19. Such further work is also necessary because in the previous course of the JPIC process some theological questions have remained open, or have only now been clearly asked and are in need of clarification. Among them, in the view of the central committee, are the ideas of covenanting and conciliarity; also the question of how ethics and ecclesiology tie up with each other. The plans for future work proposed by the Joint Working Group between the Roman Catholic Church and the World Council of Churches in its sixth report may also be useful in this connection — namely, clarification of what we mean by "the place and mission of the church in God's saving and transforming action" and the examination of ethical questions as new causes for divisions in the church.[13]

## A vital and coherent theology

20. The last assembly voiced a clear disquiet about the lack of concentrated theological work in the whole field of the programmes of the World Council:

> The theological diversity among the units and sub-units of the Council is perceived by some as a sign of vitality, by others as a sign of too little integration and too much division.[14]

It is true that in the World Council many different theological traditions jostle with each other and need to be heard. It is also true that there are new theological approaches and unfamiliar modes of biblical exegesis which have emerged in another cultural environment or on the basis of specific experiences and questionings. And we are also discovering that our traditional theological paradigms are still not yielding any convincing answers to new challenges nor enabling us to make progress. So in the World Council one cannot wonder at finding a diversified theological picture which is often really confusing. But the Vancouver assembly did not want the various theological traditions and experimental thinking to remain an incoherent jumble. It was concerned that "there should be interaction between the diversity of theological approaches".[15] In this way we should end up by developing a "vital and coherent theology". At the end of the road from Vancouver to Canberra it must be said that despite all the efforts so far made the task we were set still remains ahead of us.

21. Admittedly it has been hard to agree about what was meant by a "vital and coherent theology" and how these terms could be turned into our many working languages. If my understanding is correct, what the assembly meant was that the relation between theology and life, between the scholarly discussion of questions of faith and the actual experiences of conflict which people have in the world of today, must be more strongly stated. Literally:

> For some there is still too great a distance between the daily struggles and anguish of human life and the technical theological discussion of traditional doctrinal questions.

Of course it was at once added:

> Others fear the disruption of careful theological deliberation precisely because of the introduction of these struggles into the deliberation process.[16]

The two concerns thus expressed are not unjustified; they are repeatedly voiced from both sides; and they are still with us. In my view the question of our success in taking the one concern into account without neglecting the other is an exacting test of our capacity for fellowship. So we are talking about theological thinking which is related to the actual life of our churches and which will on the one hand help them to become one and on the other hand promote their common action and mutual solidarity in the struggle for justice, peace and the integrity of creation.

22. The assembly in Vancouver had proposed the formation of a theological advisory group which would be "representative of all units, sub-units, and theological perspectives in the WCC and drawn from the membership of working groups and commissions" and to "consider the place, diversity and interaction of theological work in all dimensions of the WCC through critical and constructive evaluation".[17]

The discussions before and during the central committee of 1984 led to the conviction that the purpose of developing a vital and coherent theology would probably not be best served by the creation of a separate, permanent task force. Instead, existing consultative structures should be more fully used for the necessary theological discussion: for instance, the central committee itself, the committees of the programme units and the regular staff meetings in Geneva. The general secretary therefore invited a number of ecumenically experienced and theologically qualified persons who have developed their reflections and suggestions on the subject in meetings and conversations with the staff in Geneva. Among them were our former president, Dr José Míguez Bonino, our present president, Metropolitan Paulos Mar Gregorios, and our former moderator, Dr M.M. Thomas. Their contributions, with some others from those on the Geneva staff, were published in our journal, *The Ecumenical Review*, April 1988. The executive committee in February 1989 at its meeting in Geneva also gave the theme thorough consideration in a discussion which appears in print as an appendix to the relevant minutes of the meeting.

23. We must therefore increase our efforts so that there can be continuous theological discussion from all sides in the World Council.

BEM, the Lima convergence document on *Baptism, Eucharist and Ministry*, demonstrates our growth in mutual understanding and our ability to reach at least an intermediate stage in common convictions — but so in their way do the ten affirmations of the world convocation in Seoul. The need for further theological clarification has revealed itself in other ways too in our work on our programmes. Thus the Larnaca conference of 1986 was sure that reflection on the theological fundamentals of diakonia should be intensified. As I have already said, theological and ecclesiological studies on the understanding and practice of covenanting belong to our process of mutual commitment to justice, peace and the integrity of creation. More work must be done on a common theological understanding of creation and on an ecumenical social ethics which takes account of the questions of human survival that are being asked, even beyond the relatively narrow circle of our member churches. Finally, the growing, independent theological contribution of women in our churches and in the World Council represents a challenge to our traditional theological thinking which calls for both unprejudiced attention and critical care.

24. Let me add here two comments on the question of a vital and coherent theology. First, however much we have to listen on the one hand to the new approaches and insights of contextual theology, it is equally

necessary on the other hand to stay within the overall theological tradition of the church since its beginnings. Throughout the ages it has been legitimate in the preaching of the church to adopt new theological insights and answers which relate to changed historical situations, cultural contexts or spiritual and intellectual challenges. But this history of the transmission of the faith embraces also at the same time critical testing to see whether what is new stands in a living relationship to the original gospel as that has been transmitted to us by the apostles.

## Communion as a leitmotif

25. Second, we must not look on the effort to find a "vital and coherent theology" as a purely theoretical exercise in thinking theologically. Common theologizing develops out of common experiences both in worship and prayer and in common commitment to the preaching of the faith or the achievement of justice and peace. Thus a vital and coherent theology has to do with the ecumenical experience of community. Community, communion or koinonia, in any event, seems to be the central concept or rather the decisive reality of life on which everything is meant to converge and which should be served by all our thoughts and plans, by all we ask God for and by everything we do together in the World Council of Churches. All the great programme undertakings in the World Council are aimed at community, communion, koinonia: the unity of the church, the missionary proclamation of the gospel by word and deed; the struggle for justice and peace, training in a life-style of healing and sharing; the defence of human rights; full participation in the life of the church; the dialogue with other faiths; and the integrity of creation; and so on. Can the sending of the Son by the Father in the power of the Holy Spirit be better described than the coming of God to human beings for the healing and restoration of communion with God and among each other in a new heaven and a new earth? So we find that our theological thinking will become "vital and coherent" when we base it on the experience of the fellowship which we already have been given and relate it to the gift of complete communion which we expect as God's promise to the church. It seems to me that *The Unity of the Church as Koinonia: Gift and Calling*, the statement prepared for the assembly by the Commission on Faith and Order at the request of the central committee, gives an apt description of where our churches stand in the quest for unity: between the unity that is a gift and the unity that is lost, between a renewed experience of communion and a communion which is still to be realized.

## New dimensions of ecclesial self-understanding

26. Among the programme guidelines in Vancouver was growing towards new dimensions of the churches' self-understanding — this "in response to their deepening participation in the ecumenical movement".[18] I find it particularly difficult to report on whether there has been progress in this direction, because one can measure only with difficulty this expansion into new dimensions of ecclesial self-understanding. Moreover it is for the churches themselves to be answerable for this. I therefore think it would be worth having a mutual exchange of ideas among the delegates of our churches and all other participants at this assembly to ascertain whether and how far the self-understanding of their own churches has been extended, enriched and deepened and in short has become "more ecumenical" through participation in the ecumenical movement generally and in the work of the World Council of Churches in particular. It can only be that ecumenical cooperation exercises a pervasive influence on all who participate in it and on our churches as a whole — an influence which will have its effects only in the long term and for the most part imperceptibly. Through ecumenical encounter, discussion and acting together in common as Christians and as churches, all of us have begun to learn to reflect in a different way on each other and learn from each other in the fields of devotion, theological work, worship and diakonia. We have also begun to feel mutually responsible for each other. This is reflected in intercession, visits, mutual aid and also in critical discussions with each other. In many respects we are indeed still separate churches and we continue to bear the marks of our confessional, cultural and even national identity. Nevertheless, the dividing walls have become lower and we are increasingly becoming aware that our divisions do not "go down to the roots".

27. This movement into new dimensions of our self-understanding as churches is aptly expressed in the study document appended to the sixth report of the Joint Working Group between the Roman Catholic Church and the World Council of Churches under the title "The Church: Local and Universal". We read there in sections 33-34:

> All churches which participate actively in the ecumenical movement agree that even where eucharistic fellowship and full communion are not yet achieved between churches, nevertheless forms of communion do exist. The churches are no longer living in isolation from each other. They have developed mutual understanding and respect. They pray together and share in each other's spiritual experience and theological insights. They collaborate in

addressing the needs of humanity. Through bilateral and multilateral dialogues they have achieved remarkable convergences with regard to previously divisive issues of doctrine and church order. They share, in different degrees, in the basic elements of communion. It is, therefore, possible to speak of an existing real though imperfect communion among the churches — with the understanding that the degrees of expressions of such communion may vary according to the relationships between individual churches.

This recognition of an already existing though imperfect communion is a significant result of ecumenical efforts and a radically new element in twentieth-century church history...

## A common understanding of the WCC

28. The World Council of Churches seeks to help the churches as they grow into new forms of community and is at the same time an expression of this growth. In the last few years, not least because of the fortieth anniversary of the WCC in 1988, the question has again arisen as to how our churches understand their membership of the World Council of Churches and whether we can reach a common understanding of our fellowship in the World Council. Because of this the central committee asked the general secretary, after discussions at its last meetings in Moscow and Geneva, to initiate a process of consultation with the member churches on the common understanding of the World Council of Churches. An exchange of ideas among the delegates at this assembly is also envisaged, the results of which should flow into the further course of this process of consultation. Can we together, humbly and conscientiously, without either anxiety regarding dogma or ecumenical exuberance, state the measure of community which has developed or has once more become recognizable, of which at any rate we have become aware — in the course of the present century in the ecumenical movement and through cooperation in the World Council of Churches? An answer to this question does not suggest itself primarily because we are on the road from the fortieth anniversary of the World Council and moving towards its fiftieth in 1998, but rather for reasons of faith; for we pray for the unity of the church, we confess God's renewing activity in our midst and we seek to let ourselves be obediently guided farther by the Holy Spirit and we should be ready to openly acknowledge this under God.

## Participation

29. In our churches a changed self-understanding has developed to an increased degree in another respect — towards the church as a participatory community. Here the programme guidelines mentioned

the development of a community of healing and sharing within the WCC and the member churches where women, men, young people and children, able and disabled, clergy and laity, *participate fully* and minister to one another...[19]

I should like to make only the following few brief remarks.

30. In the last few years in the governing bodies of the WCC we have consciously striven with, I believe, increasing success, to achieve a better balance in our centre at Geneva between women and men, between the various confessional traditions and the individual regions of the world. The same holds good for the composition of our programme commissions and that of those who take part in our consultations and conferences. Our concern was to apply the principle of full competent participation, equal rights and eligibility for all in the work of the World Council. Some of us may be put off by the fact that specific quotas were laid down, but it has kept us mindful that the aim should not be lost to view. It has also helped us to come closer to it, even if we have not yet actually hit the target hoped for. Thus, unfortunately, the proportion of women among the delegates at this assembly will still not be the forty percent and the number of young people will still not amount to the twenty percent which the central committee in Hanover had envisaged and recommended to the churches.

## Solidarity with women

31. The Ecumenical Decade of the Churches in Solidarity with Women was inaugurated at Easter 1988. It is slowly gaining an entry in the churches and calls on them to acknowledge the crucial contribution of women in church and society and to put into practice the insights gained from the study on the community of men and women in the church as Vancouver 1983 asked.[20] The decade is intended to draw the churches' attention also to the still existing discrimination against women in society and help them to see it as part of their calling to support women in their struggle against poverty, exploitation and deprivation. But above all it is important to achieve, or at least promote decisively, the full cooperation of women, with equal rights, in the theological work, the decision-making bodies and the moulding of the life of the church. We are to a great extent still only in the initial stage of realizing these objectives. For the further progress of the World Council, therefore, the tasks described here will continue to exist beyond this assembly in Canberra.

**Young people and the differently-abled**

32. This also applies to the full and fitting participation of young people from our member churches in the life of the World Council and in the ecumenical movement as a whole. The ecumenical global gathering of youth and students, planned for the end of 1992 with Brazil as the probable venue, can and must give this a substantial impetus. It is being prepared by our Youth department in cooperation with other Christian global associations of young people and has set itself the target of reconstructing and revitalizing the ecumenical youth movement. We can only welcome this. We have to ask ourselves — and rightly — whether we can talk about wholeness and unity in the life of the church so long as young people, like women, are denied the place that is rightfully theirs and enables them to contribute the whole range of their gifts and experience, and of their commitment. Incidentally this applies also in far greater measure to the disabled, who form as much as ten percent of the world's population — another fact not reflected at all among us in the World Council.

**Common confession and common learning**

33. The assembly in Vancouver had named "growing towards a community of confessing and learning" as a fifth programme guideline. A strong drive towards greater commitment in the cooperation of the member churches in the World Council can be observed in this connection. We might also speak of an urge to move out of relative lack of committedness. This has been plain to see at the various conferences of the last few years. In Larnaca in 1986 and El Escorial in 1987 those taking part chose the language of self-commitment in the final statements. At the world conference on mission and evangelism in San Antonio at the end of May 1989 "Acts in Faithfulness" were adopted in which a concrete commitment confessed by the delegates is set forth. The final acts of the world convocation for "Justice, Peace and the Integrity of Creation" which took place rather less than a year ago have all the more the nature of a commitment — not just the four "acts of covenanting" that went into this; the ten "basic affirmations" of the faith call for and contain specific commitments to practical action. This is a new feature in the life of the World Council which for many still raises important questions which call for a joint effort of clarification.

**Committedness**

34. This drive towards committedness is in my judgment not only understandable and necessary in view of the challenges we must meet on

the basis of our faith and in obedience to the biblical gospel, say in the field of justice, peace and the integrity of creation. I see here too a justified attempt to give provisional but concrete expression to the vision of the "one fully committed fellowship" which since the third assembly of the WCC in New Delhi in 1961 has been defined as the goal to which "all in each place who are baptized into Jesus Christ and confess him as Lord and Saviour"[21] are being brought by the Holy Spirit.

These attempts at steps and acts of greater committedness in our common witness to the gospel and in the struggle for human dignity, justice, peace and the preservation of creation have taken place in various forms in the areas covered by the programmes I have mentioned. But it is of crucial importance to the whole fellowship that churches and movements within the WCC's fellowship seek and try out ways of achieving greater commitment in cooperation. I think it is time that we pay special attention to these questions. That could be something of importance in the process of consultation with the member churches on a common understanding of the World Council of Churches.

35. Another feature which can be noted in the work of the World Council during the last few years is the effort to give a comprehensive expression to the calling of the churches in this world.

Of course this is by no means new. The decision to unite the two great ecumenical forerunner movements, "Life and Work" and "Faith and Order", and found the World Council of Churches, which should have taken place exactly fifty years ago but because of the second world war did not happen till 1948, is proof that from the start the oneness of the ecumenical movement was affirmed and its division into an "ecclesiastical and theological" and a "political and social" branch was disallowed. The tension thus created has of course continued to have its effects through the years. It could be felt at the last assembly too:

> ...we have sensed a tension between some of those who are concerned with the unity of the church and others concerned with the desperate need for justice, peace and reconciliation in the human community.[22]

So it is greatly to be welcomed that the Commission on Faith and Order is continuing to work on its great study on "The Unity of the Church and the Renewal of Human Community", through which the relations between these two basic concerns of the ecumenical movement are examined from the overall perspective of the promise of the kingdom of God and hopefully can be convincingly illuminated for everyone.

**A holistic mission**

36. Thus the world mission conference in San Antonio at the end of May 1989 was also concerned with developing a holistic understanding of the mission of the church today. Using the theme of the cry in the Lord's prayer, "your will be done", it was looking for a means of expressing "mission in Christ's way". Here the central commitment of the church was affirmed, of preaching the good news of God's saving love in Jesus Christ to the millions of people who have still had no opportunity to hear the gospel and to respond to it;[23] but to do so together in unity. Here God's command, "to do justly, and to love mercy" (cf. Mic. 6:8) was recognized as equally binding;[24] in solidarity of course with those who suffer and are struggling for their dignity as human beings. Probably for the first time at a world mission conference responsibility for creation and the just distribution of the riches of the earth was numbered among the tasks of the churches' mission.[25] But what is part and parcel of a "mission in Christ's way" and what alone makes it holistic is the spirit of humility in which it takes place, the will to examine oneself and to renew the churches in regard to their relations with each other, but also with people of other faiths or without any religious convictions at all. And this is not just because critical encounters in the ecumenical movement have made us very conscious of the conflicting accompanying phenomena of the modern history of mission but because we affirm the calling to fulfill mission "in Christ's way" who was himself "humble in heart" (Matt. 11:29).[26]

**Financial limits**

37. Finally let me say something about the limits we experience in the work of the World Council; limits which are not new, which we come up against time and again, which we have not succeeded in overcoming, if indeed we do not simply have to live with them.

In the financial report of the sixth assembly we read of "the financial problems that face the Council in the years to come".[27] It cannot be foreseen that this will fundamentally change in the coming years, so we are confronted with the question how we can bring the scope of our programme work into line with our actual income, which has not increased to the desired extent. We can follow different approaches to this, either setting priorities clearly — which of course may mean ending or drastically cutting our existing programme work — or else restructuring the whole of the programme work, with which the central committee concerned itself at its last two meetings in the summer of 1989 at Moscow and at the beginning of 1990 in Geneva, without coming up with any decisions. This will be the task of the new central committee to be elected by this assembly. Naturally we also want to try to open up new sources for funds. In any case that will only be attended to some time from now. Finally we should also ask the member churches to increase their membership fees as the Vancouver assembly also did. To a remarkable extent that appeal has been complied with. However, these considerable increases in the contributions of our member churches have unfortunately not led, when all is said, to increased income for the World Council because of the movements in exchange rates and the general rise in costs. In my view it is imperatively urgent that the assembly in discussing the future work of the Council should remain aware of these constricting financial conditions.

38. Here I should like to add that, in view of the recommendation of the last assembly that a statement of the financial responsibilities of membership should be presented for inclusion in the Rules of the World Council of Churches,[28] the central committee at its meeting in Moscow in 1989 approved a relevant section headed "Responsibilities of Membership" and included it in the Rules at present in force. Naturally the duties of the members of the World Council of Churches cover much more than supporting its work financially. They involve among other things active cooperation in its programme work and active two-way communication. But in this connection there is a need to stress that all member churches have to support the budget of the World Council financially too, no matter how modestly, after conscientiously evaluating what they are able to do. Unhappily this still does not happen everywhere, and we should look for ways of implementing this in future.

## Reception in the churches

39. In the last few years we have held a large number of conferences and consultations, among them a number of world conferences; in 1986 on diakonia 2000 in Larnaca, on ecumenical sharing in El Escorial in 1987, the world mission conference in San Antonio in 1989, and the world convocation for "Justice, Peace and the Integrity of Creation" in Seoul in 1990. We may legitimately ask, and must ask, whether on an overall view that is not too much; whether we have not asked too much of ourselves and our churches, above all in regard to the reception of all the results of our work. When here at this assembly we take account of what has happened in the World Council since the last assembly in Vancouver in 1983, we should likewise try to do so also for how much of our work

has been received in our member churches and by their church agencies in the movements and groups, and could be really made use of.

We should furthermore ask whether because of the fullness and diversification of our programmes individually the coherence and transparency of the work of the WCC as a whole has become unclear or is in danger of going altogether by default. This is not a new question. The fact that it is being asked again at the end of the road between Vancouver and Canberra shows that we have not finished work on it. I hope we can conduct discussion on the guidelines for the years ahead from the standpoint of how the wholeness and unity of the work of the World Council can make itself felt.

## Limitations to what we say

40. We came up against a very painful limitation to our ability to speak and act together when it was necessary to find a clear word in public on the situation of political oppression and violation of human rights in Romania, to help and encourage the victims of an arbitrary political system and ideological dictatorship which was also paralyzing our member churches in that country. Here despite intensive consultations and debates we did not find in our community the freedom and authority which were called for. Such situations, where tension is pushed to breaking point between making allowances for the difficult position of member churches and commitment to clear support for justice and peace and for the victims of human rights violations, are not a new experience for the World Council, because it presented itself for instance at the assembly in Nairobi in 1975 when the issue was freedom of belief in the Soviet Union. We will face such challenges in future too, in which we may hopefully succeed better in finding with wisdom and fearlessness the right word for truth and freedom, for the safeguarding of justice and of fellowship.

## Prayer for the Holy Spirit

41. "Come, Holy Spirit — Renew the Whole Creation". That is a prayer. And I find that its choice as the main theme for this seventh assembly of the World Council of Churches expresses a general and very profound experience of a boundary situation. It is the first time in the history of the World Council that an assembly is being held with a prayer as its leitmotif, that we turn with our prayer and reflection to the person and work of the Holy Spirit and that we seek to become aware of our moral, theological and missionary responsibility for the whole of God's creation. All in all I see us as being in deep need, a need for God, which

Martin Luther expressed in a pithy sentence in his famous hymn "A safe stronghold our God is still": "With force of arms we nothing can". In all our strivings for the unity of the church, and for a truly renewed Christian life, for justice, peace and the integrity of creation, for a new fraternal order of coexistence for the many peoples, cultures and faiths on our earth, do we not come up against limits, boundaries, frontiers which we cannot overcome in our own knowledge and strength? We are most deeply in need of the divine power of the Holy Spirit. We are dependent on the coming of the Spirit and on the Spirit's work of renewal in us and among ourselves.

But that is not everything that is to be said here. In his hymn Martin Luther also said: "Er ist bei uns wohl auf dem Plan, mit seinem Geist und Gaben" — "He has indeed appeared in our midst with his Spirit and his gifts". The Holy Spirit is at work and we believe in the promise that the power of the Spirit will be given to those who ask for it. For that reason I want to close with a prayer to the Holy Spirit (adapting the words of Anselm of Canterbury):

Come, Holy Spirit,
come, teacher of the humble, judge of the arrogant,
come, hope of the poor, refreshment of the weary...
come, star on the sea, rescuer of the shipwrecked;
come, most splendid adornment of all living beings,
the sole salvation of all who are mortal.
Come, Holy Spirit, have mercy on us;
prepare us for your work,
imbue our lowliness with your power,
meet our weakness with the fullness of your grace;
healer of wounds and purifier of sins,
You who keep our soul in felicity and comfort us in our distress!

NOTES

[1] *Gathered for Life*, ed. David Gill, Geneva, WCC, 1983, p.250.
[2] *Ibid.*, p.252.
[3] *Faith and Order 1985-1989: The Commission Meeting at Budapest 1989*, ed. Thomas F. Best, Geneva, WCC, 1990, p.26.
[4] *Gathered for Life, op. cit*, p.253.
[5] *Ibid.*, p.253.
[6] *Sharing Life*, report of the WCC world consultation on "Koinonia: Sharing Life in a World Community", Geneva, WCC, 1987, p.27.
[7] *Gathered for Life, op. cit.*, p.255.
[8] *Ibid.*, p.251.

[9] *Diakonia 2000 — Called to be Neighbours*, report of the Larnaca consultation 1986, Geneva, WCC, 1987, p.124.

[10] Programme to Combat Racism, *Review 1989*, Geneva, WCC, p.86.

[11] *Gathered for Life, op. cit.*, p.255.

[12] *Minutes of the Forty-First Meeting of the Central Committee*, Geneva, WCC, 1990, p.97.

[13] Joint Working Group between the Roman Catholic Church and the World Council of Churches, *Sixth Report*, Geneva-Rome, 1990, p.18.

[14] *Gathered for Life, op. cit.*, p.249.

[15] *Ibid.*, p.254.

[16] *Ibid.*, p.249.

[17] *Ibid.*, p.254.

[18] *Ibid.*, p.252.

[19] *Ibid.*, p.255.

[20] *Ibid.*, p.256.

[21] *The New Delhi Report*, Geneva, WCC, 1962, p.116.

[22] *Gathered for Life, op. cit.*, p.49.

[23] *The San Antonio Report*, ed. Fred Wilson, Geneva, WCC, 1991, p.36.

[24] *Ibid.*, p.22.

[25] *Ibid.*, pp.54,55,58.

[26] *Ibid.*, p.22 (...and to walk humbly with our God); cf. pp.26-28.

[27] *Gathered for Life, op. cit.*, p.241.

[28] *Ibid.*, p.243.

*Dr Jacquelyn Grant preaching at the celebration of the Lima liturgy.*

# 4.3. REPORT OF THE GENERAL SECRETARY

## *Emilio Castro*

**Introduction**

1. My initial responsibility is to share with you the process of wrestling with the main theme, of the interaction that has taken place between the theme and the changing world contexts. Let us remember that we selected the theme about four years ago under the full sway of the Cold War, the threat of nuclear catastrophe, a prevailing mood of powerlessness. The invocation of the Holy Spirit was conceived as an affirmation of faith in God's resources to lead us into the unknown and uncertain future. Then came the acceleration of history in 1989, with winds of freedom breaking the rigidities of history and opening doors and windows to our creative imagination. The Spirit theme — the invocation — became a clear encouragement to full participation in the renewal of all human history. And now, do we have new demons replacing the old ones? With all the talk about "holy war" and "just war" we are again acutely aware of historical ambiguities. How will the prayer for the Spirit to come bring about renewal in a world where sin, broken relations and mistrust remain as tragic realities?

**I. "Come, Holy Spirit — Renew the Whole Creation": the context of our prayer**

2. Four years ago, when the theme was chosen, we could hardly have imagined the kind of far-reaching changes that have since then overtaken us. Ideologies have collapsed and barriers broken down. Winds of change have swept over Eastern Europe and South Africa. But the end of the Cold War has not ushered in a new era of peace. The prayer we chose as our theme continues to be as relevant today as it was when we chose it.

3. Hunger and poverty continue to be the lot of great majorities of the world's population. People live in despair, or resort to revolt and protest. Religious and ethnic conflicts, intolerance and violence are as much in evidence as ever before. No doubt there are signs of hope. Among these is the dynamism of young people seeking solutions for the problems of the world, and ideals to guide them into the future. Among them is also the revolution — we can use no lesser word — that calls for the recognition of the gifts that God has given equally to women and men and demands that these gifts should have full opportunity to be used in the life of

society and in the church. The unheard-of progress of modern science and of technology gives us visions of a world where the great enemies of human health may well be conquered.

4. The great religions of humanity, providing meaning and direction to millions of people, offer the possibility of creative pluralism but also lead to widespread conflicts. The vitality of the Christian community has shifted towards the southern continents where poverty, youth and faith combine to produce new calls to obedience and to be the church.

5. In such a context, the prayer "Come, Holy Spirit — Renew the Whole Creation" is at once a recognition of the inadequacy of all human resources and the affirmation of the faith that God lives. The Spirit, who hovered over creation like a protective mother bird over her young, is active and present today in all of creation. Our prayer expresses the conviction that the human "No" cannot be more powerful than the creative and renewing "Yes" of God.

6. Yesterday we had the courage to affirm that the Cold War could be overcome. We had the courage to struggle against racism alongside the victims of apartheid. We entered into dialogue with people of other living faiths as part of our Christian presence in the world. Our churches launched a decade of solidarity with women so that all of us together may grow into a community of women and men. As a fellowship of churches we were able to be an instrument of peace in situations of conflict, and to be a witness of solidarity in the defence of human rights. Let us pray that in this assembly we may recognize those challenges that are calling for our responses today, and that we are empowered to follow the guidance of the Spirit, as a people together committed to the service of the coming kingdom. Let us listen to what the Spirit says to the churches.

## II. Some questions

7. This contribution to the discussions of the assembly will be limited to clarifying four fundamental questions which have arisen in the course of its preparation. Our answers to them in this assembly will identify what witness our churches are called to bear in the world today, and lead us to a vision of the World Council of Churches which will shape its future, spiritually, programmatically and structurally.

A. HOW DO WE COMMUNICATE THE THEME?

8. A group of journalists asked recently: "How do we report on an assembly centred on a prayer addressed to the Holy Spirit? When the World Council of Churches makes statements on racial, social or political

problems, or on issues such as women's liberation, we know how to present them. But the 'Spirit' is more than we can cope with. It is a different language altogether, and our audiences wouldn't know what to do with it either."

9. It is more than a matter of communication. How indeed can we talk about the Spirit when we are under the sway of "instrumental reason", which weighs, measures, monitors and controls everything? It is important to answer that question if we are to be engaged in what Lesslie Newbigin calls "a global missionary encounter with modernity". He writes:

> I am asking that the WCC should be and should be seen to be an enabler of the church's universal mission to make Christ known, loved and obeyed throughout this entire global city of which we are all a part. And I am asking that the WCC recognize that it is not enough to address the *symptoms* of modernization; we have to address the causes, the underlying belief systems which sustain it. We need a theological clarification of the issues involved in a global missionary encounter with modernity.
>
> *The Ecumenical Review*, Vol. 42, No. 1, January 1991, p.6

10. In this missionary situation, the notion of the Spirit is a fundamental challenge. By invoking the Holy Spirit we affirm communion, justice, solidarity and accountability as against the pragmatic notions of instrumentality, efficiency and profitability which characterize much of contemporary socio-economic discussions. The notions of chance — arbitrariness — and necessity figure frequently in contemporary philosophical and scientific discussions; our prayer claims a place for the notions of purpose, freedom and responsibility.

### a) The Spirit and the created order

11. As we reflect on the doctrine of creation and affirm the Holy Spirit as the One who energizes the whole creation, we rediscover the radical interdependence of human beings and the rest of nature. The eschatological vision of the coming kingdom points to the transformation of the whole cosmic order and not only of human life. In the Orthodox emphasis on theosis — a way of life in the risen Christ which finally leads to the divinization of humanity — the renewal of human life is proclaimed in the total context of the transformation of all reality. That is to say, we have come to understand more clearly, both theologically and scientifically, the interdependence of humanity and the rest of creation. Humankind is not the owner of creation. It is part of it. Nature is precious, not only because of its instrumental service to humankind but also because of its reflection of God's glory.

12. This sense of interdependence is enriched by our belief that human beings are created in the image and likeness of God (Gen. 1:27). It is this specificity that enables humanity to accept responsibility for and interdependence with the rest of nature. The awareness that all creation is God's creation must transform our attitudes towards it. We do not contemplate it from outside it; we are part of it. We do not seek new ways to exploit it; we seek new ways to relate to it in an attitude of caring respect. Our spirituality is to be lived out in the service of the transforming and redeeming purpose of God which embraces the whole of creation.

*b) The Spirit and our humanness*

13. Closely related to this is our affirmation of the sacred, transcendent character of human life. Human beings are more than producers, consumers, citizens. They are unique, unrepeatable beings, created in the image of God, animated by the Spirit, and not just objects of social engineering. For example, when we talk of responsible parenthood this is precisely what we stress, our spirituality and our humanity and the quality of interpersonal relationships. Thus when we enter into the scientific debate on experiments with embryos we know we are on holy ground. When we struggle for the justice due to the powerless we are drawing attention to the fact that in them Jesus Christ himself comes to meet us. In the experience of common worship and in personal prayer, we respond to God's call to repentance and to God's offer of love. The presence of the Holy Spirit, helping us to discover time and time again the image of God in every human being, will enable us to consider in these debates not merely what is most desirable in social engineering, but what is most in keeping with the dignity and freedom of each human being.

*c) The Spirit and community*

14. In the third place, we must enter into a serious debate on the spiritual character of our interpersonal and community relations. The Holy Spirit in Christian theology is the creator of communion, of fellowship; the Spirit is the bond of union between the Father and the Son and the One who ensures the unity of humankind in God. We must develop along these lines an adequate theology of the family, of friendship, and of human society.

15. This is particularly urgent at the present time when massive migrations of people, growing individualism and the struggle for women's liberation, are all calling in question traditional understandings of friendship and love.

16. Christian ethics cannot be dependent solely on sociological considerations, statistics and opinion polls; these cannot define what is good and what is evil. But the changes taking place even in Christian families call for a deeper analysis of the values which the church has traditionally sought to promote and protect. We need to identify those values of loyalty, faithfulness and mutuality which are the gifts of the Spirit, setting them free from the sometimes oppressive social forms in which they were preserved in the past. Human beings, as spiritual beings, are created for communion, for fellowship. The bonds of relationship with one's neighbour — not only those involving religious or even church solidarity — and the natural bonds of mutual belonging derive from the Spirit. One of the main efforts of the WCC to articulate this theological perspective is to be found in the search for an inclusive community of women and men both in church and society. We are called into community. Our relation with neighbours is not merely "social"; it is a response to the call of the Spirit.

17. This is true not only of interpersonal relations: it is also important for the type of community we want to create as a national or worldwide human society. A philosophy of society which assumes that economic growth will provide automatic answers to social needs has to be challenged in the perspective of the spirit of love manifested in Jesus Christ. A Trinitarian spirituality demands communion, justice, solidarity, participation and openness.

18. In trying to answer the journalist's question I have simply described the ongoing task of evangelism which belongs to the Christian church and the ecumenical movement. Our fundamental task is to tell a story which begins in a manger and, through the cross, reaches its climax on the resurrection morning. We believe that here we have the key to human existence.

19. The World Council of Churches is a fellowship of churches which without reserve affirms the Trinitarian faith. We pray, we worship, we affirm the revealed mystery of God's presence in the world. We are called to a missionary task: to announce new life in the Spirit in polemic confrontation with the prevailing value systems. Is it difficult to talk about the Holy Spirit? Undoubtedly it is. But if we start from this vision of the Holy Spirit active in the life and death of Jesus Christ, then to talk about the Spirit is to talk about reality.

20. It is participation in the struggle for the defence of life. It is sharing in the promise of life in all its fullness (John 10:10). In one sense our difficulty in communicating a Spirit-centred theme is a judgment on

our communication values. For it is the Spirit who makes communication possible.

## B. WILL THE LANGUAGE OF THE SPIRIT TURN US INWARD?

21. Journalists are not the only people who have problems with our theme. For example, social activists are afraid that the language of the Spirit will distance us from our social responsibility. They ask: are we not opening the door to abstruse discussions far removed from the existential reality of struggle and suffering? When social life becomes complicated and conflictive, are we not escaping to religiosity? Is the language of the Spirit appropriate for talking of conflicts, of social struggles? Is it not better suited for talking about peace and reconciliation? Behind these questions lies a serious concern: will the World Council of Churches not become so "spiritual" that it loses its identity, its raison d'etre?

### a) The Spirit of dynamism

22. These questions reflect the stereotypes and caricatures which prevail even in our own church circles. How can the theme of the role of the Holy Spirit distance us from the reality of conflict in history when the creator God who redeems and sanctifies is the God who acts in history? Creation is an act of divine will (Gen. 1:2; Job 26:13; Ps. 104:30).

23. The energies which sustain the universe are a manifestation of the Spirit. The apostle Paul talks of the eager longing of creation (Rom. 8:21f.) for the liberation that is to come. "To long for" and "to anticipate" are not passive responses; they represent spiritual attitudes of active expectation, a willingness to participate in bringing about that which is awaited. Jesus tells us that the Spirit will speak on our behalf before tribunals (Mark 13:11). It is the Holy Spirit who equipped Jesus for his messianic mission (Luke 4:18-19). The Holy Spirit is power for mission and for witness (Acts 1:8), calling the church into being, and equipping her with gifts, charisms, for public proclamation (Acts 2). Justice, peace and joy are thoroughly "earthly" realities which belong in the Holy Spirit (Rom. 14:17). The body is the temple of the Spirit (1 Cor. 6:19).

24. Confessing Jesus Christ as Lord in the midst of the "many lords" who claim ultimate obedience is possible only through the presence of the Holy Spirit (1 Cor. 12:3). The symbols of the Holy Spirit in the Bible are symbols of action, movement and struggle. The Spirit is breath, wind, the dove, fire, the finger of God. It is our faith in the Holy Spirit the Giver of Life which places us in the midst of situations of conflict. The Spirit leads us into the wilderness, as Jesus was led, where we find that all our human

resources are exhausted. Leading us out of our obsession to possess, through the wilderness of self-emptying, the Spirit helps us to say no to temptations, whether they are religious, economic or political.

25. The church, called into being at Pentecost by the coming of the Holy Spirit, is a dynamic missionary body sent to serve in the whole world in the discipleship of Jesus Christ. The WCC, which is a Spirit-inspired fellowship of churches, never sought to escape from historical controversies. The Holy Spirit obliges us to be in solidarity with the downtrodden, to proclaim peace, to uphold human rights, to challenge all historical reality that seems to militate against the vision of the kingdom. When UNICEF talks of forty million children dying for lack of sufficient food, when we see hundreds of thousands of homeless children sleeping in the streets, we find ourselves confronted with sin against the Spirit. Racism, sexism, ethnic conflicts and foreign debt are far more than social or economic problems. They are spiritual problems, an affront to the Spirit that provokes the wrath of God. In the experience of the WCC we have learned to speak of a spirituality for struggle/combat, to indicate the engaging, sacrificial character of our faith.

*b) The Spirit of liberation*

26. The poor know that the Holy Spirit is present in their conflicts and struggles. From the black churches in America we have received the treasure of the "Negro Spiritual" — biblical spirituality, consolation in moments of oppression. It also gave power in due time to ferment and shake the whole life of the American society. "There is a balm in Gilead to heal my sin-sick soul...", but that balm is also powerful to motivate marches, boycotts, protests, affirmations, liberation. In the Latin American experience the people are poor and believers; they see no dichotomy between their demand for social change and the expression of their religious faith. The oppressed go on struggling and hoping because of their awareness of the presence of God. They can say with Job: "I have heard of thee by the hearing of the ear, but now mine eye sees thee" (Job 42:5).

27. The Holy Spirit opens our eyes to see the injustice of the world and strengthens our spirits to confront it. The Spirit helps us to recognize the sinful nature of oppression. Our struggle, as the letter to the Ephesians says, is against principalities and powers. (A warning is necessary here. In the present conflict in the Gulf there are many attempts to "demonize" the enemy, to equate our cause with God's cause. Paul does not provide justification for any calling to a holy war, or a "just war". He does not

refer to "principalities and powers" to anathemize historical adversaries, but to discern in every conflict both the manifestation of human sinfulness and the need for spiritual resources to resist, endure and overcome. It is also a way to denounce evil structures of power that we produce in spite of best personal intentions (Eph. 6:10-17).

28. Many Christian groups are prisoners of individualistic interpretations of the gospel and have difficulties to understand the structural dynamics in the life of human society. We easily sacralize ideologies which deify economic success. A fundamental ecumenical task is to challenge each other, to learn from each other's experience, to overcome provincialism, to create solidarity which expresses our common belonging to the dynamic of the Spirit. In fact, one of the basic aspects of our ecumenical time is the growing solidarity among churches and peoples' organizations in the search for a common liberation. In the days ahead we shall have the opportunity to analyze the conciliar process for Justice, Peace and the Integrity of Creation. There, the aim is to bring the realities of our historical solidarities to the centre of our ecclesial fellowship and communion. I would also like to call your attention to the importance of our reflection on resource-sharing which is not simply a sharing of the goods which some may have and others may need; it means a new sense of belonging together in the movement of the Spirit to confront the powers of evil.

29. We hear so much today about the philosophy of the market. The role of the market as a place, a centre of communication between human beings, can and should be recognized and protected. But we seem to have lost sight of the spiritual dimension of the market. While the role of the market as a regulative mechanism for demand and supply may be defended in terms of its economic successes, it is dangerous to raise the market to an ideology which defines human life as a whole. Insofar as it denies the full participation of people in ethical and political decisions, it becomes a tyrannical force. The tyranny of the foreign debt — the main murderer in the world today — cannot be overcome by allowing the very mechanisms that created that situation to continue to operate freely. A clear denunciation of the greed, arrogance and the moral self-justification of the beneficiaries of the present international system belongs to the ecumenical tradition. It is a situation of collective sin where we are called to repentance. The Old Testament understanding of the Jubilee Year of the Lord does yield deep insights as we consider this problem. The Spirit will amplify the cry of the powerless, will facilitate alliances which multiply the capacity to confront this calamity and will

stimulate our intelligence to develop responsible mechanisms to overcome this tragedy.

*c) The Spirit of hope*

30. In the Spirit we "hope against all hope". The Spirit leads us to look beyond ourselves to a reality yet to come, and beyond all powers and principalities. Waiting on the Spirit, we discover a world of untapped resources, and of resistance and hope, which defies analysis in mere instrumental terms. The Holy Spirit who is the source of our hope also makes it possible for us to find allies we are unable to identify intellectually. It is the Holy Spirit who makes it possible to humanize our struggle. We are not out to destroy our adversary, but to transform and to actively hope for redemption.

31. The renewal of the church takes place where we find the Spirit at work in the world:

> Come, Holy Spirit — upset our routine, upset our conformism; enable us to discover and identify those areas of dehumanization where a word or an action in your name would make it possible to bear witness to the Spirit in our human relations. But give us also those new dimensions of solidarity which will enable us to strengthen networks of mutual aid, and to challenge more strongly the structures which violently dispossess people. Give us that life in you, that life in the Spirit which will enable us to work actively for the coming kingdom, for the renewal of all things in Christ.

## III. Discerning the Spirit at work in our time

32. Our prayer recognizes the work of the Spirit of God in the history of the human race, shaping that history and opening it up to new possibilities. But can we really hope that in and through and with the Spirit, new openings and new beginnings in our history can be produced? We hear cynical talk about "the end of history"; we are asked to acknowledge the ambiguity of everything that exists and to accept that we can only have pragmatic solutions to the immediate problems we face. But the ecumenical movement, on the basis of our faith in the Triune God, has always maintained an expectant attitude, and earnestly tried to see the hand of God in historical events. Thus the message of the WCC presidents for Pentecost 1990 said:

> The wind of the Spirit is blowing today, in us, in our churches, and in historical events where barriers are falling down and where there are possibilities of new beginnings. With the people of Namibia we celebrate their

independence; with the people of Chile their democracy; with the people of Central and Eastern Europe their newly acquired freedom. Glory be to God whose gift of dignity is affirmed through the recovery of freedom by these peoples and who opened in these events new avenues for the service and testimony which the church renders to Christ in the Spirit.

33. Here we have an interpretation of historical events as manifestations of the wind of the Spirit. But a Latin American theologian protests: "In this paragraph Namibia, Chile and the countries of Central and Eastern Europe are placed on the same level. I find it regrettable that what in my view are errors of political judgment should appear in an official letter."

34. The Pentecost message points to the possibility of interpreting historical events from the standpoint of faith. Starting with ideological presuppositions far removed from those of my Latin American friend, a group of Christian ethicists have expressed their concern about unqualified statements of the kind found in reports of our conferences, which give the impression of insisting on a single ethical norm that excludes all others. They make an emphatic call for moderation, and say that "our faith rarely prescribes specific answers to the complex problems of the world".

A. THE CALL TO DISCERN

35. Logically, any interpretation of history on the basis of theological convictions is an act of faith. It does not deny the data of human dialogue and the insights of the social sciences but dares to say a word that calls to action and supports us when we act. There is a risk, but is it not a lesser risk than that of neutrality or passiveness that borders on indifference? It is a risk, but one we live with in the light of the promise that the Holy Spirit will guide us into all truth (John 4:26; 16:13). We recall that it was through the Holy Spirit that Elizabeth blessed the child in the womb of Mary (Luke 1:40-42), and Simeon recognized God's salvation in the little refugee child (Luke 2:27f.).

36. The prophets received a precise command: "Speak." Perhaps we have been guilty of speaking even when we received no such command? When we speak, however, in obedience to God's command, the ecumenical community has the advantage that what it says comes out of a dialogue situation and with the participation in particular of those who suffer in their local situations and will be living with the consequences of what it says. This in itself is no guarantee of the rightness of the interpretation or

of the course of action that is recommended. The ambiguity of this issue is illustrated by three discussions at central committee meetings in Hanover, Moscow and Geneva on the situation in Romania. In the analysis of the situation there were no basic differences, but on the course of action to be taken we had a divided mind. Journeying together ecumenically provides opportunity for mutual support and correction.

B. THE CALL TO VENTURE

37. The second question with regard to historical interpretation relates to the present content of our reading of history. When we say that the Holy Spirit is active in history, we are saying that facts or events at a particular moment create an openness and liberation from the past which represent new possibilities for humanization and evangelism. We see the work of the Spirit, the divine wisdom, interweaving events, making possible links which liberate this or that society from its bondage and open up new possibilities. Thus, for instance, the people of Namibia have not solved all their economic, social and political problems. Reconciliation is not complete. But the people have a new beginning, a new space for participation; there is a new chance for people to take part in the shaping of their own destiny. Thus too the people of Romania, where the situation is perhaps even more ambiguous, experienced a little over a year ago the events we all know about — the heroic "disobedience" of a pastor, the courage of a people — which made it possible for them to shake off the chains of oppression and open up history. Now there is the fear that all may be lost, that the demon that has been expelled may be replaced by seven worse demons. But there are the possibilities of participation by the people and of a new witness by the church of Jesus Christ.

38. No situation represents the goal or climax of history; every situation, when considered in relation to the work of the Spirit, is a point of departure, an opening up. But this creation of spaces of freedom in history has to be accompanied by a liberation from the weight of past guilt, so that the new may really be seen as new.

39. In several countries we have experienced the transition from military dictatorship to systems of liberal democracy. The end of the dictatorship was joyfully welcomed by people and by the ecumenical movement. But the building of just societies and a climate of participation and social responsibility is hampered not only by international and socio-political factors but also by the difficulty of overcoming the cruelties and sufferings of yesterday. When we come to 1992, it will be very hard to

forget the genocide of the indigenous nations in the Americas and the importation of African people as slave labour. We cannot change that history but we should be able to redeem its memory and transform the present if, on the basis of that history, we open ourselves to the Spirit who calls us to build together that which is new. We cannot undo the shoa, the horror of the extermination camps, or eradicate it from the Jewish people's or humanity's memory. But we can accept this witness to grief and infamy and turn it into a passionate solidarity in overcoming anti-semitism and all oppressive racism.

40. There is no easy reconciliation, no facile forgiveness. Only the victim on the cross was able to pronounce the authentic word of forgiveness. Only the Aboriginals in Australia, the indigenous peoples elsewhere, the blacks of America will be able to pronounce this word of forgiveness.

41. Neither the church nor the fellowship of churches can promise that through human efforts we shall build the kingdom on earth, but we can and must proclaim that the Spirit opens up history and that it is always possible and necessary to search for ever more justice and peace. The opening for freedom is always an opening for participation and new creation.

## IV. Looking to the future

42. Every church is called to discern the manifestation of the renew-ing Spirit in the life of their nations. The ecumenical family provides a forum for reciprocal inspiration and correction. The interaction between the local and the global is essential to keep our discernment of the Spirit both relevant and responsible. But from time to time issues seem to be so pressing that the churches demand an ecumenical concerted response to them. We have heard the following issues as pressing demands on all the churches and particularly on the WCC.

A. RELIGIOUS PLURALITY

43. Interfaith coexistence is a reality of our life everywhere, but here, as elsewhere, we carry with us the burden of the past. One of the tragic misinterpretations of the Gulf crisis is to see in it a religious conflict. But the fact that this could be interpreted in such a way and that we need to clarify time and time again the total absence of religious motivations in the present conflict, is an indication of the seriousness of this concern.

44. For churches in Africa, the relation with other religions — in particular with Islam — has become the most pressing concern. Is there

perhaps in the new pluralism that we see developing everywhere in the world, due to migrations, a possible way out, a way forward, a possibility to develop styles of conviviality or living alongside one another, that could take us beyond the conflicts, from coexistence to an attitude of reciprocal pro-existence? We would like to see this new pluralism as a hopeful sign, but we need to raise the question: is it only a secular world-view that could affirm tolerance and collaboration among religious traditions? We have gone far in dialogue with friends of other religious convictions, but now, in the perspective of the Spirit, could we not discern signs of the Spirit's actions in other people's religious experience? This was a dividing theme in Vancouver as some of you will remember.

45. But it is evident that we need to develop a theological understanding of other people's convictions that could undergird a process of constructive co-participation in the building of human societies. The reading of the situations needs to be done in concrete national and local situations. It is very easy for us to pontificate from Geneva, or from any other part of the world, on the attitude that should be manifested by Christians in conflict situations. Those churches and Christians in their situation need a theological perspective that could be developed in ecumenical reflection, from a Trinitarian perspective, to provide recognition of the value and role and vocation of other religions in God's providential plan, and at the same time to integrate our testimony to Jesus Christ, the incarnate Word of God, in that recognition.

46. But here, as elsewhere, we carry with us the burdens of the past. Where are we to begin our history? With the conquest and conversion to Islam of North Africa? With the crusades of the middle ages? With Western colonization and Christian proselytism? If we believe that the Spirit is at work, we shall go to meet the other, longing to find new manifestations of the Spirit, perceptions of truth, that will help us to grow in our faith and our commitment to witness to God in Jesus Christ — which is our specific contribution to the spiritual store of humanity. We must listen to the Spirit calling us to community and shared goals. This task is not easy. Cultural and religious diversities and their relation to power will always be a source of tension and polemics. We are already in a situation of interdependence. But this is not enough; very often "interdependence" hides the reality of paternalism or even religious imperialism. As we invoke the Spirit we are praying for openness, trust, the willingness to risk, to share and to love.

B. ALTERNATIVE COMMUNITIES

47. We shall look forward to new studies and theological reflections, searching for guidelines for new social alternatives. During this year, when the Roman Catholic Church is celebrating the centenary of *Rerum Novarum*, the first encyclical on social issues, we expect a new encyclical from the Holy See.

The reflections on JPIC and the deliberations of this assembly will also contribute to the processes that would facilitate thinking and participation by all Christians in the exploration of possible social alternatives.

48. But simultaneously it is essential in our day to identify the work of the Spirit in creating little cells of humanization. Neighbourhood groups, cooperatives, base communities, prayer groups, monastic orders, women's movements, centres of artistic creation — all these are creative elements in a civil society which do not fall within the sphere of the state or within the power of macro-economic structures. It could be that our churches, our local parishes, might become similar communities of health and healing. The WCC's Christian Medical Commission is engaged in study and work in this area.

49. Writing in the early 1930s, Nicholas Berdyaeff, the Orthodox theologian and philosopher, published a book with the suggestive title *Toward a New Middle Ages*. Looking at the situation of the world, especially Europe, going towards the abyss of barbarism and new paganism, he reminded the world of the important role played by the monastic communities in the early middle ages.

Those communities could not stop or avoid the chaotic political and social situation of the time. They did not have any power to control or change history in its macro dimensions, but they were able to preserve the real tradition of the church and to offer refuge, protection, hospitality and spirituality. Philosophy, the arts, the sciences, but also love, hospitality, liturgy, were protected in those monasteries as values to cherish and from this the power was received to endure in those difficult situations, the waiting and the hoping for the day when a new missionary potential would be developed from this internal and spiritual richness.

50. Something similar is happening today, and it is essential that we should recognize this spiritual phenomenon. In the present wilderness, in the absence of alternative utopias, when voices are raised to proclaim the "end of history", it is basic to recognize and to search for the action of the Spirit creating centres of communion, of prayer, of cure, of sanctification.

51. We already see signs of an alternative reality which perhaps foreshadows the church of tomorrow and/or the more humane society of the future. I refer to those voluntary movements which offer protection against anonymity and the loss of individuality. In Western Europe we witness the dynamic expansion of movements like the Kirchentag and Taizé; centres and communities of worship, reflection and service; new religious orders full of the Spirit and of ecumenical commitment. These islands of humanity are emerging both within the churches and outside. They are deeply spiritual movements where people are struggling for peace, for safeguarding the environment, for helping refugees, for over-coming concrete injustices — all movements of the Spirit creating new alternatives, transcending our protective and divisive barriers in an ecumenism which is sometimes called "wild" but which perhaps we should see as the first-fruits of the coming kingdom. It is important for us to equip ourselves spiritually and theologically to receive and encourage these old and new manifestations of the Spirit.

52. Let us pray that here in this assembly, in the small groups which will be formed, the Holy Spirit will be powerfully present, creating links of commitment and genuine covenants of humanization.

C. The Search for Unity

53. The last issue to which I want to direct our attention carries our prayer for renewal in the Spirit over to the specific field of our calling as the World Council of Churches, the unity of the church. Are we really looking for something new, something different, in our quest for unity, or shall we continue in the routine of discussion without reaching fundamental decisions?

54. Do we expect a real breakthrough in the search for the unity of the church as a response given by God to our prayer for the Spirit, a spirit of unity and renewal? Here the search for the unity of the church is a real test of the seriousness of our prayer. Unless we expect something to happen in this domain where we have a specific responsibility, it will be difficult to dream of the renewal of the whole creation, it will be difficult to carry credibility.

55. This is an important question, because when we pray we expect that our prayer will be answered. And when in the spirit of our Lord's prayer we pray for the unity of the church, part of the answer to the prayer is our responsibility. When we celebrate communion and invoke the Holy Spirit in our prayer, we are asking for a meal to be turned into an encounter with Christ himself. And we believe that our prayer is ans-

wered and Christ is present! We must pray for the unity of the church with the same certainty.

56. The Spirit we invoke, and whose unifying work we await, is the Spirit of unity (Eph. 4:3). There is only one Spirit just as there is only one body. Section III will be considering in detail the problem of the unity of the church and of reconciliation in the world, the very intimate relation between our vocation to work for the unity of the church and our search for the renewal of the whole human family. The quest for church unity needs also to be considered from the eschatological perspective of uniting "all things in Christ" (Eph. 1:10).

57. Has there been any progress in the journey towards church unity? Doubtless one can point to many things — the encouraging process of the BEM reception; the increasing participation of the Roman Catholic Church in regional and national councils of churches; the recent meeting of the Christians of South Africa after thirty years of separation; the entry of new member churches into the family of the World Council of Churches; the meetings between representatives of the Christian churches in the two Koreas; the welcome presence here of a delegation from the China Christian Council; the recent theological agreements concluded by representatives of the Eastern Orthodox and the Oriental Orthodox families, bringing them close to full communion after 16 centuries of separation; the conciliar process for Justice, Peace and the Integrity of Creation, with its regional meetings, and the world convocation in Seoul. No doubt you can all add to this list which tells us that the ecumenical climate is very different from what it was a few years ago. And yet two concerns should receive renewed attention:

### a) The need to move towards our goal

58. Although cooperation between the churches is increasing, the processes of unity are slowing down. The relationship between Rome and the WCC has reached a level of mutual acceptance of differences in nature and structures and a mutual appreciation of the constraints on each. The question of the Roman Catholic Church's inclusion in a world ecumenical structure — whether the present WCC or whatever new body would be created to facilitate this integration — is no longer a pressing issue. The Ecumenical Patriarch Dimitrios I raised this question when he visited the WCC in 1987 but we have not been able to follow up on the hopes he expressed. It is not, however, just a question of this loss of enthusiasm for unity between ecclesiastical centres. The problem is more serious. It looks as though, with the growth of the means of communica-

tion and an increasingly conscious option for plurality, our division is more and more accepted as an inevitable fact of life.

59. Not that there is any lack of good will for church unity. But there is a lack of ardour and impatience. It is taken for granted that we cannot get beyond our confessional divisions. Thank God there is no dearth of groups living in Christian obedience who recognize themselves as members of the church of Jesus Christ and dare to proclaim and live out a unity which the authorities of their churches are not yet ready to recognize. Thank God we have a growing number of confessionally mixed marriages which are proving to be ecumenically significant. As the World Council of Churches we need to call for the presence of the Spirit, shaking our confessional complacency and awakening in us the zeal for the full manifestation of the unity of the body of Christ.

> Come, Holy Spirit — renew in your people the hunger for unity; renew the sense of guilt over division; renew the awareness of our unity in You, and heighten our imagination and our will to try to express this unity in forms which may be recognizable to the world for which we wish to bear testimony so that it may believe in the Christ who sends us.

## b) The need to express the communion we have

60. The second great concern has to do with the obvious fact that convergence towards doctrinal unity does not necessarily imply corresponding progress in the field of unity. Particularly through Faith and Order and bilateral dialogues the contemporary ecumenical movement has worked systematically on the doctrinal differences which developed in the course of history. But doctrinal unity does not seem to succeed in overcoming the divisions of history. Thus the reconciliation of our histories — of the interpretations of our common history — is indispensable for the unity of the church. Over the centuries we have emphasized so much the heresies of others that when we are called to express solidarity we have to conquer images of separation which have no place in an ecumenical age.

61. When we see the difficulties Christians have in understanding each other or, worse still, when we listen to stories of violence against Orthodox Christians in the Ukraine, or of the secular authorities in Slovakia ordering a hundred church buildings to be handed over to the Greek Catholic Church — with the immediate corollary that the Orthodox communities have no place where they can worship — we are in the realm of counter-witness, the fundamental negation of the gospel. Here it is not theological differences that separate us, or prevent people from using the

same church building at different times of day. Here we are in the realm of emotions, histories, caricatures, political manipulations and mutual ignorance. We shall have to address ourselves specifically to the places of conflict, so that a spirit of fraternity and prayer may help build the bridges which will make it possible to overcome history for the sake of the new project the Holy Spirit wants to achieve. The WCC has a ministry in the world's conflict situations and we send delegations and organize encounters to overcome such conflicts, maybe it will become necessary to organize a similar kind of service so that churches can help churches in overcoming their internal divisions and their conflicts with their Christian neighbours.

62. Allow me to refer to a particular concern close to our heart. The main aim of the ecumenical movement is to promote the unity of the churches in one "eucharistic fellowship". It is more and more frustrating that this has not been realized. We are able to be together in confronting the most divisive problems of humankind, but we are not able to heal our own history and to recognize each other within our common tradition. This came very painfully to me when praying for peace in the Gulf region. We participated in services of eucharist where half of the Christians present could only be passive participants. How can we expect to overcome divisions of life and death in the world when we are not even able to offer together the sacrifice of the Lord for the salvation of the world? If we affirm that the people of faith, the church, is called to witness to the saving and liberating purpose of God for the whole creation (Eph 3:8-11), if the unity to which the Lord calls us is "so that the world may believe" (John 17:21), then the church should be able to fully intercede for the salvation of the whole world (1 Pet. 2:9). The one church is and should be a parable and a reality anticipating the one humanity. We still have much doctrinal work to do, but we also need to keep alive this nostalgia for the table of the Lord. This should be the last assembly with a divided eucharist! It is not only a passionate *cri de coeur*... it is also the awareness of our real spiritual danger to prolong an ecumenism without openness to the surprises of the Spirit. Our common pilgrimage will not endure long without the holy anticipation of the kingdom.

63. I do not elaborate on other fundamental issues of the search for unity which will be developed in depth in Section III. Here I only refer to the relation between the table of the Lord and the "liturgy after the Liturgy", that sharing of life, that witness to God's love which is the fundamental vocation of the church. We cannot renounce the unity we are given in Christ. Our one way forward is dialogue, encounter, reconcilia-

tion and the visible unity of the church. We cannot take refuge in old injunctions which ban praying with heretics. We have already prayed with them and the Spirit has answered our prayer! The past cannot have proprietory rights over the present: we cannot be prisoners of our divided history.

*c) An opportunity to renew our commitment*

64. The WCC will be organizing its world conference on Faith and Order in 1993 — thirty years after Montreal. There we shall seek to recover enthusiasm for the unity of the church and to concentrate our thinking and prayer on the search for possible models of unity.

65. But every aspect of our life and work needs to wrestle with these questions: What does the experience of communion in grassroot faith communities, the spirituality of the poor, say, teach, demand the united church to be? What does the renewed commitment to the community of women and men say for our model of unity? What have we learned in the struggle against racism, in the search for the healing community, in the joint proclamation of the gospel, in the attempts to affirm human rights and in the overcoming of human conflicts? What do the youth say to divisions in the body of Christ? What is the impact of our actual encounter with people of living faiths on our search for church unity? How will a divided church help solve the ethical dilemmas confronted by modern science and technology? What has the reality of our communion, of the unity already being experienced in our sharing of resources and our common responses to human need, to teach us? How does our common prayer life in the WCC reflect and reinforce our search for unity? Every one of our churches has to face the question: What are we as a church contributing to the search for unity?

66. Ardently seeking unity in those places of conflict between Christians, we shall recover something of the moral authority to proclaim unity to the people of the world. The church is called to be a sign and instrument of the reconciliation of all of humankind. Here in Canberra we have gathered to celebrate our unity. In the power of the Spirit let us resolve to pursue it at all times, so that the church may truly become what our Orthodox friends call it: "the permanent epiclesis of the Holy Spirit".

## V. Epilogue

67. So let us pray: "Come, Holy Spirit — Renew the Whole Creation!" We are called to be one missionary movement engaged in dialogue and discussion, courageously confronting the value systems

prevailing in our world today. We are called to be stewards of life in relation both to nature and humanity; we are called to be committed followers of the Spirit in the historical events, opening space, building the future, redeeming the past; we are called to manifest the first-fruits of the *una sancta* to come, to indicate by the reality of our fellowship and by the intensity of our prayer the anticipation of the coming kingdom.

> We are seeking the true community of Christ which works and suffers for his kingdom. We seek the charismatic church which activates energies for salvation (1 Cor. 12). We seek the church which initiates actions for liberation and supports the work of other liberating groups without calculating self-interest. We seek a church which is the catalyst of God's saving work in the world, a church which is not merely the refuge of the saved but a community serving the world in the love of Christ.
> Minutes and report of the assembly of CWME, Bangkok, p.89

Here is the challenge that lies before us as we seek a "common understanding of the role and nature of the World Council of Churches". This assembly in which we are already experiencing the reality of being in communion is a foretaste and a promise of what God will be doing in the future through the vivifying and transforming activity of the Spirit.

Amen.

# 4.4. REPORT OF THE REFERENCE COMMITTEE

## I. The moderator's report

1. The Committee wants to express its gratitude to the moderator for his report which gave a thorough and balanced analysis of the many achievements, and challenges still to be met, in the life of the WCC since Vancouver. Particular attention should be given to the call to achieve greater committedness in the cooperation of the churches and full expression to it in the areas of unity, holistic mission, reception of WCC work, and financial support to ecumenical endeavours.

2. We welcome the moderator's proposals to continue the Justice, Peace and the Integrity of Creation (JPIC) process beyond the Canberra assembly. Especially, the Committee acknowledges the need to clarify the terms of covenanting and conciliarity, so that the relation between ethics and ecclesiology may become evident.

3. The Committee acknowledges the efforts that have been made to implement the request of the Vancouver assembly to develop a "vital and coherent theology" in order to bring into a coherent perspective the theological work being done in all the programmes of the WCC. Despite all efforts made so far, this task still remains unfinished. The Committee suggests that the future development of a "vital and coherent theology" within the WCC should be in relation to the continuing JPIC process, BEM reception and other basic tasks.

4. The Committee also commends the challenge to promote visible unity and to assess the ecumenical experience of community/communion and its implications for the total life of the WCC, for our ecclesial self-understanding and new vision about the future of the ecumenical movement.

5. In this context, with the moderator, the Committee urges continued support for the WCC's commitment to the Ecumenical Decade of the Churches in Solidarity with Women. Similar encouragement should be given to the participation of youth and the differently-abled in decision-making, including within the WCC.

## II. The general secretary's report

1. The Committee responded with enthusiasm to the general secretary's visionary call to perceive the work of the Holy Spirit in persons, communities and countries, as it opens up possibilities or confronts the misuse of creation.

2. We acknowledge his reminder that matters are more complex than they appear; that interdependence may mask paternalism; that in some places there is no sense of urgency over issues of unity and mission; that political situations may be so complex that no single course of action may be argued.

3. The Committee takes into consideration the general secretary's positive attitude of looking to the future, towards religious plurality as a basic framework for the churches' work and self-understanding. We share his desire to develop styles of conviviality that could take us beyond conflicts, from co-existence to an attitude of reciprocal pro-existence. However, the Committee recognizes the need to enter into further discussion with the aim of clarifying the interaction between gospel and culture (e.g. the issue of syncretism).

4. We respect with gratitude Dr Castro's passionate plea to promote the unity of the churches in one "eucharistic fellowship". We share his

frustrations that this has not been realized and his wish that Canberra should be the last assembly with a divided eucharist.

## III. Relationships with member churches

1. Since Vancouver extensive team visits involving staff and members of the central committee, commissions and working groups have been organized. In the immediate future preference should be given to those member churches who have not been visited during the past seven years. In view of the financial limitations, any such visits must be carefully prepared and followed up. The development, cultivation and coordination of two-way relationships between the WCC and its member churches, as well as with groups and movements within the churches, should receive priority attention in terms of staff time and resources.

2. The essential growth in relationship between the WCC and the member churches depends largely on the degree of information which the member churches have on the major issues being discussed within the WCC. At this time when the WCC is reorganizing its communication services, it must take clear account of this aspect. A possible contribution here could be the publication of an official quarterly newsletter informing the member churches of the major issues, and giving the most important documentation on the agenda of the various commissions and committees of the Council.

3. Since the Vancouver assembly the participation of both Eastern and Oriental Orthodox churches in the life of the Council has grown. The involvement of representatives of Orthodox churches in WCC programmes, conferences and consultations has become more dynamic, ecumenically committed and creative. This was clearly illustrated and acknowledged by primates and eminent representatives of Orthodox churches, particularly during the visit of His All Holiness the Ecumenical Patriarch Dimitrios I to the WCC headquarters in 1987. The commitment to strengthen ecumenical cooperation was also reflected in the decisions of the third preconciliar pan-Orthodox conference (Geneva, 1986) and in other documents and publications. These events prepare a new perspective on sharing the common responsibilities with other WCC member churches for the future of the ecumenical movement.

4. The Committee shares the joy of both the Eastern and Oriental Orthodox families at their coming closer to restoration of full unity. The WCC has been instrumental in providing a forum for dialogue and mutual commitment of the Orthodox churches. Their experience can provide a

model to advance and celebrate unity among sister churches which have been divided for many centuries.

5. The Committee commended united and uniting churches which have played a special role in the fulfilment of the functions and purposes of the WCC. Their efforts towards structural expression of unity and the inter-relationship of theology and action should be an example for many other churches.

6. Recently the WCC has followed closely its relationships with churches in Central and Eastern Europe as they received religious freedom and are facing new problems. The Committee would like to ask for a more coherent ecumenical approach to urgent issues and missionary tasks in Eastern Europe, in cooperation with the Conference of European Churches and other ecumenical partners in Europe.

## IV. The unity of the church as koinonia: gift and calling

This document, requested by the central committee, prepared by the Faith and Order Commission, discussed and amended by section III at the Canberra assembly, is recommended for adoption by the assembly and transmission to the churches.

### THE UNITY OF THE CHURCH AS KOINONIA: GIFT AND CALLING

1.1 The purpose of God according to holy scripture is to gather the whole of creation under the Lordship of Christ Jesus in whom, by the power of the Holy Spirit, all are brought into communion with God (Eph. 1). The church is the foretaste of this communion with God and with one another. The grace of our Lord Jesus Christ, the love of God, and the communion of the Holy Spirit enable the one church to live as sign of the reign of God and servant of the reconciliation with God, promised and provided for the whole creation. The purpose of the church is to unite people with Christ in the power of the Spirit, to manifest communion in prayer and action and thus to point to the fullness of communion with God, humanity and the whole creation in the glory of the kingdom.

1.2 The calling of the church is to proclaim reconciliation and provide healing, to overcome divisions based on race, gender, age, culture, colour, and to bring all people into communion with God. Because of sin and the misunderstanding of the diverse gifts of the Spirit, the churches are painfully divided within themselves and among each other. The scandalous divisions damage the credibility of their witness to the world in worship and service. Moreover they contradict not only the church's witness but also its very nature.

1.3 We acknowledge with gratitude to God that in the ecumenical movement the churches walk together in mutual understanding, theological convergence, common suffering and common prayer, shared witness and service as they draw close to one another. This has allowed them to recognize a certain degree of communion already existing between them. This is indeed the fruit of the active presence of the Holy Spirit in the midst of all who believe in Christ Jesus and who struggle for visible unity now. Nevertheless churches have failed to draw the consequences for their life from the degree of communion they have already experienced and the agreements already achieved. They have remained satisfied to co-exist in division.

2.1 The unity of the church to which we are called is a koinonia given and expressed in the common confession of the apostolic faith; a common sacramental life entered by the one baptism and celebrated together in one eucharistic fellowship; a common life in which members and ministries are mutually recognized and reconciled; and a common mission witnessing to the gospel of God's grace to all people and serving the whole of creation. The goal of the search for full communion is realized when all the churches are able to recognize in one another the one, holy, catholic and apostolic church in its fullness. This full communion will be expressed on the local and the universal levels through conciliar forms of life and action. In such communion churches are bound in all aspects of their life together at all levels in confessing the one faith and engaging in worship and witness, deliberation and action.

2.2 Diversities which are rooted in theological traditions, various cultural, ethnic or historical contacts are integral to the nature of communion; yet there are limits to diversity. Diversity is illegitimate when, for instance, it makes impossible the common confession of Jesus Christ as God and Saviour the same yesterday, today and forever (Heb. 13:8); and salvation and the final destiny of humanity as proclaimed in holy scripture and preached by the apostolic community. In communion diversities are brought together in harmony as gifts of the Holy Spirit, contributing to the richness and fullness of the church of God.

3.1 Many things have been done and many remain to be done on the way towards the realization of full communion. Churches have reached agreements in bilateral and multilateral dialogues which are already bearing fruit, renewing their liturgical and spiritual life and their theology. In taking specific steps together the churches express and encourage the enrichment and renewal of Christian life, as they learn from one another, work together for justice and peace, and care together for God's creation.

3.2 The challenge at this moment in the ecumenical movement as a reconciling and renewing movement towards full visible unity is for the seventh assembly of the WCC to call all churches:
— to recognize each other's baptism on the basis of the BEM document;
— to move towards the recognition of the apostolic faith as expressed through the Nicene-Constantinopolitan Creed in the life and witness of one another;
— on the basis of convergence in faith in baptism, eucharist and ministry to consider, wherever appropriate, forms of eucharistic hospitality; we gladly acknowledge that some who do not observe these rites share in the spiritual experience of life in Christ;
— to move towards a mutual recognition of ministries;
— to endeavour in word and deed to give common witness to the gospel as a whole;
— to recommit themselves to work for justice, peace and the integrity of creation, linking more closely the search for the sacramental communion of the church with the struggles for justice and peace;
— to help parishes and communities express in appropriate ways locally the degree of communion that already exists.

4.1 The Holy Spirit as promoter of koinonia (2 Cor. 13:13) gives to those who are still divided the thirst and hunger for full communion. We remain restless until we grow together according to the wish and prayer of Christ that those who believe in him may be one (John 17:21). In the process of praying, working and struggling for unity, the Holy Spirit comforts us in pain, disturbs us when we are satisfied to remain in our division, leads us to repentance, and grants us joy when our communion flourishes.

* * *

## V. National Christian councils (NCCs)

Since the Vancouver assembly 22 churches and 10 NCCs have joined the fellowship of the WCC. Relationships with NCCs were nurtured by frequent contacts and strengthened through a world consultation in 1986. The Reference Committee endorses the plans for a third world consultation or a smaller meeting with leaders of NCCs to be held in 1992. A permanent framework of relationships with NCCs as communities of churches rooted in a specific context has to be set up in the near future. The question of mutual accountability between the WCC and churches or councils requires further attention. The Committee recommends that the agenda of the central committee in 1991 include an item concerning relationships between the WCC and NCCs with particular reference to the involvement of NCCs in drawing up proposals for the restructuring of the WCC.

## VI. Regional ecumenical organizations (REOs)

1. The Committee acknowledged that efforts have been undertaken since the last assembly to bring more clarity and transparency into the relationships between the various ecumenical bodies. However, concern was expressed that the relationships between the WCC and the regions were still lacking in coherence and that earlier patterns of thinking in terms of "centre" and "periphery" were not fully overcome. The regions set their own priorities and cannot easily be fitted into a global framework. In addition, there are more and more examples of inter-regional cooperation without mediation through the WCC. This will ultimately have to be reflected in the way programmes are being formulated and resources allocated.

2. The Committee noted that the WCC El Escorial consultation (1987) and the JPIC process provided a solid basis and perspective for good ecumenical coordination and cooperation. It further welcomed the proposals submitted to the staff on "Guiding Principles for Relationships and Cooperation between the Regional Ecumenical Organizations and the World Council of Churches".

The Committee recommends the acceptance of the four affirmations in the "Guiding Principles":

The REOs and the WCC affirm that:

1. The oneness of the ecumenical movement implies the recognition of the principle of complementarity in their relationships and functions, globally, regionally, nationally and locally.

2. The ecclesial nature of the councils or conferences of churches confers a preferential character on their relationships with each other, with churches and church organizations.

3. Their primary function within the one ecumenical movement is to serve, enable and challenge the local churches, in the one common mission which includes the manifestation of visible unity amongst the churches.

4. Their relationship is one of partnership based on sharing of information, mutual trust, help and reciprocity.

In this regard the Committee places particular emphasis on the following points: (a) the oneness of the ecumenical movement; (b) our openness for contact beyond the REOs and the WCC; (c) how we relate to one another as partners in a complementary and non-hierarchical manner.

The Committee is convinced that steps need to be taken urgently to translate the affirmations into a commonly agreed policy spelling out the criteria that should guide everyday cooperation. It is, therefore, recommended that an agreement on procedures for cooperation be worked out in consultation with the general secretaries of REOs to be submitted to the central committee at its meeting in 1992. It is further recommended that in the future allocation of staff resources provision be made for the strengthening of cooperation between the WCC and the REOs.

## VII. Christian world communions (CWCs)

1. The Committee is pleased that since Vancouver the relationships with CWCs have been marked by growing participation, mutual trust and closer cooperation. The WCC and the CWCs have developed and enriched their relationships in the framework of the annual conference of CWCs, common agenda of reflection and discussion, statements on common concerns, mutual consultation, visits and participation in each other's major events. It was agreed that this process was enhanced by the several official visits to Geneva, especially the historic visit of His Holiness Pope John Paul II, and by regular consultation among the CWCs with headquarters in the Ecumenical Centre. This applies especially to relationships between the WCC and the Lutheran World Federation (LWF). The CWCs' specific ecumenical tasks are undertaken in relation to the broader ecumenical activities of the WCC. The partners seek to engage in programmes of common ecumenical interest, sharing resources and avoiding duplication.

2. The Committee noted the increase in the number of bilateral and multilateral dialogues and welcomed the fact that these dialogues, which used to be held primarily in emergency situations, are now regarded as normal events in ecumenical relationships.

3. The Committee appreciates the results of the fourth and the fifth forum on bilateral dialogues (1985, 1990) and recommends that the WCC, as facilitator of these forums, take the necessary steps to document

the interaction and complementary role of bilateral and multilateral dialogues.

## VIII. Relationships with other world bodies and ecumenical partners

1. The Committee encouraged the continued collaboration between the WCC and various Christian organizations such as the WSCF and the YMCA/YWCA which place emphasis on ecumenism among lay persons. The Committee strongly recommends that the WCC intensify its efforts to develop an ecumenical consciousness among lay members of the church and their active participation in the ecumenical movement.

2. The Committee commends also development of relationships and collaboration with the Frontier Internship in Mission, the World Conference on Religion and Peace, and some Roman Catholic organizations. It noted with appreciation that the WCC has given greater attention to evangelical organizations particularly the World Evangelical Fellowship and the Lausanne Committee for World Evangelization as well as to "evangelicals" within the WCC. While the Committee recognized and welcomed the existence of much good will and some progress, the need was expressed for a stronger collaboration between the WCC and the evangelical bodies (cf. *Vancouver to Canberra*, pp.12-13).

## IX. Relationships with the Roman Catholic Church (RCC)

Ever since the fourth assembly of the WCC at Uppsala (1968), following shortly after the conclusion of the Second Vatican Council, it has become a regular feature of WCC assemblies to welcome an official delegation of representatives of the Roman Catholic Church. The presence of this delegation symbolizes the closeness of relationships in the one ecumenical movement between the RCC and the WCC. Archbishop E. Cassidy, president of the Pontifical Council for Promoting Christian Unity, brought a message from Pope John Paul II. We express our gratitude for the presence of our Roman Catholic sisters and brothers among us and for their manifold contributions to this assembly.

### A. A survey of the state of relationships

Throughout this assembly, in plenary sessions, sections, groups, etc., frequent reference has been made to the fact that the deepening of relationships between member churches of the WCC and the RCC is a notable feature of the ecumenical movement at the present time. Reports indicate that there has been siginificant progress in relationships in all regions, particularly on the local level. Ecumenism is alive at the base where people live and struggle together.

One significant manifestation of this new state of relationships is the growing number of national (35) and regional (3) ecumenical organizations with full Roman Catholic membership. More recently new ecumenical instruments including the RCC have been created for Britain and Ireland as well as separate instruments for England, for Scotland and for Wales, and in France, where the new Council provided the framework for a joint declaration on the Gulf war together with Muslim and Jewish leaders.

Some contradictory signals, however, remain. Thus, it was reported from a number of situations that relationships were still — or once again — rather formal and limited to contacts on the official level of church leaders without touching the lives of people. Urgent concern was expressed about the dramatic deterioration of relationships between the RCC and Orthodox churches in several countries due to problems created by Greek-Catholic (Uniate) communities, in spite of the official agreement reached in the context of the Orthodox-Roman Catholic official dialogue.

While this Committee had to concentrate its discussion on the structured relationships between the RCC and the WCC at world level as they are reflected in the sixth report of the Joint Working Group, it is important that such reflections be placed in the wider context of developing ecumenical relationships on the local, national and regional level. No single pattern or uniform set of criteria would apply to all these relationships, which develop very much in response to the needs of Christian communities in their particular context. It is important, however, that the WCC use all the means at its disposal, i.e. through regular contacts with national and regional ecumenical organizations and through exchange with member churches, to monitor and to foster the growth of ecumenical relationships with the RCC.

## B. Response to the sixth report of the JWG

The sixth report presents an impressive survey of the joint activities between the RCC and the WCC since the Vancouver assembly. The report gives due visibility to a number of accomplishments, but at the same time does not seek to hide difficulties or failures. While some would have liked to receive through the report a fuller and more differentiated picture of the ecumenical situation (cf. I), the report does point to the important factors which have influenced this particular relationship in the past period.

A number of features of the report deserve to be mentioned specifically:

1. Within the priority of the "Unity of the Church — the Goal and the Way" the JWG has commissioned two special studies on "The Church: Local and Universal" and on the notion of "Hierarchy of Truths". Both studies have resulted in reports which have been published together with the sixth report of the JWG. While they do not pretend to present final conclusions, both study documents promise to stimulate common ecumenical discussions and are, therefore, commended to the churches for close attention.

2. Still in the area of unity of the church, but closely linked to the concerns of social collaboration, the JWG has begun to explore whether and how ethical issues (e.g. nuclear armaments and deterrence, abortion and euthanasia, procreation, genetic engineering and artificial insemination) can become new sources of potential division. This project, which has begun with surveys in selected local contexts, deserves fullest attention and support (cf. III.A.1c).

3. Mention should also be made of the initiatives which have been undertaken in close contact with, or directly through, the JWG aiming at: (1) a deeper reflection on the significance of the growing number of national and regional ecumenical organizations with RC membership; (2) a renewed exploration of the question of "mixed marriages" and their ecclesiological significance for the ecumenical movement (cf. III.A.1d+e).

4. The concern for common witness has been at the heart of the work of the JWG during these last 15 years. This was highlighted especially through the joint declaration published on the occasion of the visit by Pope John Paul II to the Ecumenical Centre in Geneva (1984). Many of the initiatives in this area, some of them identified specifically in the JWG study document on common witness (1982), have developed further and given a new profile to local and national ecumenical cooperation (cf. II.A.3a+b).

5. Much of the regular cooperation between various departments of the WCC and the Vatican is hardly noticed any more but taken for granted. The sixth report provides a very helpful survey of this close and intensive network of cooperation that has developed between the parent bodies of the JWG. This is the place to express gratitude for the dedicated work of staff and committee members on both sides which in many instances serves as inspiration and gives legitimacy to similar efforts in local and national situations.

These positive and encouraging developments should not, however, cover up the fact that the report points to a number of unresolved difficulties and recurring obstacles:

6. The fifth report of the JWG had recommended that one of the priority areas of common study and reflection be the task of ecumenical education and formation. Unfortunately, this initiative could not be brought to a conclusion so far, in spite of considerable effort on the part of the JWG. Since the urgency of the matter has not diminished, every attempt should be made to conclude the work begun as early as possible. (cf. III.A.2).

7. After the termination of the mandate of SODEPAX the JWG formed the Joint Consultation Group on Social Thought and Action (JCG). It was intended to provide a flexible framework for exploring concrete possibilities of social collaboration between the departments directly concerned on either side. In spite of considerable effort the JCG did not prove to be workable and had to be dissolved. This underlines the particular difficulties existing for collaboration in the field of social thought and action.

8. The problems became sharply visible in the context of the ecumenical process on Justice, Peace and the Integrity of Creation, and particularly regarding the invitation extended to the RCC to be a co-sponsor for the JPIC world convocation in Seoul (March 1990). In the negative response to this invitation attention was drawn once again to "the different nature of the two bodies". Nevertheless, the Roman Catholic Church not only sent a group of twenty qualified advisers to the Seoul convocation, but has contributed substantially to the process on world level, including the decision to provide staffing and financial support. There are indications that the RCC is prepared to remain actively involved in any continuation of the JPIC process.

With these observations and responses the Reference Committee recommends that the assembly receive the sixth report of the JWG and express its appreciation to all who have contributed to this important task.

## C. The way ahead

1. More than 25 years have passed since the establishment of the JWG. Most of its original mandate has been fulfilled and Roman Catholic participation in the ecumenical movement has become a normal feature. After the decision not to pursue any further — at least for the time being — the question of "membership", the mandate, structure, working style and composition of the JWG were reviewed at the time of the Nairobi

assembly in 1975. It would seem now that another review is called for as has been suggested by the WCC central committee at its meeting in 1990.

2. The sixth report of the JWG makes several proposals for strengthening the role of the JWG (cf. IV.1). This is being echoed by the central committee which asks that the mandate of the JWG not be limited only to collaboration between the departments in the WCC and the Vatican, but that it should give "permanent and careful attention to ecumenism at local and regional level" (*Minutes* 1990, p.82). The central committee also asked that the status of the JWG be redefined and that the composition include more representatives of the different regions.

3. This call for a strengthened, more effective and more visible role of the JWG has been made several times in the course of the last 15 years without much response. There are objective reasons which have prevented a change of policy on the part of the parent bodies of the JWG (especially lack of funds). Officially, the JWG is expected to focus on the task to promote, monitor and coordinate relationships and cooperation between the RCC and the WCC on the official, structural level. For this task, which of course needs to be placed in, and informed by, the wider context of ecumenical relations at all levels, a coordinating group, mainly at staff level, would be sufficient.

4. The sixth report has strongly recommended that the agenda of the JWG be more limited and focused. The group should, therefore, be liberated from the task of monitoring ongoing collaboration. Rather, a newly composed JWG should be requested to concentrate its attention on a substantive review of the relationships between the RCC and the WCC. It should, in particular, analyze more deeply the obstacles which have prevented the relationships from developing even more fully. Based on the affirmations made in the recent study report on "The Church: Local and Universal" regarding the understanding of ecclesial communion (cf. No. 26ff.) and referring back to the statement on "the common ground" included in the fourth report of the JWG (1975), the JWG should aim at a common acknowledgment of the ecclesial character of the relationship which has grown between the RCC and the fellowship of churches in the WCC, and suggest ways of giving more substantive expression to it. The JWG should investigate possibilities to set up visible signs of collaboration between WCC member churches and the RCC, examining in particular whether on the threshold to the next millennium a pre-conciliar conference could be held which would seek binding steps towards complete unity.

5. It is therefore recommended:

a)  that the Joint Working Group between the RCC and the WCC be reconstituted for a period of up to six years with the primary task of assessing afresh the basis and common ground shared by the RCC and the WCC and developing new perspectives for giving shape to this relationship;

b)  that the JWG seek to carry out this task in close contact with CWCs in dialogue with the RCC, and also place it in the context of the ongoing process of redefining the vision and self-understanding of the WCC;

c)  that in addition to this primary task the JWG direct and supervise the completion of the unfinished initiative in the area of "ecumenical formation" (cf. III.A.2 and IV.2B) and "ethical issues as new sources of potential divisions" (cf. III.A.1c and IV.2A);

d)  that no new major project of the JWG be undertaken until its primary task is completed and a report presented to the parent bodies allowing them to agree on a new framework for the relationship; this process is expected to be completed by the time of the next WCC assembly at the latest;

e)  that the task of monitoring and promoting regular cooperation between departments in the WCC and the Vatican be entrusted to a small coordinating group;

f)  that the JWG be composed of six persons from either side representing the constituency and two members of staff. Given the specific task entrusted to the JWG (5.1), due consideration should be given to the special competence needed to deal with these issues. The two co-moderators together with the four members of staff shall form the "coordinating" group. Both groups shall be entitled to invite consultants as their agenda requires;

g)  that the JWG set up a formal relationship with the JWGs within regional ecumenical organizations and consult fully with NCCs where the RCC is a full member or which work closely with the RCC, with a view to gathering experience in undertaking the primary task of the JWG.

\* \* \*

The Reference Committee wishes to express appreciation for the work of WCC staff in the area of relationships with member churches and other partners in the ecumenical movement.

# 4.5. REPORT OF THE
# PROGRAMME POLICY COMMITTEE

## I. Mandate of the Committee on Programme Policy (CPP)

a) to receive and evaluate the official report of the central committee, *Vancouver to Canberra*, and to propose formal action on this report;

b) to formulate policy for future WCC programmes, taking careful note of proposals that emerge at various points in the assembly;

c) to prepare a report which, together with the Message (prepared by the Message Committee) and the assembly report (prepared by the Report Committee), will summarize the essential findings of the assembly.

## II. *Vancouver to Canberra*

The CPP recommends that the assembly receive the report *Vancouver to Canberra 1983-1990* with appreciation for the clear, concise and comprehensive manner in which it is presented, and with gratitude to the governing bodies, the general secretary and staff of the WCC for faithfully carrying out most of the mandate of the Vancouver assembly.

The CPP makes the following comments about the report:

A. The report offers a helpful overview of the work of the WCC since the sixth assembly. The preface by the moderator, the introduction by the general secretary and "A Reader's Guide" from the editor establish a good basis for understanding the specifics of the work described in the report. The theme concerning the centrality of Jesus Christ as the Life of the World is evident throughout the work.

However, we propose that future reports give (a) fuller assessment of the impact of programmes on member churches; (b) better evaluation of the work of the units indicating emerging trends; (c) fuller assessment of how the policies have been implemented in the programmes; (d) an overview of the relationships between the WCC and its member churches.

B. The Vancouver mandate relative to fuller participation of women and youth has been addressed in the work of the WCC since Vancouver. The Ecumenical Decade of the Churches in Solidarity with Women and the global youth gathering scheduled for 1992 are evidence of this. However, the report indicates that these goals are yet to be achieved, and therefore must remain priorities. The 1993 world conference on Faith and Order should provide for the full participation and contribution of women and youth.

The Committee regrets that there is no substantive report on the basis on which to evaluate how we have grown in the area of gospel and culture. Further the CPP observes with regret that there is only one area of the report that gives an account of the important contribution of youth in the WCC.

C. The CPP notes the critical financial situation of the WCC due to problems of exchange rates, inflation and insufficient growth in the financial support from member churches proportionate to increased programme costs. The fact that one-third of the member churches take no financial responsibility for the Council is a matter of great concern.

## III. A review of the implementation of the Vancouver guidelines

### A. *Growing towards unity*

We have yet to develop adequate criteria and indicators by which to assess progress in relationships among member churches. The CPP notes with satisfaction that the response to the *Baptism, Eucharist and Ministry* document from member churches has been very encouraging. The evaluation of the responses from 185 churches reveals a broad measure of convergence in regard to the basic Christian convictions as articulated in the document. It has enabled the churches to look critically at their own traditions and to be willing to change their attitudes towards other churches. This certainly is a step towards unity. Other documents may also go through this process of study and comment by member churches.

Sharing of ecumenical resources is also part of our growth towards unity. El Escorial 1987 is a landmark on this road though in actual practice we have a long way to go. The fellowship of mutual sharing is something we can achieve while we continue to work for fellowship in faith and in sacramental life. We regretfully recognize, however, that for some of our member churches, some activities of the WCC lead to tensions and questions, but through these tensions and questions we should grow towards greater mutual understanding and unity.

### B. *Growing towards justice and peace*

The Vancouver assembly said that commitment to justice, peace and the well-being of the whole creation should be one of the purposes of all programmes of the WCC. In general, sub-units had this aim before them in their programmes. The specific effort made through the JPIC process has served to awaken member churches to the urgency of the issues.

In the last seven years we have seen important movement towards liberation, justice and peace for which we give thanks to God. The WCC's share in inspiring some of these changes has not been insignificant. Periodic actions and public statements, letters from the general secretary, visits to areas of conflict by WCC teams, support to churches and groups in their struggle against poverty, oppression and racism, have all been helpful.

### C. Growing towards a vital and coherent theology

Our common faith in the Triune God, and in the incarnation, death and resurrection of our Lord Jesus Christ is the common core that holds us together in our diversity, and should be the basis for coherence in our different theological expressions. While Faith and Order deals with this directly, the other programmes have also been involved in finding a common ground for action. Some lack of coherence is natural in a fellowship like the WCC. Nevertheless, the quest for a coherent theology is crucially important and must remain a priority. In this context, it is important to bring contextual theologies into dialogue with "classical" theologies in order to develop an ecumenical way of doing theology. Such a method must be faithful to the apostolic faith and appreciative of local cultures through which the gospel is expressed and lived.

### D. Growing towards new dimensions of the churches' self-understanding

It is difficult to specify whether anything concrete has been achieved in this area. Has there been a developing self-understanding by each of the member churches as a result of association with other member churches of the World Council? In the general secretary's words: "This challenge is one which we will continue to explore together."

### E. Growing towards a community of confessing and learning

Confessing Jesus Christ is integral to our being an ecumenical family. All programmes of the WCC serve this vocation. Consultations on world mission and evangelism have signalled that confessing Jesus Christ as Lord and Saviour in a pluralistic world requires unity in mission. The whole process of JPIC seeks to be a witness to the love of God for all humanity manifested in Jesus Christ. Our programmes for the struggle against racism are a testimony to the power of the gospel to break all chains of oppression.

The CPP also notes that meaningful learning has taken place during the period under review. WCC has produced some materials in forms suitable for use at the congregational level, and promoting participatory, experiential and interdisciplinary methods of learning. The Bible study resources produced in preparation for the meetings of Larnaca, El

Escorial, San Antonio, Seoul and this assembly have been particularly important.

## IV. Vision for the future work of the WCC

The vision from the assembly for the future work of the Council must be related to the functions of the WCC as given in its constitution, namely the goals of visible unity, the common witness of the churches and the service of human need. We must begin by reaffirming and concentrating on these goals.

### A. *Unity of the church*

The unity of the church is not something we create but a gift of God which we should receive humbly, promote responsibly and enjoy gratefully. Our common commitment to the fundamentals of Christian faith continues to call and hold us together. That commitment permits us to appreciate the richness of our diversity of gifts, traditions, cultures and races. At this assembly we have experienced powerful reminders that the Holy Spirit breaks down barriers and restores community. But we have also experienced painful reminders of continuing brokenness. We understand the role of the WCC to be at the service of the churches in responding to the call of the Holy Spirit to make visible our unity in Christ.

This gift of unity requires that we give attention to all that fragments the body of Christ. The Holy Spirit calls us to acknowledge the unity that exists among us and to overcome all barriers in order to be able to share our gifts and ministries while on our common spiritual journey towards visible unity. Our ability to enable the truthful sharing of differences among us is a sign of the strength of our unity of faith.

Only through this unity in Christ are we able to express our calling to be in mission in a suffering and hurting world. We welcome the call for common theological reflection and a comprehensive discussion on the nature and mission of the church in the perspective of unity as koinonia in the Holy Spirit. Through our participation in struggles for justice and liberation we share a common unity through solidarity with all of humanity and can become ecumenical in the fullest sense.

### B. *Justice, peace and the integrity of creation*

In this assembly we have realized more intensely that the Holy Spirit lays upon us the task which Jesus himself accepted. The Holy Spirit opens our eyes to see the injustice of the world and strengthens us to resist and struggle against oppression and the devastation of creation.

The Holy Spirit calls us to work together towards just social systems and towards a sustainable environment. We seek a world of social and economic justice and care for those who are vulnerable and dispossessed. We seek a world in which all participate in decisions which affect their lives. We seek a world based on the biblical vision of economic and ecological reconciliation. The vision of justice, peace and the integrity of creation needs to become embodied in the realities of our contextual situation. This calls for a broad cooperation with secular groups, between the churches, and with people of other faiths.

We confess that nations which claim to be Christian shoulder a substantial part of the blame for the present global military-industrial-technological civilization insofar as it breeds injustice, ferments wars and disrupts the eco-balance. The struggle for justice, peace and the integrity of creation may entail the questioning of some of the values on which this civilization is based. This vision should enable the WCC to focus on the central ethical concerns of our time.

Working towards justice, peace and the integrity of creation will help the churches understand their task in the world, provided we develop a rigorous social analysis, deepen our theological reflection and vigorously promote these concerns. This has emerged as the central vision of the WCC and its member churches as they face the next assembly when they can give an account of their efforts to fulfill the covenants made for JPIC.

At Vancouver it was assumed that *participation* was implied in the concept of justice, because justice includes participation in power; however, participation in itself has not received the attention it should. Our future work must be based on local, national, regional and inter-regional contexts. We need to intensify and deepen concrete analysis of the root causes and institutional structures of injustice. Inter-racial, inter-regional and multicultural interaction is essential to new understanding and action without domination of one culture by the other.

## C. *Wholeness of the mission of the church*

A reconciled and renewed creation is the goal of the mission of the church. This mission requires that the search for the sacramental communion of the church be more closely linked with the struggle for justice and peace. Both these dimensions point to the church as the healing communion in Christ through the Holy Spirit. Wholeness of mission requires that barriers be broken down locally and globally.

The mission of the church must include other issues for the sake of its wholeness. First, at this assembly we have frequently addressed the way in which the gospel inter-relates with culture. Too often the mission of the church has been a rationale for injustice to indigenous peoples. Particularly today, it is important to remember this as we look towards the commemoration of the conquest of Latin America five hundred years ago in the name of the gospel, a misuse of mission.

A second concern for a mission with wholeness is the just sharing of resources among all members of the body of Christ. We seek to better utilize the rich insights and guidelines for resource-sharing already available to the WCC.

A reconciled and renewed creation requires attention to these and many other issues which challenge the wholeness of the community of the people of God.

As we seek to share the message of Christ in word and deed, may we express a holistic evangelism as an ecumenical task of the whole church, rather than of some particular individuals, remembering also that each church acting in mission is acting on behalf of the *whole* church. The WCC should undertake the task of helping to equip the churches to fulfill their mission.

While we celebrate the presence of the Holy Spirit in the churches, we are aware that the Spirit is not confined to the churches. We rejoice in our experience of salvation in Christ but recognize the possibility of the presence of the Spirit of God among people of other faiths.

In increasingly plural societies where inter-religious conflict is often a source of injustice and violence, there is a new urgency for interfaith dialogue and for joint action for the well-being of humanity and the creation. The Holy Spirit calls us to engage in dialogue to mutually share our faiths, and to work together for justice, peace, and the integrity of creation.

The wholeness of mission lays on us the necessity for encounters of gospel and culture and witness in a secularized world.

## V. Style of work

### A. *Assembly*

There is full justification for meeting together once every seven years to celebrate our common faith and witness; however, the cumbersome nature and the current patterns of the assembly call for serious evaluation of the role of the assembly as an efficient way of democratic policy-making. There is need for solid biblical and theological input which could become the primary thread that binds the assembly together. Intensive biblical studies should accompany our prayers for renewal. Less time should be spent in presentation plenaries where the delegates can only be passive observers and more time given to plenaries and other formats that promote intensive participation in assembly processes which will better enrich the assembly experience. Delegates should be strongly encouraged to study the theological and other materials that the WCC and their churches publish in preparation for the assembly.

## B. Committees, consultations and other events

Emphasis on participation is crucial. Careful planning and leadership preparation are essential to enable maximum participation.

Large world conferences should be kept to a minimum. Every attempt should be made to bring different programme concerns into one conference or to have regional conferences. Financial restrictions facing the WCC demand more careful budget planning for all events.

## C. Participation of the whole people of God

We are convinced that the participation of the laity must be strengthened through increased emphasis on lay training and formation in all aspects of ecumenical learning.

We expect that the participation goals for women and youth will be maintained in all events and in membership of committees. The central committee should assure funding only for those activities which reflect approved goals of inclusiveness.

We also encourage increased participation of differently-abled persons and persons of varying theological traditions including charismatics, pentecostals and evangelical Christians with ecumenical perspectives.

We urge that greater attention be given to the needs of persons from different cultural and language groups and that the WCC language policy be reviewed.

We urge that ways be found to encourage participation in the ecumenical movement and vision without continually underlining and reinforcing the divisions we wish to overcome.

## D. Staff operations

More effective and efficient use of staff resources is needed. The current financial situation underlines the need for improved coherence of the work of different programmes. We therefore:

— question the need for so many sub-units;
— encourage cooperation and sharing;
— urge that duplication be avoided.

We are aware that the outgoing central committee has addressed some of these issues of institutional strengthening. Given the urgency of concerns facing the WCC and the limited financial resources available, we urge that the central committee give continued attention to these matters.

The Committee acknowledges that the recommendations for programme emanating from this assembly will need to be prioritized. This will be a task for the new central committee.

## VI. Programme policies that should undergird and inspire all WCC programmes in the coming years

The Holy Spirit calls us to renewal. This renewal means bringing out the truth which was already given by the Spirit. It requires a conscientious effort to act with resolve on our long-standing commitments as well as creating new emphases. More than ever it is necessary to concentrate on the following basic concerns.

### A. Renewal through reconciliation

Christians see truth in different ways and are divided from one another by history, doctrine and culture, yet at the same time they are united in Christ and the power of the Holy Spirit. When we pray to the Spirit of unity to reconcile us we become conscious of the need for repentance, reparation and renewal.

The primary task of the WCC is to call the churches to the goal of visible unity in the context of the unity of all humankind, through programmes that foster reconciliation and healing. In the years after this assembly, member churches should study and analyze the remaining obstacles in relation to the recognition of each other's baptism, the acceptance of a common creed, mutual recognition of ministries, and eucharistic participation. While differing in our ecclesiologies we should be willing to address and challenge these differences from an ecumenical perspective. Christian movements should be able to give their contribution to this pilgrimage towards unity. More attention should be given to contextual theology, inculturation and a deeper analysis of the causes of disunity.

There can also be deep divisions between Christians and people of other faiths, even though they share a common humanity and face common challenges and tasks. Dialogue with people of other faiths must continue to be promoted, particularly for cooperation in our common quest for justice, peace and the integrity of creation. Such dialogue is urgent in situations throughout the world where religious communities are divided by fear and mistrust.

## B. Renewal through freedom and justice

The freedom which we enjoy as a gift of the Spirit is not only internal and personal. It is a freedom which we are also called to experience in community.

We must continue to address spiritual and physical ill-health evidenced in unfulfilled lives and unjust socio-economic systems that perpetuate societal barriers in our world.

The Spirit of truth re-establishes and restores the integrity of the human person and human relationships within community. However, as Christians, we constantly experience the danger of becoming captives of systems and structures that defy this truth.

Since we are free in order that we may give witness to the justice of the kingdom of God, we reaffirm our challenge to resist injustice, be it economic or political, cultural or social, of gender, race or ecology. The issues of justice, peace and the integrity of creation provide us with an effective framework for accomplishing these goals. The power of the Spirit moves us to strive for the building up of just societies within our local, regional, national and international contexts.

## C. Renewal through a right relationship with the creation

The divine presence of the Spirit in creation binds us as human beings together with all created life. But through misinterpretation of our faith and because of human greed the earth we live in is in peril. The signs of the time are an invitation to repent and to establish a right relationship with the whole creation. This requires a new vision and a new understanding of ourselves and God's creation. Therefore the WCC must address itself to the need to develop a new theology of creation which will enable the churches to play a meaningful role in the renewal of creation as part of their mission as well as a new ecumenical understanding of the relationship between ecology and economy. In carrying out this work, the WCC should seek the cooperation of others who have similar concerns. In this regard we particularly recommend that special attention be given to the struggle against racism, giving priority to the rights of indigenous people.

*D. Renewal through enabling the full participation and contribution of women*

Deepening the churches' solidarity with women in the church and in the whole society should find a central place in the continuing work of the WCC. We need to continue to strengthen the solidarity of each member church with women, to fully receive their gifts, contributions and perspectives. The goals of the Decade of the Churches in Solidarity with Women need to be visibly expressed in all activities and work by, through, and encouraged by the WCC. Churches are to *act* resolutely on this concern and to uphold the goal of visible unity in the building of a renewed community of women and men.

*E. Renewal through an ecumenical spirituality for our times*

An ecumenical spirituality must be grounded in the present realities: life-giving, rooted in scriptures and nourished by prayer, communitarian and celebrating, centred around the eucharist, expressed in service and witness, trusting and confident. Those who live by the Spirit of God must take the cross for the sake of the world, share the agony of all, and seek the face of God in the depths of the human condition.

The WCC will need to encourage ecumenical spirituality rooted in the disciplines and appropriate for contemporary Christian life. As churches draw closer to each other in the ecumenical pilgrimage, they are increasingly recognizing the significance of Christian life-style, of holiness, of a spirituality of non-violence, common prayer, liturgical life, asceticism and sharing.

**VII. Conclusion**

The Committee on Programme Policy presents this report with the hope that it be translated into WCC programmes, faithfully praying:

"Come, Holy Spirit — Renew the Whole Creation".

# 4.6. REPORT OF THE FINANCE COMMITTEE

**I. Introduction**

The Finance Committee of this assembly met with the mandate to review both the financial reports since Vancouver and the current financial situation of the WCC with a view to making recommendations to the assembly for sound financial policy for the period up to the next assembly.

The increased financial response by member churches to the needs of the WCC over the period since Vancouver has been extremely encouraging. It demonstrates an increased commitment to and involvement in the Council's aims and programmes and the Council is very grateful for that support.

In reviewing progress since Vancouver, the Committee noted with appreciation the recommendations which had been acted upon. But much more progress is needed in increasing income, and integrating finance and programme policy decision-making.

This assembly meets when the financial outlook of the Council has worsened dramatically over the last year.

Over the last eight years, many churches have increased their giving in real terms and/or protected the level of their giving against the effect of inflation in their own countries. However, the adverse effect of exchange rates, particularly the US dollar and the Deutsche mark, have combined with the rise in the cost of living to reduce the WCC's available income.

By contrast, the Council, in implementing its programme policies as mandated at Vancouver, has increased its activities and therefore the amount it wishes to spend.

In its recommendations to the assembly, the Finance Committee seeks to offer policy guidance as to how these opposing trends of reduced spending power and increased programme aspirations can be harmonized.

Programme considerations are paramount within the Council. To be effective, they must be guided by financial realism, and priority decisions must be made in deciding which programmes can be undertaken and at what cost. To survive, the WCC must organize its affairs so as to live within its means. Achieving this general policy will entail better planning, prioritizing, evaluation and control of the work undertaken, together with strengthened and effective management.

It will also depend on strengthening the relationships with member churches to ensure that the service and witness the Council provides meet their aspiration, as this is the environment in which increased commitment and financial support is likely to flourish.

## II. Income

A. FINANCIAL RESPONSIBILITIES, MUTUAL ACCOUNTABILITY

1. The Finance Committee *recommends* that the assembly *affirm* the responsibility of all member churches to make an annual financial

contribution to the WCC. The corresponding responsibility on the part of the WCC is to be accountable to the fellowship of churches in the use of these funds.

2. Recognizing that the member churches and others give greatest support to activities which they understand and which reflect their own convictions, the Finance Committee *recommends* that the assembly *instruct* the new central committee to:

a)  give more thought and personal energy to ways in which churches can develop a greater sense of obligation for supporting the work of the WCC financially;

b)  review and improve the interpretation to the churches of the range and depth of Council activity to encourage their support through a sense of programmatic and financial engagement.

3. *Member churches not currently contributing financially to the WCC:* Some member churches do not contribute financially to the WCC. Some of these churches find it difficult to make substantial contributions; others face restrictions on international currency transfers. In light of the diverse circumstances of the churches, the Finance Committee is not recommending that a minimum level of annual contribution be established at this time.

The Finance Committee *recommends* that the assembly *urge* every church not presently providing financial support to examine its commitment to the WCC and to make arrangements for some annual financial contribution.

4. *Member churches currently contributing financially to the WCC:* The Finance Committee *recommends* that the assembly *encourage* the member churches to:

a)  increase their annual undesignated contributions; and

b)  seek additional ways to provide designated funds for those programme areas presently dependent on the undesignated income. This applies particularly to the theological, dialogue, ecclesiological, renewal and youth work of the Council. In addition, support may be through direct sponsorship of specific events, publications, meetings and other activities;

c)  make any designation of funds as broad as possible so as best to support issues and activities of the Council as determined by the assembly and the new central committee.

B. INCREASING OTHER INCOME

While affirming the importance of the contributions of member churches as central to the income strategy of the WCC, the Finance Committee *recommends* that the seventh assembly:

1) *direct* the new central committee to explore other funding and co-funding possibilities for World Council of Churches programmes, including government ministries/agencies (within WCC policy guidelines and in consultation with the member churches), trusts and foundations, corporations, individuals and Christian bodies other than member churches;

2) *direct* the new central committee to:

a) establish a clear responsibility for central committee members in advocacy and fund-raising for the WCC among member churches and other funding sources in their area; training would need to be offered and reporting mechanisms to the central committee established;

b) undertake a study of what aspects of WCC programmes the member churches and outside bodies are willing to support, to aid in developing a public relations and fund-raising strategy and encourage greater identification with the range of the WCC's work;

c) commit sufficient staff resources to permit consistent, informed and effective fund-raising from non-member bodies, such as those mentioned in this report, and to establish them as regular sources of income; such efforts should be monitored in terms of results for the time and money so invested;

d) explore means of using more effectively opportunities for fund-raising at WCC assemblies and other large gatherings, including fund-raising events with opportunities for participants to contribute directly and to be encouraged to advocate giving by their churches or other sponsors;

e) reaffirm the policy established in Vancouver that if trust-fund contributors do not otherwise contribute to the programme and administration of the WCC, up to 10 % of their contribution should be retained in support of the administrative capacities of the WCC in facilitating the project support for partners around the world;

f) reaffirm the policy of strict coordination of all requests for financial support of programmes from member churches and others and review this internal function separately from the need for external funds development.

C. IN-KIND CONTRIBUTIONS

In negotiating support of the Council's programmes, the Finance Committee *recommends* that the assembly *instruct* the new central committee to:

1) continue to explore the identification of, reporting on, and encouragement for other means of contributing to the WCC in addition to cash transfers, including the provision of personnel, hospitality, external travel, information, material aid and other contributions or sponsorships which reduce the budgeted cost of Council activities;

2) assist member churches in planning their in-kind contributions to be of greatest help to the Council, particularly in situations where cash transfers are severely limited by economic or legal restraints.

D. STEWARDSHIP: MAXIMIZING THE EFFECTIVE USE OF FINANCIAL RESOURCES

*1. Investment policy*

Regarding the investment policies of the World Council of Churches, the Finance Committee *recommends* that the assembly *direct* the new central committee to:

a) pursue the policy that the portfolio should be managed in a dynamic way that maximizes income without undue risk and which conforms to the general policy of the Council on social responsibility in investment;

b) introduce a system of evaluation of the yield for each investment portfolio; this evaluation should be reported to the executive committee for review at least once per year.

*2. Designation and receipt of funds*

a) In addition to the foregoing request to member churches for increased undesignated and broadly designated financial contributions, the Finance Committee *recommends* that the assembly:

1) *reaffirm* the policy that designations on income can only be made by the churches and other bodies which contribute those funds;

2) *request* the new central committee to instruct the general secretary to establish centralized processing of all receipts to ensure that incoming funds are banked immediately, credited accurately to donor specifications and that the limited staff resources available to programmes are relieved of this work.

b) The WCC's finances are vulnerable because of the diversity of currencies in use by donors and the fluctuation of their exchange rates. The Finance Committee *recommends* that the assembly:

1) *ask* the member churches and other donors to review the level of their pledges and contributions in light of the Council's Swiss-franc budget and to consider the possibility of adjusting their giving in light of any reduction in WCC income related to changes in exchange rates;

2) *direct* the new central committee to review the effectiveness of requests in currencies other than Swiss francs or the local currency of the contributor.

## *3. Cooperation in funding*

The concern of the Council about competitive funding between various parts of the international fellowship has been restated consistently since the 1975 assembly in Nairobi. The Finance Committee *recommends* that the seventh assembly *instruct* the new central committee to:

a) explore possibilities for cooperative fund-raising with individuals, congregations, national or regional bodies; such cooperation should be aimed at minimizing competition between partners and strengthening mutual support;

b) establish coordination within the Council to help ensure clearer cooperation with the member churches and other national, regional and world church bodies, in order to prevent duplication of programme, to maximize the use of human and financial resources and to minimize competition between partners.

## III. Expenses and the budget process

### A. Budgeting procedures

The Finance Committee *recommends* that the assembly *instruct* the new central committee to develop and implement consolidated budgeting policy for all programmes of the Council which reflect the following:

a) detailed programme planning must follow estimates of income, not precede it;

b) the budgeting process must consider the possibilities of in-kind contributions and secondment of staff;

c) work should not begin nor staff be engaged until funding is assured; funds will be considered assured when pledges are received in writing;

d) guidelines should provide a range of exchange rates to be used for income projections at the time the budget is adopted, taking into consideration the level of funds available to the Council to offset any exchange losses during that fiscal year.

B. Operating funds

The present policy of the World Council of Churches regarding operating funds is as follows:

a) any annual surplus of income will be credited to operating funds;
b) annual expense budgets will be balanced to the level of expected recurring income;
c) programme entities may be authorized to use up to one-third of their operating funds to balance the budget in any given year.

The Finance Committee *recommends* that the assembly *instruct* the central committee to review these policies with a view to strengthening the general policy of living within income each year and to explore the use of fund balances for non-recurring expenses.

C. Expenditure

In order to reduce expenditure to the level of recurring income, the Finance Committee *recommends* that the assembly *instruct* the new central and executive committees to:

a) reconsider the number of consultations and world conferences, their style, function, location and numbers of participants and staffing; there should always be close liaison with local churches in the place where such meetings will be held, particularly with a view to reducing costs;
b) review present policy and practice on participation subsidies, language facilities, length and style of meetings with a view to finding more effective methods which are also appropriate to the financial resources available;
c) consider amending the by-laws to reflect the present practice of having the central committee meet no more often than every 18 months;
d) hold at least every other meeting of the central committee and executive committee in Geneva;
e) discourage the practice of one central committee undertaking special obligations or plans beyond its term which are binding on the Council;

f)  ask the member churches to assist in the redeployment of staff who will be leaving the Council;

g)  review the current pattern of "redistributed costs", determining the appropriateness of items redistributed and the basis of the redistribution; attention should also be given to the level of central services and alternative ways of funding these items or reducing their cost to the Council;

h)  encourage member churches to set aside regular reserves over the next seven years to cover all or a larger portion of their delegate expenses for the eighth assembly of the World Council of Churches as well as a contribution to the budget of that event;

i)  continue the practice of annually setting aside in the budget of the WCC an amount towards the eighth assembly reserve.

## IV. Integrated financial and programme planning

A. In affirming the importance given to the need for integrated financial and programme planning by the sixth assembly, in the context of the present financial difficulties facing the new central committee, and in the context of recommendations coming before this assembly from the Programme Policy Committee, the Finance Committee *recommends* that the assembly *instruct* the new central committee to:

1)  develop an integrated planning procedure which permits the establishment of programme priorities with appropriate staffing and structure, within present and projected financial limits;

2)  adopt a long-range planning process beginning with the recommendations of this assembly: elements of this process may include:

a)  a programme evaluation to be sent to member churches in advance of each assembly, accompanied by a financial report for each programme area;

b)  periodic requests for indications from the member churches of programme recommendations and estimates of support levels to be contributed, both financial and in-kind;

c)  such information should be provided to the programme policy and finance committees at the beginning of each assembly; the style and process of the assembly must be changed to enable greater linkage between programme evaluation, programme planning and budgeting;

d)  provide the draft programme policy and financial/budgetary guidelines to all delegates for study before the time for debate is scheduled;

3) establish a programme and budget oversight group to monitor and evaluate programmes, their impact on the lives of member churches and their financial viability, and to be responsible for the pre-assembly report to the member churches;

4) review the recommendations of the seventh assembly annually, evaluating them as to their effect and desirability.

*B. Organizational matters:* In light of the impossibility of adopting a 1992 budget with the present income projections of the WCC, an immediate review of the present organization, staffing and style of the Council is needed with a view towards reducing the number of programme cost structures. Financial projections indicate that the current number of programmes, activities and staff cannot be sustained with the funds that will be available. The Committee records the opinion that in particular the following items be reviewed:

a) the organization and working style of the Council to achieve more effective management and control;

b) the effectiveness of all the operating entities of WCC, to determine if alternative ways can be found to provide the services which those offices render at a lower cost;

c) the possible delegation of programme operations to regional councils and member churches;

d) reductions in staff (to a level of not more than 270 as proposed by the officers of the WCC in November 1990), ensuring provision for the WCC to meet contractual obligations and issues of justice and mercy;

e) development of a management plan for staff reductions which will allow the Council to achieve its priorities and make most efficient use of a smaller staff rather than continuing the current pattern of staff reductions through attrition;

f) study of the use of secretarial pools and the cost of using part-time employees;

g) exploration of possible relocation of some staff to locations less expensive than Geneva.

The Finance Committee *endorses* the action taken by the Council to initiate a management study by external specialists provided there is determined effort to act on their recommendations.

## V. Conclusion

At such a time as this, the Council is experiencing a worsening financial position common to industry, commerce and member churches worldwide, largely due to the reduced value of its income. It must react quickly and positively if it is to survive. This must involve change, which may be both substantial and painful. The very theme of the assembly suggests this but great benefits can accrue from change. This assembly and the central committee which it appoints have a duty to support the leadership, management and the staff of the Council in achieving these changes. The decision to delay the appointment of commissions and working groups until after the review scheduled for July 1991 should be strongly affirmed as a first step.

The dreams coming from this assembly now need the space to be distilled into programme policies which are achievable and affordable. Initiatives to reorganize, economize and develop improved systems to plan, budget, monitor and evaluate the work of the World Council of Churches are both necessary to balance the 1992 budget, create that space and then to begin this work.

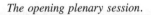
*The opening plenary session.*

# 5. Statements and Appeals on Public Issues

## 5.1. INTRODUCTION

According to the rules of the WCC, an assembly "may publish statements upon any situation or issue with which the Council or its constituent churches may be confronted". These statements have no authority except "the weight which they carry by their own truth and wisdom". Yet, as the judgment of such a widely-representative body, they may have considerable influence.

The question is always: "On which issues should an assembly speak?" Some criteria have been worked out. Priority is given, for example, to major international political developments or issues, especially those with which the WCC has had direct involvement or long-standing commitment. Statements are not offered if the issue can be or is being dealt with by the general secretary, the officers, or the central committee. Statements are also not made in cases where other forms of action (e.g. a letter or an ongoing programme) may be more appropriate.

The initial recommendation of the Business Committee at Canberra was that the Public Issues Committee prepare statements on four topics: the Gulf crisis, internal conflicts (i.e., conflicts within nations), indigenous peoples and land rights, and South Africa. Delegates subsequently proposed numerous additional topics, including global warming, anti-semitism, the debt crisis, the drug crisis, AIDS, Romania and Albania. The Business Committee determined that these issues could be handled in some other fashion, but it did agree to authorize statements or appeals on the situation in the Baltic states, the Pacific, Sri Lanka and El Salvador.

Draft statements were brought to the plenary for a first reading on 15 February, but prolonged discussion of the Nominations Committee report meant that there was no time for comments on the work of the Public Issues Committee. A special session was called for the evening of

Sunday, 17 February, though many delegates were unable to attend due to the programme of parish visits.

The revised statements and appeals were presented to the assembly on Wednesday, 20 February, by Dr Janice Love (Methodist, USA), co-moderator of the Public Issues Committee. Dr Love introduced the statement on "The Gulf War, the Middle East, and the Threat to World Peace" (5.2) and invited comments on its "preamble" (paragraphs 1-37).

Several suggestions for improvement were offered, but two issues received most attention: (1) Dr Karel Blei (Reformed, Netherlands) argued that the statement failed to recognize the threat to Israel posed by Iraq or to commend Israel for its restraint in not retaliating to Iraqi missile attacks. Paragraphs 2, 13 and 14 should be revised to reflect greater understanding of Israel's situation. Other views were also expressed. Ms Jean Zaru (Friends, Israeli Occupied Territory) contended that Israel should not get special treatment. It especially should not be commended for not retaliating since, in the current war, the US is fighting on Israel's behalf. (2) Prof. Joseph Omoyajowo (Anglican, Nigeria) objected to the reference to anti-Muslim feeling in paragraph 34. The truth, he said, is that Islam attempts in many places to humiliate other faith communities.

There was much debate about the procedure for revising paragraphs 1-37, but the assembly finally agreed simply to request the Public Issues Committee to revise that part of the text in light of the discussion.

Dr Love then moved the adoption of the second part of the statement on the Gulf war (paragraphs 38-43). Early in the discussion, Dr Konrad Raiser (United, Germany) moved to amend paragraph 39 by adding the following sentence: "We call upon [the churches] to give up any theological or moral justification of the use of military power, be it in war or through other forms of oppressive security systems, and to become public advocates of a just peace." Dr Raiser noted that the language of his amendment was taken from the final document of the 1990 JPIC conference in Seoul. The amendment was approved (268-193-79), though objection was already raised that more time should be devoted to a decision of such consequence.

Other amendments were proposed, but most were resisted by the Committee and subsequently defeated by the assembly. A motion to close debate was, at one point, approved by the delegates, but rescinded after the WCC's general secretary, Emilio Castro, intervened. Our impatience with small changes, said Dr Castro, should not keep us from hearing the mind of the assembly on such an important conflict.

The debate on this statement was more than three hours old when the assembly broke for lunch. During the break, the Public Issues Committee received seven specific amendments dealing with paragraphs 38-43. An addition to paragraph 41 — appealing to Israel to lift the blanket curfew imposed on the occupied territories at the start of the war — was accepted by the Committee and adopted by the assembly.

The Committee also accepted an amendment expressing "deep dismay that without apparent reference to the UN Security Council the USA persistently refuses to consider any offer by other parties to break the political stalemate and open new doors to negotiated settlement". Bishop Barry Rogerson (Anglican, England) objected that such "one-sided criticism" of the US would damage the WCC's credibility. If the position of the US government is thought to be incompatible with that of the UN, he added, then it is for the UN to say so. Rev. James Rogers (Reformed, Scotland) expressed alarm that the WCC is seeking to occupy some high moral ground far removed from the real world — and, therefore, will be ignored. The amendment was defeated.

Bishop Rogerson then defended a proposed amendment to link all allied cease-fire to an Iraqi withdrawal from Kuwait in accordance with UN resolutions. This amendment was also defeated.

As the assembly moved towards a final vote on the statement as a whole, several delegates expressed concern about the implications of the "Raiser amendment". Rev. John Broadhurst (Anglican, England) recalled the failure of countries to stand up to Hitler. The statement as amended is, he argued, a pacifist measure. To vote for it would be to oppose the right of Kuwait, Palestine, Cyprus, or any oppressed nation to self-defence. Landesbischof Horst Hirschler (Lutheran, Germany) agreed that there are situations in which a country may legitimately go to war against another country when all non-violent means have been exhausted. Dr Held, moderator of the central committee, also noted that, because of the Raiser amendment, he would abstain. Dr Raiser maintained that his amendment did not impose a pacifist position; but, in the end, the assembly voted to reconsider the amendment and defeated it. The delegates then voted, with some opposition, to adopt the public issue statement on the Gulf war.

By now, the assembly had spent over four hours on the report from the Public Issues Committee but had discussed only one of the eight statements and appeals. A motion was made that the delegates receive the remaining report, express their general support for the substance of the statements, and commend the statements to the central committee for final adoption. Rev. Tyrone Pitts (Baptist, USA) and Prof. Michael Horsburgh (Anglican, Australia) both argued, however, that the assembly must use this opportunity to speak on Aboriginal land rights. The statements on "Indigenous Peoples and Land Rights" and "South Africa" were subsequently adopted without discussion. The other statements were received and referred to the central committee.


## 5.2. STATEMENT ON THE GULF WAR, THE MIDDLE EAST AND THE THREAT TO WORLD PEACE


### I. Preamble

1. As we gather in the seventh assembly of the World Council of Churches (Canberra, February 1991), a war of terrible proportions is being waged in the Gulf. Kuwait was already ravaged by Iraqi invading forces. Now, both Kuwait and Iraq are being destroyed by bombardment of unprecedented intensity. Hour by hour this war claims a mounting toll of victims on all sides, combatants and non-combatants alike, our own sisters and brothers. As we met, news was received of the horrible bombing of a shelter in Baghdad killing hundreds of people who sought refuge there, many of them children and women. At this very moment, preparations are being made for a ground battle which is certain to cause greater destruction and loss of life. It is a war of ominous dimensions which threatens the destruction of the land and the people it seeks to liberate. Day by day the war escalates, drawing in more and more nations of the Gulf, the Middle East, and other parts of the world. It squanders the resources of rich and poor countries alike, and no end is in sight.

2. Intensive efforts were made around the world to prevent this war and avoid its escalation. Urgent appeals were made by leaders of nations not to abandon non-violent efforts to cause Iraq to withdraw unconditionally from Kuwait and resolve its differences with its neighbour through negotiations. The churches pleaded with the leaders of their nations not to aggravate further the long-standing conflict in the Middle East which time and again has brought war and violence to the region; created a climate of fear and mistrust between Israel and the Arab nations; led to the suffering of Jews, Christians and Muslims alike, and to the continuing occupation of Palestinian territories and parts of Lebanon and to the invasion and

partial occupation of Cyprus; inflicted suffering upon the Palestinian people who have been deprived of their rights to self-determination, statehood and national dignity, and exacerbated conflicts within the countries of the region, delaying justice for national minorities like the Kurdish people.

3. War promises no lasting solution for the festering wounds of the Middle East, no just, peaceful and durable regional or world order, but rather continued insecurity, pain and conflict.

4. It is never too soon nor too late to seek peace and a comprehensive settlement. So once again, together, our hearts cry out to the leaders of the nations, especially to those of the coalition forces led by the United States of America and of Iraq: Cease the bombing! Still the missiles! Stop the fighting! Restrain your armies! Negotiate! Trust in the promise of peace!

*Peace-making, the believers' calling*

5. We confess that many of us and our churches have for too long been confused, timid and unfaithful in the face of the daunting complexity of the decades-long problems confronting the Middle East. We have failed to disassociate ourselves from the institutions of militarism which view war either as a solution to human conflicts or as a necessary evil, or to avoid complicity with the powers who trust more in armed might than in the rule of law or the ability of the human spirit to achieve justice by peaceful means.

6. During this assembly we have sought to open our hearts and minds to one another and to the Holy Spirit, and we have renewed our resolve to be peace-makers, conscious of the cost of being disciples of the Prince of Peace.

7. The participants in the WCC world convocation on "Justice Peace and the Integrity of Creation" (Seoul, 1990) declared: "We will resist doctrines and systems of security based on the use of, and deterrence by, all weapons of mass destruction, and military interventions and occupations." It is imperative that the churches hear and respond now to this challenge.

8. The first assembly of the World Council of Churches (Amsterdam, 1948) was delayed by a looming world war, and every subsequent assembly has been confronted with the prospect or reality of war. Yet, consistently and persistently, the World Council of Churches has sought lasting peace through efforts to eliminate injustices which give rise to war, to create and strengthen institutions capable of safeguarding

international peace and security and, in the event of war, to aid the victims.

9. The peace we seek, as the Vancouver assembly (1983) reminded the churches, "is not just the absence of war. Peace requires a new international order based on justice for and within all the nations, and respect for the God-given humanity and dignity of every person. Peace is, as the Prophet Isaiah has taught us, the effect of righteousness."

10. We trust in the knowledge that the world belongs to God, not to the powers of this world, and we take courage and hope from God's promise of peace, righteousness and justice which was embodied in Jesus Christ and made present among us through the work of the Holy Spirit. With God's help, peace is possible even now.

*The churches' advocacy for a just peace in the Gulf and the Middle East*

11. The World Council of Churches has repeatedly advocated respect for international law and a peaceful resolution of this conflict. It has:
a) strongly opposed Iraq's invasion and annexation of Kuwait;
b) welcomed the Security Council's demand that Iraq withdraw immediately and unconditionally from Kuwait and its appeal to Iraq and Kuwait to initiate intensive negotiations for the resolution of their differences;
c) supported the application of strict sanctions banning all commercial dealings and trade with Iraq, with the exception of medical supplies and foodstuffs in humanitarian circumstances;
d) called upon the Security Council to enforce with equal vigour its earlier resolutions on the territorial integrity of Lebanon, the division and occupation of Cyprus, Israel's withdrawal from the territories it occupied in 1967, and the right of every state in the area, including Israel, to live in peace within secure and recognized boundaries free from threats or acts of force;
e) appealed for the withdrawal of all foreign forces from the region and the exploration of all avenues for negotiations to defuse the crisis and obtain a peaceful settlement;
f) declared as morally unacceptable the holding of foreign nationals in Iraq and Kuwait, appealed to the Iraqi government to facilitate the departure of all foreign nationals desiring to do so, and appealed for strict application of international norms for the protection of refugees.

12. Around the world, member churches and regional ecumenical bodies took the lead in pressing for peace along these same lines:

a) The Middle East Council of Churches sought a regional solution to the conflict, at the same time expressing hope for a comprehensive, just resolution for all the conflicts and occupations in the region in order to bring harmony and peace among Muslims, Christians and Jews in the region. It contributed significantly to assisting the refugees and other victims of the conflict.

b) The National Council of the Churches of Christ in the USA appealed repeatedly to the US Administration and Congress not to abandon sanctions as a means to obtain an end to the occupation of Kuwait, warning against the rapidly escalating military response of the US government to the crisis and the apparently open-ended nature of US military involvement in the region. A delegation of US church leaders travelled to Iraq and other states of the region in an expression of ecumenical concern and solidarity.

c) The Canadian Council of Churches issued similar appeals to its own government and also sent a delegation to the region, meeting with leaders of churches and of other religious faith communities.

d) The Conference of European Churches and national councils of churches in Europe warned against acceptance of the inevitability of war, recalling the conviction of the European churches, expressed at the European Ecumenical Assembly (Basel, 1989), that war is against the will of God and that everything should be done to further peaceful resolution of conflicts.

e) The Latin American Council of Churches urged the UN to redouble efforts for a peaceful solution, and churches in Asia, Africa, the Caribbean and the Pacific drew attention to the grave effects of the crisis on their nations and cautioned governments against military or economic support for efforts to achieve a military solution.

*The widening effects of the conflict in the Middle East*

13. When Iraq refused to withdraw from Kuwait, massive forces of the coalition led by the United States were deployed in the Gulf and three months later began bombing both Kuwait and Iraq. Iraq launched missiles on Israel, some of which fell in Palestinian areas. This has caused fear and suffering in Israel, which has not retaliated. But it has imposed a blanket curfew in the Occupied Territories, further worsening the already desperate plight of Palestinians who feel unprotected, abandoned by the world community and fear for their future, and heightening tensions in the whole region.

*Orthodox liturgy at morning worship on 16 February.*

*Milos Vesin from Yugoslavia, one of the worship animators.*

*Morning worship on Ash Wednesday.*

*The opening worship in the tent.*

The officers of the central committee elected at Canberra: left, Archbishop Aram Keshishian (Lebanon), moderator; centre and right, Pastora Nélida Ritchie (Argentina), and Ephorus Dr Soritua Nababan (Indonesia), co-moderators.

Australian prime minister Bob Hawke with Metropolitan Paulos Mar Gregorios at the opening plenary session.

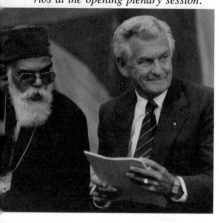

The assembly newspaper was indispensable...

Rev. Dr Emilio Castro (centre) embraces Bishop K.H. Ting (left, China Christian Council) and Rev. C.M. Kao (right, Presbyterian Church in Taiwan) after the announcement that the Chinese church had rejoined the WCC fellowship.

A painting by Aboriginal artist Wenten Rubuntja, one of the gifts from the Aboriginal people to the WCC.

Two of the stewards (photo WCC/Gordon Gray).

The procession for peace through Canberra, which preceded the all-night vigil in the worship tent.

Youth felt under-represented on the newly elected central committee.

*Press conference given by the members of the team visit to two Aboriginal communities.*

*Aboriginal dancer at the plenary on the theme presentation.*

*Children were part of the worship service on justice, peace and the integrity of creation which preceded the all-night vigil.*

14. Lebanon's hard-won, fragile peace was disrupted as missiles were launched on Israel from its territory. Israel retaliated with a renewal of heavy punitive bombing raids on Lebanese towns and villages. This has placed further obstacles in the way of the Lebanese government and army in their efforts to establish their authority over this strife-torn land.

15. Smouldering fires of tension throughout the region have been fanned as countries from the northern limits of the Middle East to the Horn of Africa. Turkey, Iran, Jordan, Sudan and others have been drawn into the sphere of confrontation. Indeed, the whole of the region, including Iraq, is armed with huge arsenals of the most modern weaponry, much of it provided by the governments and industries of countries participating in the coalition forces. The whole of the Middle East is a powder-keg which could explode in a moment. And with the presence of chemical, biological and nuclear weaponry in and around the region a conflagration could rapidly escape the confines of the Gulf.

16. All wars have serious side effects, but the oil spillage which has already occurred in the Gulf, and the estimated consequences for the global warming of the earth's atmosphere should the oil wells of Kuwait, Iraq and Saudi Arabia be set ablaze, show that the potential of this war for widespread, even global ecological destruction is exceptional.

*The global implications of the war*

17. In fact, the war already has global impact. Among its chief victims have been the poor nations of the world, many of whom are already beset by internal conflicts and massive foreign debt.

18. Their peoples were among the first to suffer. Workers in the Middle East from countries like Sri Lanka, Bangladesh, the Philippines, India and Korea were either trapped in war zones or forced to flee under excruciating circumstances. The war has added to the drain on these nations' economies, some of which depended heavily on remittances — from their nationals employed in the region — which have now been cut off.

19. The war has dealt a massive economic blow to much of the developing world, eliminating major markets for primary exports, causing prices for fuels and petroleum products and for basic foodstuffs like rice and grain to skyrocket, and making the cost of other essential imports prohibitive for the poor.

20. The war has led to new acts and threats of terrorism in several parts of the world.

21. The war has fanned the flames of religious, ethnic and regional conflicts in many countries, especially in Asia, seriously destabilizing some and giving rise to violent conflicts in others.

22. The preoccupation of the global mass media, governments, and international institutions with the war in the Gulf has distracted attention from efforts to resolve other armed conflicts raging around the world and from other massive human tragedies. It is estimated, for example, that some 20 million people are on the brink of starvation and death in the African countries of Sudan, Ethiopia, Somalia, Angola, Mozambique and Liberia. At this time of war, much of the world has turned a deaf ear to their cries for help.

*The United Nations, the Gulf war, and the "new world order"*

23. The World Council of Churches promoted the formation of the United Nations and through representatives of the member churches it was present when the Charter was adopted. Since the Amsterdam assembly (1948) it has supported the UN and, especially through its Commission of the Churches on International Affairs, a leading non-governmental organization in consultative status with the Economic and Social Council, the WCC has contributed to the success of the UN and its related agencies.

24. The achievements of the United Nations over the years have been notable in many fields. Even during the past decade of the greatest neglect by the major powers, it continued to lay the groundwork for a role in the peaceful resolution of international conflicts. Much of this work came to fruition after 1985 when the UN was instrumental in negotiating an end to the Iran/Iraq war, the war in Afghanistan, and a settlement of the long-standing dispute over Namibia and guiding it to independence; brought closer the end of apartheid in South Africa through the application of comprehensive sanctions; and played a new, more energetic role in promoting the settlement of regional conflicts in Central America and elsewhere.

25. The words of the late Bishop Bell at the first assembly (Amsterdam, 1948) remain pertinent, however. "International law", he said, "clearly requires international institutions for its effectiveness. These institutions, if they are to command respect and obedience of nations, must come to grips with international problems on their own merits and not primarily in the light of national interests... The United Nations was designed to promote friendly relations among the nations. Its purposes in these respects deserve the support of Christians. But unless the nations

surrender a greater measure of national sovereignty in the interest of the common good, they will be tempted to have recourse to war in order to enforce their claims."

26. The churches and the general public in most parts of the world supported the initial actions of the UN Security Council in condemning the invasion of Kuwait and the application of sanctions to enforce its call for Iraq's withdrawal from this occupied country. They would very much have preferred that the United Nations itself had taken all decisions and the limited actions necessary to end the aggression. Unfortunately member nations have not yet empowered the UN for such a role.

27. By adopting Security Council resolution 678, which authorized "member states... to use all necessary means to implement previous resolutions", the UN placed itself in danger of being blamed for being unduly dependent upon a powerful nation or group of nations and for appearing to authorize a large-scale war which is not in the interests of an international order of peace based on law.

28. The question of how major international decisions are made has become one of pressing urgency in the world today. The lessons learned from the way this first major world crisis in the post-Cold War era has been handled by the international community demand a critical examination of the emerging new world order. No one government or group of governments should either take or be allowed to take primary responsibility for the resolution of major conflicts beyond their own borders.

29. For the Security Council or the Secretary-General, in the exercise of his good offices, to be for some reason unable to act independently and in the true spirit of the UN Charter would be unacceptable. The community of nations cannot afford such a weakening of the UN system. For the sake of world peace, for the sake of the rule of law, for the sake of the authority of the United Nations, its position as guarantor of a comprehensive international peace order must be strengthened.

30. It is imperative, for the sake of world peace, the rule of law, and the credibility of the United Nations, that the parties to the Gulf war cease immediately the hostilities and invest their efforts in the pursuit of a negotiated peace.

31. For the sake of all peoples it is time to build a new world order of justice, the foundation stone of peace:

a)   a world economic order which ends the domination and exploitation of the poor by the rich;

b) information and communication systems which — as the world convocation on "Justice, Peace and the Integrity of Creation" (JPIC) (Seoul, 1990), said — offer all peoples truth in place of distortion, and media disposed to peace rather than violence; and which redress the concentration of control over global communications media in the hands of a few powerful nations and corporations;

c) an environmental order which respects the integrity of God's creation and controls the industrialized nations' insatiable thirst for oil — a major source of global conflict, as this war shows, and of widespread damage to the environment — and leads them to adopt new energy policies which promote conservation.

## The impact of racism and intolerance

32. The war in the Gulf reveals the tragic impact of racism on both the international and domestic policies of nations from which indigenous peoples are often the first to suffer.

33. Internationally, there is a shocking rise in discrimination against persons of Arab nationality, background or appearance. In the name of "national security" and "prevention of terrorism", many are subjected to systematic humiliation, harassment, preventive detention, and open threat of physical harm by both state authorities and private groups in many nations around the world.

34. Anti-Muslim feeling is on the increase in many Western countries, fed by the portrayal of Islam as an inherently menacing religion. As a result, many Muslims feel humiliated and angry, and the future of Christian-Muslim relations — so crucial to peace and harmony in many parts of the world — risks being gravely affected. At a time when there are manifestations of anti-semitism in a number of countries, many Jews feel great anguish.

35. A disproportionate burden is being imposed on racial and ethnic minorities in this war. According to United States Department of Defense estimates, for example, 25% of US troops deployed in the Gulf (and 29% of ground forces and 55% of women in uniform) are black. Yet African-Americans comprise only slightly more than 11% of the civilian population over the age of 16. Corresponding figures for other racial or ethnic minority groups are not readily available, but it is safe to assume that Native Americans and persons of Hispanic background are similarly over-represented in the fighting forces. Concern rises for a generation of black, Hispanic and Native American youth endangered by intense, endemic poverty, inadequate health care, the ever-rising incidence of AIDS, and

the impact of drugs and drug-related crime. Now, many of those who joined the military in search of education, stable employment and a way out of these dangers, are at peril in the Gulf.

## The situation and role of women

36. This particular conflict and the long-standing institutions of war and militarism that feed it are created, controlled, and perpetuated by men. Some women may at times support military solutions to conflicts and, increasingly, women participate as soldiers. In the rare circumstances where women lead governments, some of them promote policies leading to war. But most women and children are victimized by war and militarism. They become refugees, objects of sexual violence by occupation forces, and they are trapped in the midst of violence. Women and children are also the majority of those who are deprived of basic necessities when resources from institutions that enhance life are diverted to those that destroy it. In contrast to this victimization by forces in which they have little meaningful participation, women are often at the heart of movements for peace with justice and other activities that promote creative non-violent resolution of conflict. And women have taken the lead in urging that adversaries be recognized as full human beings rather than being made objects in enemy images.

## The impact on youth

37. Modern warfare takes a particularly terrible toll on youth and children. There are indications that the chief victims both of the occupation of Kuwait and of the bombing of Iraq in retaliation are many infants and children. Young people make up the bulk of the armed forces exposed to battle. The youth of this assembly have expressed concern that young men and women from many countries are called to fight in the Middle East in a war not of their making, and that young people are among the first to suffer from the economic deprivation and strife it is causing.

## II. Appeals and affirmations

38. Out of deep human concern for all those who are victimized by the war in the Gulf: the poor, the racially oppressed, women, youth, civilian victims, and those who out of loyalty or due to circumstance are engaged in conflict as members of the armed forces; out of our concern for justice, peace and the integrity of creation; and as an expression of our hope for a truly just, peaceful, democratic participatory world order and institutions

able to govern and sustain it, we at the seventh assembly of the World Council of Churches cry out: Stop the war! Pursue the way of peace!

39. To the churches:

a) We urge you to be constant in prayer and pastoral care for the leaders of the nations and particularly for all those on every side caught up in or victimized by this tragic war: innocent civilians, those involved in the fighting, families and friends who grieve the separation or loss of their loved ones, and those who reject military service on grounds of conscience.

b) We appeal especially to the churches in arms exporting and importing countries to press for immediate steps to control this trade in death and destruction. The more lethal the weapons and the larger their number, the greater the violence and destruction of wars and conflicts. This uncontrolled trade denies the sanctity of human life and defiles the planet.

c) We reiterate the affirmation of the sixth assembly: "The churches today are called to confess anew their faith, and to repent for the times when Christians have remained silent in the face of injustice or threats to peace. The biblical vision of peace with justice for all, of wholeness, of unity for all God's people is not one of several options for the followers of Christ. It is an imperative in our time."

40. To the United Nations:

a) We urge you to reassert your role as peace-maker, peace-keeper, conciliator and negotiator.

b) We urge you to act now, decisively, to stop the war and to return to the strict application of non-violent sanctions — without deadlines — against Iraq, whose actions are in violation of international law and have been widely condemned by the nations.

c) We urge you to reconvene the Security Council on a continuing, emergency basis, to map a new course for peaceful negotiation of the dispute between Iraq and Kuwait and of the other outstanding conflicts in the region.

d) We urge you to move with all due speed to the convening of the International Peace Conference on the Middle East, called for by the 38th UN General Assembly (1983), to resolve the question of Palestine, to address the legitimate national rights of Palestinians to self-determination and an independent state of their own, and as a means to implement Security Council Resolution 242 (1967) which affirms the right of every state in the area, including Israel, "to live in peace within secure and recognized boundaries free from threats or acts of

Meanwhile, we call for international protection for the Palestinian people under occupation until such an international peace conference has done its work.

e) We also call for the initiation of a conference on peace, security and cooperation in the Middle East with the equal participation of all interested states and peoples as a further instrument for the achievement of a just and lasting settlement in the region which will bring about the mutual recognition of all states and effective guarantees for their security.

f) We urge you to be consistent in your actions to ensure the compliance of the nations with United Nations resolutions, especially those others calling for an end to illegal occupation of territory in the region of the Middle East: the Palestinian territories occupied by Israel in 1967, Lebanon, and Cyprus.

41. To the nations and their leaders:

a) We commend those nations who have exerted efforts to seek a negotiated solution to this conflict both before and after the engagement of the war, and encourage you to pursue them now with even greater vigour.

b) We call urgently and insistently on both Iraq and the coalition forces led by the United States to cease fire immediately and to work for a negotiated solution of the Iraq-Kuwait dispute within the context of the United Nations.

c) We urge all nations involved in the war to respect international norms for the protection of non-combatants in situations of armed conflict.

d) We appeal to the government of Iraq to signal its intention and offer guarantees that it will comply with Security Council Resolution 660 by withdrawing completely and unconditionally from the territory of Kuwait immediately upon the cessation of hostilities.

e) We call upon all external powers to withdraw all forces from the Middle East — except those required to perform a peace-keeping role under UN command — as a means to help restore a climate propitious for the pursuit of a lasting settlement of the region's conflicts.

f) We appeal to the government of Israel to lift the blanket curfew that has been imposed on the Occupied Territories since the war began.

42. To peoples of other faiths:

In the presence of the representatives of other faiths who have been our guests during this assembly, we commit ourselves to refuse to be separated from brothers and sisters of other faiths as a result of this war, and to reject especially any effort to divide Christians, Muslims and Jews whose faiths originated in the Middle East, and to join with them in prayers and common endeavours for peace in anticipation of the day when all may live together in peace and mutual respect.

43. Ever mindful that God rules with righteousness over all, we pray:

Come, Holy Spirit
transform our lives,
lift and sustain us in this day.
Give wisdom and faith
that we may know
the great hope to which we are called.
Come, Holy Spirit,
renew the whole creation.

# 5.3. STATEMENT ON INDIGENOUS PEOPLES AND LAND RIGHTS — MOVE BEYOND WORDS

1. "Come, Holy Spirit — Renew the Whole Creation!" We have come to Australia, the land of our Aboriginal sisters and brothers, the original inhabitants who call it the land of the spirit. We have come to listen and learn. We have come to celebrate together that which the Holy Spirit gives to us. We have been graciously received by the Aboriginal people and Torres Strait Islanders who have shown great leadership and wisdom. We have worshipped together. They have shared their stories with us. They have shared their lives with us, their pain of stolen land and stolen children, poverty and oppression. Despite all they have endured, they have survived and continue to thrive. We salute them and stand in solidarity with them in their courageous struggle for equality and justice.

2. For the last twenty years, voices of indigenous peoples throughout the world have spoken to the churches through programmes and gatherings sponsored by the WCC. Most recently, in the Darwin consultation and San Antonio encuentro (both in 1989), the WCC highlighted anew indigenous peoples' struggles for international recognition of their sovereignties, self-determination, traditional religious practices and land rights. Indigenous peoples request that the churches join them in these struggles, remembering that some churches for too long have helped justify actions and acted in concert with oppressive governments, but

knowing also that some churches have begun to take steps to support these struggles.

3. While we acknowledge the immense profit and privilege which often accrued to the churches when early missionary undertakings accompanied the exploitation of indigenous peoples, churches have also been a prophetic voice seeking justice for indigenous communities. The WCC calls its member churches to conversion, active and ongoing repentance and reparation for past sins as a prelude to reconciliation. Only by so doing can we hope to gain or retain and be worthy of the trust and respect of indigenous people. We must continue to confront our own role as an accessory and even accomplice in the historic and contemporary acts of injustice against indigenous peoples.

4. To that end the WCC should continue to work with indigenous peoples to ensure that issues identified by them, their communities and organizations, will be heard and acted upon. We affirm the growing consciousness of indigenous peoples' struggle for freedom, including those of the Dalits of India. We realize that wounds that had their beginnings 500 years ago with invasion, conquest, colonization and missionary zeal, will take time to heal. Recognizing that oppression of indigenous peoples is racism and that issues of racism in all parts of the world are linked, the WCC should intensify its efforts to pursue racial justice.

5. Working towards the goal of justice through sovereignty, self-determination and land rights for indigenous peoples, the seventh assembly of the World Council of Churches (Canberra, February 1991) calls upon member churches to move beyond words to action, specifically:

a) to negotiate with indigenous peoples to ascertain how lands taken unjustly by churches from indigenous peoples can be returned to them;

b) to recognize, acknowledge and vigorously support self-determination and sovereignty of indigenous peoples, as defined by them, in church and society;

c) to use their influence with governments and international bodies in actively seeking the goal of justice through sovereignty and self-determination of indigenous peoples;

d) to declare the year 1992, the quincentenary of the arrival of Columbus in the western hemisphere, a year against racism with specific focus on indigenous and black peoples who in this year will mark 500 years of genocide, land theft, slavery, and oppression. We call upon the international religious community and governments to resist participating in activities celebrating 1992 designed without input from indigenous peoples and to join with indigenous peoples in any celebrations or commemorations they plan;

e) to oppose continuing and now increasing (justified by war in the Gulf) exploitation of indigenous peoples' lands and mineral resources;

f) to protect burial grounds and sacred sites of indigenous peoples from desecration and destruction and to work towards the return of ancestral remains, artifacts, sacred objects and other items belonging to indigenous peoples;

g) to protect freedom of indigenous peoples to practise their traditional religions.

## Aboriginal people and Torres Strait Islanders

6. The seventh assembly has listened carefully to the voices of the Aboriginal and Torres Strait Island people. We have been painfully reminded of their struggle for self-determination and self-management, in order to pursue freely their own economic, political, social, religious and cultural development. We recognize that indigenous peoples of Australia and the Torres Strait Islands were independent, self-governing peoples long before Europeans invaded their land, and that they have a right to regain such control over their land under their own rule.

7. We recognize that the Australian churches have begun to speak out on the issue of land rights. However, the time has come for an even more effective commitment and stance on the issues that affect Aboriginal and Torres Strait Island people. Such a commitment requires a settlement for a treaty acknowledging the rights of indigenous peoples.

8. Out of this deep concern, the World Council of Churches seventh assembly, meeting in Canberra, Australia, in February 1991:

a) supports the self-determination and self-management of the Aboriginal and Torres Strait Island people and their right to define sovereignty for themselves;

b) requests that the WCC central committee monitor and support a treaty process between Aboriginal and Torres Strait Island people and the Australian government;

c) commits itself to be in solidarity with the Aboriginal and Torres Strait Island people until their rights are established throughout Australia;

d) calls on the Australian churches to return land unjustly taken from the Aboriginal and Torres Strait Island people;

e) recalls the fourth act of covenant from the WCC world convocation on "Justice, Peace and the Integrity of Creation" (Seoul 1990) "for the eradication of racism on national and international levels...", and concretely the need "to join actively in the land rights struggles of indigenous people as they struggle against racist institutions and policies which rape the land and resources".

# 5.4. STATEMENT ON SOUTH AFRICA

## The present challenge

1. The seventh assembly of the World Council of Churches (Canberra, February 1991) takes place at a critical moment in the history of South Africa. The structures and practices of legalized racism which have dominated the social, economic and political life of the country, are trembling under the weight of growing pressure from within and without. The liberation struggle, as well as boycotts, economic sanctions and other measures which have served to isolate South Africa from the world community of nations, have combined to produce a growing momentum for change.

2. It is already becoming evident, however, that the next phase in the movement for a new, democratic and non-racial South Africa might yet prove to be the most difficult phase of all.

3. While the state president's recent decision to seek the repeal of the land act, the group areas act and the population registration act is to be welcomed, many of the discriminatory structures and practices which these acts created remain intact. The security laws which sustain apartheid and fuel township violence are still in place. In addition, the overwhelming majority of schools remain segregated by law. Political prisoners, incarcerated under apartheid laws, are still not free. The indemnity regulations gazetted in October fall far short of an amnesty. The repatriation of exiles and the release of political prisoners are, consequently, well behind schedule. Apartheid is still maintained in economic structures, in housing, education, business and finance, and health services. The recent announcement by the state president contained no promise to restore people and communities to lands from which they were forcibly removed in recent years, nor does it offer compensation for lands unjustly expropriated. There has been no commitment made to a policy of fair and just redistribution of land. The majority of South Africans are still denied the right to vote and the exercise of political power through constitutional means.

4. According to the UN Declaration on Apartheid, the system of legalized racism will end when the right of all the people "to participate in government on the basis of universal, equal suffrage, under a non-racial voters' roll, and by secret ballot" is guaranteed in a new South African constitution. To this end it is essential that the negotiating of such a constitution be carried out by a constituent assembly which is itself elected democratically and not according to racial or ethnic groupings. The free and democratic election of such an assembly will be the major political challenge of the next period.

## "Spirit of Truth — Set us Free!"

> "If you continue in my word, you will be my disciples, and you will know the truth and the truth will make you free." (John 8:32)

5. Under the sub-theme, "Spirit of Truth — Set us Free!", the Canberra assembly has considered situations of grave crisis and challenge to the church of Christ around the world. With respect to the South African situation we have discussed the ways in which God's Holy Spirit is able to break down barriers of misunderstanding and prejudice, at the same time opening people to the deeper truth which liberates and renews. These discussions have driven us back to God's word, to repentance and to the discovery of the liberating truth which comes through discipleship in Jesus Christ.

6. Through Bible study we have discerned the biblical meaning of "truth" as that which is made visible and transparent. It is through the Spirit (John 14) that we are exposed to our own sinfulness and forced to be truthful (transparent) to God about the hidden racism in our hearts and minds. Through God's word of acceptance in Jesus Christ, proclaimed during our worship together, we have sensed the Spirit's power which frees us from sin and enables us to be transparent and trusting to one another and to God.

7. We have felt a strong bond of unity in the Spirit with the churches of South Africa. With those who stand in the front line of the struggle against apartheid we share the confident hope that the one God who redeems in history will bring into being a new South Africa in which isolation and fear are overcome through mutual acceptance and trust.

## Commitments

8. We express our support and encouragement to all South Africans, both black and white, who have dedicated their energies and talents to

bring about a peaceful transition to a democratic, non-racial South Africa. We want especially to express our gratitude to Dr Nelson Mandela, deputy president of the African National Congress. Since his release from prison on 11 February 1990, he has demonstrated an ability to transcend historic animosities through a spirit of reconciliation, providing at the same time vigorous, determined leadership in the struggle. To those in the liberation movements, the trade unions and other institutions working to bring authentic democracy to South Africa, we renew our pledge to keep the faith and not to grow weary in support of their efforts until the day of freedom comes.

9. We address a special word of gratitude, encouragement and support to the churches of South Africa and to the South African Council of Churches. It can be said of many of these churches that they "are afflicted in every way but not crushed, perplexed but not driven to despair, always carrying in the body the death of Jesus" (2 Cor. 4:8-10). In their courageous witness and through their suffering they have given inspiration to the global communion of churches and have provided insight into the meaning of discipleship to Jesus Christ. We encourage them to persevere in the struggle. We pledge our support for their work of reconstruction and reconciliation when democracy is established. As the unity of the church is to be a sign of the unity of the human family, we would also challenge them to do everything possible to express visibly the unity of the church in South Africa.

10. We join in the spirit of the national conference of church leaders in South Africa, which gathered in Rustenburg in November 1990, in confessing before God and one another the ways in which we have permitted, supported and refused to resist the dehumanizing, oppressive system of apartheid. To the extent we have allowed our sisters and brothers to suffer humiliation, dispossession and death for so long under this oppressive system, we have denied the gospel of Jesus Christ and violated our unity in the Holy Spirit.

11. With our member churches in South Africa we are grieved by the escalation of violence which has since 1989 claimed thousands of lives in Natal and the Transvaal, causing considerable destruction to property, swelling the number of refugees in neighbouring countries, and creating a vast influx of displaced persons in Durban, Witwatersrand and other cities. We urge the government of South Africa to act decisively to restore peace and security, to end violence and to establish an impartial police and security force in consultation with all partners in the negotiation process. We appeal to all political organizations to restrain those who

engage in acts of violence within their ranks and to do everything possible to encourage peace, tolerance for opposing opinions and mutual respect and understanding. We express appreciation for the efforts of the South African Council of Churches and the body of church leaders in South Africa in promoting conciliation, investigating and analyzing the root causes of violence and crime, and providing support for the victims caught up in the conflict.

12. On the basis of consultation with the South African Council of Churches and other partners within the South African community, we strongly reaffirm the position of the WCC central committee on the need to maintain sanctions against South Africa until all apartheid laws have been repealed. We agree with the UN declaration on apartheid which urges that measures be undertaken "to ensure that the international community does not relax existing measures aimed at encouraging the South African regime to eradicate apartheid, until there is clear evidence of profound and irreversible changes".

## Recommendations

We request the central committee, as a matter of urgency, to initiate a consultation process with member churches in South Africa, the South African Council of Churches and the liberation movements, with a view:

a) to determining the criteria for "clear evidence of profound and irreversible changes" and to agree together on the moment when the lifting of sanctions would be justified;

b) to coordinating ecumenical action for reconstruction, reconciliation and the appropriate means to promote a free, democratic, non-racial and unitary state in South Africa.

We appeal to the South African government:

a) to repeal all repressive security legislation and to reorganize the police and security forces in a manner representative of all sectors of South African society and which is more accountable to impartial, democratic institutions;

b) to create a climate conducive to negotiations in order to engender confidence and enable participation in the process towards a democratic constitution, freed from threats of violence and intimidation;

c) to provide for the security and protection of all partners in the negotiation process, especially leading members of the African National Congress, the Pan-Africanist Congress and other anti-apartheid groups who have been subjected to harassment by right-wing vigilantes and askaris supported by the security police.

We encourage all South Africans to become involved in the process of constructive change by striving to remove all vestiges of injustice, seeking reconciliation and the healing of wounds, banishing fear and mistrust, and renewing their commitment to building a nation in which the new political order will be complemented by new attitudes, new relationships of tolerance and respect for the humanity of all people.

We call upon all member churches, councils of churches and church-related agencies to intensify their activities in support of a peaceful transition to a truly democratic South Africa by:

a) appealing to their respective governments to maintain sanctions until such time that all apartheid laws are abolished and the demise of apartheid is declared to be irreversible, while continuing campaigns of divestment from banks and transnational corporations;

b) continuing to make available to congregations and news media accurate information on the current situation in South Africa;

c) working in partnership with the South African Council of Churches to implement programmes to repatriate and resettle returnees and to develop plans for social reconstruction in post-apartheid South Africa;

d) supporting through prayer and action the churches in South Africa as they work for unity and reconciliation on the basis of the Rustenburg (1990) Declaration, "Towards a United Christian Witness in a Changing South Africa".

## 5.5. STATEMENT ON INTERNAL CONFLICTS

1. The central committee of the World Council of Churches, meeting immediately after the seventh assembly (Canberra, February 1991), notes with deep concern the proliferation and intensification of conflicts taking place within the borders of a large number of sovereign states. Most of the violent conflicts today are intra-state conflicts, often intensified by external forces. Many of them have escalated to such a degree that they pose threats to the integrity of states and to regional and international stability. Yet, the international community has — until now — not found adequate ways of dealing with these types of internal conflicts.

**Sources and effects of internal conflicts**

2. The sources of internal conflicts are complex. Many reflect genuine struggles for justice. Central to these conflicts is the sense of oppression

experienced by groups of people who have a common ethnic, cultural, linguistic, national or religious identity. These groups seek to escape domination by the state or other groups, or to evolve new forms of relationships within or outside existing state structures, whereby they are able to safeguard and manifest their own identity.

3. Religious identity can be a source of conflict between groups in society. The misuse of religion for domination and for protection of special interests has a profoundly destructive effect on particular groups and society as a whole.

4. In many societies, prevailing social and economic policies lead to the alienation of peoples from their ancestral lands, or competition between different groups for an increasingly small share of public resources, jobs, etc. Individuals and groups who find no response to, or even access to a public forum for their needs and aspirations often turn to violence, thus increasing both the militarization of societies and the polarization of political discourse within them. The effects of these conflicts include the escalation of human rights abuses, violence, massive internal displacements of people, and a large increase in the number of refugees and asylum-seekers. Such conflicts often have an impact on neighbouring states, especially as refugees move across borders.

5. Many internal conflicts are made more destructive by the intervention of other states which supply arms and financial support to the state or to one party in the conflict. Provocation and manipulation by external powers result in escalation of violence and internal repression, especially of the poor and marginalized.

## The role of churches and religious communities

6. Churches and other religious communities can play an important positive role in contributing to the resolution of internal conflicts, even if they themselves are victims of the situation. Where peoples or groups experience oppression, religious communities can become the bearers of national, ethnic or cultural identity and the guardians of the hopes and aspirations of people for peace and justice. We acknowledge, however, that churches and religious communities in some places have themselves become contributors to internal conflicts, and that religious symbols and values have been misused.

7. The churches have a special responsibility to seek resolution of interconfessional and inter-religious conflicts. Interfaith and interconfessional dialogue thus become important tools in the resolution of internal conflicts. Churches must also guard against the kind of relationships with

the state that protect the social and economic privileges of an elite while others, invariably the poor, are abandoned. Churches need to be able to provide early warning about potential conflicts and to assist in seeking solutions which safeguard the legitimate rights and identities of all groups.

## International response

8. The solving of internal conflicts has so far been seen as the responsibility of the affected nation state. The United Nations has been inhibited from being an effective instrument for resolving internal conflicts or even for providing humanitarian assistance to the internally displaced, because member states wish to protect their sovereignty. The result is that internal conflicts are dealt with through the use of force, other forms of oppression, or even attempts to destroy or annihilate groups which the state identifies as a threat or a problem.

9. In some instances, the United Nations has been able to assist in the resolution of conflicts and has helped to safeguard the rights of minorities and other groups within states through the use of international human rights mechanisms. Nevertheless, the increased number of people caught in oppressive and violent situations of conflict urgently demands the development of new instruments for resolving internal conflicts.

## Recommendations

The central committee of the World Council of Churches:

1. Calls upon member churches:
a) to make serious efforts to be peace-makers in situations of internal conflict through such means as prayer, education on peaceful resolution of conflicts and the promotion of interconfessional and interfaith dialogue;
b) to intensify their work for the protection of human rights with particular attention to collective rights and the rights of minority groups who are victims;
c) to intensify their advocacy work and humanitarian assistance to the victims of internal conflicts such as refugees and internally displaced persons;
d) to monitor situations carefully and to provide early warning about potential conflicts;
e) to undertake self-examination of their role in internal conflicts in order to identify where they have been helpful in resolving them, and where

they have directly or indirectly impeded resolution of conflicts or even encouraged them;

f)  to assist, wherever possible, in processes at the national level leading to comprehensive and lasting peace.

2. Calls upon the United Nations and other intergovernmental bodies:

a)  to give urgent attention to developing mechanisms within the United Nations framework for resolving internal conflicts;

b)  to intensify its work on the draft Declaration on the Rights of Persons belonging to National or Ethnic, Religious or Linguistic Minority Groups, and to promote efforts for the protection of minority rights;

c)  to monitor and limit the supply or sale of arms, as well as financial and other assistance by outside powers to warring parties in internal conflicts.

# 5.6. STATEMENT ON THE PACIFIC

1. As the assembly of the World Council of Churches met for the second time in the region of the Pacific Ocean (Canberra, 1991), its attention was drawn again to the urgency of the manifold issues of the Pacific. Recalling the resolution on the region at the sixth assembly in Vancouver, Canada (1983), the central committee, meeting immediately after the assembly, notes with alarm that the international community has failed to address the critical problems which concern the Pacific.

2. Outside powers are intensifying their exploitation of the region's economic and geopolitical significance. Covering one-third of the earth's surface, the Pacific Ocean provides replacements for raw materials as traditional resources are depleted. The vast distances and sparse population make it a convenient place for testing, dumping of nuclear and industrial waste, storing and disposal of long-range missiles, and weapons of mass destruction such as nuclear, chemical and biological arms. The combination of economic, strategic and military factors has turned the "ocean of peace" into a "nuclear lake" and one of the most militarized regions of the world. The Pacific Ocean has been aptly termed a "playground of the great powers", and these powers show no regard for the spiritual and economic significance of the ocean and land for the Pacific peoples.

3. The peoples of the Pacific islands, in most cases a majority in their own lands, are powerless minorities when faced with the political domination, economic strength and military might of the great powers. One of the poorer regions of the world, the Pacific states are dependent on external aid which is too often inappropriate and elitist for their fragile and exploited economy.

4. The inadequacy of the international response to these serious problems has added to several adverse developments for the peoples of the Pacific. Notable among these are: the beginning of the destruction of chemical weapons and toxic waste on Johnston Atoll; the grave health hazards including the contamination of the aquatic food chain as a result of nuclear and industrial waste pollution across the region; the ecological repercussions of the "greenhouse effect" which threaten the existence especially of low-lying countries; massive drift-net fishing of precious pelagic resources; increasing tourism that benefits primarily external interests, and heightened political instability arising from unjust economic policies, discriminatory statutes denying human rights, political assassinations and coups d'etat.

5. Against this backdrop of turmoil and upheaval, the seventh assembly stands with the peoples of the Pacific and gives thanks to God for the witness of the churches in the Pacific. It expresses its deep gratitude to the Pacific Conference of Churches and the Catholic Bishops' Conference of the Pacific for their leadership in drawing the attention of the South Pacific Forum and the ecumenical community to these developments. In supporting their concerns, the central committee:

a) reaffirms the right of the Pacific people to a nuclear-free and independent Pacific;

b) renews its call to governments and transnational corporations immediately to cease all weapons testing, nuclear or conventional, dumping of nuclear and toxic waste, and calls on the United Nations to take all appropriate measures;

c) urges the respect of the rights of the peoples of the Pacific to have the principal authority for decisions which affect the region;

d) reaffirms its support for greater autonomy and independence for those Pacific island peoples still under colonial domination;

e) reiterates the need for safeguarding indigenous values in the political and socio-economic life of the Pacific societies through the elimination of colonial and neo-colonial structures reflected in the activities of transnational corporations, foreign media and tourism;

f) calls on the World Health Organization and scientific, academic and research institutes to study and monitor the effects of nuclear testing and waste dumping on the sea and the land, and calls on those responsible to take immediate steps to redress and prevent further ill-effects;

g) draws special attention to the disastrous consequences of global warming for the Pacific and urges the international community, as a matter of priority, to adopt concerted counter-measures;

h) asks the Pacific rim countries to involve all Pacific governments and peoples as full and equal partners in all discussions on the region;

i) calls upon WCC member churches to:

  1) continue to study the internal and external factors which contribute to the militarization of their societies;

  2) participate actively in the preparations for the 1992 convention on world climatic change, ensuring that its special significance for the Pacific is taken into account;

  3) encourage all initiatives through advocacy and education to support the aspirations of the Pacific peoples, including raising the issues with their own governments; and

  4) develop solidarity networks with the Pacific islanders and their churches with a view to engaging the international community in addressing systematically and on a sustained basis the challenges of the Pacific today.

# 5.7. STATEMENT ON THE BALTIC STATES AND OTHER REGIONS OF TENSION IN THE SOVIET UNION

The central committee of the World Council of Churches, meeting in Canberra in February 1991 immediately after the seventh assembly, has followed with grave concern the most recent developments in the Baltic states, as well as the conflicts and tensions arising from issues of national, confessional and cultural identity in many parts of the Soviet Union. The central committee brings the following to the attention of the churches for prayer and action:

## 1. The Baltic states

The Committee commends the democratically elected governments of the Baltic states and all those who are determined to avoid violence and pursue non-violent means. It affirms them as they seek just solutions to their vital concerns and take into account in the process the need to respect the integrity and aspirations of all the peoples of the Soviet Union, remembering that decisions taken in the Baltic states have far-reaching effects upon political processes throughout the Soviet Union.

The committee mourns the recent bloodshed and deaths of unarmed civilians in Lithuania and Latvia, and welcomes the enquiry by the Soviet government into the incidents which caused them. It is encouraged by the Soviet government's commitment to the Conference on Security and Cooperation in Europe, and to its Charter of Paris, signed on 21 November 1990, according to which all participating states are to "refrain from the threat or use of force" and to "settle disputes by peaceful means"; it urges them to abide by their commitment in all circumstances.

The central committee appeals therefore to all parties involved to regard the endeavour of the Baltic peoples to gain self-determination as part of the process of achieving lasting peace and reconciliation through new relationships in Europe, where basic human rights can be guaranteed, including the rights of the minorities, and where the integrity of every human person is respected; and it calls upon member churches:

a) to maintain their commitment to and support for peaceful processes in the pursuit of democracy, human rights and self-determination in the Baltic states, acknowledging the aspirations for independence;

b) to remember before God, in prayer and worship, the leaders of church and government in the Soviet Union;

c) to render every possible assistance, both material and spiritual, to the Baltic churches, especially taking into account the pastoral needs of those who refuse military service on conscientious grounds;

d) to continue to offer prayers for the people of the Baltic states as they strive for peace.

## 2. West Ukraine

Changes in legislation in the Soviet Union over the recent period have meant welcome new freedoms for Christian communities previously denied full expression of their faith. However, one disturbing result in West Ukraine arising from these developments has been the increasing confrontation between local Orthodox congregations and Catholics of the Eastern rite (Uniates). In many instances, these confrontations have led to violent clashes, and the forcible occupation by Uniates of churches formerly used as places of worship by Orthodox congregations.

Such actions, often occurring with the apparent acquiescence of the Uniate hierarchy and of the local authorities, are not only fomenting community strife and hatred, but are also hindering the proper exercise of ministry.

In expressing its profound concern, the central committee of the World Council of Churches calls upon all the parties concerned at all levels:

— to seek ways of resolving their differences by engaging in patient negotiation in a spirit of reconciliation, mutual respect and Christian love;

and calls upon the member churches:

— to pray for the leaders and people of both the Orthodox and Uniate communities in West Ukraine, that they may seek and find peaceful solutions to their difficulties, remembering that each is engaged in a dialogue leading to the recognition of the other as part of the body of Christ.

### 3. Armenia — Karabagh

The central committee expresses its concern about the worsening situation in Karabagh. The Armenian people of Karabagh have been victims of discrimination, intimidation and violence. There is continuing tension between the republics of Azerbaijan and Armenia over the region of Karabagh, historically part of Armenia.

The WCC, through statements and publications, has drawn the attention of the churches, the public and the governments to this matter.

The committee therefore appeals to all parties involved to seek ways to resolve the conflicts in the region through peaceful means.

The committee especially appeals to the leaders of the Soviet Union:

— to continue efforts to undertake peaceful steps to safeguard legitimate religious, cultural and national interests, including the right to self-determination of the Armenian people of Karabagh;

— to take steps to ensure that the human rights of all people in the region are protected.

The committee calls upon all member churches to continue to be faithful in prayer for the Armenian people as well as all people in the region as they strive for both justice and peace.

## 4. Georgia

The central committee is also concerned about the situation in Georgia where inter-ethnic tensions and conflicts in different parts of the country continue to cause suffering to the people. It supports the right of the Georgian people to self-determination, acknowledging the aspirations for independent development.

The committee appeals to all parties concerned:

— to find ways to resolve the present conflicts in a peaceful manner and through negotiations;

— to safeguard and promote human rights of all people in the region. The committee calls upon member churches to uphold in intercession all the people of Georgia and the church in Georgia at this difficult time.

# 5.8. APPEAL ON SRI LANKA

1. The central committee of the World Council of Churches, meeting in Canberra immediately after the seventh assembly (February 1991), expresses its profound concern and distress over the situation in Sri Lanka, in particular in the North and East, and in the South, rent apart by multi-faceted conflicts. The continuing violence — leading to widespread destruction, deaths and disappearances, ever-increasing numbers of refugees both inside and outside Sri Lanka, the erosion of trust and the breakdown of the country's social fabric — gives cause for grave concern.

2. The committee addresses an urgent call to the government of Sri Lanka and to all those engaged in these conflicts to bring to a halt all acts of violence. It especially appeals to the Sri Lankan government to stop immediately the bombing and strafing in the Jaffna peninsula. It urges all parties once again to seek, through peaceful negotiation, just and lasting solutions to long-standing problems. It calls upon them to reject all divisive appeals to ethnic prejudice and intolerance, and instead to explore creative ways of healing the wounds of conflict, of establishing trust and of building true multi-ethnic community based on genuine equality.

3. The commitee calls upon the member churches to be constant in prayer for all the suffering people of Sri Lanka, including those who have

taken refuge in India or other countries, and to offer them all possible humanitarian assistance.

4. It commends in particular the Christian community of Sri Lanka to the prayers of the member churches as they strive to be bearers of hope and unity in their divided land.

# 5.9. APPEAL ON EL SALVADOR

1. The churches in El Salvador have repeatedly and urgently called the attention of the worldwide ecumenical community to the suffering of the Salvadorean people under the ravages of ten years of civil war. Religious communities have bound up wounds, visited the prisoners and cried out for peace, while they themselves have been persecuted, attacked, and even suffered martyrdom for their faithful witness to the truth. The World Council of Churches has on numerous occasions expressed solidarity with our Salvadorean sisters and brothers, intervening with the authorities on their behalf, advocating their cause, paying pastoral visits, and urging the churches, governments and the United Nations and other intergovernmental organizations to attend to their plight.

2. Through its member churches in El Salvador, the WCC follows with great hope the efforts being made by the government of El Salvador and the Farabundo Marti National Liberation Front (FMLN) to negotiate terms for a cessation of armed conflict and to engage in a political process which could lead to lasting peace in the nation. Despite the agreements reached thus far on respect for human rights, fundamental guarantees of individual liberty and the integrity of the human person continue to be violated.

3. Conscious of the deep-rooted social and economic inequalities which lie behind the conflict, but also of the vast wellspring of human resources working for justice among Salvadorean civic and non-governmental organizations, the central committee of the World Council of Churches, meeting in Canberra immediately after the seventh assembly (February 1991):

a) commends and encourages the churches of El Salvador in their continuing efforts to provide humanitarian assistance and pastoral care, to defend and promote basic human rights, and to mobilize their nation's civil and social forces in the quest for lasting peace; and expresses unwavering support to the churches which persevere in their courageous witness for justice in spite of continuous persecution;

b) calls urgently upon all parties to the armed conflict to end the war;

c) offers its full support for the negotiations now being conducted under United Nations auspices;

d) appeals earnestly to the government of El Salvador, the armed forces and the Farabundo Marti National Liberation Front to respect the agreed conditions for holding free and fair elections in March 1991, and to intensify their efforts to reach further agreements which reflect the profound hopes for justice expressed by Salvadorean civil and grassroots communities, particularly those expressed by the permanent committee of the national debate for peace;

e) invites all governments, especially that of the United States of America, to support the prompt and effective demilitarization of the Central American region, and particularly of El Salvador, in accordance with the Esquipulas II Agreement, by stopping the supply of arms and military aid which is inimical to the process of democratization;

f) reiterates the appeals of the churches to the government of El Salvador to establish a system of justice capable of protecting the human rights of all citizens, and to show its good faith by completing full investigations of the murders of Archbishop Romero and many other religious and lay leaders, and by bringing all those responsible to trial;

g) reaffirms its strong support for the churches and social movements in El Salvador as they work to build peace among the poorest of the poor, witnessing to the creative power of the Spirit to bring unity, love, reconciliation and dignity for all.

## 5.10. FOR INFORMATION

*Notes regarding actions on proposals for public issues received from assembly delegates*

1. *Public statements / appeals* on the Baltic States, West Ukraine, Armenia-Karabagh, Sri Lanka and El Salvador.

2. *Global warming and related environmental problems* – Message from the officers of the central committee to concerned UN bodies. This issue is highlighted in the report of section I.

3. *Anti-semitism* – Letter from the general secretary to the member churches dated 8 August 1990.

4. *Debt crisis and other economic issues* – to be dealt with through the Commission on the Churches' Participation in Development which is preparing a major statement for the central committee in September 1991.

5. *East Timor* – Officers of the central committee to follow up the issue in consultation with churches concerned.

6. *Aids* – Major issue addressed by several WCC sub-units. Information from the Christian Medical Commission.

7. *Death penalty* – Major policy statement by the central committee, Geneva, March 1990.

8. *Cyprus* – Referred to in the statement on "The Gulf War, the Middle East and the Threat to World Peace".

9. *Drug crisis* – Being dealt with in ongoing programmes.

10. *Albania* – The central committee in March 1990 expressed its concern on the situation in Albania. While some worship services have recently been allowed, the constitutional provision prohibiting religion has not been changed. Recommended: statement by the officers of the WCC calling for the support of member churches to ensure religious freedom in Albania; the General Secretariat and the Commission of the Churches on International Affairs to pursue the matter in cooperation with the Conference of European Churches.

11. *Romania, with special reference to ethnic minorities* – Statement on the issue made by central committee, Geneva, March 1990. The Conference of European Churches, in cooperation with the WCC, has initiated a process of conversations and discussions among the various churches and different ethnic communities in Romania. The WCC should continue to support this.

12. *UN Conference on Environment and development* – Message from the officers of the WCC to the preparatory committee of the conference assuring support and participation in the preparations for this significant event.

# 6. The Report of the Seventh Assembly

## 6.1. INTRODUCTION

As noted in 3.1, reports from each of the four sections were "received" by the assembly. Comments from the plenary discussions have been appended to the section reports, but these reports were not revised on the basis of the discussions or formally "adopted" by the assembly. Instead, a "report" integrating the work of the sections was produced by one of the nine committees and presented to the full assembly for adoption. WCC assemblies have always prepared "messages" to the churches, but this is the first time that an assembly has produced such an integrated report.

The report was presented by committee co-moderators, Ms Khushnud Azariah (United, Pakistan) and Dr Paul Crow (Disciples, USA). The text, said Ms Azariah, attempts to capture the spirit of the assembly and to identify major issues that have surfaced in the sections. It is not a consensus document. Attention is called to a number of issues that remain unresolved.

Unfortunately, discussion of the report did not begin until past the time when the assembly was to have adjourned. Several brief suggestions for revision were offered. The committee accepted all but one — a proposal to insert a paragraph urging churches to adopt inclusive language with reference to both humanity and God. The ecumenical movement is still struggling with the appropriate use of such language, said Dr Crow. The proposed paragraph assumed a level of agreement that simply does not exist at this time.

The report was adopted in substance and referred to the central committee for final editing in response to the plenary discussion. The referral was necessary since there was no opportunity for the revised report to be returned to the assembly.

## 6.2. REPORT OF THE REPORT COMMITTEE

1. "Come, Holy Spirit — Renew the Whole Creation!" With this prayer on their hearts Christians from around the world gathered 7-20 February 1991 in Canberra, Australia, for the seventh assembly of the World Council of Churches. This southern "Land of the Spirit"[1] — a land of stark beauty, where the air is filled with the sharp cries of birds and the pungent smell of eucalyptus leaves — formed the background to this new stage of the churches' search for visible unity, for words of prophecy and wisdom, and for common witness and service to the world.

2. We met at a pivotal point in history, a time of disappointed visions of peace, of wars and rumours of wars, of threats to planet earth and to all the creatures which it bears. We were sustained by a deep hope in the renewing energy of the Holy Spirit. We confessed the Holy Spirit as one with the Father and with Christ, undivided, indivisible, embracing the whole created order within its life-giving, reconciling and redemptive love. Yet we recognized, too, the need for discernment and the danger of speaking too easily and quickly about the presence of the Spirit, of identifying the Spirit with our own priorities and programmes. We were challenged to submit all that we are and all that we do to the Spirit's purifying judgment, waiting for the Spirit to reveal all truth.

3. This assembly as those before it was shaped by the context in which it met. Through the presence and testimony of the original inhabitants of this land we learned of their history, suffering and hope for a future marked by the full recognition of their unique identity and dignity. We learned of serious efforts towards this end by both the church and the wider society, but recognize that much remains to be done. There were moving moments of reconciliation when Aboriginal Christians invited non-Aboriginal Australians to join in working for a just society, and when at the celebration of the Lima liturgy officers of the World Council of Churches and Aboriginal Christians shared the eucharist together.

4. Our life and work were warmly supported by the Australian churches, and for many a high point of the assembly will remain the dramatic presentation "Under the Southern Cross" which presented the vitality and diversity of Australian culture and the important role which the churches play within it. There were many cherished chances to meet

---

[1] From the title of a book written in preparation for the assembly on the Australian religious experience.

Australian Christians, and many participants took the opportunity to experience the worship and wider life of a local church. For all the care shown and work done on our behalf, we are profoundly grateful. We register our deep gratitude also for the presentation made to the assembly by the prime minister of Australia, and for the cooperation and support extended by the civil authorities of this land.

5. We were nurtured in this assembly by a rich worship life both solemn and festive, and by Bible study which drew us together in reflection on the theme and sub-themes. In prayer and praise of the Triune God, in confession together of the faith, and in common reflection upon the scriptures, we experienced the unity which is already ours in the Spirit. We met with gratitude and joy many Christians from diverse confessions and cultures, forging and renewing bonds of friendship and affection.

6. The sixth assembly in Vancouver in 1983 had envisioned the churches growing more and more into Jesus Christ; at Canberra they were called to grow in their relations one with another, to grow into a deeper communion in faith and life. This requires bringing cherished traditions and convictions to the discussion, listening and learning from one another, and worshipping and working together. It may require that we offer — or admit that we need to receive — a costly forgiveness.

7. The concern for a speedy end to the conflict in the Persian Gulf, and a just resolution of the situation there, was constantly on our minds. There were differences of opinion as to how this should be achieved, but we were united in our anguish for all who suffer and resolute in our prayer and witness for peace.

8. The theme of gospel and culture arose with new force as we heard how concepts and images from particular cultures are being used as vehicles for Christian truth. We affirm that the church is called to communicate the gospel message intended for all humankind so that it may be heard, understood and accepted in all cultures. Such handing on of God's truth requires faithfulness to the apostolic faith of the church, creative application of the gospel to contemporary issues and situations, and self-criticism of efforts to communicate the gospel in fresh ways. We continue to search for a common understanding of how to live out these criteria in different contexts.

9. This more than any previous assembly sought to embrace the full diversity of God's people. There was serious commitment to sharing leadership among women and men, young and old, ordained and lay. Strenuous efforts were made to bring new persons into the ecumenical

community. This very openness has raised fundamental questions of participation and representation both for the World Council of Churches and for its member churches, questions which must be addressed in the years ahead.

10. There was at this assembly a fresh awareness of our divisions as wounding the body of Christ. For many the greatest pain was felt when we were unable to express fully our communion by sharing the eucharist. It was asked: how may we help overcome the divisions of the world when we cannot even celebrate together our Lord's sacrifice for its salvation? Here and elsewhere we need desperately a mobilizing portrait of visible reconciled life that will hold together an absolute commitment to the unity and the renewal of the church and an absolute commitment to the reconciliation of God's world — and that will show us the inseparable relation between them.

11. In these and other areas we are practising a costly growing together. Both hurting and healing are held within the circle of Christian community, that healing may prevail. Holding fast to one another, bearing the cost of our divisions, we seek from the Spirit of unity the gift of reconciliation and renewal.

\* \* \*

12. The heart of the assembly was the work done in its four sections, exploring aspects of the theme relating to creation, to truth and freedom, to unity and reconciliation, and to transformation and renewal. Several issues and questions emerged in more than one section; these included the nature and role of the church, the activity of the Holy Spirit, the relation of the gospel to other cultures, the search for a renewed community of women and men, and the transformation of the international economic order.

### Section I: Giver of Life — Sustain Your Creation!

"In the beginning God created the heavens and the earth... And God saw everything that God had made, and behold, it was very good" (Gen. 1:1,31).

13. The universe in all its beauty and grandeur manifests the glory of the Triune God who is the source of all life. All things have been made in Christ, in whom God's creation comes to fulfilment. The divine presence of the Spirit in creation binds us as human beings together with all created life. We are accountable before God in and to the community of life, so

that we understand ourselves as servants, stewards and trustees of the creation. We are called to approach creation in humility, with reverence, respect and compassion, and to work for the mending and healing of creation as a foretaste and pointer to the final gathering up of all things in Christ (cf. Eph. 1:10).

14. The earth was created by God out of nothing in a pure and simple act of love, and the Spirit has never ceased to sustain it. Yet our earth is in grave peril, the very creation groaning and travailing in all its parts (Rom. 8:22). This is a "sign of the times", calling us to return to God and to ask the Spirit to re-orient our lives. Through misunderstanding — and sometimes through deliberate choice — Christians have participated in the destruction of nature, and this requires our repentance. We are called to commit ourselves anew to living as a community which respects and cares for creation.

## *The theology of creation: a challenge for our time*

15. What is our place as human beings in the natural order? The earth itself, this little watery speck in space, is about 4.5 billion years old. Life began about 3.4 billion years ago. We ourselves came on the scene some 80,000 years ago, just yesterday in the twinkling of the Creator's eye. It is shocking and frightening for us that the human species has been able to threaten the very foundations of life on our planet in only about 200 years since modern industrialization began. So where do we belong in the Creator's purpose?

16. The Christian scriptures testify that God is the Creator of all, and that all that was created "was very good" (Gen. 1:31; cf. 1 Tim. 4:4). God's Spirit continually sustains and renews the earth (Ps. 104:30). Humanity is both part of the created world and charged to be God's steward of the created world (Gen. 1:26-27, 2:7). We are charged to "keep" the earth and to "serve" it (Gen. 2:15), in an attitude of that blessed meekness which will inherit the earth.

17. Human sin has broken the covenants which God has made and subjected the creation to distortion, disruption and disintegration — to "futility" (Rom. 8:20). In our own day we have brought the earth to the brink of destruction. But we confess that the redemptive work of Christ was the renewal not only of human life, but of the whole cosmos. Thus we confidently expect that the covenant promises for the earth's wholeness will be fulfilled, that in Christ "the creation itself will be set free from its bondage to decay and will obtain the glorious freedom of the children of God" (Rom. 8:21).

18. The sacramental Christian perspective influences our approach to the creation; we confess that "the earth is the Lord's and all that is in it, the world, and those who live in it" (Ps. 24:1). In the whole of the Christian life we take up the created things of this world and offer them to God for sanctification and transfiguration so that they might manifest the kingdom, where God's will is done and the creation glorifies God forever.

19. We agree that some past understandings have led to domination, to forms of control which have been destructive of life, and to views of nature which regard it as subject to human "ownership" and unqualified manipulation. Many streams of the tradition have misunderstood human "dominion" (Gen. 1:28) as exploitation, and God's transcendence as absence. The more theology stressed God's absolute trancendence and distance from the material sphere, the more the earth was viewed as an "unspiritual" reality, as merely the object of human exploitation. While we repudiate these consequences of some theologies of creation, we also know that they are closely related to ways of life which have received theological sanction and support.

20. We are one in our confession of the Holy Spirit as the Source and Giver of Life, and have rejoiced in exploring together at this assembly the presence and the power of the Spirit. But much remains to be explored. How do we understand the relationship between the presence of the Spirit and "sustainability", and indeed the meaning of that word and relationship for our common life? These are life and death questions for humanity and for the planet as a whole.

21. Our exploration of a Spirit-centred theology of creation has led us to deeper understanding. The heritage of indigenous peoples and non-Western cultures, especially those who have retained their spiritualⁱty of the land, offers new insights for all. Worldwide, women and the land have often been seen and treated in parallel ways. The Spirit works to heal the wounds of both. Women's experience is invaluable in helping us to understand and to heal our relationships with the earth and with each other. The poor, who invariably suffer first and most from a degraded environment, also teach us things we must know for an adequate theology of creation. In a world so intimately interconnected, their struggles are the critical starting point for all. The community of scientists is also indispensable, for they carry the single most powerful set of tools for our understanding nature and nature's fragility in the face of human onslaught. And beyond this, our sense of the mystery of life and our awe and wonder at the Creator's handiwork is deepened by what we learn

from science. We thank God for all these sources of insight, wisdom and understanding.

22. Opinion is divided, however, on how to relate inherited faith claims to the new cultural perspectives of emerging Christian voices, on how to relate Christian accounts of creation to creation stories from other traditions, and on how to relate faith to science in the continuing dialogue on creation.

23. Surely the Spirit blows where it wills. We hope that the WCC as a whole will join our plea to stand in its refreshing breezes, even as we carry on the necessary task of discerning together the spirits to see if they are of God. There are new perspectives and new partners in today's world. We cannot turn our back on them.

*Towards an ethic of economy and ecology*

24. In the institutions of the sabbath, the sabbatical year and the jubilee year, the Bible has shown us how to reconcile economics and ecology, how to recreate people and society (Ex. 23, Lev. 25). Effective economics and stewardship of the earth's resources must be seen together. Law and mercy, discipline and social justice complement one another.

25. Reducing the destructive human domination over creation calls for a new, inclusive experience of community and sharing. The biblical vision is of an intimate and unbreakable relationship between development, economy and ecology. This vision is dimmed when progress is seen as the production and consumption of more and more material things, while development is equated with growth. The vision vanishes when wealth is cut off from the needs of the poor, and the world is divided between North and South, industrialized and non-industrialized nations. Exploitation of nation by nation, of people by companies, and of those who have only the work of their hands to offer by those who have access to powerful economic resources, leads inevitably to conflict. The unfair distribution of resources brings starvation to our neighbours, while destroying the integrity of our souls. In efforts to increase the gross *national* product, the gross *natural* product is diminished.

26. Any policy or action that threatens the sustainability of creation needs to be questioned. We cannot ignore the burden of debts that can never be repaid, bio-technologies through which human beings usurp powers that belong to the Creator, or the fact that the root causes of population growth lie largely in the poverty and lack of social security still prevailing in two-thirds of our world. In facing these and other

crucial issues we need the dynamic power of the Spirit which integrates faith and life, worship and action to overcome our fear of change.

27. The free-market economy facilitates rapid response to needs expressed in financial terms. But markets and prices do not possess any inherent morality. The vast and shameful arms trade illustrates clearly the immorality of our world economic order; it is one of the root causes of the Gulf war. The international ecumenical movement has for years criticized the lack of economic democracy, social injustice, and the stimulation of human greed. But flagrant international inequality in the distribution of income, knowledge, power and wealth persists. Acquisitive materialism has become the dominant ideology of our day. The irresponsible exploitation of the created world continues. Changes will come only by active opposition and informed and responsible social pressure. We are now more than ever aware that the market economy is in need of reform, and to that end we suggest the following means:

28. *Local self-empowerment:* Around the world we see that small groups of people of all races and classes, filled with courage and hope, can make a difference. These small local communities try to live against the trends of an acquisitive society in which individual greed and social and ecological exploitation predominate. Those forms of local direct action often bring a new quality of life based not primarily on acquiring goods, but on living in right relation with all of creation. A similar change in values is even more necessary on the part of those who enjoy more privileged life-styles.

29. *Government control:* Today the limits of bureaucratic control are easily seen. Legislation is effective only if it is part of a full process of social change, applied within a properly functioning legal system. In many countries more could be done to promote the effectiveness and democratic character of governmental control. Without both political and economic democracy there will be no genuine respect for creation. The effective investigation, public prosecution and punishment of ecological crimes is a matter of urgent concern.

30. *Rethinking economics:* We should not lose sight of how the world community must be accountable to the whole creation, and how it is responsible for the economic and ecological choices to which the world system of trade leads. Market prices rarely reflect real long-term scarcities. Prices should reflect the need to conserve and to regenerate what nature offers; a market economy price is based on demand and supply, which are both being calculated on a very narrow, short-term basis. Non-

material needs receive no price; hence they are often not satisfied through consumption, but only increased.

31. What we need, therefore, is a new concept of value, one based not on money and exchange but rather on *sustainability* and *use*. We need likewise a new concept of development as opposed to simple growth, a development which results in a self-sustaining whole. What is "just" and "right", then, must be found in social, biological, and physical relationships involving humanity and the earth. Such a true development focuses on the level of the eco-system as a whole.

32. *A universal declaration on human obligations towards nature:* The existing Universal Declaration of Human Rights serves as a moral standard for those charged with the responsibility of exercising power. In June 1992, the second United Nations Conference on Environment and Development that will take place in Brazil will present a plan for an "earth charter". It would comprise an international agreement on the obligations and responsibilities of governments to the global environment and to future generations. We think that the charter should include a section on the obligations of industrial and agricultural producers of goods and services, with special reference to global corporations, and a section on the responsibilities of consumers. There should be judicial mechanisms for the implementation of the charter from international to local levels. And an international organization, comparable to Amnesty International, should be formed to expose violations of the charter and to mobilize the public conscience. Collective action by consumers would be very helpful to this end.

33. *Education:* We need to educate ourselves, each other and our children in the new ecological values and responsibilities. Such learning should take place in the home, school, church and work place. And beyond this, we need a spirituality which will enable us to resist the forces which treat us only as acquisitive, exploiting creatures. We need to catch the biblical vision of development, ecology and social justice. Then we must go out into the world and, as a new type of missionary, challenge every economic, social and political structure which does not conform to the standards of the gospel.

## *The church: for the life of all creation*

34. The church, a redeemed community which is a sign of the "new creation" in Christ, is called by God to a crucial role in the renewal of creation. Empowered by the Spirit, Christians are called to repent of their misuse and abuse of nature and to reflect critically upon the ways of

understanding the Bible, and the theological systems which have been used to justify such abuse.

35. A new appreciation of the theology of creation and a fresh awareness of Christian responsibility towards all of creation may deepen the faith, and enrich the life and work, of the church.

## Section II: Spirit of Truth — Set us Free!

"For freedom Christ has set us free... For you were called to freedom, brothers and sisters..." (Gal. 5:1,13).

### Christian witness to the liberating Spirit of God

36. Freedom is a gift of the Holy Spirit. By the action of the Spirit in Christ men and women are set free from sin and from captivity to the principalities and powers of this world, from the forces of evil which tempt all human beings to do injustice to others. The Holy Spirit frees us, opens us to new possibilities, and calls us to work for the freedom of others.

37. "When the Spirit of Truth comes he will guide you into all truth" (John 16:13). The Spirit of Truth in bearing witness to Jesus Christ convinces the world of sin. Sin has brought division, discord and confusion into the created universe. Truth is often not told and is often hard to tell; but we need to know the truth before we can be truly free. The Spirit of Truth re-establishes and restores the integrity of both persons and communities. By the Spirit we are able to know the truth and this sets us free to live a life based on love, which resists unjust dominations of all kinds.

38. As individuals and as churches we have at times forgotten our Christian vocation to witness to the gospel of freedom and truth. The Holy Spirit calls us to recognize our responsibilities for the divisions in the church and in the world and to follow the path of repentance. *Metanoia* and *te' shuvah*, the biblical terms for repentance, mean a radical change of mind, a transformation. Such repentance is the way leading to reconciliation, sanctification, and salvation in Christ.

39. The Spirit of freedom and truth moves us to witness to the justice of the kingdom of God and to resist injustice in the world. We manifest the life of the Spirit by striving for the release of those who are captive to sin and by standing with the oppressed in their struggles for liberation, justice and peace. Liberated by the Spirit we are empowered to understand the world from the perspective of the poor and vulnerable and to give ourselves to mission, service and the sharing of our resources.

40. Our theological perspective convinces us that we need to affirm the vision of an inhabited world *(oikoumene)* based on values which promote life for all. As Christians we seek a world of social and economic justice. We believe that the WCC and its member churches can witness to the liberating Spirit of God by joining their efforts with those of national and international organizations which strive for justice and freedom, and against the abuse of human rights. We believe that the gospel calls Christians to be active in the promotion and defence of human rights: the rights of women and children, the rights of minorities, the rights of those oppressed by racism and economic injustice. We are especially concerned about the human rights of young people who so often suffer disproportionately the effects of war, poverty, racism, unemployment, drugs and other social problems.

## Towards a world in which justice prevails

41. Through the six preceding assemblies the World Council of Churches has called attention to the need to renew the international economic order. The ecumenical process on Justice, Peace and the Integrity of Creation (JPIC) confirmed the view that prevailing models of economic growth and world trade do not create conditions for a just and sustainable world society but rather destroy the ecological systems of the world, provoke massive migrations and lead to wars. The organization of the international market in ways which would promote life and justice for all remains a major challenge. We look for a review leading to more accountable and just economic and monetary structures, within the jurisdiction of the United Nations and the International Court of Justice. The creation of a just world economic order may require the creation of new international organizations.

42. Closely linked to the present economic order and the organization of the international market is the ongoing debt crisis which, since the end of the 1970s, has meant the impoverishment of the most deeply-indebted nations of Africa, Asia, the Caribbean, Latin America, and the Pacific. The debt crisis also threatens the economic prospects of the former "socialist" nations of Eastern Europe and is introducing tensions, financial instability and economic recession in North America, Western Europe and Japan. In this very serious situation the WCC and its member churches are called to share their energies and resources with those who suffer the effects of the world economic system. The critical reformulation of this system must be one of our priorities.

43. As Christians we seek a world of social and economic justice. This includes the empowerment of the victims of injustice and respect and care for those who are vulnerable, oppressed and dispossessed. The networks of concern that churches and Christian communities can build together and with other organizations can play a positive role in this process.

44. Racism, one of the terrible sins of humankind, is incompatible with the gospel of Christ. It is not simply exercised through personal prejudice but is also embodied in the structures and institutions of society. When members of one race or group seek to dominate those of another they are not truly free but are enslaved by their own fear and desire for control. Being oppressed and being an oppressor are both spiritually disabling. We see the need for both individual repentance of the sin of racism and for changes to abolish structural and institutional racism. The liberating voice of the Spirit calls us to embrace all our sisters and brothers in love and with justice.

45. Some specific aspects of racism which concern us are: the suffering of the black diaspora within predominantly white societies, the increased racial tensions occurring as the result of massive migration of peoples, and the disturbing currents of racism in many regional conflicts, including the present conflict in the Middle East. We need also to recognize the particular vulnerability of women and children, who often suffer double discrimination.

46. The ethnicity which is newly emerging in Europe poses another challenge to our churches as ethnic groups are often defined in religious terms as well as by language and origin. Christianity runs the risk of being a divisive rather than a unifying force within the new political situations, and here dialogue with the Roman Catholic Church is essential.

47. At this assembly in Australia we are particularly conscious of the struggles of our Aboriginal brothers and sisters for a recognition of their history, culture, spirituality and land rights. We affirm the efforts towards justice and reconciliation made by some churches and other groups. We support all those who seek justice for indigenous peoples in Australia and in other countries.

48. The Spirit of truth calls us to know and to tell the truth about our histories and to repent of racism in the past as well as in the present. Anniversaries, such as the 500th anniversary of the arrival of Columbus in the Americas in 1992, are a particular opportunity for churches to reflect soberly on their history in the light of the gospel, and to consider what actions are appropriate to achieve reconciliation and justice.

49. Communication in the light and power of the Spirit supports and sustains the building of a community of justice and equips us to challenge the powers which are opposed to the Spirit of truth. Our communication as Christians must be prophetic, serving the cause of justice, peace, and the integrity of creation. We are to communicate with one another in love, speaking the truth and listening to hear what is truly being said, rather than what we want to hear.

50. The mass media are powerful means of control, where the truth is often not told and we are unable to exercise an informed and free judgment. Control may be exercised by governments, the market, or the dominant culture. We are specially concerned about the influence on children of the media's promotion of violence, pornography and obscenity. Churches can seek ways to educate people to be discerning listeners, viewers and readers and to develop people's participation in communication. We encourage our churches to find ways to develop communications for liberation, to promote good interpersonal communication and the telling of the stories of the people. We encourage individual Christians who work in the field of communications to exercise their Christian witness in the work-place.

51. The search for lasting peace and meaningful security presents different challenges in the various regions of the world. The Seoul covenant (from the JPIC process) with its four interlocking elements of protection of the environment, alleviation of debts, demilitarization of international relations and the rejection of racism, provides us with a helpful framework for our Christian commitment to peace with justice.

52. We affirm the roles of the United Nations and the International Court of Justice, and believe that these and other constructive international instruments for peace and security need to be developed and strengthened.

53. Churches are called to serve as examples of peace-making, not least by making peace among themselves. They must resist the use of religious factors to cause or exacerbate conflict, and we urge that they strengthen their regional solidarity in work for peace. The World Council of Churches could play a greater role in education for peace and in working for reconciliation in situations of conflict between churches and states.

54. The relationship between men and women is fundamental to the human condition although there are major cultural differences in the expression of such relationships. Sexual difference is a gift of God in creation but our human societies are often distorted by sexism (that is,

discrimination based on gender). Specific aspects of sexism which concern us are the economic injustice experienced by many women and the growing phenomenon of the feminization of poverty (in other words the fact that increasingly the poor are women). In the work-place women are not only frequently underpaid and exploited but also are often forced to participate on male terms, which take little notice of their special needs and responsibilities. At work, at home and in society generally it is common for women and children to be the victims of male violence.

55. The Ecumenical Decade of the Churches in Solidarity with Women is an urgent call to the churches to give creative support to women's movements and groups which challenge oppressive structures in the global community and in the local community and church. The form which solidarity with women will take depends very much on local circumstances and on the needs and aspirations of women themselves, but we are sure that the full participation of women in our churches and societies will encourage the renewal of community.

56. As we affirm that "in Christ there is neither male nor female" (Gal. 3:28) we call on Christian communities and families to strive for equality in relationships, for mutual respect, a sharing of tasks and responsibilities and new models of caring and sharing. We acknowledge that churches differ in their approaches to the question of the ordination of women. Some see it as an issue of justice while others do not. In this situation we urge mutual respect for the other's position in the spirit of love and understanding.

57. Facing situations of tyranny and oppression, striving for justice and peace, we often tend to lose heart and hope. As Paul exhorts the Galatian Christians not to give in to the desires of human nature, so we are called to stand fast in the freedom of Christ, to be obedient to the truth, and to walk by the Spirit. All this is made possible by the power of the Holy Spirit.

## Section III: Spirit of Unity — Reconcile Your People!

"Through Christ God reconciled us to himself and gave us the ministry of reconciliation" (2 Cor. 5:18).

58. Christians see truth in different ways and yet at the same time are united in the power of the Holy Spirit. Our rich diversity of insights and practices is a gift of the Holy Spirit. Sadly all too often diversity is a cause of division even in the life of the church. Yet as members of the body of Christ we are already united by our common baptism; guided by the Holy Spirit, we are drawn into a koinonia (communion) rooted in the giving

and receiving life of the Holy Trinity. What we work towards is unity of faith, life and witness. In this process it will be especially important to face up to the divisions which prevent us from sharing the eucharist together, and make it impossible for churches to recognize each other's ministries.

59. Christians are even more deeply divided from people of other faiths and ideologies, even though we share a common humanity and face common challenges and tasks. There are also deep divisions within and between other living faiths and ideologies.

60. From the depth and pain of our divisions we cry "Spirit of unity — reconcile your people". Reconciliation happens when there is honest recognition of the actual sin committed against our neighbour and when practical restitution has been made for it. When costly repentance meets costly forgiveness the Holy Spirit can lead us into community (koinonia).

*Christian community as koinonia in the Spirit*

61. In developing perspectives on ecclesiology, in discussing the nature and mission of the church, the idea of koinonia can be most helpful. This is so particularly as we reflect upon the identity of our own church in relation to ecumenical developments such as the text *Baptism, Eucharist and Ministry (BEM),* which has received encouraging responses from so many churches. Koinonia in the Holy Spirit is based on sharing in the life of the Trinitarian God and is expressed by sharing life within the community. It becomes possible through reconciliation with God and with one another in the power of the Holy Spirit.

62. Unity and diversity are twin elements in Christian koinonia, but that diversity must have its limits. For example, amidst all diversity the confession must be maintained of Jesus Christ as God and Saviour, the same yesterday, today and forever. And a diversity that divides and excludes, thus destroying the life of the body of Christ, is unacceptable.

63. The gospel finds its historical expression in many cultures, which are transformed, renewed and corrected by it. Though national and ethnic identities are legitimate they should not be allowed to impair the unity of the church, or to become masks which shelter un-Christian elements.

64. In reflecting on the relationship between unity and koinonia we find a new vision in the statement entitled "The Unity of the Church as Koinonia: Gift and Calling", which was prepared by the Faith and Order Commission at the invitation in 1987 of the WCC central committee and has been adopted by this assembly.

65. The statement affirms that the purpose of God according to holy scripture is to gather, by the power of the Holy Spirit, the whole of creation under the Lordship of Jesus Christ. The church is the foretaste of this God which is promised for the whole creation. It is called to proclaim reconciliation and to provide healing, to overcome divisions based on race, gender, age, culture or colour and to bring all people into communion with God. It is a sad fact that churches have failed to draw the consequences for their own life from the degree of communion which they have already experienced, and from the agreements already achieved through the ecumenical movement.

66. The unity of the church is envisioned as a koinonia (communion) given and expressed in the common confession of the apostolic faith; a common sacramental life entered by the one baptism and celebrated together in one eucharistic fellowship; a common life in which members and ministries are mutually recognized and reconciled; and a common mission witnessing to the gospel of God's grace to all people and serving the whole of creation. The goal of the search for full communion is realized when all the churches are able to recognize in one another the one, holy, catholic and apostolic church in its fullness. This urges action, for in taking specific steps together the churches express and encourage the enrichment and renewal of Christian life.

67. A true community of women and men is God's gift and promise for humanity, which is created "in God's image" — male and female (Gen. 1:27); and the church, as sign of that which God desires for women and men, is called to embody that community in its own life. Today Christians from many traditions look together for a more complete and authentic community of women and men. We affirm that the domination of women by men does not belong to human community as intended in God's creation (Gen. 1,2) but to the consequences of sin, which distort the community of women and men as well as the relationship between human beings and nature (Gen. 3:16-19). The God who created us as women and men calls us into community. The Christ who identifies with our suffering calls us to become his body. The Spirit who empowers us to witness and serve sends us forth as God's agents, co-workers for a new heaven and a new earth.

## Towards a wider ecumenical community

68. Particularly in this century the world has witnessed the rise and growth of movements which emphasize the Holy Spirit and the gifts of the Holy Spirit (charisms) or, as they themselves like to put it, "baptism

in the Spirit" or "filling with the Spirit". They are not all of the same type but are called charismatic or pentecostal movements and, in Africa, are sometimes identified with African instituted churches.

69. In their emphases on the charisms of the Spirit described in the New Testament and their rediscovery of the ministry of healing, these movements are valid expressions of Christian faith. If seen as based on a reappropriation of the gifts received in baptism they can be integrated into the life of the churches, bringing them many gifts. They may also represent stronger faith and fellowship, increased spontaneity, openness and freedom among worshippers, all of these leading to greater participation in the life of the churches. There are, however, negative implications for the ecumenical movement if "filling with the Spirit" as a "second experience" after baptism is seen as normative for all Christians. Such teaching may be divisive, as may be an over-emphasis on the Holy Spirit as working independently of the Father and the Son.

70. There is often misunderstanding between Pentecostals and Christians of other traditions. Some Pentecostals have rejected the traditional churches in a desire to enliven their own worship; some have rejected the ecumenical movement as a "human" attempt to produce Christian unity, or because of genuine theological differences about the nature of the Christian faith and its expression in the modern world. But others have sought fellowship with Christians outside their boundaries, particularly with evangelicals. They have begun to take an interest in questions of visible church unity; traditional churches have in turn become more open to the spiritual and theological insights that Pentecostals bring. In Latin America, for example, Pentecostals (now the numerically dominant form of Protestantism in the region) take part in the Latin American Council of Churches. Similar dialogue has been taking place in other areas as well. These hopeful signs bode well for future efforts to bring the churches closer together.

*The Christian community in mission*

71. A reconciled and renewed creation is the goal of the church's mission. The vision of God uniting all things in Christ (Eph. 1:10) is the driving force of the church's life of sharing, motivating all efforts to overcome economic inequality and social divisions.

72. Whatever our approach to mission at home or abroad, our mission needs to be "in Christ's way". Wholeness of mission demands a will to break down barriers at every level, and involves the whole people of God in sharing, serving and renewal in a spirit of love and respect. Each

church acting in mission is acting on behalf of the whole body of Christ. At the same time we affirm local ecumenical endeavours in mission. Always we need to remember our original understanding of mission, which is preaching, teaching and healing. It is best done together, and should never divide, alienate or oppress. Our conviction is not hesitant or partial that Jesus Christ through the action of the Holy Spirit is God's saving presence for *all*.

73. Since the church's mission is to reconcile all with God and with one another, sharing can be recognized as part of mission in Christ's way. It includes sharing faith, sharing power, sharing material resources. Such sharing encourages reconciliation. We affirm that what we call "ours" is given by God in love, and is given to be shared. At times sharing offers up and receives emptiness and suffering as well as fullness and joy. There can and must be no barriers to sharing, whether giving or receiving. In this spirit we affirm the WCC "Guidelines for Sharing" as an important means towards common mission and service.

74. The gospel of Jesus Christ must become incarnate in every culture. When Christianity enters any culture there is a mutual encounter, involving both the critique of culture by the gospel and the possibility of the culture questioning our understanding of the gospel. Some of the ways in which the gospel has been imposed on particular cultures call for repentance and healing. In each case we need to ask: Is the church creating tension or promoting reconciliation?

*The Christian community in relation to others*

75. The Holy Spirit works in ways that surpass human understanding. The Bible testifies to God as sovereign of all nations and peoples. God's love and compassion include everyone. We witness to the truth that salvation is in Christ, but we seek also to remain open to other people's expression of truth as they have experienced it.

76. Today in many parts of the world religion has become a divisive force, with religious language and symbols being used to exacerbate conflicts. Ignorance and intolerance make reconciliation difficult. We seek to live in respect and understanding with people of other living faiths, and to this end we need to build mutual trust and a "culture of dialogue". This begins at the local level as we relate to people of other faiths, and take common action especially in promoting justice and peace. The first step is to come to know and to trust each other, telling our stories of faith and sharing mutual concerns. Both the telling and the hearing of faith are crucial in discerning God's will. Dialogue is an authentic form of

Christian witness and ministry. As Christians we affirm the Holy Spirit counselling us to hold fast to the revealed Christ, to keep faith, and to encounter the other's faith.

77. Ideologies may be constructive or destructive; but both types tend to demand absolute loyalty and to ignore the essential ingredient of accountability, thus causing conflict. In recent years this has most strongly affected churches in Marxist-influenced societies. Now we have experienced the collapse of this system; but this is no reason for triumphalism about the free-market system, as we are increasingly confronted with its negative effects throughout the world. We all, as Christians, need to analyze and understand the ideologies under which we live. Some are "hidden" — not openly acknowledged and discussed — yet deeply rooted and influential in society. Among these are wealth and achievement-oriented value systems which ignore human and personal factors. The task of the community of faith is to apply prophetic, biblical values to all ideologies.

78. Ideological trends can be found in fundamentalism and nationalism. We must learn to distinguish between fundamentalism as an approach to biblical hermeneutics and fundamentalism (whether Christian or non-Christian) which is an intolerant ideological imperialism, closed to other approaches and realities. Nationalism is positive when it unites people in the struggle for cultural, religious and political self-determination, but it is negative when used to dominate some and to exclude others. It may be even more oppressive when it contains elements that equate faith with a particular nationality.

## Section IV: Holy Spirit — Transform and Sanctify Us!

"Do not be conformed to this world but be transformed by the renewal of your mind..." (Rom. 12:2)

79. It has been said that spirituality is organizing one's life so as to allow the Holy Spirit room to act. It has to do with setting priorities, with the calendars and rhythms of life which affect how communities and individuals express their spirituality. Different experiences of God's presence through the Holy Spirit in word, in the church and in daily life also determine our understanding of spirituality. We have a spiritual hunger to become what we were through creation and already are in Christ. We long for the freedom which is given through the Holy Spirit.

80. Christian spirituality is rooted in baptism, whereby we are grafted into the death and resurrection of Christ, become members of his body and receive the gifts of the Holy Spirit to lead a life consecrated to the

service of God and God's children. Christian spirituality celebrates God's gifts but, taking up the cross, agonises with Christ for the sake of all God's children: made in the image of God, we are growing into the likeness of Christ (Gen. 1:27, 2 Cor. 3:18; cf. Eph. 4:24). An ecumenical spirituality should be incarnational, here and now, life-giving, rooted in the scriptures and nourished by prayer; it should be communitarian and celebrating, centred around the eucharist. Its source and guide is the action of the Holy Spirit. It is lived and sought in community and for others.

81. The Holy Spirit cannot be understood apart from the life of the Holy Trinity. Proceeding from the Father, the Holy Spirit points to Jesus of Nazareth as the Christ, the Messiah, the Saviour of the world. The Spirit is the power of God, energizing the people of God, corporately and individually, to fulfill their ministry. The Holy Spirit is "holy" by virtue of the very nature of the Holy Trinity. It is distinct from other "spirits" in this world, whether benign or demonic (1 John 4:1-6). The Holy Spirit is gloriously free, unbinding God's people from the structures and strictures of this world. The challenge to God's people is to discover, accept, and live in this freedom. To live in the Holy Spirit is to yield one's life to God, to take spiritual risks; in short, to live by faith.

82. Since Pentecost a visible Christian community of repentant and redeemed believers has been constituted by the work of the Holy Spirit, so that this community may become the fullness of the body of Christ in history, a sign and sacrament of the kingdom of God among the nations. We believe in the church, holy and becoming holy by the work of the Spirit, a place where sanctification and transfiguration really can occur. The church's holiness is experienced as reconciliation, peace and justice, which are to be realized within the life of the community. There are various forms of Christian communities (house churches, prayer groups, base Christian communities and so on) which complement parish life by focusing on particular aspects of the kingdom such as a simpler life-style, a concern for personal or cultural identity or political justice.

## Responding to the Holy Spirit

83. We respond to the Holy Spirit in humility and penitence. The Holy Spirit enables us to empty ourselves, to receive forgiveness, peace and joy and the grace to live for the sake of others. The church, impelled and empowered by the Holy Spirit, is called to proclaim the gospel. We share in mission and evangelism, open and sensitive to the contribution of other churches. Nominally Christian nations in the North need the help of

churches in the South as they seek to relate to large numbers of immigrants and refugees of different faiths and cultures. New religions and alternative forms of spirituality present a further challenge to many of our churches and to the ecumenical movement.

84. Churches need to recover the notion of sacred time, allowing God's time, the *kairos*, to enter the *chronos* of the mundane world, enabling and empowering new visions and fresh opportunities. The Genesis affirmation of God's resting on the seventh day (Gen. 2: 1-3) has built the principle of rest into the very structure of the cosmos. The observance of liturgical times, rites and rhythms supports many kinds of Christian spirituality. The sabbath principle serves as a protection against unlimited activity and unrelenting desire for profit. The sabbath year, coming once in fifty years, was intended to break the spiral by which "the rich become richer and the poor poorer" (cf. Lev. 8:8-17). It is relevant to apply this in the debt-ridden parts of the international community. If debts are not lifted and forgiven, there can be finally no balance, no justice.

85. In a world where misery and despair mark many lives, Christians, by humble perseverance in their work and witness for justice, raise signs of hope in Jesus Christ. The example of the "great cloud of witnesses" kindles and encourages the Christian life of many. The Holy Spirit offers us the precious and vulnerable gift of hope, reinforcing the discipleship of those identifying with the cause of liberation. There is an authentic spirituality maturing in the midst of struggle, nourished by the One who gave himself up for the freedom of others.

86. Throughout history it is the Holy Spirit who has drawn the churches out of isolation and division into unity. The Holy Spirit calls us now to acknowledge the unity which exists among us, and to overcome all confessional barriers in order to be able to share our energies, gifts and ministries on a common spiritual journey towards visible unity. Charismatic renewal movements, women's groups and youth groups sometimes challenge churches to greater openness and press towards the breaking of denominational barriers.

87. As the churches — enabled to initiate dialogue with the help of national, regional and international councils of churches — move towards each other on their ecumenical pilgrimage, the Holy Spirit calls us to repent of past stances and actions and to engage in a process of forgiveness. We need to acknowledge the occasions when our churches have failed to respect the "Lund principle" (1952) that they should act together except where conscience compels them to act separately. For without repentance and forgiveness no "new creation" as reconciled

communities can emerge among and between the churches. The Holy Spirit has been evident in enabling churches to forgive, to reconcile their histories and to come to communion in God in Christ. Two current examples of churches participating in this process are the Eastern and Oriental Orthodox churches, and the Reformed and Mennonite communities.

88. The Holy Spirit has been active in strengthening the relationships between the Roman Catholic Church and national and regional councils of churches. The Basel ecumenical assembly in 1989, organized by a regional council of churches and the regional conference of Roman Catholic Episcopal Conferences, might provide a useful model of cooperation.

89. We need integrity in word and action. Sanctification means a continuous commitment to the life of visible community and a continuous search to overcome the stumbling blocks to full and visible unity.

90. The Holy Spirit, the Giver of Life, continues to breathe life into all creation. As all life emanates from God and ultimately will return to God (Ps. 104), the ethos of holiness requires an attitude towards all that exists as by nature belonging to God. We do not "own" ourselves, our bodies, our lives, the air, the soil: all is given by God.

91. Though inseparably belonging to creation, we are in the world as stewards and as priests of creation. We are endowed with the privilege of offering creation back to its Creator. The church is now challenged to define the relationship of humanity to the rest of creation. Anthropomonism (the idea that human beings are God's only real concern) denies the integrity of the creation. However, sacralizing nature may lead towards pantheism and a denial of the uniqueness of men and women as created in the image of God (Gen. 1:27).

92. The Holy Spirit, giver of life, is at work among all peoples and faiths and throughout the universe. With the sovereign freedom which belongs to God the wind blows wherever it wants. Recognizing this, the church rejoices in being nourished by the ministry of the Holy Spirit through the word and sacraments.

93. Spirits must be discerned. Not every spirit is of the Holy Spirit. The prime criterion for discerning the Holy Spirit is that the Holy Spirit is the Spirit of Christ; it points to the cross and resurrection and witnesses to the Lordship of Christ. The biblical list of "fruits" of the Spirit, including love, joy and peace, is another criterion to be applied (Gal. 5:22). These criteria should be remembered in our encounters with the often-profound spirituality of other religions.

*The people of God: transformed and transforming*

94. The church is the entire people *(laos)* of God, empowered by the Holy Spirit. As the laity of the church, whether women or men, young or old, live in the world they are ambassadors of the Holy Spirit, transforming society by their witness and service. They need — but do not always receive — all the support the church can give.

95. For many it is especially the family that provides an appropriate space and ethos for spiritual development. We need to explore diverse models of family spirituality and to find appropriate structures for prayer life and spiritual formation.

96. The church is called to demonstrate God's all-inclusive love. In practice this is often difficult. In the fellowship of a local congregation in a small community, including persons seems natural — until an "outsider" tries to join in. In other situations the human factors of language, race, sex, caste, or economic status may seem insurmountable barriers to those seeking to join the Christian community. What we mean by "inclusive" needs to be defined by those who are, or who feel, excluded. We need to become "intensive" listeners, hearing and heeding the voice of the Holy Spirit who so often speaks through the pain of the person "on the other side of the road" (Luke 10:30-37). A truly inclusive community values every human being equally, including the marginalized. The Spirit challenges us to an *active* inclusivity, urging us to reach out in faith and love to minorities and oppressed people.

97. Another manifestation of Christian spirituality is a peace-oriented life-style, exploring the power of active non-violence, for the transformation of society. In any exercise of power the church must always point towards love as the better way. The challenge for us is to translate Spirit-led peace-making and peace-living from personal to congregational and community life.

98. A eucharistic spirituality which is actually lived out by a local Christian community is, in itself, the most valuable diaconal service that can be given. It is a missionary witness of immeasurable significance. Christian spirituality expresses itself as we participate fully in the liturgical life of the people of God, gathering around word and sacrament in fellowship and prayer (Acts 2:42). Worship both stimulates and results from our inner relationship with the Spirit. It is a life-giving means of evangelism and local ecumenism.

99. The Holy Spirit frees people to committed stewardship in relation to creation, church and community. In a world which values things more than relationships, and wealth and health more than service in love, the

Holy Spirit calls us personally and corporately to live for God and for the gospel. We give thanks to God for the spiritual renewal that has been evident in the life of the worldwide church. This renewal needs to be continued and strengthened by mutual sharing with those inside and outside our churches and through the ecumenical movement.

\* \* \*

100. "For in hope we are saved" (Rom 8:24). We who live in the Spirit live by hope. In spite of all the dangers and difficulties of the world we are moved not to despair but to joy in the promises of the Triune God. Created by God, saved by Christ, we rejoice in the power of the Holy Spirit, the Spirit of freedom and truth, the Spirit at work in history, the Spirit which continually opens the future before us.

Come, Holy Spirit, have mercy on us; renew and empower us to be your witnesses in the world!

*Metropolitan David of the Georgian Orthodox Church speaking during the special session on public issues.*

# 7. *Additional Documents*

*New WCC* [*Central Committee officers*] Presidents

*Prof. Anna Marie
Aagard, Denmark*

*Bishop Vinton
Anderson, USA*

*Bishop Leslie Boseto
Solomon Islands*

*Mrs Priyanka Mendis
Sri Lanka*

*His Beatitude
Parthenios, Egypt*

*Rev. Eunice Santana
Puerto Rico*

*His Holiness
Pope Shenouda, Egypt*

*Dr Aaron Tolen
Cameroon*

# 7.1. ASSEMBLY PROGRAMME AND AGENDA

*Thursday, 7 February*

9.30 Opening worship

11.30 Meeting of Nominations Committee

14.30 Plenary business session: opening actions; election of new member churches; reception of churches which have joined since Vancouver

16.30 Plenary session: address by the prime minister of Australia; report of the general secretary; appointment of assembly committees

18.30 Business Committee

21.30 Evening prayers


*Friday, 8 February*

7.45 Worship

8.45 Sub-sections

10.45 Regional meetings

12.30 Midday preaching service

12.30 Committee meetings (Credentials and Nominations)

14.30 Plenary session on assembly theme: H.B. Patriarch Parthenios of Alexandria; Prof. Dr Chung Hyun Kyung

16.30 Plenary session on assembly sub-themes: Dr Pauline Webb; Metropolitan John of Pergamon; Rev. Dr David McDonald: Rev. Dr Philip Potter; Dr Mary Tanner

18.30 Business Committee

21.30 Evening prayers


*Saturday, 9 February*

7.45 Worship

8.45 Section meetings

12.30 Midday preaching service

12.30 Committee meetings

14.30 Plenary session: appointment of remaining assembly committees; first report of the Credentials Committee; first report of the Nominations Committee; announcement of public issues; presentation: "The Spirit Speaks to the Churches"

16.30   Plenary session: welcome by Australian national organizing committee; presentation: "Covenanting for Life"
18.00   Procession for peace from convention centre to worship tent
20.00   JPIC celebration of service and commitment; all-night vigil of prayer and fasting for peace with justice

*Sunday, 10 February*
 9.30   Celebration of the Lima liturgy
12.00   Celebration of the Armenian Orthodox liturgy
19.30   "Gathering under the Southern Cross"

*Monday, 11 February*
 7.45   Worship
 8.45   Sub-sections
12.30   Midday preaching service
12.30   Committee meetings
14.30   Plenary session: welcome to guests of other faiths; report of the moderator of the central committee
16.30   Plenary session: discussion of reports of the moderator and general secretary; preliminary finance report
18.30   Business Committee

*Tuesday, 12 February*
 7.45   Worship
 8.45   Sub-sections
12.30   Midday preaching service
12.30   Committee meetings
14.30   Plenary session: presentation of new revised standard version of the Bible; second report of the Nominations Committee; presentation: "Without a Vision People Perish"; exchange of gifts with the Aboriginal people of Australia
18.30   Business Committee
20.00   Pacific evening with worship

*Wednesday, 13 February*
 7.45   Worship
 8.45   Regional groups in sections
12.30   Midday preaching service

12.30   Committee meetings
14.30   Plenary session: messages from the children and from the youth;
        presentation: "Sharing our Life — Towards New Community"
16.30   Plenary session: greetings received by the assembly; presenta-
        tion: "Land Rights and Identity"
18.30   Business Committee
20.00   Aboriginal evening
21.30   Evening prayers

*Thursday, 14 February*
 7.45   Worship
 8.45   Sub-sections
12.30   Midday preaching service
12.30   Committee meetings
14.30   Section meetings
18.30   Business Committee
20.00   Regional meetings
21.30   Evening prayers

*Friday, 15 February*
 7.45   Worship
 8.45   Sub-sections
12.30   Midday preaching service
12.30   Committee meetings
14.30   Plenary business session: presentation of gifts to participants;
        second report of the Credentials Committee; third report of the
        Nominations Committee
16.30   Plenary session: messages received by the assembly; presenta-
        tion: "Churches in Solidarity with Women"
18.30   Business Committee
20.00   Concert sponsored by WomenSpace
21.30   Evening prayers

*Saturday, 16 February*
 7.15   Eastern Orthodox liturgy
 8.45   Section meetings
12.30   Midday preaching service
12.30   Committee meetings
14.30   Plenary discussion on theme presentation
18.30   Business Committee
20.00   Sing-a-long

*Sunday, 17 February*
     Visits to local congregations
17.00    Black churches celebration
18.30    Business Committee

*Monday, 18 February*
 7.45    Worship
 9.45    Plenary business session: application for membership; report of finance committee
11.45    Plenary business session: report of Section I
14.30    Plenary business session: greetings to and message from the stewards; third report of the Credentials Committee; fourth report of Nominations Committee; election of central committee
16.30    Plenary business session: nominations report; election of presidents
18.30    Business Committee
20.00    Meeting of newly elected central committee
21.30    Evening prayers

*Tuesday, 19 February*
 7.45    Worship
 9.45    Plenary business session: report of Section II
11.45    Plenary business session: report of Reference Committee
14.30    Plenary business session: report of Reference Committee (continued)
16.30    Plenary business session: report of Section III (continued); report of Section IV; report of Programme Policy Committee
18.30    Business Committee
21.30    Evening prayers

*Wednesday, 20 February*
 7.45    Worship
 9.45    Plenary business session: report of Programme Policy Committee (continued); deliberative session on public issues
11.45    Plenary deliberative session: public issues (continued)
14.30    Plenary business session: public issues
16.30    Plenary business session: election of presidents (continued); Report Committee report; youth resolution; communicating the assembly; closing actions; adjournment
20.00    Closing worship

# 7.2. MESSAGES FROM CHURCH LEADERS

## DIMITRIOS I, ECUMENICAL PATRIARCH

To the Rev. Dr Emilio Castro, general secretary of the World Council of Churches, grace and peace from God the Father and our Lord Jesus Christ.

For our holy Orthodox Church, the theme of the seventh assembly of the World Council of Churches, convened by the grace of God in Canberra — the capital of the blessed Australian commonwealth — in itself constitutes a major reason for joy and for profound praise of the name of our Lord. For it is well known throughout the Christian world, both in the East and the West, that in the Christian faith the subject of the Holy Spirit was nurtured particularly by the Eastern Tradition which, with admirable consequence, based its entire *worship, theology* and *popular piety* upon this firm foundation of Christian truth, which — if it be permitted to adopt an image — constitutes the umbilical cord between the uncreated Trinitarian God and his creation.

One may recall how persistently and vigorously the Orthodox, immediately after the foundation of the World Council of Churches, brought forward the vital theological demand for enlarging the constitutional basis of the World Council of Churches from a mainly Christological to a more expressly Trinitarian one. This was achieved, by the grace of God, in 1961 at the New Delhi assembly. Therefore, one can easily understand why worldwide Orthodoxy, as well as all Christians respecting the quintessence of the gospel, regardless of their denominational background, rejoice over the selection of the theme for the seventh assembly.

The Holy Spirit, in its relationship with the whole of creation, its wholeness, its role in sanctification and salvation, undoubtedly constitutes the most inclusive synopsis of the entire Christian message to the world. What we call "theological Trinity" in the divine revelation would remain an unproductive and inactive word, that is, a word unable to offer consolation, without what we name "economic Trinity", as the God-bearing church fathers correctly discerned. For this they struggled with all their strength to develop and formulate in doctrine, in the most godly manner, all the consequences of the saving "kenosis" of divinity in the various stages of divine economy.

However, our Orthodox Church has yet another, equally important reason to rejoice over the theme of the seventh assembly, namely the invocational formulation of the theme, which renders clear, from the outset, that Christians cannot study the relationship of the Holy Spirit to the entire creation in some philosophically detached manner, that is in a non-participatory and merely theoretical way, but only in the contrition and compunction of prayer, invoking the heavenly illumination, can we see and accordingly confess the wonders of God around us and in all creation. Thus, we remember anew and obey the golden rule in order to attain true theology. As Evagrios Ponticos from most ancient Christian times stated: "If you are a theologian you will pray truly, and if you pray truly, you are a theologian."

Rightly, therefore, and in a God-pleasing manner, the World Council of Churches has for some years focused its theological study on the most crucial theme of *pneumatology*. Following the Melbourne world conference on mission and evangelism, in May 1980, which with its theme "Your Kingdom Come" linked the notion of *invocation* and *salvation*, it was absolutely within the logic of matters to bring this entire development into a festive declaration of ultimate hope in the Holy Spirit for all Christians from the platform of the assembly.

Such a declaration from the supreme and most official platform of the World Council of Churches certainly will remind the member churches that the only Comforter between the "Ascension" and the "Parousia" always remains the Holy Spirit, and help them respond creatively to today's worldwide ecological movement of many ideological variations by pointing out that, if its requests are exhausted on the *horizontal* level, neglecting the *vertical*, it will in no way benefit the animate and inanimate creation, which groans in deep pain nowadays. For truly "there is salvation in no one else" except "in the name of Jesus Christ" (Acts 4:12 and 10) and "no one can say Jesus is Lord except in the Holy Spirit" (1 Cor. 12:3).

Therefore from Canberra, the cry of the World Council of Churches may be summarized in the sacred principle of life or death expressed in the simple statement: without *invocation* there is no *supplication*.

Wishing, together with my most reverend and beloved brothers who constitute the Holy Synod, that the deliberations in Canberra will be blessed by both the *inspiration* and the *validation* of the Comforter, we entrust to the head of our delegation, the Most Reverend Metropolitan Bartholomew of Chalcedon, to read this message and to address to all the participants of the seventh assembly our heartfelt blessing as well as the fraternal greetings of our holy apostolic and patriarchal ecumenical throne.

May the grace of our Lord Jesus Christ and the love of God the Father and the communion of the Holy Spirit be with you all. Amen.

Constantinople, 13 February 1991

## ALEXY II, PATRIARCH OF MOSCOW AND ALL RUSSIA

Dear brothers and sisters, delegates and all other envoys of the world ecumenical community, gathered for the seventh assembly of the World Council of Churches in Canberra: "The grace of the Lord Jesus Christ and the love of God and the fellowship of the Holy Spirit be with you all" (2 Cor. 13:14).

I greet you on behalf of the Russian Orthodox Church which is now being revived for a new life having entered the second millennium of its ministry.

Renewal in the life of our church and our society goes on under complex and difficult circumstances.

There takes place a painful but extremely necessary transformation of the recent historical context of our church and social life and a discovery of reassuring prospects for bringing about a new historical context in the life of our church and our community as well as in the European life.

This process of the old dying and of the new being born opens up great opportunities for the Christian witness of the church, but at the same time it is God's challenge and his call for us to repent and make radical renewal of life. "Put off your old nature" (Eph. 4:22) so that "we might walk in newness of life" (Rom. 6:4).

We ask for your holy prayers of love and Christian solidarity with us in this challenge of our revival and renewal.

On our part, we and our church as a whole will incessantly pray for you who have gathered in Canberra, as we know that after Canberra the World Council of Churches and the ecumenical movement as a whole will enter a new phase of their development which might well be of crucial importance for their future.

We welcome the fact that the assembly's attention and programme are focused on the main theme "Come, Holy Spirit — Renew the Whole Creation"; we are convinced that this renewal in the Spirit demands that all humanity and especially we, Christians, should "come to ourselves", "go to our Heavenly Father" and repent for our great historical sin of going away from him to a "distant" country (cf. Luke 15:17-19) and for our irresponsible treatment of the richness of his creation entrusted to us.

Renewal in the Spirit demands not only ecology in "nature", in the environment and space, but first of all, ecology of the spirit, ecology in the social milieu of human relations.

While invoking the Holy Spirit to renew his whole creation, we ourselves, "who have the first-fruits of the Spirit" (Rom. 8:23), must feel our responsibility and duty, "for we are fellow workers with God" (1 Cor. 3:9).

In this fellow work with God, the Holy Spirit "helps us in our weakness... and the Spirit himself intercedes for us with sighs too deep for words" (Rom. 8:26).

"He who searches the hearts of men knows what is the mind of the Spirit" (Rom. 8:27). The Spirit says to the church: "Remember then from what you have fallen, and repent" (Rev. 2:5).

Dear brothers and sisters, while reviewing the past of the ecumenical movement in Canberra and reflecting on a new period in the life and work of the World Council of Churches, we should always bear in mind "what the Spirit says to the churches" (Rev. 3:13) and unceasingly search our conscience and ask whether the Holy Spirit says to the churches what he said to the church of Laodicea in the Revelation of St John the Theologian.

The message of Canberra will be a new Christian witness in the divided world only when we, Christians, and our churches hear the call of the Holy Spirit to us.

Let us base all new directions and structures of the World Council of Churches on this call to renewal in the Holy Spirit, always mindful of what the Apostle said: "No other foundation can anyone lay than that which is laid, which is Jesus Christ" (1 Cor. 3:11).

We pray that the World Council of Churches may remain faithful to its original and major vocation, to be the council of churches searching together for the fulfilment of their common calling to attain unity in faith and eucharistic communion, and to remain, in the spirit of the Toronto declaration, the council of churches which the Russian Orthodox Church joined at its third assembly in New Delhi thirty years ago.

With love in the Lord and beseeching the Spirit of Truth, the Comforter, to set us on the path of truth in the unity of spirit and in the union of peace and love.

Moscow, 1 February 1991

## POPE JOHN PAUL II

On the occasion of the seventh assembly of the World Council of Churches I send warm greetings to you and all the participants, and assure you of my closeness in prayer as you gather to consider the theme: "Come, Holy Spirit — Renew the Whole Creation".

The fact that the World Council of Churches has chosen for its assembly a theme dedicated to the Holy Spirit is both significant and opportune. It calls to mind the abiding presence of the Spirit who has been with the church throughout her history and who is among us now in fulfilment of the words of our Lord Jesus Christ who said: "The Holy Spirit, whom the Father will send in my name... will teach you all things, and bring to your remembrance all that I have said to you" (John 14:26).

The ecumenical movement, of which your assembly is an important forum, has been "fostered by the grace of the Holy Spirit" (*Unitatis Redintegratio* 1). It is in fact the Spirit who sustains our prayer, our openness to conversion in mind and heart, and our faithfulness to the word of life transmitted in the gospel and in the church. We can truly state that progress towards the restoration of unity among Christians depends above all on the guidance of the Holy Spirit.

In the seven years since your last assembly the Spirit has brought us further along the road towards unity. My visit to the World Council of Churches in 1984 and your subsequent visit to Rome underlined the significant efforts towards unity in which we are engaged. At Assisi in 1986, when the representatives of many Christian communities and of other religious traditions generously responded to my call for a Day of Prayer for Peace, we had a moving experience of the direction in which the Spirit is leading us.

Theological dialogue too has made important contributions to the search for unity and is helping to clarify issues which need to be further studied. In this connection, I am mindful of the value of the consultation undertaken with regard to the document *Baptism, Eucharist and Ministry*.

Such positive aspects of our search for visible unity in faith are surely a sign of the Holy Spirit drawing us closer to the unity which Christ wishes for his disciples. The difficulties which we experience in our ecumenical efforts should not discourage us but rather impel us to commit ourselves anew to the task in hand. May your assembly be an occasion for a renewed awareness of the Spirit's gifts in this regard.

The present tragic situation of our troubled world confirms once again humanity's need for reconciliation, its need for an ever more authentic witness to the biblical message of peace, justice and the integrity of creation. But the sad fact is that our testimony to these values is less convincing to the degree that the world continues to be confronted by our divisions. Herein lies the urgency of the ecumenical task.

It is my prayer that the Lord will bless your assembly and that the Holy Spirit will guide our common efforts towards unity of faith. May the same Spirit enlighten all those gathering in Canberra to reflect together on the great issues of our times in the light of the Word of God. "The grace of the Lord Jesus Christ and the love of God and the fellowship of the Holy Spirit be with you all" (2 Cor. 13:14).

Vatican, 30 January 1991

## 7.3. MESSAGE FROM THE PRE-ASSEMBLY WOMEN'S MEETING

### At Such a Time as This...

At such a time as this, a time of wars, of distress, of grief and of fear, we gathered together for the pre-assembly women's meeting of the seventh assembly of the World Council of Churches. Over 300 women, and a few invited men, from member churches throughout the world, met in Canberra, Australia, 3-6 February 1991. In the leadership and input made by women to this meeting, we affirmed and celebrated the many gifts women have to offer to the church.

We discussed, from our perspectives as women, the theme "Come, Holy Spirit — Renew the Whole Creation". We knew that this Spirit was among us as the enabling energy of God, identified as *Ruach*, the feminine Hebrew word for Spirit. *Ruach* hovered over the waters before God created the world. We knew that we were close to and carried by the Spirit, an energy which permeates God's whole creation. Through our worship, discussions and Bible study, we were challenged to greater responsibility as partners in caring for God's creation. We drew inspiration from the courage of Esther and Vashti, Eve and Mary and the community of women and men in the early church.

At such a time as this we are painfully aware that God's creation is being violated by a war that ravages the Gulf region. Women, youth and children who are the primary victims of any war are at the centre of our concern. This brings to our consciousness the wars and the war-like situations in other parts of the world. We call for an immediate ceasefire and peaceful solutions to conflict in the Gulf region, as well as in other situations of conflict. We urge our churches to make clear to our governments that we will actively resist the militarization and trade in armaments that make war inevitable.

We know that this war of unprecedented proportions is placing even greater burdens on a crisis-ridden global economic order. As a consequence, marginalized and poor women, youth and children including those from wealthy nations but particularly in Africa, Asia, Latin America and the Pacific, are the hardest hit. In addition to this, women and children experience the violence generated by a militaristic culture even in the privacy of their homes.

We affirm our commitment to make every effort to use non-violent means to resolve conflicts on all levels.

At such a time as this, our Aboriginal sisters shared their experiences of suffering in a context where their land has been wrested from them and their culture undermined. We were moved to solidarity with indigenous peoples all over the world who engage in struggles to reclaim their lost heritage and to reaffirm their spirituality and identity. We were reminded of women in many parts of the world oppressed by the continuing sins of racism and caste-ism.

We shared with each other stories of struggle — the Holy Spirit moving among women around the world, empowering them to challenge forces of death and destruction. Women's demands for peace with justice manifest themselves in new forms of resistance in people's movements everywhere. We stand in solidarity with all women, including women of other faiths, in seeking the renewal of human community and the renewal of all creation. These expressions of hope inspired us in our discussions.

Three years after the initiation of the Ecumenical Decade of the Churches in Solidarity with Women by the World Council of Churches in 1988, we recognize that it has been launched by many churches around the world. Women have embraced the Decade with great enthusiasm — as an opportunity to share their gifts to build a prophetic community of women and men. However, when we heard the testimonies of our sisters in the pre-assembly meeting we recognized that the total church has not adequately claimed the Decade as its own or responded to the challenges the Decade poses to be in solidarity with women. We urge the churches to act resolutely so as to bring about change in the remaining years of the Decade.

At such a time as this, drawing from our spiritual experience we express our deep hope in the renewing energy of the Holy Spirit and commit ourselves to continue our struggle for a community which will work for justice, peace and the integrity of creation.

# 7.4. MESSAGE FROM THE PRE-ASSEMBLY YOUTH EVENT

"And afterward, I will pour out my Spirit on all people. Your sons and daughters will prophesy, your old people will dream dreams, your young people will see visions. Even on my servants, both men and women, I will pour out my Spirit in those days" (Joel 2:28-29, Acts 2:17-18).

## Introduction

We the youth of the seventh assembly of the World Council of Churches — more than 300 stewards, delegates, observers and advisers — have gathered to wrestle with the theme "Come, Holy Spirit — Renew the Whole Creation" in a pre-assembly youth event here in Canberra, 2-5 February 1991. We have struggled with and celebrated our diversity of nations, cultures, languages, theologies and denominational backgrounds. We have worshipped together, listened to each others' stories and formed links of global solidarity to sustain us in the future.

## Aboriginal and indigenous peoples

From the opening of our gathering, we have acknowledged that we are on Aboriginal land. We have committed ourselves to struggle in solidarity with all indigenous peoples and to respect and learn from their deep spiritual and cultural traditions; we call on the whole assembly to do likewise.

## Vision and struggle

We believe that our lives are a continuous experience of Pentecost: the Holy Spirit gives us vision and the gift of prophecy. It is this same Spirit which empowers and challenges us to confront the evil of sin both personal and corporate. As we realize the image of God within us and the indwelling of the Holy Spirit, we are empowered to be co-workers with God in renewing the whole creation.

As young people we are alarmed at the extent of environmental degradation of the world which we are inheriting — the destruction of rain forests, the dumping of toxic wastes, nuclear-weapons testing, global warming, and the thinning of the ozone layer — to name but a few areas. We acknowledge that the cause of these problems is our own greed, especially in the first world where wasteful consumption is accepted as normal because we see ourselves as the owners rather than as the stewards of creation. We ask the Giver of Life to empower us in our commitment to renouncing greed and to seeking alternate life-styles, both personal and corporate. Let us start with this assembly, by eliminating the use of disposable cups and by recycling the vast quantities of paper we use.

As young people we know that the freedom given to us by God is often denied to us by human structures of sin. As young people we feel the greatest burden of human rights abuses, of economic and social injustice, of apartheid, of civil and international war, and other forms of corporate evil. These structures force millions of us to become refugees or displaced peoples, inside or outside our own countries. In Asia, Latin America, Africa and Eastern Europe we lead the struggle against authoritarian and repressive governments, and suffer accordingly. From many countries we are called to fight in the Middle East, in a war not of our own making; all of us suffer and will continue to suffer from the economic strife it causes. But regardless of where we come from and what form our oppression takes, we know that the Spirit of Truth is with us in our struggle for justice, peace and freedom. Our hope and prayer is that the churches will intensify their efforts to translate this movement of the Spirit into concrete solidarity and support.

As young people, and especially young women, we are often deprived of freedom by our churches which render us voiceless, powerless and marginalized in the name of "experience" and "knowledge". We believe, however, that experience and knowledge are not wisdom, and that the Spirit of Truth is not limited to any age, gender, or other category of person. We deplore the fact that our representation at this assembly (10 percent of delegates) is even lower than in Vancouver (13 percent) and only half the level that the member churches have committed themselves to reaching. We acknowledge the effort of this assembly to remedy this imbalance in the selection of the various committees, but we urge the member churches to take their own commitment more seriously at all levels of selection.

As young people we have felt the Spirit calling us to reconciliation and unity as God's people. We recognize that reconciliation is a costly process, that there is no easy way of overcoming the differences which have divided us for so long. Indeed, we recognize that we can and must LEARN from our diversity of perspectives, and have done so in concrete ways during our pre-assembly gathering. One thing we know: there can be no reconciliation without justice, and justice requires both repentance and renewal. We therefore call on the member churches to seriously repent of their own participation in building barriers that divide — young from old, rich from poor, men from women, powerful from powerless, one race from another, one tradition within our own Christian faith from another. We further call for the churches to renew and intensify their commitment to overcoming these barriers through concrete programmes of action. We believe that without repentance and renewal, we cannot pray "Spirit of Unity — Reconcile your People!"

## Conclusion

And yet we know that the Holy Spirit is within each of us as individuals and all of us as a community, urging and enabling us to transform and sanctify ourselves. Then we may indeed dream dreams and see visions with which to guide our lives in this world. With this hope we now join with the entire seventh assembly of the World Council of Churches in praying, "Come, Holy Spirit — Renew the Whole Creation".

# 7.5. STATEMENT FROM
# DIFFERENTLY-ABLED PERSONS

As persons who are differently abled, we have great concern that the World Council of Churches (WCC) continue concrete, viable efforts to include our gifts and graces in working towards the healing of our world community.

We draw your attention to the Vancouver assembly's efforts to include 10 percent of persons who are differently abled in the life of the WCC, through its programme policy bodies and committees. This has not happened here at the Canberra assembly. We currently have only two delegates and there is no representation of persons with disabilities on any of the assembly committees at this time.

We have come and want to share our gifts and graces. We also want to be a vital part of the assembly's ongoing work, to share its leadership and to feel the wholeness of the body of Christ. We call your attention to the fact that there are over 500 million people in the world who are disabled, needing to become differently-abled. God, embodied in Jesus, uses the differently-abled to demonstrate effectively the power of the Holy Spirit to renew creation. Therefore, we call all people of God to be reminded of this and to assist us in abolishing the attitudes of exclusiveness and indifference.

We understand that there are other mechanisms for augmenting membership on the central committee and working groups so that disability issues can be represented. With this in mind, we call on you to fully endorse and to ensure our full participation in the life of the WCC and the church worldwide. We ask you, therefore, to invite an adviser to be present and to participate at the core group meeting in July 1991 and at the central committee in September.

Again, our issues belong to everyone. Statistics provided by the World Health Organization a decade ago indicate that the 500 million people in the world who have some disability or other are among the most oppressed, marginalized and poverty-stricken in our societies. Causes include — but are not limited to — poverty, famine, inadequate health care, malnutrition, disease, natural and human-made accidents, war, effects of nuclear radiation, torture, violence, etc. Ninety-eight percent of persons with disabilities live in the developing countries and only two percent of these people receive any support at all. Since the causes are directly related to the issues of justice, peace and the integrity of creation, this concern clearly touches in some way the work of every sub-unit and programme of the WCC, and in this assembly the work of every section, sub-section and plenary presentation.

Persons who are differently abled look to you and the assembly for assistance in helping us to be a part of the whole, by including persons with disabilities in the decision-making processes, in the life of WCC events, and as resource people in the various areas in which we have gifts to share apart from disability-related concerns.

We call upon the WCC to include persons who are differently abled in their official criteria for selection of participants, along with youth, women, Orthodox and regional balances.

# 7.6. STATEMENT REGARDING WCC ACTION ON ABORIGINAL CONCERNS

We, the Indigenous owners and occupiers of Australia, call on the WCC assembly to recognize our rights:

1. Aboriginal sovereignty over Australia.

2. To self-determination and self-management, including the freedom to pursue our own economic, political, social, religious and cultural development.

3. To permanent control and enjoyment of our ancestral lands.

4. To protection of, and control of, access to our sacred sites, sacred objects, artefacts, designs, knowledge and works of art.

5. To the return of the remains of our ancestors, that are all over Australia and other countries of the world, for burial in accordance with our traditions.

6. To respect for and promotion of our Aboriginal identity, including the traditional law, cultural, linguistic, religious and historical aspects, and including the right to be educated in our own languages and in our own culture and history.

7. In accordance with the Universal Declaration of Human Rights, the International Covenant on Economic, Social and Cultural Rights, the International Covenant on Civil and Political Rights, and the International Convention on the Elimination of All Forms of Racial Discrimination, to rights of life, liberty, security of person, food, clothing, housing, medical care, education and employment opportunities, necessary social services and other basic rights.

8. To a justice system which recognizes our customary laws and frees us from discrimination, cultural genocide and activity which may threaten our identity or security or interfere with our freedom of expression or association, or otherwise prevent our full enjoyment and exercise of universally recognized human rights and fundamental freedoms.

In order to support our claims as listed above, we strongly request the WCC assembly to take the following steps:

1. In the imminent restructuring of the WCC that an Indigenous desk be established *immediately*:

a) managed and staffed by Indigenous peoples;

b) ensuring adequate representations of the Indigenous people of Australia on any working parties and any following committees of this desk.

2. To lobby the United Nations for the sovereign rights of Indigenous peoples ensuring that international laws encompass Indigenous values and cultural, economic, religious and legal concepts practised and recognized by Indigenous peoples.

3. To establish an Indigenous peoples' centre in Geneva to provide housing accommodation and information resources to Indigenous people meeting on Indigenous peoples and land-rights issues.

4. While welcoming the government's initiative for a council of Aboriginal reconciliation, we insist that there can be no reconciliation unless we first have justice and recognition. We cannot negotiate reconciliation unless Aboriginals are guaranteed equal bargaining powers and status. This process needs to be community-based and not government-based, observed by international bodies i.e. the United Nations, the World Council of Churches.

5. To urge the Australian churches to:
   a) take action against those pushing church religion in Aboriginal communities to the detriment of the Indigenous culture;
   b) help to develop Aboriginal spirituality, and the regeneration of Indigenous education, i.e. language, history and culture, through adequate resources;
   c) return land they have taken from Indigenous people;
   d) observe the "pay-the-rent" concept for mission lands they acquired;
   e) observe the "Zacchean principle": that is giving a percentage of their income to the Indigenous people;
   f) believe that each denomination within Australia must have an Indigenous body which will be given decision-making powers, finances and resources to carry out the decisions made;
   g) request the Australian Council of Churches to convene a meeting of Indigenous Christians of Australia to encourage the formation and development of an Indigenous church.

6. To ensure that only Indigenous peoples represent and speak on Indigenous concerns and issues, nationally and internationally.

7. To ensure that a representation of Indigenous peoples from all the churches are delegates to the WCC assembly and also that Indigenous members are appointed to the central committee especially, as well as other WCC committees.

8. [For the WCC Assembly] To strongly urge the Australian government:

   a) to recognize "Aboriginal sovereignty over Australia", maintain its commitment to negotiate an appropriate resolution, i.e. treaty or instrument of reconciliation, with Aboriginal people, and ensure that adequate resources, both finances and international expertise, be made available to the Aboriginal people in order that they be able to make a free and informed decision;

   b) to introduce national legislation to ensure that Aboriginals have sole control, ownership of, and responsibility for all decisions relating to Aboriginal heritage, artefacts, sacred sites and knowledge; and that Aboriginal skeletal remains be returned to Aboriginal burial grounds. This legislation should facilitate the establishment of sacred sites/heritage commissions in each state/territory, administered and controlled by Aboriginal people. These commissions should be empowered to declare "sacred sites" of significance to Aboriginal people, as well as to address all matters associated with Aboriginal heritage, knowledge and artefacts;

   c) to honour the mandate given to it by the 1967 referendum to exercise powers on Aboriginal affairs (the power of the states should not militate against the Aboriginal people to their detriment);

   d) to take action to stop the trade in X-rated pornographic videos which promote domestic violence and abuse in many communities;

   e) to respond to Aboriginal people's needs to combat alcohol and substance abuse and related problems;

   f) that the WCC condemn the obvious irreverence that the federal government of Australia has shown and continues to show for the loss of Aboriginal lives in *custody*, and call upon the government to immediately utilize its legislative powers granted in the 1967 referendum to intervene with the state governments to stop deaths in custody. The WCC should also urge the commonwealth government to pressure the state governments into implementing recommendations of the Royal Commission into Deaths in Custody.

# 7.7. REFLECTIONS OF ORTHODOX PARTICIPANTS

## I. Introduction

The Eastern Orthodox and Oriental Orthodox delegates and participants at the seventh assembly of the World Council of Churches, meeting in Canberra, Australia, want to communicate with all in attendance through this statement in order to express to them some concerns. We preface our comments with an expression of appreciation to the World Council of Churches for its many contributions to the development of dialogue among churches, and to assisting all members in making efforts to overcome disunity. As Orthodox, we appreciate the assistance given over decades in the process of dialogue leading towards the full communion of Eastern and Oriental Orthodox churches.

We also recognize the contributions of the WCC in the work it has done in its Commissions on Faith and Order and on Mission and Evangelism (CWME), its contribution to the Renewal of Congregational Life (RCL), its relief work through the Inter-Church Aid, Refugees and World Service (CICARWS), and in the Justice, Peace and the Integrity of Creation programme (JPIC).

Yet, our experience at this assembly has heightened a number of concerns that have been developing among the Orthodox since the last assembly. We want to share these with the Canberra assembly and to tell you where these are now leading us.

The Orthodox concern about these issues should not be understood as implying a reluctance to continue dialogue. The present statement is motivated not by disinterest or indifference towards our sisters and brothers in other churches and Christian communities, but by our sincere concern about the future of the ecumenical movement, and of its goals and ideals, as they were formulated by its founders.

## II. Orthodox concerns

1. The Orthodox churches want to emphasize that for them, the main aim of the WCC must be *the restoration of the unity of the church*. This aim does not exclude relating church unity with the wider unity of humanity and creation. On the contrary, the unity of Christians will contribute more effectively to the unity of humanity and the world. Yet the latter must not happen at the expense of solving issues of faith and order, which divide Christians. *Visible unity*, in both the faith and the

structure of the church, constitutes a specific goal and must not be taken for granted.

2. The Orthodox note that there has been an *increasing departure from the Basis* of the WCC. The latter has provided the framework for Orthodox participation in the World Council of Churches. Its text is: "The World Council of Churches is a fellowship of churches which confess the Lord Jesus Christ as God and Saviour according to the scriptures and therefore seek to fulfill together their common calling to the glory of the one God, Father, Son and Holy Spirit" (Constitution). Should the WCC not direct its future work along these lines, it would be in danger of ceasing to be an instrument aiming at the restoration of Christian unity and in that case it would tend to become a forum for an exchange of opinions without any specific Christian theological basis. In such a forum, common prayer will be increasingly difficult, and eventually will become impossible, since even a basic common theological vision will be lacking.

3. The tendency to marginalize the Basis in WCC work has created some dangerous trends in the WCC. We miss from many WCC documents the affirmation that Jesus Christ is the world's Saviour. We perceive a growing *departure from biblically-based Christian understandings* of: (a) the Trinitarian God; (b) salvation; (c) the "good news" of the gospel itself; (d) human beings as created in the image and likeness of God; and (e) the church, among others.

Our hope is that the results of Faith and Order work will find a more prominent place in the various expressions of the WCC, and that tendencies in the opposite direction will not be encouraged. The Orthodox, consequently, attribute special significance to the work of the Faith and Order Commission of the WCC, and view with concern each tendency to undermine its place in the structure of the Council.

4. The Orthodox follow with interest, but also with a certain disquiet, the developments of the WCC towards the broadening of its aims in the direction of *relations with other religions*. The Orthodox support dialogue initiatives, particularly those aiming at the promotion of relations of openness, mutual respect and human cooperation with neighbours of other faiths. When dialogue takes place, Christians are called to bear witness to the integrity of their faith. A genuine dialogue involves greater theological efforts to express the Christian message in ways that speak to the various cultures of our world. All this, however, must occur on the basis of theological criteria which will define the limits of diversity. The biblical faith in God must not be changed. The definition of these criteria

is a matter of theological study, and must constitute the first priority of the WCC in view of its desired broadening of aims.

5. Thus, it is with alarm that the Orthodox have heard some presentations on the theme of this assembly. With reference to the theme of the assembly, the Orthodox still await the final texts. However, they observe that some people tend to affirm with very great ease the presence of the Holy Spirit in many movements and developments without discernment. The Orthodox wish to stress the factor of sin and error which exists in every human action, and separate the Holy Spirit from these. We must guard against a tendency *to substitute a "private" spirit, the spirit of the world or other spirits for the Holy Spirit* who proceeds from the Father and rests in the Son. Our tradition is rich in respect for local and national cultures, but we find it impossible to invoke the spirits of "earth, air, water and sea creatures". Pneumatology is inseparable from Christology or from the doctrine of the Holy Trinity confessed by the church on the basis of divine revelation.

6. The Orthodox are sorry that their position with regard to eucharistic communion has not been understood by many members of the WCC, who regard the Orthodox as unjustifiably insisting upon *abstinence from eucharistic communion*. The Orthodox once more invite their brothers and sisters in the WCC to understand that it is a matter of *unity in faith and fundamental Orthodox ecclesiology*, and not a question of a triumphalistic stance.

For the Orthodox, the eucharist is the supreme expression of unity and not a means towards unity. The present situation in the ecumenical movement is for us an experience of the cross of Christian division. In this regard, the question of the ordination of women to the priestly and episcopal offices must also be understood within a theological and ecclesiological context.

7. Finally, our concern is also directed to the *changing process of decision-making* in the WCC. While the system of quotas has benefits, it may also be creating problems. As Orthodox we see changes that seem to increasingly weaken the possibility of an Orthodox witness in an otherwise Protestant international organization. We believe that this tendency is to the harm of the ecumenical effort.

8. For the Orthodox gathered at this assembly, these and other tendencies and developments question *the very nature and identity of the Council*, as described in the Toronto statement. In this sense the present assembly in Canberra appears to be a crucial point in the history of the ecumenical movement.

We must, therefore ask ourselves: *Has the time come for the Orthodox churches and other member churches to review their relations with the World Council of Churches?*

We pray the Holy Spirit to help all Christians to renew their commitment to visible unity.

# 7.8. EVANGELICAL PERSPECTIVES FROM CANBERRA

*A Letter to Churches and Christians Worldwide from Participants Who Share Evangelical Perspectives*

We wish to share with you the challenges we have received, the lessons we have learned and our observations on the assembly.

**Background**

The sixth assembly of the WCC at Vancouver in 1983 made increased dialogue, with participation by evangelicals in WCC activity, a priority. The WCC expressed this commitment by seeking greater involvement from evangelicals within the member churches of the WCC, promoting interchange with evangelical consultations such as Lausanne II at Manila, and increased input in WCC consultations and working groups from those in charismatic, evangelical and pentecostal movements both within and beyond the WCC.

**Our experience**

Evangelical participants at Canberra accepted the invitation of the WCC to participate in its deliberations on the theme: "Come, Holy Spirit — Renew the Whole Creation". We felt welcomed in the dialogue and were able to contribute in concrete ways and at all levels. We were listened to, for example, as the assembly worked on a biblically informed theology of creation, relevant to the eco-crisis we face. As the assembly discussed the process of listening to the Spirit at work in every culture, we cautioned, with others, that discernment is required to identify the Spirit as the Spirit of Jesus Christ and thus to develop criteria for and limits to theological diversity. We argued for a high Christology to serve as the only authentic Christian base for dialogue with persons of other living faiths. Some drafts of assembly documents appear to show reluctance to use straightforward biblical language, but the opportunities for evangelical perspectives to find inclusion in the reports of the assembly represented real progress in the dialogue begun in Vancouver.

Despite such a sincere commitment to take more seriously that major segment of the worldwide church which those with evangelical perspectives represent, evangelicals remain under-represented at Canberra, at the level of plenary presentation and in leadership of sections. For this reason, we have asked the leadership of the WCC to address structural deficiencies in the Council by welcoming an evangelical presence on every commission, just as women's and Orthodox perspectives have been solicited, and to establish a monitoring group composed both of WCC staff and evangelical advisers from member and non-member churches.

We who hold evangelical perspectives, however, must share the responsibility for the present theological imbalance within the WCC.

There is presently insufficient commitment to ecumenical activity by evangelicals in member churches of the WCC and in churches in the wider Christian communion. This has helped perpetuate the divisive stereotype that the WCC can only assist churches with regard to issues of justice and human rights while organizations like the Lausanne movement and the World Evangelical Fellowship should be turned to for insight concerning evangelism. In fact, insofar as all these organizations claim to express the whole gospel, they all need to listen to and learn from one another.

## Theological concerns

The moderator of the central committee of the WCC identified in his report that the WCC has remained unable to develop a "vital and coherent theology". Our experience of the assembly confirms this. The ecumenical movement needs a theology rooted in the Christian revelation and is relevant to contemporary problems. At present, there is insufficient clarity regarding the relationship between the confession of the Lord Jesus Christ as God and Saviour according to scripture, the person and work of the Holy Spirit, and legitimate concerns which are part of the WCC agenda. We share many of these concerns, such as those related to justice, peace and the integrity of creation, to the contextualization (or inculturation) of the gospel, and to religious pluralism. This theological deficit not only conspires against the work of the WCC as a Christian witness but also increases the tensions among its member churches.

We encourage individuals and churches with evangelical concerns to engage themselves in serious theological reflection to fill the existing gap. The challenge is to develop a theology forged in the midst of obedient action for the sake of the gospel, so as to bring together the apostolic faith and the suffering of the oppressed, the personal and the social, the private and the public, justification by faith and the struggle for peace with justice, commitment to Christ and action empowered by the Holy Spirit in the midst of the crises facing the modern world.

## Practical challenges

1. We have been challenged again by the call for Christian unity which the WCC has had as its vocation. We call those with evangelical concerns to place high priority on visible expressions of Christian unity.

2. Evangelicals need to take a more active part in ecumenical events, both evangelicals who are part of member churches and those who are outside; for example we draw attention to the WCC youth event in 1992 in which we hope that the evangelical youth movements will also be able to participate. Evangelical youth movements have a long experience of empowering young people.

3. In light of the assembly theme, "Come, Holy Spirit — Renew the Whole Creation", we were concerned at the failure of the assembly to highlight the significant contribution of pentecostal and charismatic Christians to the renewal of the church in its life and worship. Fearing that we too are all too often guilty of treating them in the same way, we urge non-pentecostal evangelicals to work towards greater respect, harmony and cooperation with pentecostal and charismatic Christians.

4. The assembly challenged us to respond more adequately to the needs of indigenous and marginalized peoples in our own contexts. It alerted us to the special predicament of Aboriginal people in Australia. Aboriginal evangelicals who participated in our meeting shared their pain and anguish and the lack of support for their churches received from evangelicals in general. They call on evangelicals to support their aspirations for recognition as a people with a culture shaped by the interaction between their traditional culture and the biblical perspective, for their right to self-determination, and to support their struggle for justice and land rights.

5. The experience provided by the assembly of work in sub-sections enabled evangelicals and those from other perspectives to discover each other not as antagonists but as believers together. In particular we recognized the many common theological commitments and concerns

with the Orthodox. We strongly urge that conversations and encounters between evangelicals and the Orthodox be fostered as soon as possible to explore common ground and address differences.

6. We have been challenged to pursue the examination of our own experience and expression of the syncretism between Christianity and cultural traditions. We cannot address the charge of syncretism to the religious experiences of people in the two-thirds world without at the same time examining afresh the degree to which Christianity in the Western world has easily assimilated aspects of its own culture such as rationalism and individualism.

7. Very inadequate attention was given in the assembly to the dramatic and far-reaching changes that have taken place in Eastern Europe. It raised questions about the way in which sections of the ecumenical movement supported the ruling ideologies in Eastern Europe. We were challenged to examine ways in which Christians are tempted to align themselves uncritically with the spirit of the age. We were also encouraged by the witness of those Christians in Eastern Europe whose testimony witnesses to the power of the Holy Spirit to sustain God's people and to bring new life amidst death and adversity.

8. The debates on the Gulf war forced us to recognize the inadequacy of the traditional just-war theory which evangelicals have by and large embraced, except for those from the peace tradition. We are challenged to work afresh on a Christian approach to war and peace-making in a modern context.

9. The inadequacy of theological reflection in the handling of complex issues regarding justice, peace and the integrity of creation challenges us to recognize the lack of such reflection on those themes among evangelicals and the need for intensive theological reflection in these areas.

10. We have been challenged by the leadership of women in this assembly. Women were visible and active participants in the full programme of the assembly including worship (both preaching and administering the eucharist); section work, plenary sessions, business and committee actions as well as the educational offerings of the visitors' programme. The assembly was enriched by the participation of these many gifted women. This challenges the evangelical movement to re-assess its theological understanding of women's spiritual giftedness and to take care that it does not unwittingly quench the activity of the Holy Spirit.

We thank God for the opportunity we have had to be involved in this assembly. We humbly encourage evangelical Christians everywhere to join us in praying "Come, Holy Spirit — Renew the Whole Creation" and begin with us.

Chris Ambrose, Churches of Christ in Australia (press)
Walter Arnold, Evangelical Lutheran Church of Wurttemberg (central committee)
George Austin, Church of England (delegate)
Ray Bringham, Church of God, USA (guest)
John Broadhurst, Church of England (delegate)
Bjørn Bue, Church of Norway (central committee)
David Coffey, Baptist, Union of Great Britain (delegate)
Donald Dayton, Wesleyan Theological Society, USA (observer)
John Evans, Presbyterian Church of New Zealand (accredited visitor)
Douglas Fondell, Evangelical Covenant Church USA (accredited visitor)
Ben Fubara-Manuel, Presbyterian Church of Nigeria (youth delegate)
Malcolm Hanson, United Reformed Church in the United Kingdom (adviser)
Sue Horner, Evangelical Covenant Church, USA (adviser)
Jim Houston, Anglican Church of Australia (visitor)
Robert Johnston, Evangelical Covenant Church, USA (delegated observer)
Peter Kuzmic, Evangelical Church, Yugoslavia (adviser)
Robert McNaughton, Evangelical Covenant Church, USA (observer)
John McKinlay, Presbyterian Church of New Zealand (accredited visitor)
Vijay Menon, Church of England (delegate)
John Mullen, Evangelical Covenant Church, USA (accredited visitor)
David Parker, Baptist Union of Australia (accredited visitor)
Jeff Powell, Presbyterian Church (USA) (press)
Cecil M. Robeck, Assemblies of God, USA (accredited visitor)
Margaret Rodgers, Anglican Church of Australia (delegate)
Vinay Samuel, Church of South India (observer)
Rachel Shirras, Church of England (youth delegate)
William Showalter, Presbyterian Church (USA) (accredited visitor)
Chris Sugden, Church of England (press)
Margaret Swinson, Church of England (delegate)

# 7.9. ASSEMBLY PARTICIPANTS

## PRESIDENTS OF THE WCC

*Barrow*, H.E. Dame R. Nita (Barbados),* Methodist Church in the Caribbean and
the Americas [Antigua]**
*Bührig*, Dr Marga, Swiss Protestant Church Federation
*Gregorios*, H.E. Metropolitan Dr Paulos Mar, Malankara Orthodox Syrian
Church (India)
*Hempel*, Landesbischof Dr Johannes W., Federation of Evangelical Churches
[Germany]
*Ignatios IV*, His Beatitude, Greek Orthodox Patriarchate of Antioch and All the
East [Syria] (absent)
*Makhulu*, Most Rev. W.P. Khotso, Church of the Province of Central Africa
[Botswana]
*Wilson*, Very Rev. Dr Lois M., United Church of Canada

## OFFICERS OF THE WCC

*Moderator of central committee*
*Held*, Rev. Dr Heinz Joachim, Evangelical Church in Germany

*Vice-moderators of central committee*
*Chrysostomos of Myra*, H.E. Metropolitan, Ecumenical Patriarchate [Turkey]
*Talbot*, Dr Sylvia, (Virgin Islands USA) African Methodist Episcopal Church
[USA]

*General secretary*
*Castro*, Rev. Dr Emilio, (Switzerland) Methodist Church in Uruguay

## DELEGATES FROM MEMBER CHURCHES

*Abbey-Mensah*, Rev. Mrs Dinah, fo, Evangelical Presbyterian Church, Ghana
*Abdelsayed*, Archpriest Gabriel, mo, (USA), Coptic Orthodox Church [Egypt]

---

m = male; f = female; o = ordained; l = lay; y = youth.
* Indicates country of residence where it is other than that specified in the name of the
church.
** Square brackets indicate that this is not part of the name of the church.

*Abel*, Miss Carol, fl, Church in Wales

*Abou Edou*, Pasteur Samuel, mo, Presbyterian Church of Cameroon

*Aboud*, Mrs Heather, fl, (Australia), Greek Orthodox Patriarchate of Antioch and All the East [Syria]

*Abraham*, Prof. Annama, fl, (India), Syrian Orthodox Patriarchate of Antioch and All the East

*Abraham*, Mr Pulukuri, ml, Samavesam of Telugu Baptist Churches [India]

*Abraham*, Mrs Ruth, fl, Ethiopian Evangelical Church Mekane Yesus

*Abramides*, Mr Elias, ml, (Argentina), Ecumenical Patriarchate of Constantinople [Turkey]

*Aco*, Sra Graciela, fl, Methodist Church in Brazil

*Adams*, Dr Charles, mo, Progressive National Baptist Convention Inc. [USA]

*Adejobi*, Ms Adedoja, yfl, Church of the Lord Aladura [Nigeria]

*Adejobi*, Primate Emmanuel, mo, Church of the Lord Aladura [Nigeria]

*Ademola*, Deaconess Isabella, fl, Methodist Church [Nigeria]

*Aden*, Ms Margaretha, fl, Kalimantan Evangelical Church (GKE) [Indonesia]

*Adhikari*, Mr Susanta, ml, Bangladesh Baptist Sangha

*Agger*, Rev. Eskil, mo, Evangelical Lutheran Church of Denmark

*Aguiar*, Sr Anibal, yml, (Uruguay), Evangelical Church of the River Plate [Argentina]

*Aguilar*, Ms Elizabeth, yfl, United Church of Christ [USA]

*Aherrera*, Mrs Lydia, fl, (Philippines), United Methodist Church [USA]

*Ahn Chu Hye*, Miss, yfl, Korean Methodist Church

*Ahrén*, Rt Rev. Dr Per-Olov, mo, Church of Sweden

*Ailenei*, Mr Alexandru, ml, Romanian Orthodox Church

*Ajalat*, Mr Charles, ml, (USA), Greek Orthodox Patriarchate of Antioch and All the East [Syria]

*Akande*, Rev. Dr S.T. Ola, mo, Nigerian Baptist Convention

*Akanle*, Mrs Abosede, fl, Church of Nigeria

*Akinola*, Mrs Aduke, fl, Nigerian Baptist Convention

*Al Laham*, Mr Samer, ml, Greek Orthodox Patriarchate of Antioch and All the East [Syria]

*Al Zehlaoui*, Rev. Fr Joseph, mo, (Cyprus), Greek Orthodox Patriarchate of Antioch and All the East [Syria]

*Alemayehu*, Ato Lulsegged, ml, Ethiopian Evangelical Church Mekane Yesus

*Alesana*, Rev. Enoka, mo, Congregational Christian Church in American Samoa

*Allsop*, Rev. Ian, mo, Churches of Christ in Australia

*Almasi*, Dr Stefan, ml, Reformed Church of Romania

*Ambrosius of Joensuu*, Bishop, mo, Orthodox Church of Finland

*Amouzou*, Pasteur Komla, mo, Evangelical Church of Togo

*Anderson*, Mr Alexander Ross, ml, Church of Scotland

*Anderson*, Bishop Vinton, mo, African Methodist Episcopal Church [USA]

*Anderson*, Mrs Vivienne, fl, African Methodist Episcopal Church [USA]

*Andersson*, Rev. Krister, mo, Mission Covenant Church of Sweden

*Andrea*, Ms Helene, fl, (Lebanon), Greek Orthodox Patriarchate of Antioch and All the East [Syria]

*Andrews*, Rev. James, mo, Presbyterian Church (USA)

*Anggui*, Rev. Andreas, mo, Toraja Church [Indonesia]

*Annobil*, Rt Rev. Theophilus, mo, (Ghana), Church of the Province of West Africa [Liberia]

*Arends*, Rev. Samuel, mo, (South Africa), United Congregational Church of Southern Africa

*Arnold*, Oberkirchenrat Walter, mo, Evangelical Church in Germany

*Ashjian*, Archbishop Mesrob, mo, (USA), Armenian Apostolic Church (Cilicia) [Lebanon]

*Asuoha*, Mrs Ezinne, fl, Presbyterian Church of Nigeria

*Attia*, Mr Maged, yml, (Australia), Coptic Orthodox Church [Egypt]

*Audi*, Metropolitan Elias, mo, (Lebanon), Greek Orthodox Patriarchate of Antioch and All the East [Syria]

*Auriaria*, Deaconess Rakera, yfl, Methodist Church in Fiji

*Austin*, Ven. George, mo, Church of England

*Avramides*, Rev. Stephen, mo, Church of Greece

*Avvakumov*, Rev. Fr Yuri, mo, Russian Orthodox Church

*Awasom*, Rev. Henry, mo, Presbyterian Church in Cameroon

*Aykazian*, Rev. Fr Viken, mo, (Switzerland), Armenian Apostolic Church (Etchmiadzin) [USSR]

*Ayres Mattos*, Bispo Paulo, mo, Methodist Church in Brazil

*Azariah*, Mrs Khushnud, fl, Church of Pakistan

*Baah*, Miss Maria, yfl, (Trinidad), African Methodist Episcopal Church [USA]

*Babirye*, Miss Sarah, fl, Church of Uganda

*Bärlund*, Ms Catarina, fl, Evangelical-Lutheran Church of Finland

*Baffoe*, Mr Stephen, yml, Methodist Church, Ghana

*Baiin*, Rev. Chita, mo, Pasundan Christian Church (GKP) [Indonesia]

*Bailey*, Mrs Joyce, fl, (Jamaica), Methodist Church in the Caribbean and the Americas

*Baker*, Rev. Christina, fo, United Church of Canada

*Bakhomios*, Metropolitan, mo, Coptic Orthodox Church [Egypt]

*Bakkevig*, Rev. Dr Trond, mo, Church of Norway

*Balfour*, Rev. Penny, fo, Scottish Episcopal Church

*Baliozian*, Bishop Aghan, mo, (Australia), Armenian Apostolic Church (Etchmiadzin) [USSR]

*Bannister*, Mrs Kathryn, yfl, United Methodist Church [USA]

*Barbier*, Pasteur Jean-Pierre, mo, Evangelical Lutheran Church of France

*Barcroft*, Miss Janet, fl, Church of Ireland

*Bartholomeos of Chalcedon*, Metropolitan, mo, Ecumenical Patriarchate of Constantinople [Turkey]

*Bartsch*, Dr Hans-Joachim, ml, Federation of Evangelical Churches [Germany]

*Basarab*, Dr Mircea, mo, (Germany), Romanian Orthodox Church

*Basmajian*, Ms Nancy, fl, (USA), Armenian Apostolic Church (Etchmiadzin) [USSR]

*Bass*, Bishop Richard, mo, Christian Methodist Episcopal Church [USA]

*Baur*, Herr Peter, ml, (Switzerland), United Methodist Church [USA]

*Bazett*, Barbara, fl, Canadian Yearly Meeting-Society of Friends

*Bebis*, Prof. Dr George, ml, (USA), Ecumenical Patriarchate of Constantinople [Turkey]

*Becker*, OLKR Henje, mo, Evangelical Church in Germany

*Bendza*, Prof. Dr Marian, ml, Autocephalic Orthodox Church in Poland

*Beredi*, Bischof Dr Andrej, mo, Slovak Evangelical Church-Augsburg Confession in Yugoslavia

*Bertrand*, Pasteur Michel, mo, Reformed Church of France

*Best*, Mrs Marion, fl, United Church of Canada

*Beukenhorst*, Pasteur Martinus, mo, United Protestant Church of Belgium

*Bezchasny*, Rev. Fr Sergey, mo, Russian Orthodox Church

*Bhintarto*, Drs Andrew Lucius, mo, Indonesian Christian Church (GKI)

*Bichkov*, Rev. Dr Alexei, mo, Evangelical Christian Baptist Union of the USSR

*Binas-O*, Miss Rosemarie, yfl, Philippine Independent Church

*Birmelé*, Prof. Dr André, mo, Evangelical Church of the Augsburg Confession of Alsace and Lorraine [France]

*Bishoy*, Bishop, mo, Coptic Orthodox Church [Egypt]

*Björnsdottir*, Mrs Adda, fl, Evangelical Lutheran Church of Iceland

*Blei*, Rev. Dr Karel, mo, Netherlands Reformed Church

*Bobrova*, Mrs Nina, fl, Russian Orthodox Church

*Boots*, Ms Nora, fl, United Methodist Church [USA]

*Borovoy*, Protopresbyter Vitaly, mo, Russian Orthodox Church

*Bosenberg*, Sra Cristina, yfl, Evangelical Church of the River Plate [Argentina]

*Boteler*, Rev. Mary-Gene, fo, Presbyterian Church (USA)

*Bottoms*, Rev. Ruth, yfo, Baptist Union of Great Britain

*Boukis*, Mr Dimitris, yml, Greek Evangelical Church

*Boyadjian*, Ms Manoushag, fl, Armenian Apostolic Church (Cilicia) [Lebanon]

*Bozabalian*, Archbishop Nerses, mo, Armenian Apostolic Church (Etchmiadzin) [USSR]

*Brandner*, Herr Tobias, yml, Swiss Protestant Church Federation

*Bredt*, Rev. Violet, fo, United Church of Zambia

*Brendel*, Herr Thomas, ml, Federation of Evangelical Churches [Germany]

*Bresch*, Pasteur Thomas, mo, Reformed Church of Alsace and Lorraine [France]

*Briggs*, Mr John, ml, Baptist Union of Great Britain

*Brink*, Rev. Agnete, fo, Evangelical Lutheran Church of Denmark

*Broadhurst*, Rev. John, mo, Church of England

*Brown*, Dr Katheryn Middleton, fl, African Methodist Episcopal Church [USA]

*Brown Christopher*, Bishop Sharon, fo, United Methodist Church [USA]

*Browning*, Most Rev. Edmond, mo, Episcopal Church [USA]

*Bruce*, Mrs Anne, fl, United Free Church of Scotland

*Bruce*, Rev. Graeme, mo, United Free Church of Scotland
*Bryce*, Rt Rev. Jabez, mo, (Fiji), Church of the Province of New Zealand
*Bubeer*, Mr Andrew, yml, Baptist Union of Great Britain
*Buchanan*, Rt Rev. Duncan, mo, (South Africa), Church of the Province of Southern Africa
*Bue*, Bishop Bjørn, mo, Church of Norway
*Buevsky*, Dr Alexei, ml, Russian Orthodox Church
*Burnham*, Ms Rachel, fo, United Reformed Church in the UK
*Bussert*, Rev. Joy, fo, Evangelical Lutheran Church in America
*Butler*, Rt Rev. Dr Thomas, mo, Church of England
*Buys*, Rev. Jameson, mo, Dutch Reformed Mission Church [South Africa]
*Cabildo*, Rev. Arcadio, mo, Evangelical Methodist Church in the Philippines
*Camba*, Bishop Erme, mo, United Church of Christ in the Philippines
*Cameron*, Miss Annabelle, yfl, Presbyterian Church in Canada
*Campbell*, Dr Dennis, mo, United Methodist Church [USA]
*Carey*, Rt Rev. George, mo, Church of England
*Carol*, Ms Anisoara, fl, Romanian Orthodox Church
*Carpenter*, Mrs Jennifer, fl, Methodist Church [UK]
*Carvalho*, Mr Ari, yml, United Methodist Church [USA]
*Caspary*, Pfarrer Heinrich-Nikolaus, mo, Evangelical Church in Germany
*Casserstedt Lundgren*, Mrs Gunilla, yfl, Church of Sweden
*Castro*, Bishop George, mo, Evangelical Methodist Church in the Philippines
*Chandrasekaran*, Prof. Edna, fl, United Evangelical Lutheran Churches in India
*Chatupa*, Mr Timothy, ml, United Church of Zambia
*Chilstrom*, Bishop Herbert, mo, Evangelical Lutheran Church in America
*Chiwanga*, Mrs Gladys, fl, Church of the Province of Tanzania
*Chovanova*, Rev. Dana, fo, Slovak Evangelical Church of the Augsburg Confession in the CSFR
*Christenson*, Mrs Joyce, fl, Evangelical Lutheran Church in Canada
*Christodoulos of Demetriados*, Metropolitan, mo, Church of Greece
*Chrysanthos of Limassol*, Metropolitan, mo, Church of Cyprus
*Chrysostomos of Myra*, Metropolitan, mo, (Greece), Ecumenical Patriarchate of Constantinople [Turkey]
*Chrysostomos of Peristerion*, Metropolitan, mo, Church of Greece
*Chryssavgis*, Rev. Dr John, mo, (Australia), Ecumenical Patriarchate of Constantinople [Turkey]
*Cioconea*, Mr Cristian, ml, Romanian Orthodox Church
*Coffey*, Rev. David, mo, Baptist Union of Great Britain
*Colley*, Mrs Carol, fl, United Methodist Church [USA]
*Coman*, Rev. Prof. Constantin, mo, Romanian Orthodox Church
*Conley*, Mrs Judith, fl, Episcopal Church [USA]
*Contreras Hernandez*, Sra Susana, fl, Methodist Church of Mexico
*Correia*, Profesora Evanilza de Barros, fl, Episcopal Church of Brazil

*Cosma*, Mother Filoteia, fl, Romanian Orthodox Church

*Coutret*, Therese, fl, Friends General Conference [USA]

*Cragg*, Rev. Dr Donald, mo, (South Africa), Methodist Church of Southern Africa

*Craston*, Rev. Canon Colin, mo, Church of England

*Crow, Jr*, Rev. Dr Paul, mo, Christian Church (Disciples of Christ) [USA]

*Csete-Szemesi*, Senior István, mo, Reformed Christian Church in Yugoslavia

*Csiha*, Dr theol. Kálmán, mo, Reformed Church of Romania

*Curnow*, Rev. Andrew, mo, Anglican Church of Australia

*Dabala*, Sr Mario, ml, (Uruguay), Waldensian Church [Italy]

*Daciuk*, Ms Anna, yfl, Autocephalic Orthodox Church in Poland

*Dadayan*, Mr Khatchig, ml, (Canada), Armenian Apostolic Church (Cilicia) [Lebanon]

*Daley*, Rev. Oliver, mo, (Jamaica), United Church of Jamaica and Grand Cayman

*Daniel of Moldavia and Bukovina*, Metropolitan, mo, Romanian Orthodox Church

*Danquah*, Ms Beatrice, yfl, Presbyterian Church of Ghana

*Darmoutomo*, Mr Prayudi, ml, Indonesian Christian Church (GKI)

*David of Suchumi and Abkhazeti*, Metropolitan, mo, Georgian Orthodox Church [USSR]

*Davies*, Rev. Noel, mo, Union of Welsh Independents

*Davison*, Mrs Beverly, fl, American Baptist Churches in the USA

*Daw*, Ms Diana, fl, Myanmar Baptist Convention

*Dawd-El-Khoury*, Mrs Mahat, fl, Greek Orthodox Patriarchate of Antioch and All the East [Syria]

*De Boer-De Leeuw*, Drs Jeannette, fl, Netherlands Reformed Church

*De Gaay Fortman*, Prof. Dr Bastiaan, ml, Reformed Churches in the Netherlands

*De La Torre*, Mrs Catalina, fl, Philippine Independent Church

*Deenik-Moolhuizen*, Rev. Jeannette, fo, Netherlands Reformed Church

*Denecke*, Pfarrerin Ulrike, fo, Evangelical Church in Germany

*Devasagayam*, Prof. Swamiraj, ml, Church of South India

*Dickson*, Rev. Prof. Kwesi, mo, Methodist Church, Ghana

*Dionysios of Neapolis*, Metropolitan, mo, Church of Greece

*Dipko*, Rev. Dr Thomas, mo, United Church of Christ [USA]

*Doig*, Mrs Margaret, fl, Church of Scotland

*Dometian of Vidin*, Metropolitan, mo, Bulgarian Orthodox Church

*Domingues*, Pastor Jorge, ymo, Methodist Church in Brazil

*Du*, Mrs Norma, fl, Philippine Independent Church

*Ebelle Ekanga*, Mme Nicole-Christine, fo, Evangelical Church of Cameroon

*Edgar*, Pauline, fl, Friends General Conference [USA]

*Edwards*, Very Rev. Dr David, mo, Church of England

*Edwards*, Ms Donnalie, yfl, (Barbados), Church in the Province of the West Indies

*Efthimiou*, Rev. Dr Milton, mo, (USA), Ecumenical Patriarchate of Constantinople [Turkey]

*Eidson*, Mr Ryan, yml, United Methodist Church [USA]

*Elia*, Mr David, yml, (Australia), Syrian Orthodox Patriarchate of Antioch and all the East [Syria]

*Elia*, Miss Rima, yfl, (Australia), Syrian Orthodox Patriarchate of Antioch and All the East [Syria]

*Endri Kusruri Karsanto*, Dra, fl, Javanese Christian Churches (GKJ) [Indonesia]

*Eneme*, Mrs Grace, fl, Presbyterian Church in Cameroon

*Engel*, Frau Edeltraud, fl, Evangelical Church in Germany

*Engelen*, Ms Irma, fl, Evangelical Church of Sangir Talaud (GMIST) [Indonesia]

*Epting*, Kirchenrat Dr Karl-Christoph, mo, Evangelical Church in Germany

*Erari*, Dr Karel, mo, Evangelical Christian Church in Irian Jaya [Indonesia]

*Eriksson*, Ms Annika, fl, Mission Covenant Church of Sweden

*Espino Zuniga*, Reverendo Oscar, mo, Baptist Convention of Nicaragua

*Estes*, Mr Tolly, ml, Episcopal Church [USA]

*Etienne*, Mrs Emmy, fl, (Seychelles), Church of the Province of the Indian Ocean

*Faa'alo*, Rev. Puafitu, mo, Tuvalu Christian Church

*Fabini*, Mrs Alida, fl, (Romania), Evangelical Church of the Augsburg Confession in Romania

*Familiaran*, Rev. Moley, mo, American Baptist Churches in the USA

*Farfan Figueroa*, Pastor Erasmo, mo, Pentecostal Mission Church [Chile]

*Fjärstedt*, Rev. Dr Biörn, mo, Church of Sweden

*Florea*, Mr Petru, ml, Romanian Orthodox Church

*Fortes*, Ms Raquel, yfl, Episcopal Church of Brazil

*Foster*, Rev. Robert, mo, Moravian Church in Jamaica

*Foth*, Ms Birgit, yfl, Mennonite Church [Germany]

*Fouras*, Mrs Maria, fl, (Australia), Church of Cyprus

*Francisco*, Rev. Julio, mo, Evangelical Congregational Church in Angola

*Francois*, Mrs Edith, fl, Presbyterian Church of Ghana

*Fraser*, Mr Craig, yml, Church of Scotland

*Frazier*, Mrs Bonnie, fl, Christian Church (Disciples of Christ) [USA]

*Fry*, Rev. Dr Franklin, mo, Evangelical Lutheran Church in America

*Fubara-Manuel*, Rev. Benebo, ymo, Presbyterian Church of Nigeria

*Gabriel*, H.G. Archbishop, mo, Ethiopian Orthodox Church

*Gabriel of Larissa*, Bishop, mo, (Australia), Greek Orthodox Patriarchate of Antioch and All the East [Syria]

*Gagua*, Mr Boris, ml, Georgian Orthodox Church [USSR]

*Galfy*, Dr Zoltán, mo, Reformed Church of Romania

*Gallay*, Mme Rose-Marie, fl, Swiss Protestant Church Federation

*Gam*, Rt Rev. Getake, mo, Evangelical Lutheran Church of Papua New Guinea

*Ganaba*, Mrs Olga, fl, Russian Orthodox Church

*Garima*, H.G. Archbishop, mo, Ethiopian Orthodox Church

*Garlington*, Ms Thelma, fl, International Evangelical Church [USA]

*Garrett*, Dr Maxine, fl, Moravian Church, USA (Northern Province)

*Gcabashe*, Mrs Virginia, fl, (South Africa), Methodist Church of Southern Africa

*Gedisa*, Ms Gabby, fl, Evangelical Lutheran Church of Papua New Guinea

*Geil*, Bishop Georg, mo, Evangelical Lutheran Church of Denmark

*Geil*, Ms Mette, yfl, Evangelical Lutheran Church of Denmark

*Geiser*, Pfarrer Daniel, mo, Mennonite Church [Germany]

*Georges*, Rev. Judith, fo, Church of the Brethren [USA]

*Gerka*, Prof. Dr Milan, mo, Orthodox Church of Czechoslovakia

*Gerny*, Bischof Hans, mo, Old Catholic Church of Switzerland

*Gerritsma*, Drs Nynke, yfl, Reformed Churches in the Netherlands

*Gerschau*, Ms Jutta, fl, Evangelical Church in Germany

*Ghose*, Most Rev. John, mo, Church of North India

*Giampiccoli*, Pastor Franco, mo, Waldensian Church [Italy]

*Giannopoulos*, Archimandrite Theofilos, mo, Greek Orthodox Patriarchate of Jerusalem

*Gilbert*, Dr Helga, fl, Evangelical Church in Germany

*Gill*, Mr Mehboob, ml, Church of Pakistan

*Girsang*, Rev. Kamonangan, mo, Simalungun Protestant Christian Church (GKPS) [Indonesia]

*Giultsis*, Prof. Vassilios, ml, (Greece), Greek Orthodox Patriarchate of Alexandria [Egypt]

*Gomez*, Rt Rev. Drexel, mo, (Barbados), Church in the Province of the West Indies

*Goncharov*, Rev. Fr Georgy, mo, (Czechoslavakia) Russian Orthodox Church

*Gondarra*, Rev. Djiniyini, mo, Uniting Church in Australia

*Gonzalez*, Mr Hector, ml, American Baptist Churches in the USA

*Gorski*, Obispo William, mo, Evangelical-Lutheran Church in Chile

*Grant*, Rev. James, mo, Church of Scotland

*Gregorios*, Metropolitan Dr Paulos Mar, mo, Malankara Orthodox Syrian Church [India]

*Grey-Smith*, Ms Ruth, fl, Anglican Church of Australia

*Grove*, Bishop William, mo, United Methodist Church [USA]

*Grumm*, Ms Christine, fl, Evangelical Lutheran Church in America

*Guibunda*, Mr Humberto, ml, (Mozambique), United Methodist Church [USA]

*Guli*, Rev. Dr John, mo, Church of the Brethren in Nigeria

*Gulo*, Rev. Lala'aro, mo, Nias Protestant Christian Church (BNKP) [Indonesia]

*Gutierrez*, Obispo Sinforiano, mo, Free Pentecostal Mission Church of Chile

*Habib*, Rev. Dr Samuel, mo, Synod of the Nile of the Evangelical Church [Egypt]

*Hallewas*, Dr Edward, mo, Evangelical Lutheran Church [Netherlands]

*Hanna*, Dr Marcelle, fl, (USA), Coptic Orthodox Church [Egypt]

*Hannon*, Rt Rev. Brian, mo, Church of Ireland

*Hanse*, Mr Willem, yml, (Namibia), African Methodist Episcopal Church [USA]

*Han Wenzao*, Mr, ml, China Christian Council

*Harahap*, Rev. Daniel, mo, Batak Protestant Christian Church (HKBP)
[Indonesia]

*Hargrave*, Mr James, yml, Church of England

*Harper*, Rev. Blanton, mo, National Baptist Convention of America

*Harris*, Mrs Dorothy, fl, Uniting Church in Australia

*Harteveld*, Mr Teunis, ml, Remonstrant Brotherhood [Netherlands]

*Hartmann*, Mme Henriette, fl, Swiss Protestant Church Federation

*Hatendi*, Rt Rev. Dr Ralph, mo, (Zimbabwe), Church of the Province of Central
Africa

*Havea*, Rev. Dr Sione, mo, Methodist Church in Tonga

*Hayes*, Rev. Stephen, mo, Presbyterian Church in Canada

*Hearn*, Rev. Woodrow, mo, United Methodist Church [USA]

*Hebmüller*, Mr Paulo, yml, Evangelical Church of Lutheran Confession [Brazil]

*Heilmann*, Herr Friedrich, ml, Federation of Evangelical Churches [Germany]

*Held*, Rev. Dr Heinz Joachim, mo, Evangelical Church in Germany

*Henseler*, Rev. Sarah, fo, Reformed Church in America

*Hirata*, Mrs Makiko, fl, United Church of Christ in Japan

*Hirschler*, Landesbischof Horst, mo, Evangelical Church in Germany

*Hoare*, Sir Timothy, ml, Church of England

*Hoekema*, Rev. Alle, mo, General Mennonite Society [Netherlands]

*Hösli*, Pfarrerin Sabina, fo, Swiss Protestant Church Federation

*Hoggard*, Bishop J. Clinton, mo, African Methodist Episcopal Zion Church
[USA]

*Holland*, Rev. Prof. Angus, mo, (Australia), Presbyterian Church of Southern
Africa

*Horsburgh*, Prof. Michael, ml, Anglican Church of Australia

*Horstman*, Bishop Teunis, mo, Old Catholic Church of the Netherlands

*Houmbouy*, Monsieur Béalo, ml, Evangelical Church in New Caledonia and the
Loyalty Isles

*Hromádka*, Dr Josef, mo, Evangelical Church of Czech Brethren

*Huang Chao-Hung*, Dr, ml, Presbyterian Church in Taiwan

*Humbert*, Rev. Dr John, mo, Christian Church (Disciples of Christ) [USA]

*Hunsinger*, Mme Béatrice, fl, Evangelical Church of the Augsburg Confession of
Alsace and Lorraine [France]

*Hutasoit*, Dra Rumondang, fl, Indonesian Christian Church (HKI)

*Huttunen*, Fr Heikki, mo, Orthodox Church of Finland

*Hwang Wha Ja*, Dr fl, Presbyterian Church of Korea

*Hye Yeon Yoo*, Ms, yfl, Presbyterian Church of Korea

*Hylleberg*, Rector Bent, mo, Baptist Union of Denmark

*Iannuariy*, Archimandrite, mo, Russian Orthodox Church

*Ibrahim*, Metropolitan Gregorios Yohanna, mo, Syrian Orthodox Patriarchate of
Antioch and All the East [Syria]

*Ieremia*, Mrs Tifilelei, fl, Congregational Christian Church in Samoa

*Ihorai*, Pasteur Jacques, mo, Evangelical Church of French Polynesia

*Ikuta*, Rev. Cynthia, fo, United Church of Christ [USA]

*Inangorore*, Mme Jennifer, fl, (Burundi), Church of the Province of Burundi, Rwanda and Zaire

*Ionita*, Rev. Fr Ioan, mo, (USA), Romanian Orthodox Church

*Iriney*, Metropolitan, mo, (Austria), Russian Orthodox Church

*Isho*, Mrs Susan, yfl, (Australia), Apostolic Catholic Assyrian Church of the East [Iraq]

*Iso*, Mr Malaipa, yml, (Papua New Guinea), United Church in Papua New Guinea and the Solomon Islands

*Istavridis*, Prof. Dr Vasil, ml, Ecumenical Patriarchate of Constantinople [Turkey]

*Ivanov*, Archpriest Vladimir, mo, (Germany), Russian Orthodox Church

*Izard*, Miss Rosemary, yfl, Methodist Church [UK]

*Jabbour*, Mr Tony, ml, (Australia), Greek Orthodox Patriarchate of Antioch and All the East [Syria]

*Jackson*, Mr J. Rhett, ml, United Methodist Church [USA]

*Jacobs*, Mrs Lorraine, fl, Associated Churches of Christ in New Zealand

*Jacobsen*, Ms Anna, fl, Church of Norway

*Jägers*, Mrs Maryon, fl, (Netherlands), Church of England

*Jäggi*, Pfarrer Paul, mo, Swiss Protestant Church Federation

*Jagusch*, Herr Karl-Heinz, ml, Federation of Evangelical Churches [Germany]

*James*, Rev. Prof. Arthur, mo, United Presbyterian Church of Pakistan

*Jarjour*, Mrs Rosangela, fl, (Cyprus), National Evangelical Synod of Syria and Lebanon

*Jathanna*, Miss Sukumari, fl, Church of South India

*Jefferson*, Rev. Ruth, fo, Anglican Church of Canada

*Jenkins*, Rev. David, mo, United Reformed Church in the UK

*Jensen*, Rev. Russell, mo, Baptist Union of New Zealand

*Jeremias*, Bishop, mo, Autocephalic Orthodox Church in Poland

*Jessiman*, Dr Jon, ml, United Church of Canada

*Jock*, Rev. John, mo, Presbyterian Church in the Sudan

*John of Finland*, Archbishop, mo, Orthodox Church of Finland

*John of Pergamon*, Metropolitan, mo, (Greece), Ecumenical Patriarchate of Constantinople [Turkey]

*Johnson*, Bishop S. Tilewa, mo, (Gambia), Church of the Province of West Africa

*Johnston*, Prof. Alexandra, fl, Presbyterian Church in Canada

*Jones*, Rt Rev. Alwyn Rice, mo, Church in Wales

*Jones*, Rev. Barry, mo, Methodist Church of New Zealand

*Jones*, Ms Catherine, yfl, Methodist Church of New Zealand

*Jones*, Dr Mac Charles, mo, National Baptist Convention of America

*Jones, Jr*, Rev. Robert, mo, National Baptist Convention of America

*Jongeneel-Touw*, Drs Magritha, fl, Netherlands Reformed Church

*Jonson*, Rt Rev. Dr Jonas, mo, Church of Sweden

*Joseph*, Rev. Winston, mo, (Trinidad), Church in the Province of the West Indies

*Juanitez*, Rt Rev. Julian, mo, Philippine Independent Church

*Jung*, Dr Hans-Gernot, mo, Evangelical Church in Germany

*Juras*, Mr Jan, ml, Slovak Evangelical Church-Augsburg Confession in the CSFR

*Kaessmann*, Rev. Dr Margot, fo, Evangelical Church in Germany

*Kalayci*, Deacon Hrisostomo, mo, Ecumenical Patriarchate of Constantinople [Turkey]

*Kalinik of Vratsa*, Metropolitan, mo, Bulgarian Orthodox Church

*Kambodji*, Rev. Djatu, mo, Christian Church of Central Sulawesi (GKST) [Indonesia]

*Kang Byoung Hoon*, Dr, mo, Korean Methodist Church

*Kangrga*, Dr Nedeljko, ml, Serbian Orthodox Church [Yugoslavia]

*Kao Chun-Ming*, Rev., mo, Presbyterian Church in Taiwan

*Karaisarides*, Rev. Constantine, mo, Church of Greece

*Karickam*, Prof. Abraham, ml, Mar Thoma Syrian Church of Malabar [India]

*Karpenko*, Rev. Fr Alexander, mo, (Switzerland), Russian Orthodox Church

*Kathii*, Rev. Henry, mo, Church of the Province of Kenya

*Kathindi*, Mrs Nangula, fl, (Namibia), Church of the Province of Southern Africa

*Katonia*, Citoyen Tusange, yml, Episcopal Baptist Community [Zaire]

*Kazilimani*, Mr Jason, ml, (Zambia), Church of the Province of Central Africa

*Kea*, Mrs Charlotte, fl, Church of the Province of Kenya

*Keim*, Frau Christine, yfl, Evangelical Church in Germany

*Kelly*, Ms Emily, yfl, Presbyterian Church (USA)

*Kennedy*, Rev. John, mo, (UK), Methodist Church

*Keshishian*, Archbishop Aram, mo, Armenian Apostolic Church (Cilicia) [Lebanon]

*Ketuabanza*, Mme Mfutu, fl, Baptist Community of West Zaire

*Khelendende*, Maman Ndota, fl, Mennonite Community [Zaire]

*Khumalo*, Rev. Dr Samson, mo, Presbyterian Church of Africa [South Africa]

*Kidess*, Rev. Fr Issa, mo, Greek Orthodox Patriarchate of Antioch and All the East [Syria]

*Kidu*, Rev. Edea, mo, (Papua New Guinea), United Church in Papua New Guinea and the Solomon Islands

*Kidu*, Mrs Taboro, fl, (Papua New Guinea), United Church in Papua New Guinea and the Solomon Islands

*Kikalao*, Mr Nashon, yml, Evangelical Lutheran Church in Tanzania

*Kim Hyung Ki*, Mr, ml, Presbyterian Church in the Republic of Korea

*Kim Hyung Tae*, Very Rev. Dr, mo, Presbyterian Church of Korea

*Kimhachandra*, Rev. Sint, mo, Church of Christ in Thailand

*Kimijima*, Rev. Yozaburo, mo, United Church of Christ in Japan

*Kinnunen*, Mrs Mari, yfl, Evangelical-Lutheran Church of Finland

*Kirby*, Ms Ellen, fl, United Methodist Church [USA]

*Kirill of Smolensk*, H.E. Archbishop, mo, Russian Orthodox Church

*Kirkpatrick*, Rev. Clifton, mo, Presbyterian Church (USA)

*Kirov*, Mr Dimitre, ml, Bulgarian Orthodox Church

*Kishkovsky*, Very Rev. Leonid, mo, Orthodox Church in America

*Kisku*, Most Rev. Sagenen, mo, United Evangelical Lutheran Churches in India

*Kitahara*, Ms Yoko, yfl, United Church of Christ in Japan

*Klaiber*, Bischof Dr Walter, mo, (Germany), United Methodist Church [USA]

*Klapsis*, Rev. Dr Emmanuel, mo, (USA), Ecumenical Patriarchate of Constantinople [Turkey]

*Klein*, Bischof Dr Christoph, mo, Evangelical Church of the Augsburg Confession in Romania

*Knall*, Bischof Dr Dieter, mo, Evangelical Church of the Augsburg and Helvetic Confessions [Austria]

*Koenig*, Oberkirchenrätin Irene, fo, Federation of Evangelical Churches [Germany]

*Koffeman*, Dr Leendert, mo, Reformed Churches in the Netherlands

*Kolowa*, Bishop Sebastian, mo, Evangelical Lutheran Church in Tanzania

*Konach*, Mr Wsiewolod, ml, Autocephalic Orthodox Church in Poland

*Korhammer*, Dr Rita, fl, Evangelical Church in Germany

*Koshiishi*, Rev. Samuel, mo, Anglican-Episcopal Church in Japan

*Koshy*, Prof. George, ml, Church of South India

*Kosieng*, Pastor Beka, mo, Evangelical Lutheran Church of Papua New Guinea

*Kostic*, Very Rev. Milun, mo, (UK), Serbian Orthodox Church [Yugoslavia]

*Koukoura*, Dr Dimitra, fl, (Greece), Greek Orthodox Patriarchate of Alexandria [Egypt]

*Kovacevich*, Bishop Christopher, mo, (USA), Serbian Orthodox Church [Yugoslavia]

*Kraft*, Bischof Dr Sigisbert, mo, Catholic Diocese of Old Catholics in Germany

*Krco*, Bishop Longin, mo, (Australia), Serbian Orthodox Church [Yugoslavia]

*Kreyer*, Rev. Virginia, fo, United Church of Christ [USA]

*Krusche*, Generalsup. Dr Günter, mo, Federation of Evangelical Churches [Germany]

*Küttler*, Superintendent Thomas, mo, Federation of Evangelical Churches [Germany]

*Kumar*, Miss Rachel, fl, Methodist Church in India

*Kumar*, Mr Uttam, ml, United Evangelical Lutheran Churches in India

*Kumari*, Miss B. Samarpana, yfl, Church of South India

*Kunuk*, Assist. Sup. Methusalah, ml, Anglican Church of Canada

*Kuria*, Rev. Dr Plawson, mo, (Kenya), Presbyterian Church of East Africa

*Kurian*, Fr Dr Jacob, mo, Malankara Orthodox Syrian Church [India]

*Kyrill*, Archimandrite, mo, (UK), Ecumenical Patriarchate of Constantinople [Turkey]

*L'Huillier*, Archbishop Peter, mo, Orthodox Church in America

*Labajova*, Ms Vlasta, yfl, Silesian Evangelical Church-Augsburg Confession [CSFR]

*Labi*, Rev. Fr Kwame, mo, (Ghana), Greek Orthodox Patriarchate of Alexandria and All Africa [Egypt]

*Labiro*, Dra Paulina, fl, Christian Church of Central Sulawesi (GKST) [Indonesia]

*Laham*, Me Albert, ml, (Switzerland), Greek Orthodox Patriarchate of Antioch and All the East [Syria]

*Laidlaw*, Mrs Catherine, fl, Church of Scotland

*Lakew*, Mrs Zewditu, fl, Ethiopian Orthodox Church

*Lal*, Rev. James, mo, Methodist Church in India

*Larsson*, Dr Birgitta, fl, Church of Sweden

*Lasaro Rakuka*, Rev. Manasa, mo, Methodist Church in Fiji

*Le Roux*, Ms Yvette, yfl, (South Africa), Methodist Church of Southern Africa

*Lee*, Prof. Dr Samuel, ml, Presbyterian Church of Korea

*Lefringhausen*, Dr Klaus, ml, Evangelical Church in Germany

*Lenz-Matthies*, Frau Hildegard, fl, Evangelical Church in Germany

*Lethunya*, Mrs Sebolelo, fl, Lesotho Evangelical Church

*Leuluaialii*, Rev. Siatua, mo, (Western Samoa), Methodist Church in Samoa

*Leuluaialii*, Mrs Nefara, fl, (Western Samoa), Methodist Church in Samoa

*Lewis*, Rev. Dr Kingsley, mo, (Antigua), Moravian Church, Eastern West Indies Province

*Libbey*, Rev. Dr Scott, mo, United Church of Christ [USA]

*Liddell*, Dr Shirley, fl, Christian Methodist Episcopal Church [USA]

*Lind*, Mrs Hilda, fl, Church of Sweden

*Llewellyn*, Dr Hallett, mo, United Church of Canada

*Lodberg*, Mr Peter, ml, Evangelical Lutheran Church of Denmark

*Lofton*, Dr Fred, mo, Progressive National Baptist Convention Inc. [USA]

*Lossky*, Prof. Nicolas, ml, (France), Russian Orthodox Church

*Love*, Dr Janice, fl, United Methodist Church [USA]

*Lumenta*, Rev. Dirk, mo, Protestant Church in Indonesia

*Lutz*, Mr Charles, ml, Evangelical Lutheran Church in America

*Lynn*, Ms Stephanie, yfl, United Church of Canada

*M'Imathiu*, Bishop Lawi, mo, Methodist Church in Kenya

*Mackenzie*, Ms Vanessa, fl, (South Africa), Church of the Province of Southern Africa

*Maeda*, Ms Keiko, fl, Anglican-Episcopal Church in Japan

*Mäkeläinen*, Dr Heikki, mo, Evangelical-Lutheran Church of Finland

*Makikon*, Mrs Leionney, fl, Presbyterian Church of Vanuatu

*Makonnen*, Ato Gabre Christos, ml, Ethiopian Orthodox Church

*Malcolm*, Rt Rev. Arthur, mo, Anglican Church of Australia

*Malpas*, Mrs Jan, fl, Anglican Church of Australia

*Maltzahn*, Ms Kathleen, yfl, Uniting Church in Australia

*Mandeng*, Rev. Dr David, mo, Presbyterian Church of Cameroon

*Mandysová*, Mrs Nadeje, fl, Evangelical Church of Czech Brethren

*Mani*, Bishop Emmanuel, mo, Church of Nigeria

*Manik*, Elder Ingan, ml, Karo Batak Protestant Church (GBKP) [Indonesia]

*Mantik-Mingkid*, Mrs Annette, fl, Protestant Church in Indonesia

*Mapanao*, Miss Maryssa, fl, United Church of Christ in the Philippines

*Maraki*, Rev. Pakoa, mo, Presbyterian Church of Vanuatu

*Marc*, Mme le pasteur Isabelle, fo, Reformed Church of France

*Martelli*, Rev. Claudio, mo, Evangelical Methodist Church of Italy

*Martinez*, Rev. Joel, mo, United Methodist Church [USA]

*Masal*, Rev. Edwin, mo, Kalimantan Evangelical Church (GKE) [Indonesia]

*Mashao*, Mr Zachariah, ml, (South Africa), Evangelical Lutheran Church in Southern Africa

*Mategyero*, Rev. Stanley, mo, Church of Uganda

*Mathew*, Mrs Rachel, fl, Mar Thoma Syrian Church of Malabar [India]

*Mathew*, Miss Rebecca, fl, (USA), Malankara Orthodox Syrian Church [India]

*Matsinhe*, Rev. Carlos, mo, (Mozambique), Church of the Province of Southern Africa

*Matumbyo*, Mr Christopher, yml, Church of the Province of Tanzania

*Mawhinney*, Rev. Edmund, mo, Methodist Church in Ireland

*May Mya Tun*, Ms, yfl, Church of the Province of Burma

*Mayland*, Mrs Jean, fl, Church of England

*Mba Nzue*, Pasteur Emmanuel, mo, Evangelical Church of Gabon

*Mbelolo*, Prof. Ya Mpiku, ml, Evangelical Community [Zaire]

*Mbise*, Ms Loe Rose, fl, Evangelical Lutheran Church in Tanzania

*Mbugo*, Mr Andrew, yml, Province of the Episcopal Church of the Sudan

*Mburu*, Mr Saphiah Kiania, ml, (Kenya), Presbyterian Church of East Africa

*McGonigle*, Dr George, ml, Episcopal Church [USA]

*McKenzie*, Mr Tyrone, ml, (UK), Church in the Province of the West Indies

*Meade*, Miss Alfreda, fl, (Montserrat), Church in the Province of the West Indies

*Mehlape*, Mrs Mabel, fl, (South Africa), Evangelical Lutheran Church in Southern Africa

*Mekarios*, H.G. Archbishop, mo, Ethiopian Orthodox Church

*Melchizedek*, H.G. Bishop, mo, Ethiopian Orthodox Church

*Meletios of Nikopolis*, Metropolitan, mo, Church of Greece

*Melnik*, Sister Liubov, fl, Russian Orthodox Church

*Menon*, Mr Vijay, ml, Church of England

*Messakh*, Rev. Thobias, mo, Protestant Evangelical Church in Timor (GMIT) [Indonesia]

*Mészáros*, Bishop Dr István, mo, Reformed Church in Hungary

*Mezmer*, Pfarrer Otto, mo, Evangelical Synodal Presbyterial Church of the Augsburg confession in Romania

*Mghwira*, Ms Anna, fl, Evangelical Lutheran Church in Tanzania

*Michael*, Mr Rajkumar, ml, Methodist Church in India

*Mikó*, Dr Eugen, mo, Reformed Christian Church in Slovakia [CSFR]

*Miletich*, Theologian Srboljub, ml, (Australia), Serbian Orthodox Church [Yugoslavia]

*Miller*, Dr Donald, mo, Church of the Brethren [USA]

*Miller*, Mrs Peggy Reiff, fl, Church of the Brethren [USA]

*Miller-Keeley*, Archdeacon Diane, fo, Church of the Province of New Zealand

*Mirza*, Rt Rev. Dr Zahir-Ud-Din, mo, Church of Pakistan

*Misukka*, Ms Marina, yfl, Orthodox Church of Finland

*Mitchell*, Dr Mozella, fl, African Methodist Episcopal Zion Church [USA]

*Mitsides*, Dr Andreas, ml, Church of Cyprus

*Moderow*, Sup. Hans-Martin, mo, Federation of Evangelical Churches [Germany]

*Mogoba*, Bishop Mmuthlonyane, mo, (South Africa), Methodist Church of Southern Africa

*Mogwe*, Miss Alice, fl, (Botswana), Church of the Province of Central Africa

*Moraitini*, Mrs Aliki, fl, (Switzerland), Ecumenical Patriarchate of Constantinople [Turkey]

*Moran*, Ms Cecilia, fl, Presbyterian Church (USA)

*Moraru*, Rev. Prof. Alexandru, mo, Romanian Orthodox Church

*Morris*, Ms Anne, fl, Church of England

*Morris Jones*, Rev. Derwyn, mo, Union of Welsh Independents

*Moseme*, Rev. Dr Abiel, mo, Lesotho Evangelical Church

*Motel*, Pfarrer Hans-Beat, mo, European Continental Province of the Moravian Church — Western District [Germany]

*Motsoeneng*, Mr Tseliso, yml, Lesotho Evangelical Church

*Moukouyou-Kimbouala*, Monsieur Michel, ml, Evangelical Church of the Congo

*Mourad Malak*, Mrs Jacklin, yfl, (Australia), Coptic Orthodox Church [Egypt]

*Moussa*, Bishop, mo, Coptic Orthodox Church [Egypt]

*Müller-Stöver*, Dr Irmela, fl, Evangelical Church in Germany

*Mulder*, Dr Edwin, mo, Reformed Church in America

*Mules*, Mr Glen, ml, Orthodox Church in America

*Mundi*, Mrs Regina, fl, Presbyterian Church in Cameroon

*Mungania*, Rev. John, mo, Methodist Church in Kenya

*Munir*, Mr Shahzad, yml, United Presbyterian Church of Pakistan

*Muñoz Moraga*, Pastor Luis, mo, Pentecostal Church of Chile

*Munro*, Rev. Gavin, mo, Associated Churches of Christ in New Zealand

*Munteanu*, Mr Ioan, ml, Romanian Orthodox Church

*Musinskis*, Propst Laimons, mo, (Australia), Evangelical Lutheran Church of Latvia in Exile [Canada]

*Musuamba*, Mme Bilenga, fl, Presbyterian Community [Zaire]

*Muttiah*, Rev. Dr Thesiganesan, mo, Methodist Church [Sri Lanka]

*Muwanika*, Ms Harriet, yfl, Church of Uganda

*Muzau*, Pasteur Kitangwa, mo, Baptist Community of West Zaire

*Mwondha*, Mrs Faith, fl, Church of Uganda

*Mya Han*, Most Rev. Andrew, mo, Church of the Province of Burma

*Nababan*, Ephorus Dr Soritua, mo, Batak Protestant Christian Church (HKBP) [Indonesia]

*Nacpil*, Bishop Emerito, mo, (Philippines), United Methodist Church [USA]

*Najarian*, Rev. Fr Haigazoun, mo, (USA), Armenian Apostolic Church (Etch-miadzin) [USSR]

*Nakashian*, Mrs Anoush, fl, (Jerusalem), Armenian Apostolic Church (Etchmiad-zin) [USSR]

*Naniye*, Chanoine Alfred, mo, (Burundi), Church of the Province of Burundi, Rwanda and Zaire

*Neevel*, Rev. Mary Ann, fo, United Church of Christ [USA]

*Neliubova*, Ms Margarita, fl, Russian Orthodox Church

*Nestor*, Hieromonk, mo, Russian Orthodox Church

*Ngcobo*, Rev. Samuel, mo, (South Africa), Reformed Presbyterian Church of Southern Africa

*Ngoda*, Mrs Joyce, fl, Church of the Province of Tanzania

*Ngoie-Wa-Banze*, Diaconesse, fo, Episcopal Baptist Community [Zaire]

*Nguema Mvie*, Monsieur César, ml, Evangelical Church of Gabon

*Ngugi*, Rt Rev. James, mo, African Christian Church and Schools [Kenya]

*Niederhoffen*, Rev. Zoltán, mo, Reformed Church in Hungary

*Nieminski*, Rt Rev. Dr Joseph, mo, (Canada), Polish National Catholic Church [USA]

*Nifon of Ploiesti*, Bishop, mo, Romanian Orthodox Church

*Nikolaj of Dalmatia*, Bishop, mo, Serbian Orthodox Church [Yugoslavia]

*Niphon of Philipopolis*, Bishop, mo, (USSR), Greek Orthodox Patriarchate of Antioch and All the East [Syria]

*Njike*, Pasteur Charles, mo, Evangelical Church of Cameroon

*Nontawasee*, Mrs Prakai, fl, Church of Christ in Thailand

*Norgate*, Rt Rev. Richard, mo, Church of the Province of Tanzania

*Norman*, Ms Virginia, fl, (Dominican Republic), Episcopal Church [USA]

*Nwokafor*, Mr Anthony, ml, Methodist Church [Nigeria]

*Nyawo*, Mrs Edith, fl, Evangelical Presbyterian Church in South Africa

*Nyirabukara*, Mme Josette, fl, Presbyterian Church of Rwanda

*O'Connor*, Rev. Canon Michael, mo, Church of England

*Odenberg*, Rev. Christina, fo, Church of Sweden

*Oettel*, Frau Christine, fl, Federation of Evangelical Churches [Germany]

*Okine*, Mrs Naomi, fl, Methodist Church, Ghana

*Okullu*, Rt Rev. Dr J. Henry, mo, Church of the Province of Kenya

*Olf*, Ms Vivian, fl, (Netherlands), European Continental Province of the Mora-vian Church — Western District [Germany]

*Oliveira*, Reverendo Deaõ Orlando, mo, Episcopal Church of Brazil

*Omodunbi*, Bishop Amos, mo, Methodist Church [Nigeria]

*Omoyajowo*, Very Rev. Prof. Joseph, mo, Church of Nigeria

*Oneka*, Mr Joseph, ml, Church of Uganda

*Onema*, Evêque Fama, mo, (Zaire), United Methodist Church [USA]

*Orach*, Mrs Esther, fl, Presbyterian Church in the Sudan

*Orlova*, Ms Tatyana, fl, Evangelical Christian Baptist Union of the USSR

*Orteza*, Mrs Edna, fl, (USA), United Church of Christ in the Philippines

*Osipov*, Prof. Alexei, ml, Russian Orthodox Church
*Osnaya Jimenez*, Ms Saraí, fl, (Mexico), Episcopal Church [USA]
*Ostrowski de Núñez*, Dra Margarita, fl, Evangelical Church of the River Plate [Argentina]
*Otello*, Consenior Jerzy, mo, Evangelical Church of the Augsburg Confession in Poland
*Ottley*, Rt Rev. James, mo, (Panama), Episcopal Church [USA]
*Ovcharenko*, Ms Alevtina, yfl, Russian Orthodox Church
*Owen*, Mrs Brenda, fl, Presbyterian Church of Wales
*Owen*, Rev. David, mo, Presbyterian Church of Wales
*Page*, Rev. Dr Ruth, fo, Church of Scotland
*Pahl*, Ms Cerise, fl, Evangelical Church of Lutheran Confession [Brazil]
*Pajula*, Erzbischof Kuno, mo, Estonian Evangelical Lutheran Church [USSR]
*Palmer*, Mr Samuel, ml, Methodist Church of Sierra Leone
*Panteleimon of Zakyntos*, Metropolitan, mo, Church of Greece
*Papaderos*, Dr Alexandros, ml, (Greece), Ecumenical Patriarchate of Constantinople [Turkey]
*Papazian*, Prof. Hakob, ml, Armenian Apostolic Church (Etchmiadzin) [USSR]
*Park Jong-Wha*, Prof. Dr, mo, Presbyterian Church in the Republic of Korea
*Park Pong Bae*, Rev. Dr, mo, Korean Methodist Church
*Parvey*, Rev. Constance, fo, Evangelical Lutheran Church in America
*Pasco*, Obispo Maximo Tito, mo, Philippine Independent Church
*Pashaian*, Mrs Kariné, fl, Armenian Apostolic Church (Etchmiadzin) [USSR]
*Patelos*, Prof. Constantine, ml, (Greece), Greek Orthodox Patriarchate of Alexandria and All Africa [Egypt]
*Patton*, Dr Janet, fl, Presbyterian Church (USA)
*Paul*, Ms Jenny, fl, Province of the Episcopal Church of the Sudan
*Paula*, Bishop, mo, Coptic Orthodox Church [Egypt]
*Paulin*, Rev. Rachel, fo, Presbyterian Church of New Zealand
*Pavlovic*, Metropolitan Jovan, mo, Serbian Orthodox Church [Yugoslavia]
*Peacocke*, Rev. Dennis, mo, International Evangelical Church [USA]
*Peers*, Most Rev. Michael, mo, Anglican Church of Canada
*Pereeti*, Rev. Tekere, mo, Cook Islands Christian Church
*Peter*, Mrs Joyce, fl, Presbyterian Church of Africa [South Africa]
*Petersoo*, Most Rev. Udo, mo, Estonian Evangelical Lutheran Church [Canada]
*Petliuchenko*, Archpriest Viktor, mo, Russian Orthodox Church
*Pheidas*, Prof. Vlasios, ml, Church of Greece
*Phenya*, Rt Rev. Rassie Gladwin, mo, (South Africa), Presbyterian Church of Southern Africa
*Pickens*, Dr Larry, mo, United Methodist Church [USA]
*Pihkala*, Rev. Dr Juha, mo, Evangelical-Lutheran Church of Finland
*Pikulski*, Pfr Dr Kazimierz, mo, Polish Catholic Church in Poland
*Pilton*, Ms Linda, yfl, Churches of Christ in Australia
*Piske*, Rev. Meinrad, mo, Evangelical Church of Lutheran Confession [Brazil]

*Pitakoe*, Mr Luke, ml, (Solomon Islands), United Church in Papua New Guinea and the Solomon Islands

*Pitts*, Rev. Tyrone, mo, Progressive National Baptist Convention Inc. [USA]

*Poblete Molina*, Sr Manuel, ml, Pentecostal Church of Chile

*Poe*, Ms Margaret, yfl, United Methodist Church [USA]

*Pogo*, Rt Rev. Ellison, mo, (Solomon Islands), Church of Melanesia

*Pons*, Sra Mariela, yfl, Evangelical Methodist Church [Argentina]

*Popescu*, Mr Cristian, yml, Romanian Orthodox Church

*Popescu*, Rev. Prof. Dimitru, mo, Romanian Orthodox Church

*Popov*, Prelate Alexander, mo, (Australia), Bulgarian Orthodox Church

*Post*, Herr Martin, yml, Evangelical Church in Germany

*Posumah*, Rev. Jedida, fo, Christian Evangelical Church in Minahasa (GMIM) [Indonesia]

*Powell*, Rev. Staccato, mo, African Methodist Episcopal Zion Church [USA]

*Predele*, Ms Aida, fl, Evangelical Lutheran Church of Latvia [USSR]

*Premasagar*, Rt Rev. Victor, mo, Church of South India

*Psiachas*, Metropolitan Dionysios, mo, (New Zealand), Ecumenical Patriarchate of Constantinople [Turkey]

*Pullam*, Ms Ruth, fl, United Church of Canada

*Rabe Ranjanivo*, Mlle Mialy-Tiana, yfl, Malagasy Lutheran Church

*Rabenirina*, Mgr Rémi, mo, (Madagascar), Church of the Province of the Indian Ocean

*Rabetokotany*, Monsieur Miarilaza, yml, Church of Jesus Christ in Madagascar

*Racimo*, Rev. Fr Primitivo, mo, Philippine Independent Church

*Rada*, Dr Heath, ml, Presbyterian Church (USA)

*Raiser*, Prof. Dr Konrad, mo, Evangelical Church in Germany

*Raiwalui*, Mrs Vasiti, fl, Methodist Church in Fiji

*Rakic*, Protodeacon Radomir, mo, Serbian Orthodox Church [Yugoslavia]

*Rakotomanga*, Mlle Lucile, yfl, Church of Jesus Christ in Madagascar

*Rakotomaro*, Pasteur Jean-Baptiste, mo, Malagasy Lutheran Church

*Ramambasoa*, Mme Florentine, fl, Church of Jesus Christ in Madagascar

*Ramambasoa*, Pasteur Joseph, mo, Church of Jesus Christ in Madagascar

*Rambaran*, Drs Fred, mo, Moravian Church in Suriname

*Rani*, Ms V.R. Vidhya, fl, United Evangelical Lutheran Churches in India

*Ranorosoalalao*, Mme Simone, fl, Malagasy Lutheran Church

*Rantakari*, Mrs Birgitta, fl, (Zambia), Evangelical-Lutheran Church of Finland

*Rastan*, Miss Simin, fl, (Iran) Episcopal Church in Jerusalem and Middle East

*Ravololoson*, Mme le pasteur Esther, fo, Church of Jesus Christ in Madagascar

*Rayner*, Most Rev. Dr Keith, mo, Anglican Church of Australia

*Reber*, Dr Robert, ml, United Methodist Church [USA]

*Regul*, Oberkirchenrat Jürgen, mo, Evangelical Church in Germany

*Rehm*, Ms Jennifer, yfl, Episcopal Church [USA]

*Reid*, Ms Evelyn, fl, National Baptist Convention of America

*Reitsma*, Mr Bernard, yml, Netherlands Reformed Church

*Rhaburn*, Mrs Violet, fl, (Panama), Methodist Church in the Caribbean and the Americas

*Richaud*, Mme Vahi, fl, Evangelical Church of French Polynesia

*Richmond*, Rev. Helen, fo, Uniting Church in Australia

*Rights*, Dr Graham, mo, Moravian Church, USA (Southern Province)

*Riini*, Mrs Mona, fl, Presbyterian Church of New Zealand

*Ritchie*, Pastora Nélida, fo, Evangelical Methodist Church [Argentina]

*Robbins*, Rev. Dr Bruce, mo, United Methodist Church [USA]

*Robins*, Ms Zaiga, fl, (USA), Evangelical Lutheran Church of Latvia [USSR]

*Robinson*, Mr Keith, ml, Scottish Episcopal Church

*Rodgers*, Deaconess Margaret, fl, Anglican Church of Australia

*Röder*, Pfarrer Thomas, mo, (Germany), United Methodist Church [USA]

*Rogerson*, Rt Rev. Barry, mo, Church of England

*Romanides*, Prof. John, mo, Church of Greece

*Rondo*, Rev. Kelly, mo, Christian Evangelical Church in Minahasa (GMIM) [Indonesia]

*Roric* Jur, Rt Rev. Gabriel, mo, Province of the Episcopal Church of the Sudan

*Rose*, Mr Mark, yml, Evangelical Lutheran Church in Canada

*Roskovec*, Rev. Jan, ymo, Evangelical Church of Czech Brethren

*Rotgans*, Ms Rosalien, fl, Moravian Church in Suriname

*Ruiz Avila*, Obispo Raul, mo, Methodist Church of Mexico

*Rumbergs*, Dr Daina, fl, (Australia), Evangelical Lutheran Church of Latvia in Exile [Canada]

*Rumsarwir*, Rev. Willem, mo, Evangelical Christian Church in Irian Jaya [Indonesia]

*Ruoff*, Ms Kerstin, yfl, Evangelical Church in Germany

*Rusch*, Rev. Dr William, mo, Evangelical Lutheran Church in America

*Russell*, Mrs Cheryl, fl, United Methodist Church [USA]

*Rusterholz*, Pfarrer Heinrich, mo, Swiss Protestant Church Federation

*Saga*, Mr Stewart, ml, Methodist Church in Malaysia

*Sahade*, Rev. Fr Ignacio, mo, (Argentina), Greek Orthodox Patriarchate of Antioch and All the East [Syria]

*Sahiouny*, Rev. Dr Salim, mo, (Lebanon), National Evangelical Synod of Syria and Lebanon

*Sahuburua*, Mr Zeth, ml, Protestant Church in the Moluccas (GPM) [Indonesia]

*Sakaian*, Miss Christine, yfl, (Australia), Armenian Apostolic Church (Etchmiadzin) [USSR]

*Salamate*, Rev. Eldad, mo, Evangelical Church of Sangir Talaud (GMIST) [Indonesia]

*Samban*, Prof. Dr Jacob, ml, Toraja Church [Indonesia]

*Samuel*, Archbishop Athanasius, mo, (USA), Syrian Orthodox Patriarchate of Antioch and All the East [Syria]

*Sandelin*, Mr Holger, yml, Church of Sweden

*Sandiford*, Ms Audrey, yfl, Anglican Church of Canada

*Sano*, Bishop Roy, mo, United Methodist Church [USA]

*Sapina*, Mr Miroslav, ml, (Austria), Serbian Orthodox Church [Yugoslavia]

*Sasaujan*, Mr Mihai-Simion, yml, Romanian Orthodox Church

*Sauca*, Rev. Prof. Ioan, mo, Romanian Orthodox Church

*Schaad*, Pastor Juan Pedro, mo, (Paraguay), Evangelical Church of the River Plate [Argentina]

*Schaefer*, Pfarrer Hermann, mo, Evangelical Church in Germany

*Scott*, Dr Beverly, fl, American Baptist Churches in the USA

*Scott*, Mr Paul, ml, International Council of Community Churches [USA]

*Scoutas*, Mrs Patricia, fl, (Australia), Ecumenical Patriarchate of Constantinople [Turkey]

*Scouteris*, Prof. Constantine, ml, Church of Greece

*Seddoh*, Mme Nenevi, fl, Evangelical Church of Togo

*Seim*, Dr Turid Karlsen, fl, Church of Norway

*Semen*, Rev. Prof. Petre, mo, Romanian Orthodox Church

*Sens*, Okr Dr Matthias, mo, Federation of Evangelical Churches [Germany]

*Serapion*, Bishop, mo, Coptic Orthodox Church [Egypt]

*Sergei of Solnechnogorsk*, Archbishop, mo, (Switzerland), Russian Orthodox Church

*Serote*, Bishop Ntwampe, mo, (South Africa), Evangelical Lutheran Church in Southern Africa

*Shahbazian*, Prof. Parguev, ml, Armenian Apostolic Church (Etchmiadzin) [USSR]

*Shava*, Rev. Naison, mo, Evangelical Lutheran Church in Zimbabwe

*Shen Yi-Fan*, Bishop, mo, China Christian Council

*Shenouda*, His Holiness Pope, mo, Coptic Orthodox Church [Egypt]

*Shenouda*, Rev. Fr Antonious Thabit, mo, (UK), Coptic Orthodox Church [Egypt]

*Sherry*, Rev. Dr Paul, mo, United Church of Christ [USA]

*Shiolashvili*, Rev. Fr David, mo, Georgian Orthodox Church [USSR]

*Shirras*, Ms Rachel, yfl, Church of England

*Shotwell*, Rev. J. Ralph, mo, International Council of Community Churches [USA]

*Siahaan*, Rev. Oberlin, mo, Christian Protestant Church in Indonesia (GKPI)

*Sieunarine*, Rt Rev. Everson, mo, (Trinidad), Presbyterian Church in Trinidad and Tobago

*Silalahi*, Mrs Ribur, fl, Indonesian Christian Church (HKI)

*Silitonga*, Mrs S. Ame, fl, Batak Protestant Christian Church (HKBP) [Indonesia]

*Silk*, Ven. Robert, mo, Church of England

*Simangunsong*, Rev. Harlen, mo, Indonesian Christian Church (HKI)

*Simic*, Prof. Pribislav, mo, Serbian Orthodox Church [Yugoslavia]

*Sinulingga*, Rev. Musa, mo, Karo Batak Protestant Church (GBKP) [Indonesia]

*Siratt*, Mr Sabam, ml, Batak Protestant Christian Church (HKBP) [Indonesia]

*Sjoberg*, Bishop Donald, mo, Evangelical Lutheran Church in Canada

*Skarrie Elmquist*, Mrs Marie, fl, Mission Covenant Church of Sweden

*Skulason*, Rt Rev. Olafur, mo, Evangelical Lutheran Church of Iceland

*Sliwa*, Metropolitan Mar Gewargis, mo, (Iraq), Apostolic Catholic Assyrian Church of the East [Iraq]

*Smith-Cameron*, Rev. Canon Ivor, mo, Church of England

*Soedjatmoko*, Mrs Sri Winarti, fl, East Java Christian Church (GKJW) [Indonesia]

*Sommers*, Rev. Dr Gordon, mo, Moravian Church, USA (Northern Province)

*Soone*, Dean Einar, mo, Estonian Evangelical Lutheran Church [USSR]

*Soplantila*, Rev. Abraham, mo, Protestant Church in the Moluccas (GPM) [Indonesia]

*Sørensen*, Ms Louise, yfl, Evangelical Lutheran Church of Denmark

*Souchon*, Mme Cécile, fl, Reformed Church of France

*Speaks*, Mrs Janie, fl, African Methodist Episcopal Zion Church [USA]

*Speranskaya*, Ms Helena, fl, Russian Orthodox Church

*Stanovsky*, Rev. Elaine, fo, United Methodist Church [USA]

*Stefanides*, Rev. Nikolaos, mo, Greek Evangelical Church

*Steffer*, Rev. Dr Robert, mo, Christian Church (Disciples of Christ) [Canada]

*Stepánek*, Bishop Vratislav, mo, Czechoslovak Hussite Church

*Stepanov*, Rev. Fr Vladislav, ml, Russian Orthodox Church

*Stöckigt*, Pastorin Beate, fo, Federation of Evangelical Churches [Germany]

*Stonawski*, Bischof Wilhelm, mo, Silesian Evangelical Church-Augsburg Confession [CSFR]

*Straw*, Rev. Gordon, mo, Evangelical Lutheran Church in America

*Striegnitz*, Herr Meinfried, ml, Evangelical Church in Germany

*Sturm*, Superintendent Herwig, mo, Evangelical Church-Augsburg and Helvetic Confessions [Austria]

*Stylianos*, Archbishop Dr, mo, (Australia), Ecumenical Patriarchate of Constantinople [Turkey]

*Sumbayak*, Mr Harrys, yml, Simalungun Protestant Christian Church (GKPS) [Indonesia]

*Supit*, Dr Bert, ml, Christian Evangelical Church in Minahasa (GMIM) [Indonesia]

*Suvarská*, Prof. Eva, fl, Orthodox Church of Czechoslovakia

*Suvarsky*, Protopresbyter Jaroslav, mo, Orthodox Church of Czechoslovakia

*Swinson*, Mrs Margaret, fl, Church of England

*Szabó*, Rev. Mrs Marianna, fo, Lutheran Church in Hungary

*Szarek*, Okr Jan, mo, Evangelical Church of the Augsburg Confession in Poland

*Szebik*, Bishop Imre, mo, Lutheran Church in Hungary

*Tabart*, Dr Jill, fl, Uniting Church in Australia

*Taburimai*, Rev. Koae, mo, Kiribati Protestant Church

*Tagoilelagi*, Mrs Iolesina, fl, (New Zealand), Congregational Christian Church in Samoa

*Talbert*, Bishop Melvin, mo, United Methodist Church [USA]

*Talbot*, Bishop Frederick, mo, (Virgin Islands USA), African Methodist Episcopal Church [USA]

*Talbot*, Dr Sylvia, fl, (Virgin Islands USA), African Methodist Episcopal Church [USA]

*Tallie*, Ms Patrina, yfl, Christian Church (Disciples of Christ) [USA]

*Tanielu*, Rev. Laau, mo, Congregational Christian Church in Samoa

*Tapia Gleisner*, Sra Marcela, yfl, Evangelical-Lutheran Church in Chile

*Tarasar*, Dr Constance, fl, Orthodox Church in America

*Tate*, Mrs Hazel, fl, Progressive National Baptist Convention Inc. [USA]

*Taufatofua*, Rev. Sela, fo, Methodist Church in Tonga

*Taylor*, Mr Victor, ml, Christian Methodist Episcopal Church [USA]

*Taylor*, Rev. Walter, ymo, Christian Church (Disciples of Christ) [USA]

*Teklehaimanot*, Rev. W/Giorgis, mo, Ethiopian Evangelical Church Mekane Yesus [Ethiopia]

*Telaumbanua*, Mr Tuhoni, ml, Nias Protestant Christian Church (BNKP) [Indonesia]

*Terefe*, Ato Haddis, ml, Ethiopian Orthodox Church

*Tetelepta*, Dr Hesina, fl, Protestant Church in the Moluccas (GPM) [Indonesia]

*Thawley*, Rev. Michael, mo, Presbyterian Church of New Zealand

*Theodoros of Kyrini*, Bishop, mo, (USSR), Greek Orthodox Patriarchate of Alexandria and All Africa [Egypt]

*Thomas*, Prof. Mary, fl, Malankara Orthodox Syrian Church [India]

*Thompson*, Rev. Kenneth, mo, (Australia), Methodist Church in Ireland

*Thompson*, Ms Kristine, yfl, Presbyterian Church (USA)

*Tillmann*, Mrs Norma, fl, Evangelical Church of Lutheran Confession [Brazil]

*Timotheos*, H.G. Archbishop, mo, Ethiopian Orthodox Church

*Timotheos of Kerkyra*, Metropolitan, mo, Church of Greece

*Ting*, Bishop K.H., mo, China Christian Council

*Tobing*, Mrs Alida, fl, Batak Protestant Christian Church (HKBP) [Indonesia]

*Tobing*, Dr Victor, ml, Christian Protestant Church in Indonesia (GKPI)

*Tökés*, Bishop László, mo, Reformed Church of Romania

*Tolentino*, Ms Joy, yfl, (Philippines), United Methodist Church [USA]

*Tóth*, Bishop Dr Károly, mo, Reformed Church in Hungary

*Totomarovario*, Mme Laurette, fl, (Madagascar), Church of the Province of the Indian Ocean

*Toy*, Rev. Fran, fo, Episcopal Church [USA]

*Trenaman*, Ms Dianne, yfl, Uniting Church in Australia

*Truhachev*, Rev. Fr Sergej, mo, Russian Orthodox Church

*Tsetsis*, Very Rev. Dr Georges, mo, (Switzerland), Ecumenical Patriarchate of Constantinople [Turkey]

*Tshibulenu*, Pasteur Sakayimbo, mo, Mennonite Community [Zaire]

*Tshihamba*, Rev. Dr Mukome, mo, Presbyterian Community [Zaire]

*Tuomi*, Ms Helgma, fl, Evangelical-Lutheran Church of Finland

*Turner*, Rev. Dr Eugene, mo, Presbyterian Church (USA)

*Turner*, Mrs Rua, fl, Methodist Church of New Zealand
*Tveter*, Ms Anne, yfl, Church of Norway
*Twagirayesu*, Pasteur Michel, mo, Presbyterian Church of Rwanda
*Udo*, Rev. Okokon, mo, Presbyterian Church of Nigeria
*Um*, Ms Mary, fl, Korean Methodist Church
*Urban*, Frau Ursula, fl, Evangelical Church in Germany
*Vadic of Srem*, Bishop Vasilije, mo, Serbian Orthodox Church [Yugoslavia]
*Valent*, Pfarrer Jan, mo, Slovak Evangelical Church of the Augsburg Confession in Yugoslavia
*Van Ee*, Mr Daniel, yml, Netherlands Reformed Church
*Varghese*, Mr Varghese, yml, Malankara Orthodox Syrian Church [India]
*Varipatis*, Deacon Constantine, mo, (Australia), Church of Cyprus
*Vasili*, Dr Nick, ml, (Australia), Church of Cyprus
*Vasquez*, Sra Denise, fl, (Puerto Rico), Evangelical Lutheran Church in America
*Veem*, Ms Katarina, fl, (Sweden), Estonian Evangelical Lutheran Church [Canada]
*Viczian*, Rev. Dr Janos, mo, Baptist Union of Hungary
*Vidal*, Dr Daniel, mo, Spanish Evangelical Church
*Vikström*, Archbishop Dr John, mo, Evangelical-Lutheran Church of Finland
*Vörös*, Rev. Eva, fo, Reformed Church in Hungary
*Vogelmann*, Mme le pasteur Rose, fo, Episcopal Baptist Community [Zaire]
*Vogt*, Ms Franziska, yfl, Old Catholic Church of Switzerland
*Voicu*, Archdeacon Dr Constantin, mo, Romanian Orthodox Church
*Voksö*, Mr Per, ml, Church of Norway
*Vollprecht*, Pfarrer Frieder, mo, Moravian Church, Herrnhut [Germany]
*Von Loewenich*, Oberkirchenrat Hermann, mo, Evangelical Church in Germany
*Voumina*, Monsieur Guillaume, ml, Evangelical Church of the Congo
*Vun*, Rev. Cheong-Fui, mo, (Malaysia), Church of England
*Wahono*, Rev. Prof. S. Wismoady, mo, East Java Christian Church (GKJW) [Indonesia]
*Walker-Smith*, Rev. Angelique, fo, National Baptist Convention USA Inc.
*Walters*, Rev. Muru, mo, Church of the Province of New Zealand
*Waltschanow*, Prof. Slawtscho, ml, Bulgarian Orthodox Church
*Wang Hsien-Chih*, Rev. Dr, mo, (Taiwan), Episcopal Church [USA]
*Waters*, Rev. Robert, mo, Congregational Union of Scotland
*Watley*, Rev. Dr William, mo, African Methodist Episcopal Church [USA]
*Weber*, Herr Jürgen, ml, Evangelical Church in Germany
*Weber*, Frau Sibylle, yfl, Federation of Evangelical Churches [Germany]
*Webster*, Ms Alison, yfl, Methodist Church [UK]
*Weerasuriya*, Ven. Coultas, mo, Church of Ceylon
*Weiss*, Rev. Dr Daniel, mo, American Baptist Churches in the USA
*Welch*, Rev. Elizabeth, fo, United Reformed Church in the UK
*Wennes*, Bishop Howard, mo, Evangelical Lutheran Church in America

*Werkström*, Archbishop Bertil, mo, Church of Sweden
*Werner*, Pfarrer Dietrich, mo, Evangelical Church in Germany
*Westra*, Drs Aukje, fl, Reformed Churches in the Netherlands
*Wickramasinghe*, Ms Lydia, yfl, Church of Ceylon
*Widmann*, Prof. Peter, mo, Evangelical Lutheran Church of Denmark
*Williams*, Mrs Tungane, fl, Cook Islands Christian Church
*Willie*, Rev. David, mo, Methodist Church [UK]
*Wilson*, Obispo John, mo, Moravian Church in Nicaragua
*Wolde Eyesus*, Dr Markos, mo, Ethiopian Orthodox Church
*Woldeyes*, Prof. Asrat, ml, Ethiopian Orthodox Church
*Wood*, Rev. Dr D'Arcy, mo, Uniting Church in Australia
*Woods*, Mr Derick, ml, Moravian Church in Great Britain and Ireland
*Wuwungan*, Rev. Dr O.E., mo, Protestant Church in Indonesia
*Yacoub*, Rev. Kamal Youssef, mo, Synod of the Nile of the Evangelical Church
    [Egypt]
*Yando*, Pasteur Emmanuel, mo, Protestant Methodist Church [Ivory Coast]
*Yannoulatos*, Bishop Anastasios, mo, (Kenya), Church of Greece
*Yesehaq*, H.G. Archbishop, mo, (USA), Ethiopian Orthodox Church
*Youmshajekian*, Rev. Krikor, mo, Union of the Armenian Evangelical Churches
    [Lebanon]
*Yung Kok-Kwong*, Rev., mo, Church of Christ in China, Hong Kong Council
*Zabala*, Rt Rev. Artemio, mo, Philippine Episcopal Church
*Zacharias Mar Theophilos*, Bishop, mo, Mar Thoma Syrian Church of Malabar
    [India]
*Zahirsky*, Mrs Valerie, fl, Orthodox Church in America
*Zaia*, Bishop Joseph, mo, (Australia), Apostolic Catholic Assyrian Church of the
    East [Iraq]
*Zamen*, Dr Mrs Grace, fl, Church of North India
*Zau Yaw*, Rev. M., mo, Myanmar Baptist Convention
*Zerihun*, Archpriest Teshoma, mo, Ethiopian Orthodox Church
*Zverev*, Rev. Nikolai, mo, Evangelical Christian Baptist Union of the USSR

# DELEGATED REPRESENTATIVES
## OF ASSOCIATE MEMBER CHURCHES

*Akhura*, Rev. Levi, mo, African Church of the Holy Spirit [Kenya]
*Blake*, Sr Jorge, ml, Church of the Disciples of Christ [Argentina]
*Brandon González*, Sra Adriana, fl, Evangelical Methodist Church [Uruguay]
*Diaz*, Obispo Roberto, mo, Evangelical Methodist Church [Costa Rica]
*Gnadt*, Obispo Hellmut, mo, Methodist Church of Chile
*Gomez*, Obispo Medardo, mo, Salvadorean Lutheran Synod
*Guarna*, Pastor Severio, mo, Evangelical Baptist Union of Italy

*Harahap*, Bishop Ginda, mo, Christian Protestant Angkola Church (GKPA) [Indonesia]

*Huacani Nina*, Obispo Carlos, mo, Evangelical Methodist Church in Bolivia

*Kim Hyung Shik*, Rev., mo, Korean Christian Church in Japan

*Loayza*, Pastor German, mo, Bolivian Evangelical Lutheran Church

*Mendez*, Rev. Hector, mo, Presbyterian Reformed Church in Cuba

*Mondal*, Rt Rev. Barnabas, mo, Church of Bangladesh

*Salvador*, Pastor José da Silveira, mo, Evangelical Presbyterian Church of Portugal

*Sánchez*, Pastor Carlos, mo, Baptist Association of El Salvador

*Santos*, Rev. Cleves Emerich dos, mo, United Presbyterian Church [Brazil]

*Sardiñas*, Sr Manuel, ml, Methodist Church in Cuba

*Sipoto*, Pastor Jaime, mo, Reformed Church of Equatorial Guinea

*Soares*, Dr Fernando, mo, Lusitanian Catholic-Apostolic Evangelical Church [Portugal]

*Veira*, Pastor Ricardo, mo, United Evangelical Lutheran Church [Argentina]

*Waspada*, Bishop Dr I Ketut, mo, Protestant Christian Church in Bali (GKPB) [Indonesia]

# MEMBERS OF THE RETIRING CENTRAL COMMITTEE

*Abayasekera*, Ms Annathaie, fl, Church of Ceylon

*Athanasios of Beni-Souef*, Archbishop, mo, Coptic Orthodox Church (Egypt]

*Heyward*, Rt Rev. Oliver, mo, Anglican Church of Australia

*Jesudasan*, Rt Rev. Isaiah, mo, Church of South India

*Jornod*, Pasteur Jean-Pierre, mo, Swiss Protestant Church Federation

*Julkiree*, Ms Boonmee, fl, Church of Christ in Thailand

*Kaddu*, Mrs Joyce, fl, Church of Uganda

*Kim Choon Young*, Rev. Dr, mo, Korean Methodist Church

*Kruse*, Bischof Dr Martin, mo, Evangelical Church in Germany

*McCloud*, Rev. Dr J. Oscar, mo, Presbyterian Church (USA)

*Newell*, Kara, fo, Friends United Meeting [USA]

*Post*, Rev. Dr Avery, mo, United Church of Christ [USA]

*Richardson*, Rev. John E., mo, Methodist Church [UK]

*Rogers*, Rev. Dr James, mo, Church of Scotland

*Russell*, Rt Rev. Philip, mo, (South Africa), Church of the Province of Southern Africa

*Sabug, Jr*, Mr Fructuoso, ml, Philippine Independent Church

*Seah*, Rev. Dr Ingram, mo, Presbyterian Church in Taiwan

*Skuse*, Ms Jean, fl, Uniting Church in Australia

*Sowunmi*, Prof. Mrs Adebisi, fl, Church of Nigeria

*Thorogood*, Rev. Bernard, mo, United Reformed Church in the UK

*Tolen*, Dr Aaron, ml, Presbyterian Church of Cameroon
*Van der Veen-Schenkeveld*, Rev. Marja, fo, Reformed Churches in the Netherlands

# DELEGATED REPRESENTATIVES
# OF WCC ASSOCIATE COUNCILS
# AND OF OTHER ORGANIZATIONS

*Abraham-Williams*, Rev. Gethin, mo, Cytun-Churches Together in Wales
*Ada*, Pasteur Samuel, mo, Evangelical Community for Apostolic Action
*Anderson*, Rev. Dr Donald, mo, Anglican Consultative Council
*Banks*, Dr Trevor, ml, Disciples Ecumenical Consultative Council
*Basdekis*, Dr Athanasios, ml, Council of Christian Churches, Germany
*Beach*, Dr Bert, mo, General Conference of Seventh-day Adventists
*Bisnauth*, Rev. Dale, mo, Caribbean Conference of Churches
*Bleakley*, Rt Hon. David, ml, Irish Council of Churches
*Boll*, Rev. Godofredo, mo, National Council of Christian Churches in Brazil
*Boseto*, Bishop Leslie, mo, Pacific Conference of Churches
*Braidwood*, Mr Norman, ml, World Alliance of YMCAs
*Brown*, Dr Stuart, ml, Canadian Council of Churches
*Carino*, Dr Feliciano, mo, National Council of Churches in the Philippines
*Chikane*, Rev. Dr Frank, mo, South African Council of Churches
*Chipenda*, Rev. José, mo, All Africa Conference of Churches
*Chipesse*, Rev. Augusto, mo, Angolan Council of Evangelical Churches
*Craig*, Rev. Maxwell, mo, Action of Churches Together in Scotland
*Dartey*, Rev. David, mo, Christian Council of Ghana
*Delteil*, Monsieur Jean-François, ml, World Student Christian Federation
*Fischer*, Mr Jean, ml, Conference of European Churches
*Forsbeck*, Rev. Rune, mo, Swedish Ecumenical Council
*Gape*, Mr Churchill, ml, Botswana Christian Council
*Gayle*, Mrs Rubye, fl, Jamaica Council of Churches
*George*, Mr Varghese, ml, Council of Churches of Malaysia
*Gill*, Rev. David, mo, Australian Council of Churches
*Guy*, Lt-Col. David, mo, The Salvation Army
*Hale*, Dr Joe, mo, World Methodist Council
*Hamilton*, Mr James, ml, National Council of Churches USA
*Hesse Steel*, Mrs Elaine, fl, World YWCA
*Horsholt Pedersen*, Mrs Sigrid, fl, Ecumenical Council of Denmark
*Ingelstam*, Mrs Margareta, fl, International Fellowship of Reconciliation
*Jarjour*, Rev. Dr Riad, mo, Middle East Council of Churches
*Kamara*, Mr A.F., ml, United Christian Council of Sierra Leone
*Kerepia*, Mrs Anne, fl, Melanesian Council of Churches

*Kutjok*, Rev. Ezekiel, mo, Sudan Council of Churches
*Kwon Ho Kyung*, Rev., mo, National Council of Churches in Korea
*Lidgett*, Mrs Helen, fl, Conference for World Mission
*Lulias*, Very Rev. Fr Nikitas, mo, Syndesmos
*Lumbama*, Rev. Elijah, mo, Christian Council of Zambia
*Lungmuana*, Rev. Khawlhring, mo, National Council of Churches in India
*Meissner*, Okr Herbert, mo, Protestant Association for World Mission in
    Germany
*Moyer*, Rev. John, mo, Frontier Internship in Mission
*Munroe*, Ms Judy, fl, Ecumenical Development Cooperative Society
*Ondra*, Mr Jaroslav, ml, Czechoslovak Ecumenical Council
*Opocensky*, Rev. Dr Milan, mo, World Alliance of Reformed Churches
*Pattiasina*, Rev. Joseph, mo, Communion of Churches in Indonesia
*Peñaranda*, Mr Miguel, ml, International Christian Youth Exchange
*Peter*, Mrs Navamani, fl, International Committee for World Day of Prayer
*Prasad*, Rev. Andrew, mo, Council for World Mission
*Reardon*, Rev. John, mo, Council of Churches in Britain and Ireland
*Rusama*, Rev. Dr Jaakko, mo, Finnish Ecumenical Council
*Samuel*, Bishop John, mo, Christian Conference of Asia
*Saroia*, Mr Yousaf, ml, National Council of Churches in Pakistan
*Schlegel*, Pfarrer Joachim, mo, Ecumenical Missionary Liaison Committee,
    Germany
*Schlosser*, Frau Magdalena, fl, Swiss Protestant Missionary Council
*Schmauch*, Rev. W. Christoph, mo, Christian Peace Conference
*Schmidt-Lauber*, Prof. Dr Hans-Christoph, mo, Ecumenical Council of Churches
    in Austria
*Shejavali*, Dr Abisai, mo, Council of Churches in Namibia
*Siyachitema*, Rt Rev. Jonathan, mo, Zimbabwe Council of Churches
*Staalsett*, Rev. Dr Gunnar, mo, Lutheran World Federation
*Stephen*, Rev. George, mo, National Christian Council of Sri Lanka
*Svensson*, Rev. Bertil, mo, Swedish Missionary Council
*Tapuai*, Rev. Fa'atauva'a, mo, National Council of Churches of American
    Samoa
*Thomas*, David, ml, Friends World Committee for Consultation
*Thomas*, Rev. Dr Kenneth, mo, United Bible Societies
*Tranda*, Bischof Zdzislaw, mo, Polish Ecumenical Council
*Tso Man-King*, Rev. Dr, mo, Hong Kong Christian Council
*Valle*, Rev. Carlos, mo, World Association for Christian Communication
*Van Butselaar*, Dr Jan, mo, Netherlands Missionary Council
*Van der Zee*, Rev. Willem, mo, Council of Churches in the Netherlands
*Van Houten*, Dr Richard, ml, Reformed Ecumenical Council
*Vose*, Dr Noel, mo, Baptist World Alliance
*Williamson*, Rev. Dr Raymond, mo, Australian Council of Churches/Mission
*Win Tin*, Rev., mo, Myanmar Council of Churches

## DELEGATED OBSERVERS

*Bouwen MAFR*, Rev. Fr Frans, mo, (Jerusalem), Roman Catholic Church
*Clark*, Rt Rev. Alan, mo, (UK), Roman Catholic Church
*\*Coste*, Rev. Père René, mo, (France), Roman Catholic Church
*Cross*, Rev. Dr Peter, mo, (Australia), Roman Catholic Church
*Dsouza*, Bishop Patrick, mo, (India), Roman Catholic Church
*Fitzgerald*, Rev. Fr Michael, mo, (Vatican), Roman Catholic Church
*Ganaka*, Bishop Gabriel, mo, (Nigeria), Roman Catholic Church
*Geernaert*, Sister Donna, fl, (Canada), Roman Catholic Church
*Goldie*, Dr Rosemary, fl, (Italy), Roman Catholic Church
*Heather*, Bishop Bede, mo, (Australia), Roman Catholic Church
*Jenkins CSB*, Sister Margaret, fl, (Australia), Roman Catholic Church
*Johnston*, Dr Robert, mo, (USA), The Evangelical Covenant Church
*Klein*, Prof. Dr Aloys, mo, (Germany), Roman Catholic Church
*\*Kownacki*, Rev. Fr Robert, mo, (USA), Roman Catholic Church
*Lang MM*, Rev. Fr Joseph, mo, (USA), Roman Catholic Church
*Martin*, Msgr Diarmuid, mo, (Vatican), Roman Catholic Church
*McDonnell OSB*, Rev. Fr Kilian, mo, (USA), Roman Catholic Church
*Meeking*, Rt Rev. Basil, mo, (New Zealand), Roman Catholic Church
*Mutiso-Mbinda*, Msgr John, mo, (Vatican), Roman Catholic Church
*Neefjes OFM*, Fr Felix, mo, (Brazil), Roman Catholic Church
*Nossol*, Bishop Alfons, mo, (Poland), Roman Catholic Church
*Putney*, Rev. Fr Michael, mo, (Australia), Roman Catholic Church
*Radano*, Msgr John, mo, (Vatican), Roman Catholic Church
*Sharry*, Sister Lenore, fl, (Australia), Roman Catholic Church
*Sullivan*, Miss Denise, fl, (Australia), Roman Catholic Church
*Tillard OP*, Rev. Fr Jean, mo, (Canada), Roman Catholic Church

## OBSERVERS

*Abraham*, Rev. Dr K.C., mo, Ecumenical Association of Third World Theologians
*Adcock*, Rev. Neil, mo, Baptist World Alliance
*Ajuoga*, Bishop Dr Matthew, mo, Organization of African Instituted Churches
*Apple*, Rabbi Raymond, ml, International Jewish Committee for Inter-religious Consultation
*Aschmann*, Pfarrer Hanspeter, mo, Swiss Protestant Church Federation
*Askola*, Rev. Irja, fo, Ecumenical Association of Academies and Laity Centres in Europe

---

\*Adviser to the RC delegation

*Avi*, Rev. Dick, mo, Melanesian Association of Theological Schools
*Azariah*, Rt Rev. Masilamani, mo, Church of South India
*Blanket*, Rev. Edmund, mo, Aboriginal and Islander Commission, Australia
*Blow*, Mr Reg, ml, Aboriginal and Islander Commission, Australia
*Blow*, Mrs Walda, fl, Aboriginal and Islander Commission, Australia
*Boer*, Rev. Drs Bert, mo, Commission on Interchurch Aid of the Netherlands
    Reformed Church
*Bokeleale*, Mgr Itofo, mo, Church of Christ in Zaire
*Brand*, Dr Eugene, mo, Lutheran World Federation
*Brinkman*, Dr Martien, mo, Reformed Churches in the Netherlands
*Broome*, Mrs Carol, fl, Aboriginal and Islander Commission, Australia
*Broome*, Rev. David, mo, Aboriginal and Islander Commission, Australia
*Brunson*, Mr Douglas, ml, Ecumenical Development Cooperative Society
*Buti*, Rev. Sam, mo, Dutch Reformed Church in Africa, South Africa
*Campbell*, Mr Douglas, ml, Amnesty International
*Cantell*, Rev. Dr Risto, mo, Evangelical-Lutheran Church of Finland
*Christiaens SJ*, Rev. Père Louis, mo, International Labour Office
*Coenen*, Okr Dr Lothar, mo, Evangelical Church in Germany
*Dayton*, Dr Donald, ml, Wesleyan Theological Society, USA
*De Waard*, Dr Hendrik, mo, Reformed Ecumenical Council
*Erichsen*, Rev. Jan Arnold, mo, Norwegian Church Aid
*Fernando*, Mr Marshal, ml, World Student Christian Federation
*Finau SM*, Bishop Patelisio, mo, Pacific Conference of Churches
*Flynn*, Mr Sonny, ml, Aboriginal and Islander Commission, Australia
*Forker*, Rev. Wilbert, mo, The Templeton Foundation
*Fourmile*, Fr Lloyd, mo, Aboriginal and Islander Commission, Australia
*Frankovits*, Mr André, ml, Amnesty International
*Freychet*, Pasteur Michel, mo, Protestant Federation of France
*Frieling*, Prof. Dr Reinhard, mo, Evangelical Working Group on Comparative
    Religions in Europe
*Fullerton*, Rev. Dr Gordon, mo, Presbyterian Church of Australia
*Gitari*, Bishop David, mo, Partnership in Mission International
*Gnavi*, Rev. Fr Marco, mo, Community of San Egidio, Italy
*Godoy Fernandez*, Pastor Daniel, mo, Christian Fellowship of Churches in Chile
*Goodman*, Mrs Maureen, fl, Brahma Kumaris World Spiritual University
*Guest*, Mr Kenneth, ml, United Methodist Church, USA
*Hally*, Fr Cyril, mo, Pax Christi International
*Hardung*, Dekan Wolf-Dietrich, mo, Ohne Rüstung Leben, Germany
*Heyns*, Prof. Johan, mo, Dutch Reformed Church, South Africa
*Hjerrild*, Rev. Ane, fo, Church of Denmark
*Hoath*, Mr Colin, ml, Anglican Church of Canada/Primate's Fund
*Houtepen*, Prof. Dr Anton, ml, Interuniversity Institute for Missiological
    Research
*Ibarra*, Dr Angel, ml, Salvadorean Lutheran Synod

*Irvine*, Dr Graeme, mo, World Vision International
*Jacobs*, Mr Pio, ml, Maori Council of Churches, Aotearoa/New Zealand
*James*, Rev. Canon Graham, mo, Church of England
*Janda*, Mrs Joyce, fl, Ecumenical Women's Group, Geneva
*Joseph*, Rev. Dr Ipe, mo, All India Sunday School Association
*Katoneene*, Rev. Jonah, mo, Association of Christian Lay Centres in Africa
*Kelie*, Ms Anna, fl, Curacao Council of Churches
*Kim Hyong Dok*, Mr, ml, Korean Christians Federation
*Kim Yoo Sook*, Mrs, fl, Asian Church Women's Conference
*Klabu*, Mr Roland, ml, Anglican Diocese of Kuching, Malaysia
*Ko Gi Jun*, Mr, ml, Korean Christians Federation
*Kobia*, Rev. Samuel, mo, National Council of Churches of Kenya
*Kwong*, Rt Rev. Dr Peter, mo, Anglican Diocese of Hong Kong and Macao
*Kyle*, Ms Erica, fl, Aboriginal and Islander Commission, Australia
*Lancaster*, Rev. Lewis, mo, Presbyterian Church (USA)
*Lapp*, Dr John, ml, Mennonite Central Committee
*Lemire*, Frère Emile, ml, Taizé Community
*Li Chon Min*, Mr, ml, Korean Christians Federation
*Logan*, Rev. Dr Paul, mo, Presbyterian Church of Australia
*Luyckx*, Dr Marc, ml, Commission of the European Communities
*Lythe*, Mrs Patricia, fl, Conference of Churches in Aotearoa/New Zealand
*Makambwe*, Ven. Francis, mo, Mindolo Ecumenical Foundation, Zambia
*Marcal*, Rev. Arlindo, mo, Christian Church in East Timor
*Mathaha*, Mrs Idelette, fl, Christian Council of Lesotho
*McGregor*, Archdeacon Marjorie, fl, Diakonia
*McNaughton*, Rev. Dr Robert, mo, The Evangelical Covenant Church
*Meo*, Rev. Dr Jovili, mo, South Pacific Association of Theological Schools
*Mercado*, Mrs Nellie, fl, Association of Christian Institutes for Social Concern in
    Asia
*Mills*, Dr Howard, mo, Churches Council on Theological Education, Canada
*Mofokeng*, Rev. Kenosi, fo, African Spiritual Churches Association, South
    Africa
*Moss*, Mrs Cath, fl, Ecumenical Youth Council in Europe
*Motu'ahala*, Mr Sione, ml, Pacific Conference of Churches
*Moyo*, Dr Ambrose, mo, Conference of African Theological Institutions
*Nafzger*, Rev. Samuel, mo, Lutheran Church — Missouri Synod, USA
*Neville*, Mr William, ml, Pax Romana
*Norgren*, Rev. Dr William, mo, Episcopal Church, USA
*Ocanto Sanchez*, Sra Edna, fl, World Student Christian Federation
*Oke Esono*, Pastor Samuel, mo, Reformed Church of Equatorial Guinea
*Olaitan*, Rev. Canon Samuel, mo, Chapel of the Healing Cross, Nigeria
*Om Yong Son*, Mr, ml, Korean Christians Federation
*Oskam*, Mr Cees, ml, Interchurch Coordination Committee for Development
    Projects, Netherlands

*Otte*, Prof. Dr Klaus, ml, Swiss Protestant Church Federation
*Platten*, Rev. Canon Stephen, mo, Church of England
*Potgieter*, Prof. Pieter, mo, Dutch Reformed Church, South Africa
*Potter*, Mr David, ml, World Congress of Faiths
*Quintero Perez*, Mr Manuel, ml, Ecumenical Global Gathering of Youth and Students
*Raiser*, Dr Elisabeth, fl, Ecumenical Forum of European Christian Women
*Ramcharan*, Mr Michael, ml, Collaboration for Ecumenical Planning and Action in the Caribbean
*Reitzel*, Pasteur Hans Ulrich, mo, Council of Churches of Morocco
*Rhee*, Rev. Dr Syngman, mo, National Council of Churches USA
*Rocha Souza*, Sr Enilson, ml, Ecumenical Service Commission, Brazil
*Ruhiu*, Mrs Alice, fl, World Student Christian Federation
*Samuel*, Canon Dr Vinay, mo, Partnership in Mission International
*Scambia*, Dr Francesca, yfl, Community of San Egidio, Italy
*Schnyder*, Dr Klaus, ml, Uniapac
*Schoneveld*, Dr Jacobus, mo, International Council of Christians and Jews
*Schulz*, Dr William, ml, Unitarian Universalist Association
*Senituli*, Mr Lopeti, ml, Pacific Concerns Resource Centre
*Serrano*, Rev. Luis, mo, Diaconia, El Salvador
*Sevaaetasi*, Rev. Leanavaotaua, mo, Congregational Christian Church in American Samoa
*Silva*, Pastor Orlando, mo, "Brazil for Christ"
*Simon*, Rev. Dr Christopher, mo, Sharing of Ministries Abroad
*Sinnemäki*, Rev. Maunu, mo, Evangelical-Lutheran Church of Finland
*Spencer*, Rev. Robert, mo, North American Retreat Directors Association
*Srisang*, Dr Koson, ml, Ecumenical Coalition on Third World Tourism
*Stanford*, Mrs Delphine, fl, Aboriginal and Islander Commission, Australia
*Starr*, Dr William, mo, Young Life
*Tabbernee*, Rev. Dr William, mo, Australia and New Zealand Association of Theological Associations
*Takenaka*, Prof. Masao, mo, Asian Christian Art Association
*Tanner*, Dr Mary, fl, Church of England
*Tesfay-Musa*, Ms Elsa, fl, Anglican Church of Canada
*Tetteh*, Rev. Rachel, fo, All Africa Conference of Churches
*Thompson*, Mr William, ml, World Conference on Religion and Peace
*Thomsen*, Mr Jørgen, ml, Ecumenical Council of Denmark
*Thomsen*, Rev. Jens Jørgen, mo, Danchurchaid, Denmark
*Traer*, Rev. Robert, mo, International Association for Religious Freedom
*Traitler*, Dr Reinhild, fl, Ecumenical Forum of European Christian Women
*Tu'uholoaki*, Rev. Mrs Ming-ya, fo, World Conference of Associations of Theological Institutions
*Van Baak*, Rev. Edward, mo, Christian Reformed Church, USA
*Van Eck*, Dr Arthur, mo, National Council of Churches USA

*Veres-Kovács*, Deputy Bishop Attila, mo, Reformed Church of Romania
*Vischer*, Prof. Lukas, mo, Swiss Protestant Church Federation
*Wakowako* Mr Are, ml, Fiji Council of Churches
*Wiebusch*, Rev. Robert, mo, Lutheran Church of Australia
*Wikström*, Rev. Lester, mo, Church of Sweden
*Wilkens*, Oberkirchenrat Klaus, mo, Evangelical Church in Germany
*Wilson*, Rev. Dr Henry, mo, World Alliance of Reformed Churches
*Wilson*, Rev. Nancy, fo, Universal Fellowship of Metropolitan Community
    Churches, USA
*Winckler*, Dr Michael, ml, Lutheran Church of Schaumburg-Lippe, Germany
*Yeow Choo Lak*, Rev. Dr, mo, Association for Theological Education in South-
    East Asia
*Zimmermann*, Pfarrer Jean, mo, World Evangelical Fellowship
*Zomer*, Mr Henk, ml, Dutch Interchurch Aid

# GUESTS

*Abrecht*, Rev. Dr Paul, mo, (Switzerland), American Baptist Churches in the
    USA
*Abubakar*, Dr Carmen, fl, (Philippines), Muslim
*Ajitsingh*, Mrs Charanjit, fl, (UK), Sikh
*Bath*, Commissioner Robert, mo, (Australia), The Salvation Army
*Brash*, Rev. Dr Alan, mo, Presbyterian Church of New Zealand
*Broitman*, Ms Caryn, fl, (USA), Jewish
*Carroll*, Archbishop Francis, mo, (Australia), Roman Catholic Church
*Cassidy*, Archbishop Edward, mo, (Vatican), Roman Catholic Church
*Courtney*, Joan, fl, (Australia), Religious Society of Friends
*Denton*, Mr John, ml, Anglican Church of Australia
*Dowling*, Rt Rev. Owen, mo, Anglican Church of Australia
*Emilianos of Sylibria*, Metropolitan, mo, (Switzerland), Ecumenical Patriarchate
    [Turkey]
*Engel*, Rev. Dr Frank, mo, Uniting Church in Australia
*Garrett*, Rev. Dr John, mo, (Fiji), Uniting Church in Australia
*Henderson*, Rev. Gregor, mo, Uniting Church in Australia
*Hill*, Lt.-Col. Arthur, mo, (Australia), The Salvation Army
*Jiagge*, Mrs Justice Annie, fl, Evangelical Presbyterian Church [Ghana]
*Kinloch*, Dr Hector, ml, (Australia), Religious Society of Friends
*Leonidas*, Archimandrite, mo, (Australia), Ecumenical Patriarchate [Turkey]
*Mahinda*, Ven. Deegalle, mo, (USA), Buddhist
*Maury*, Pasteur Jacques, mo, Reformed Church of France
*Meyer*, Rabbi Dr Marshall, mo, (USA), Jewish
*Míguez Bonino*, Dr José, mo, Evangelical Methodist Church, Argentina

*Miyake*, Rev. Michio, mo, (Japan), Shinto
*Oloyede*, Prof. Is-Haq, ml, (Nigeria), Muslim
*Pagura*, Obispo Federico, mo, Evangelical Methodist Church, Argentina
*Pennybacker*, Rev. Dr Albert M., mo, Christian Church (Disciples of Christ) [USA]
*Perkins*, Rev. Harvey, mo, Uniting Church in Australia
*Phillips*, Deaconess Jean, fl, Uniting Church in Australia
*Potter*, Rev. Dr Philip, mo, (Germany), Methodist Church in the Caribbean and the Americas
*Rambachan*, Dr Anantanand, ml, (USA), Hindu
*Reeson*, Rev. Ronald, mo, Uniting Church in Australia
*Reeves*, Most Rev. Sir Paul, mo, (USA), Church of the Province of New Zealand
*Shanmugam*, Dr Gangadaran, ml, (India), Hindu
*Singh*, Dr Mohinder, ml, (India), Sikh
*Singh*, Mr Ajit, ml, (UK), Sikh
*Steicke*, Rev. Dr Lance, mo, Lutheran Church of Australia
*Stubs*, Rt Rev. Alan, mo, Presbyterian Church of Australia
*Tate*, Senator Michael, ml, (Australia), Roman Catholic Church
*Timotheos*, Archbishop Aphrem Aboodi, mo, Syrian Orthodox Patriarchate of Antioch and All the East
*Uchida*, Mr Masataka, ml, (Japan), Buddhist (Rissho Kosei-kai)
*Van der Bent*, Rev. Ans, mo, (France), United Church of Christ, USA
*Webb*, Dr Pauline, fl, Methodist Church [UK]
*Wilson*, Sir Ronald, ml, Uniting Church in Australia
*Woods*, Archbishop Sir Frank, mo, Anglican Church of Australia

## ADVISERS

*Bam*, Ms Brigalia, fl, (South Africa), Church of the Province of Southern Africa
*Barbosa Dos Santos*, Mr José Carlos, ml, (Brazil), Roman Catholic Church
*Biakokoz*, Dr Irena, yfl, Autocephalic Orthodox Church in Poland
*Carmen*, Mrs Andrea, fl, American Indian Traditional Religion
*Chung Hyun Kyung*, Prof. Dr Mrs, fl, Presbyterian Church in the Republic of Korea
*Cuambe*, Mr Gaspar, ml, Free Methodist Church [Mozambique]
*De Vries*, Soeur Minke, fl, Swiss Protestant Church Federation
*Deschner*, Prof. John, mo, United Methodist Church [USA]
*Dickinson*, Prof. Richard, mo, United Church of Christ [USA]
*Eck*, Prof. Diana, fl, United Methodist Church [USA]
*Esche*, Mrs Ruth, fl, Presbyterian Church (USA)
*Falconer*, Rev. Alan, mo, (Ireland), Church of Scotland
*Foulkes*, Dra Irene, fl, Presbyterian Church in Costa Rica
*Gillespie*, Ms Judith, fl, Episcopal Church [USA]
*Grant*, Rev. Dr Jacquelyn, fo, African Methodist Episcopal Church [USA]

*Gruber*, Ms Pamela, fl, Congregational Union of Scotland
*Hanson*, Rev. Malcolm, mo, United Reformed Church in the UK
*Harakas*, Prof. Stanley, mo, (USA), Ecumenical Patriarchate of Constantinople [Turkey]
*Harling*, Rev. Per, mo, Church of Sweden
*Heryan*, Rev. Miroslav, mo, Evangelical Church of Czech Brethren
*Horner*, Mrs Sue, fl, The Evangelical Covenant Church (USA)
*Jenkins*, Ms Henni, yfl, Church of the Province of New Zealand
*Kahl*, Dr Brigitte, fl, Federation of Evangelical Churches [Germany]
*Kane CSP*, Rev. Dr Thomas, mo, (USA), Roman Catholic Church
*Keju-Johnson*, Ms Darlene, fl, United Church of Christ in the Marshall Islands
*Kim Yong-Bock*, Rev. Dr, mo, Presbyterian Church of Korea
*Kuzmic*, Rev. Peter, mo, Evangelical Church of Yugoslavia
*Kwok Pui-Lan*, Dr, fl, Anglican Diocese of Hong Kong and Macao
*Lee Ye Ja*, Ms, fl, Presbyterian Church of Korea
*Loh*, Dr I-to, mo, (USA), Presbyterian Church in Taiwan
*Manorama*, Ms Ruth, fl, Church of South India
*Manougian*, Rev. Fr Nourhan, mo, (USA), Armenian Apostolic Church (Etchmiadzin) [USSR]
*Maraschin*, Dr Jaci, mo, Episcopal Church of Brazil
*Marshall*, Hon. Russell, mo, Methodist Church of New Zealand
*McDonald*, Hon. David, mo, United Church of Canada
*McMahon*, Rev. Dorothy, fo, Uniting Church in Australia
*McMaster*, Dr Belle Miller, fl, Presbyterian Church (USA)
*Mendis*, Mrs Priyanka, yfl, Church of Ceylon
*Mkhatshwa*, Rev. Fr Simangaliso, mo, (South Africa), Roman Catholic Church
*Monteiro*, Mrs Simei, fl, Methodist Church in Brazil
*Mukarji*, Dr Daleep, ml, Church of North India
*Mxadana*, Mr George, ml, (South Africa), Church of the Province of Southern Africa
*Niguidula*, Rev. Lydia, fo, United Church of Christ in the Philippines
*Padilla*, Dr Rene, mo, Baptist Church [Argentina]
*Raditapole*, Dr Deborah, fl, Lesotho Evangelical Church
*Rasmussen*, Prof. Larry, ml, Evangelical Lutheran Church in America
*Reeves*, Rev. Kathy, fo, United Methodist Church [USA]
*Reindorf*, Mrs Dinah, fl, Methodist Church, Ghana
*Ruiz Perez*, Ms Brenda, fl, Baptist Convention of Nicaragua
*Santa Ana*, Prof. Dr Julio de, ml, Methodist Church in Brazil
*Santana*, Rev. Eunice, fo, (Puerto Rico), Christian Church (Disciples of Christ) [USA]
*Schaal*, Herr Dieter, ml, Federation of Evangelical Churches [Germany]
*Sepulveda*, Pastor Juan, mo, Pentecostal Mission Church [Chile]
*Shegog*, Rev. Eric, mo, Church of England
*Talapusi*, Rev. Dr Faitala, mo, (Fiji), Congregational Christian Church in Samoa

*Tamaela*, Rev. Christian, mo, Protestant Church in the Moluccas (GPM) [Indonesia]

*Tamez*, Dr Elsa, fl, (Costa Rica), Methodist Church of Mexico

*Taylor*, Rev. Michael, mo, Baptist Union of Great Britain

*Templeton*, Mrs Elizabeth, fl, Church of Scotland

*Tharakan*, Dr K.M., ml, Malankara Orthodox Syrian Church [India]

*Tita*, Mr Michael, ml, Romanian Orthodox Church

*Trojan*, Dr Jakub, mo, Evangelical Church of Czech Brethren

*Vesin*, Rev. Fr Milos, mo, (USA), Serbian Orthodox Church [Yugoslavia]

*Wallis*, Rev. Jim, mo, (USA), Sojourners

*Weir*, Rev. Dr Mary, fl, United Church of Canada

*Williamson*, Dr Roger, ml, Methodist Church [UK]

*Wood*, Rt Rev. Dr Wilfred, mo, Church of England

*Wood*, Rev. Bertrice, fo, United Church of Christ [USA]

*Yabaki*, Rev. Akuila, mo, (UK), Methodist Church in Fiji

*Yeboah*, Sister Yaa Biamah Florence, fl, Presbyterian Church of Ghana

*Yongui-Massok*, Mme Marie-Thérèse, fl, Presbyterian Church of Cameroon

*Zaru*, Jean, fl, (West Bank), Friends United Meeting [USA]

*Zetto*, Rev. Dr Jeffrey, mo, Evangelical Lutheran Church in America

# STEWARDS

*Abu Ghazaleh*, Mr Sami, yml, (West Bank), Evangelical Lutheran Church in the Middle East

*Abu-Absi*, Mr Michael, yml, (USA), Roman Catholic Church

*Adjaye*, Ms Stella, yfl, Methodist Church, Ghana

*Aguilar*, Mr José, yml, Methodist Church of Mexico

*Aitchison*, Ms Julia, yfl, Church of Scotland

*Algorta Baldeon*, Mr Luis, yml, Methodist Church in Brazil

*Andersson*, Mr Bengt, yml, Church of Sweden

*Angulo Cabrera*, Mr José, yml, Christian Alliance Church of Colombia

*Archibald*, Mr Timothy, yml, Presbyterian Church in Canada

*Awadzie*, Mr Atsu, yml, (Togo), Roman Catholic Church

*Baccaro*, Mr Vagner, yml, Episcopal Church of Brazil

*Backo*, Ms Kerry, fl, Uniting Church in Australia

*Barrel*, Mr Laurence, yml, (Bangladesh), Roman Catholic Church

*Batterham*, Ms Alison, yfl, Anglican Church of Australia

*Battle*, Mr Michael, ml, Episcopal Church [USA]

*Benyameen*, Ms Geneviève, yfl, Coptic Orthodox Church [Egypt]

*Beswick*, Mr Ricky, ml, Uniting Church in Australia

*Blazek*, Mr Mojmir, mo, Evangelical Church of Czech Brethren

*Calderon*, Ms Alicia, yfl, (Germany), Church of the Brethren [USA]

*Caldwell*, Ms Lynn, yfl, United Church of Canada

*Canty*, Ms Genevieve, yfl, Uniting Church in Australia

*Cardenas Alvarez*, Ms Alejandra, fl, (Argentina), Presbyterian Church in Chile

*Chang Yoon-Jae*, Mr, ml, Presbyterian Church of Korea

*Charles*, Mr Philip, yml, (St Vincent), United Methodist Church [USA]

*Chivers*, Ms Claire, yfl, Anglican Church of Australia

*Christmas*, Ms Danielle, yfl, (St Kitts), Moravian Church, Eastern West Indies Province

*Clague*, Ms Pauline, yfl, Uniting Church in Australia

*Clarkson*, Ms Sue, yfl, Uniting Church in Australia

*Clausen*, Ms Elisabeth, yfl, (Sweden), United Methodist Church [USA]

*Cossa*, Mr Azarias, yml, Presbyterian Church of Mozambique

*Dabbagh*, Ms Rouba, yfl, (Lebanon), Muslim

*Darmaputera*, Mr Arya, yml, Indonesian Christian Church (HKI) [Indonesia]

*De Jesus*, Mr Edgar, yml, (Philippines), United Methodist Church [USA]

*De Lany*, Mr Heath, yml, Anglican Church of Australia

*De Silva*, Mr Heshan, yml, Baptist Church [Sri Lanka]

*De Souza Marques*, Ms Deise, yfl, Methodist Church in Brazil

*Debra*, Mr Peter, ml, Lutheran Church in Guyana

*Deibert-Dam*, Ms Gaby, fl, Evangelical Church in Germany

*Deville*, Mr Adam, yml, Anglican Church of Canada

*Dinarte Winter*, Ms Gisela, yfl, Evangelical Methodist Church [Argentina]

*Duta*, Mr Florea, yml, Romanian Orthodox Church

*Elia*, Mr Elie, yml, (Australia), Syrian Orthodox Patriarchate of Antioch and All the East [Syria]

*Euving*, Ms Erica, yfl, Reformed Churches in the Netherlands

*Fa'Alevao*, Mr Leatulagi, ml, (Fiji), Congregational Christian Church in Samoa

*Fallot*, Ms Abigail, yfl, Reformed Church of France

*Fanta*, Mr Eskinder, yml, (USA), Ethiopian Orthodox Church

*Fernando*, Mr Udan, ml, Methodist Church [Sri Lanka]

*Flynn*, Ms Bee, fl, (Australia), Roman Catholic Church

*Garcia*, Ms Maria, yfl, Lutheran Church in Costa Rica

*Gianelli*, Mr Marcos, yml, Presbyterian Independent Church [Brazil]

*Gondarra*, Mr Alfred, ml, Uniting Church in Australia

*Graham*, Ms Kate, yfl, Uniting Church in Australia

*Habulan*, Ms Sylvia, fl, (Philippines), Roman Catholic Church

*Halley*, Mr Kirino, ml, (Fiji), Roman Catholic Church

*Heider*, Mr Martin, ml, Evangelical Church in Germany

*Hernandez Navarro*, Ms Maria, yfl, Baptist Church in El Salvador

*Jacob*, Mr Richard, yml, (Trinidad), Church in the Province of the West Indies

*James*, Ms Janice, yfl, Methodist Church [Netherlands Antilles]

*Jara*, Mr Trino, ml, Church of the Nazarene [Costa Rica]

*Jennings*, Ms Vivette, fl, (Jamaica), Church in the Province of the West Indies

*Jeyakumar*, Ms Sylvia, yfl, Church of South India

*Jonassen*, Ms Mari, yfl, Church of Norway

*Karadaglis*, Mr Demetrios, yml, Church of Greece

*Karim*, Mr Said, yml, (Ireland), Greek Orthodox Patriarchate of Antioch and All the East [Syria]

*Kazarian*, Ms Lucy, fl, Armenian Apostolic Church (Cilicia) [Lebanon]

*Kepreotes*, Mr Dimitri, yml, (Australia), Church of Greece

*Khokhar*, Ms Shamila, yfl, Church of Pakistan

*Kirkpatrick*, Mr Nigel, yml, Church of Ireland

*Kisanga*, Mr Charles, ml, (Sudan), Roman Catholic Church

*Ko Mei-Na*, Ms, yfl, Presbyterian Church in Taiwan

*Kreuter*, Mr Jens, yml, Evangelical Church in Germany

*Kuitse*, Ms Jifke, yfl, General Mennonite Society [Netherlands]

*Kusliawan*, Ms Ligysari, yfl, Uniting Church in Australia

*Kyomo*, Mr Ipyana, ml, Moravian Church in Tanzania

*Latu*, Ms Vai, yfl, Free Church of Tonga

*Lawson*, Mr Matthew, yml, Church of England

*Leafa Elia*, Ms Ake, yfl, (Western Samoa), Methodist Church in Samoa

*Lee*, Ms Tessa, yfl, Presbyterian Church of Korea

*Lee Ming-Yu*, Ms, fl, Presbyterian Church in Taiwan

*Livermore*, Ms Caroline, fl, Religious Society of Friends [UK]

*Mainprize*, Ms Diana, yfl, Anglican Church of Australia

*Martens*, Mr Warren, yml, Aboriginal and Islander Commission, Australia

*Mathew*, Mr George, yml, Malankara Orthodox Syrian Church [India]

*McConnell*, Mr Kent, yml, Presbyterian Church (USA)

*Mckim*, Capt. John, ml, (Australia), The Salvation Army

*McLean*, Ms Alison, yfl, Anglican Church of Canada

*McNally-Worrell*, Mrs Susan, yfl, Episcopal Church [USA]

*Meyer*, Mr Joel, yml, Church of the Brethren [USA]

*Mofokeng*, Mr Ernest, yml, (South Africa), Ebenezer Evangelical Church

*Moglia*, Mr Simon, yml, Uniting Church in Australia

*Morales Sanchez*, Ms Estela, yfl, Evangelical Methodist Church [Uruguay]

*Moran*, Ms Julie, yfl, (Australia), Roman Catholic Church

*Moricz*, Ms Julia, fl, Orthodox Church in America

*Mwakibinga*, Mr Silas, yml, Moravian Church in Tanzania

*Nantalo*, Ms Yasmina, yfl, (Kenya), Church of Uganda

*Nassif*, Mr Mahrous, yml, (Australia), Coptic Orthodox Church [Egypt]

*Naw Lwe Say*, Ms, fl, Myanmar Baptist Convention

*Newell*, Ms Lucinda, fl, Anglican Church of Australia

*Ngondji*, Ms Ikedji, yfl, Community of Disciples of Christ [Zaire]

*Nichols*, Ms Catherine, yfl, Christian Church (Disciples of Christ) [USA]

*Nirmal*, Mr Milind, yml, Church of North India

*Nita*, Mr Ciprian, yml, Romanian Orthodox Church

*Nkwe*, Mr Modipe, yml, (Botswana), Church of the Province of Central Africa

*Ntreh*, Mr Joseph, ml, Evangelical Presbyterian Church [Ghana]

*Nyatepe-Coo*, Ms Ehui, fl, (Togo), Protestant Methodist Church in Benin and Togo

United Methodist Church [USA]

*Ochoumare*, Ms Laure, yfl, (Senegal), Protestant Methodist Church in Benin and Togo

*Oduche*, Ms Deborah, yfl, Church of Nigeria

*Oelze*, Mr Stefan, yml, Evangelical Church in Germany

*Olayinka*, Ms Bolaji, yfl, Christ Apostolic Church [Nigeria]

*Oliva Proazzi*, Mr Walter, yml, United Evangelical Lutheran Church [Argentina]

*Omolo*, Ms Ann, yfl, Church of the Province of Kenya

*Opio*, Mr Joseph, ml, (USA), Greek Orthodox Patriarchate of Alexandria and All Africa [Egypt]

*Oyalana*, Ms Victoria, yfl, Methodist Church [Nigeria]

*Padarath*, Mr Premanand, ml, Presbyterian Church in Canada

*Parris*, Mr Ezra, yml, (Jamaica), Moravian Church, Eastern West Indies Province

*Paszkjewicz*, Ms Anna, yfl, Autocephalic Orthodox Church in Poland

*Paul*, Ms Bareli, yfl, (Papua New Guinea), United Church in Papua New Guinea and the Solomon Islands

*Payne*, Mr Christopher, ml, Uniting Church in Australia

*Pearcy*, Mr Hamish, yml, Anglican Church of Australia

*Perry*, Ms Tania, yfl, Uniting Church in Australia

*Pinter Brebovszkyne*, Rev. Marta, fo, Lutheran Church in Hungary

*Pittman*, Ms Rhonda, yfl, Church of the Brethren [USA]

*Purdy*, Ms Dawn, yfl, United Church of Canada

*Rafaele*, Mr Sikeli, ml, (Fiji), Roman Catholic Church

*Rakotoharintsifa*, Mr Andrianjatovo, ml, (Switzerland), Church of Jesus Christ in Madagascar

*Rakotonirainy*, Mlle Bakoharimisa, yfl, Church of Jesus Christ in Madagascar

*Rene*, Ms Doryn, fl, (Mauritius), Church of the Province of the Indian Ocean

*Ross*, Ms Catherine, yfl, Anglican Church of Australia

*Ruddell*, Ms Maryellen, yfl, Presbyterian Church in Canada

*Rusden*, Mrs Cathleen, yfl, Presbyterian Church of New Zealand

*Saarelma*, Mr Antti, yml, Evangelical-Lutheran Church of Finland

*Sainty*, Mr Hugh, ml, (Australia), Roman Catholic Church

*Santhosham*, Rev. Galeb, mo, (Malaysia), Evangelical Lutheran Church in Malaysia and Singapore

*Sarapik*, Rev. Aivar, ymo, Russian Orthodox Church

*Saunders*, Rev. Leith, fo, United Church of Canada

*Schalekamp*, Mr David, yml, Reformed Church in America

*Schaumburg-Müller*, Ms Marianne, yfl, Evangelical Lutheran Church of Denmark

*Shole*, Mr Samuel, ml, (South Africa), Evangelical Lutheran Church in Southern Africa

*Sigurthórsson*, Mr Kristinn, ml, Evangelical Lutheran Church of Iceland
*Silva Dos Santos*, Mr Jerry, yml, Episcopal Church of Brazil
*Simango*, Ms Gladys, yfl, (Zimbabwe), United Church of Christ [USA]
*Simon*, Mr Donald, ml, Presbyterian Church of Vanuatu
*Simunyola*, Mr Stanley, yml, United Church of Zambia
*Soliman*, Ms Miriam, yfl, (Australia), Coptic Orthodox Church [Egypt]
*Solomon*, Mr Ghebre Michael, ml, (Kenya), Ethiopian Evangelical Church
    Mekane Yesus
*Stepanov*, Mr Nikolai, ml, (USA), Russian Orthodox Church
*Supardan*, Ms Prapti, yfl, Javanese Christian Churches (GKJ) [Indonesia]
*Tangulu*, Ms Nonu, yfl, Methodist Church in Tonga
*Taufa*, Ms Tangitangi, yfl, (Tonga), Roman Catholic Church
*Teodoro*, Ms Gloria, yfl, Philippine Independent Church
*Thornhill*, Ms Betty, yfl, United Church of Canada
*Thorpe*, Mr Jeremy, yml, Anglican Church of Australia
*Tongia*, Mr Tevita, ml, (Tonga), Church of the Province of New Zealand
*Traitler-Espiritu*, Mr Sascha, yml, Evangelical Church-Augsburg and Helvetic
    Confessions [Austria]
*Tranda*, Ms Hanna, yfl, Evangelical Church of the Augsburg Confession in
    Poland
*Vaalele*, Mr Talia, ml, (Fiji), Congregational Christian Church in Samoa
*Van Katwijk*, Mr Evert-Jan, yml, Netherlands Reformed Church
*Vasechko*, Mr Valentin, ml, (USA), Russian Orthodox Church
*Visco Gilardi*, Mr Leonardo, yml, Evangelical Methodist Church of Italy
*Viviers Beltrami*, Ms Ana Laura, yfl, Evangelical Methodist Church [Argentina]
*Von Sinner*, Mr Rudolf, yml, (Germany), Swiss Protestant Church Federation
*Waszuk*, Mr David, yml, Evangelical Methodist Church [Uruguay]
*Weber*, Ms Karin, yfl, Federation of Evangelical Churches [Germany]
*Weston*, Ms Roberta, yfl, Evangelical Lutheran Church in Canada
*Whelan*, Mr Shawn, yml, (Australia), Roman Catholic Church
*Williams*, Mr Abayomi, ml, Methodist Church of Sierra Leone
*Williamson*, Ms Elizabeth, yfl, Anglican Church of Australia
*Wirakotan*, Mr Joseph, yml, Uniting Church in Australia
*Wuthiwaropas*, Mr Sutap, ml, Church of Christ in Thailand
*Yacoub*, Mr Ishak, yml, Coptic Orthodox Church [Egypt]
*Zakary*, Mr Ezzat, ml, Coptic Orthodox Church [Egypt]
*Zeballos Flores*, Ms Maria, yfl, Pentecostal "Fuente de Salvación" [Argentina]

## STAFF

*Appel*, Mrs Doris, fl, Germany
*Appiah*, Ms Evelyn, fl, Ghana
*Arai*, Rev. Tosh, mo, Japan

*Ariarajah*, Rev. Dr Wesley, mo, Sri Lanka
*Balikungeri*, Mrs Mary, fl, Switzerland
*Barth-Dadieh*, Mrs Salomey, fl, Switzerland
*Batista Guerra*, Rev. Israel, mo, Cuba
*Becher*, Mrs Jeanne, fl, USA
*Beffa*, Mr Pierre, ml, Switzerland
*Béguin-Austin*, Ms Midge, fl, Switzerland
*Berry*, Ms Victoria, fl, Canada
*Best*, Rev. Dr Thomas, mo, USA
*Blyth*, Rev. Myra, fo, UK
*Botros*, Ms Brigitta, fl, Switzerland
*Braunschweiger*, Ms Nan, fl, Switzerland
*Bria*, Prof. Ion, mo, Romania
*Brock*, Mr Peter, ml, Australia
*Brüschweiler*, Mme Patricia, fl, Switzerland
*Burgy*, Mr François, ml, Switzerland
*Buss*, Pasteur Théo, mo, Switzerland
*Cambitsis*, Mrs Joan, fl, UK
*Campbell*, Rev. Joan, fo, USA
*Cano*, Ms Andrea, fl, USA
*Castro*, Rev. Dr Emilio, mo, Uruguay
*Chan Seong Foong*, Ms, fl, Malaysia
*Chaperon*, Mme Danielle, fl, France
*Chapman*, Mrs Pamela, fl, UK
*Chapman*, Mrs Eileen, fl, Australia
*Christ*, Ms Catherine, fl, USA
*Christ*, Frau Margrit, fl, Switzerland
*Constant*, Mrs Brigitte, fl, France
*Cooney SMSM*, Sister Monica, fl, New Zealand
*Courvoisier*, Ms Maryse, fl, France
*Csupor*, Mrs Isabel, fl, Germany
*Cudré-Mauroux*, Mr Gilbert, ml, Switzerland
*David*, Rev. Canon Kenith, mo, South Africa/UK
*Davies*, Rev. Michael, mo, UK
*De Rycke*, Mrs Désirée, fl, Switzerland
*Dhanjal-Lugon*, Mrs Sophie, fl, Switzerland
*Dönch*, Ms Rosemarie, fl, Germany
*Doom*, Mr John, ml, French Polynesia
*Dorris*, Deacon Thomas, ml, USA
*Duraisingh*, Rev. Dr Christopher, mo, India
*Fanchette*, Fr Philippe, mo, Mauritius
*Faure-Clemente*, Mrs Francisca, fl, Switzerland
*Ferris*, Dr Elizabeth, fl, USA
*Fischer-Duchable*, Mrs Nicole, fl, Switzerland

*Fitzpatrick*, Ms Brenda, fl, Australia
*Fleury*, Ms Béatrice, fl, France
*Ford*, Ms Linda, fl, UK
*Freidig*, Ms Marlise, fl, Switzerland
*Friedli*, Mrs Shelagh, fl, Switzerland
*Fung*, Mr Raymond, ml, Hong Kong
*Gassmann*, Rev. Dr Günther, mo, Germany
*Gautschi-Bischof*, Ms Margret, fl, Switzerland
*Gehler*, Ms Marie-Louise, fl, UK
*Gendre*, Mrs Marie-Christine, fl, Switzerland
*George*, Rev. Dr K.M., mo, India
*Giovannini*, Mrs Maria Rosa, fl, Switzerland
*Gouel*, Ms Elisabeth, fl, France
*Granberg-Michaelson*, Rev. Wesley, mo, USA
*Green*, Ms Rosemary, fl, UK
*Greig*, Rev. James, mo, UK
*Grob*, Ms Monika, fl, Switzerland
*Haller*, Ms Erna, fl, Switzerland
*Harper*, Rev. Charles, mo, USA
*Hassink*, Mr Edwin, yml, Netherlands
*Haworth*, Ms Joan, fl, UK
*Herrmann*, Dr Rudolf, ml, Switzerland
*Hilton*, Dr David, ml, USA
*Hoppe*, Ms Anneliese, fl, Germany
*Hyatt*, Mrs Lore, fl, Germany
*Inoubli*, Mrs Catherine, fl, France
*Isaac*, Mr Samuel, ml, India
*Janda*, Rev. Canon Clement, mo, Sudan
*Jauch*, Ms Eldri, fl, Switzerland
*Jungo*, Ms Stella, fl, Switzerland
*Kaiser*, Ms Helga, fl, Germany
*Kanyoro*, Mr Francis, ml, Kenya
*Kaseje*, Dr Dan, mo, Kenya
*Katsuno*, Ms Lynda, fl, Canada
*Kemppi-Repo*, Rev. Eeva, fo, Finland
*Kerkhoff*, Ms Cornelia, fl, Germany
*Ketsela*, Ms Mulu, fl, Ethiopia
*Keulemans*, Dr Nico, ml, Netherlands
*Kifle*, Ato Melaku, ml, Ethiopia
*Kindt-Siegwalt*, Rev. Dr Irmgard, fo, Germany
*Kok*, Mr Jan, ml, Netherlands
*Komalo*, Ms Imalia, fl, Indonesia
*Konta de Palma*, Mrs Livia, yfl, Sweden
*Koshy*, Mr Ninan, ml, India

*Larson*, Rev. Dr Rebecca, fo, Canada
*Lebouachera*, Ms Yasmina, fl, Switzerland
*Leclère*, Mme Catherine, fl, France
*Lemopulo*, Mr Yorgo, ml, Turkey
*Leu*, Ms Isabelle, fl, Switzerland
*Limouris*, V. Rev. Prof. Dr Gennadios, mo, Greece
*Linn*, Pfarrer Gerhard, mo, Germany
*MacArthur*, Rev. Terry, mo, USA
*Maldonado*, Rev. Dr Jorge, mo, Ecuador
*Marquot*, Mrs Lise, fl, Switzerland
*McClellan*, Mrs Monique, fl, Germany
*McNulty*, Mrs Joyce, fl, UK
*Mizuno*, Ms Michelle, yfl, USA
*Monjol*, Mr Michel, ml, France
*Mubu*, Mr Kenneth, ml, Zambia
*Murigande*, Pasteur Richard, mo, Burundi
*Mustaklem*, Mr Costandi, ml, Jordan
*Mutambirwa*, Dr James, ml, Zimbabwe
*Nerfin*, Ms Catherine, fl, Switzerland
*Nicole*, Dr Jacques, mo, Switzerland
*Niles*, Dr D. Preman, ml, Sri Lanka
*Oduyoye*, Dr Mercy, fl, Ghana
*Oh Jae-Shik*, Dr, ml, Korea
*Oracion*, Rev. Dr Levi, mo, Philippines
*Ortega*, Rev. Ofelia, fo, Cuba
*Pache*, Mrs Thérèse, fl, Switzerland
*Padolina*, Ms Priscilla, fl, Philippines
*Palma*, Ms Marta, fl, Chile
*Park Kyung-Seo*, Dr, ml, Korea
*Payne*, Rev. Clifford, mo, Trinidad
*Perkins*, Rev. William, mo, USA
*Pettingell*, Rev. Hugh, mo, UK
*Philpot*, Mr David, ml, UK
*Pirri-Simonian*, Ms Teny, fl, Lebanon
*Pityana*, Rev. Barney, mo, South Africa
*Pobee*, Dr John, mo, Ghana
*Poerwowidagdo*, Rev. Dr Judo, mo, Indonesia
*Poser*, Dr Klaus, ml, Germany
*Pozzi-Johnson*, Mr David, ml, USA
*Rajotte*, Rev. Dr Freda, fo, UK
*Rath*, Mr Günther, ml, Germany
*Ray*, Ms Sheila, fl, UK
*Reidy*, Mrs Miriam, fl, Australia
*Reilly*, Ms Joan, fl, UK

*Restrepo*, Mrs Mercedes, fl, Switzerland
*Riekkinen*, Rev. Dr Wille, mo, Finland
*Rollman*, Mrs Helga, fl, Germany
*Ross*, Ms Dawn, fl, Canada
*Roussel*, Ms Magali, fl, Switzerland
*Rubeiz*, Dr Ghassan, ml, Lebanon
*Sabev*, Prof. Dr Todor, ml, Bulgaria
*Salter*, Mrs Elizabeth, fl, UK
*Sbeghen*, Mrs Renate, fl, Switzerland
*Scavella*, Mrs Carolyn, fl, USA
*Schmidt*, Ms Jean, fl, USA
*Schoen*, Dr Ulrich, mo, Germany
*Schweizer*, Ms Heidi, fl, Switzerland
*Scott*, Rev. Bob, mo, New Zealand
*Senturias*, Dr Erlinda, fl, Philippines
*Silenzi*, Ms Ada, fl, Italy
*Sindab*, Ms Jeane, fl, USA
*Sintado*, Rev. Carlos, mo, Argentina
*Sköld*, Ms Margareta, fl, Sweden
*Smith* Mrs Gudrun, fl, Germany
*Sovik*, Mrs Ruth, fl, USA
*Stalschus*, Ms Christa, fl, Germany
*Staudenmann*, Mrs Aurea, fl, Switzerland
*Stromberg*, Ms Jean, fl, USA
*Stunt*, Ms Heather, fl, UK
*Swai*, Mr Lalashowi, ml, Tanzania
*Talvivaara*, Ms Anu, yfl, Finland
*Tevi*, Ms Lorine, fl, Fiji
*Thiers*, Ms Odile, fl, France
*Thomas*, Ms Janet, fl, Liberia
*Thomas*, Mr T.K., ml, India
*Tierney*, Ms Claire, fl, Ireland
*Tosat-Delaraye*, Mrs Pilar, fl, Switzerland
*Ucko*, Rev. Hans, mo, Sweden
*Udodesku-Noll*, Mrs Sabine, fl, Germany
*Van Beek*, Mr Huibert, ml, Netherlands
*Van Drimmelen*, Drs Robert, ml, Netherlands
*VanElderen*, Mr Marlin, ml, USA
*Veerus de Niilus*, Mrs Malle, fl, Argentina
*Visinand*, Ms Elizabeth, fl, Switzerland
*Von Arx*, Mrs Denise, fl, Switzerland
*Vuagniaux*, Mrs Gabrielle, fl, Switzerland
*Wahl*, Mrs Margot, fl, Germany
*Wehrle*, Ms Luzia, fl, Switzerland

*Williams*, Mr Peter, ml, Denmark
*Wong*, Miss Peony, fl, Hong Kong
*Zierl*, Ms Ursula, fl, Germany

## COOPTED STAFF

*Ahn Jae-Woong*, Mr, ml, Hong Kong
*Akagawa*, Mr Keiichi, ml, Japan
*Alvarez Castillo*, Sra Beatriz, fl, Switzerland
*Alvarez Gazapo*, Sr Antonio, ml, Spain
*Amirtham*, Rt Rev. Samuel, mo, India
*Arias*, Sr Gonzalo, ml, Spain
*Baltruweit*, Pfarrer Fritz, mo, Germany
*Barua*, Ms Lucy, fl, Australia
*Beaume*, Pasteur Gilbert, mo, France
*Becker*, Prof. Dr Ulrich, mo, Germany
*Beltran Acosta*, Sra Amparo, fl, Colombia
*Best*, Mr Bruce, ml, Australia
*Binder*, Herr Thomas, ml, Germany
*Bingle*, Dr Richard, ml, UK
*Birchmeier*, Pasteur Heinz, mo, Switzerland
*Bitemo*, Monsieur Raymond, ml, Congo
*Bluck*, Rev. John, mo, New Zealand
*Borgmann*, Herr Lutz, ml, Germany
*Brennan SJ*, Fr Frank, mo, Australia
*Brown*, Rev. John, mo, Australia
*Busch*, Mr David, ml, Australia
*Byfield*, Mrs Hazel, fl, Jamaica
*Byu*, Dr Esther, fl, Japan
*Carpenter*, Ms Marj, fl, USA
*Casades Morgan*, Mrs Ana, yfl, Switzerland
*Chernykh*, Mrs Natalia, fl, USSR
*Chimelli*, Mme le pasteur Claire, fo, Switzerland
*Coates*, Rev. Anthony, mo, UK
*Coleman*, Mrs Donata, fl, UK
*Conway*, Mr Martin, ml, UK
*Corsten*, Mme Katherina, fl, Switzerland
*Crawford*, Rev. Janet, fo, New Zealand
*Cullot*, Mme Martine, fl, Switzerland
*Dalabira*, Ms Helen, fl, Greece
*Davite*, Mr Marco, ml, Italy
*Delmonte*, Sra Elisabeth, fl, Uruguay

*Demont*, Mme Christiane, fl, Switzerland
*Devadas*, Mr David, ml, India
*Douglass*, Ms Robyn, fl, Australia
*Drossou*, Mrs Paraskevi, fl, Greece
*Ducharme*, Rev. Douglas, mo, Cyprus
*Dufour*, Sr Daniel, ml, Switzerland
*Dupe*, Mr Gustaf, ml, Indonesia
*Ebner*, Mme Roswitha, fl, Switzerland
*Epps*, Rev. Dwain, mo, USA
*Ernst*, Frau Erika, fl, Germany
*Faerber*, Monsieur Robert, ml, Switzerland
*Faerber-Evdokimoff*, Mme Tomoko, fl, Switzerland
*Figuière*, Monsieur Jean, ml, France
*Fouke*, Ms Carol, fl, USA
*Gassmann*, Mme Ursula, fl, Switzerland
*Ginglas-Poulet*, Mme Roswitha, fl, Switzerland
*Gnanadason*, Mrs Aruna, fl, India
*Goertz*, Pasteur Marc, mo, France
*Gordeev*, Mr Serguei, ml, USSR
*Gorodnichev*, Mr Viacheslav, ml, USSR
*Goudswaard*, Mr Jos, ml, Australia
*Goudswaard*, Mrs Dory, fl, Australia
*Gray*, Rev. Gordon, mo, UK
*Grutzner*, Mrs Angela, fl, Australia
*Gurney*, Mr Robin, ml, Switzerland
*Haller*, Mr Mario, ml, Switzerland
*Hazard*, Mme Marie-Jo, fl, France
*Hildebrand*, Frau Bettina, fl, Germany
*Holloway*, Ms Sandra, fl, Switzerland
*Honegger*, Pasteur André, mo, France
*Hovell*, Mrs Susana, fl, Australia
*How*, Rev. Dr Gordon, mo, Canada
*Howard*, Rev. Fred, mo, USA
*Khomoutov*, Mr Sergei, ml, USSR
*Kim Ha Bum*, Mr, ml, Korea
*Kim Myung Gon*, Mr, ml, Korea
*Kinnamon*, Rev. Dr Michael, mo, USA
*Kollmar*, Pfarrer Peter, mo, Germany
*Kunde*, Sr Carlos, ml, Ecuador
*Lamberth*, Mr David, ml, USA
*Lasserre*, Mme Nelly, fl, Switzerland
*Ledger*, Ms Christine, fl, Switzerland
*Lenz*, Herr Gerhard, ml, Germany
*Lodwick*, Rev. Dr Robert, mo, Switzerland

*Lopez*, Mrs Jeannine, fl, Australia
*Lucke*, Pfarrer Hartmut, mo, Switzerland
*Luttmann*, Mme Michèle, fl, France
*Maiocchi*, Dr Renato, ml, Italy
*Makhnev*, Mr Vassily, ml, USSR
*Marshall*, Mrs Anne, fl, Australia
*Marvillet*, Ms Christiane, fl, Australia
*Mavor*, Rev. John, mo, Australia
*Méar*, Mme Christine, fl, France
*Melnikov*, Mr Aleksander, ml, USSR
*Merritt*, Dr David, mo, Australia
*Mitri*, Dr Tarek, ml, Lebanon
*Müller-Römheld*, Dr Walter, ml, Germany
*Mukasa*, Mr Paul, ml, Kenya
*Nemoto*, Mr Nobihiro, ml, Japan
*Nevskaya*, Mrs Olga, fl, USSR
*Ngoma*, Mr Jumbe, ml, Zambia
*Nolan*, Dr Elizabeth, fl, Australia
*Northam*, Mrs Inge, fl, Switzerland
*Nossova*, Mrs Zinaida, fl, USSR
*Nottingham*, Dr William, mo, USA
*Nyomi*, Rev. Setri, mo, USA
*Ortega*, Dr Hugo, mo, Argentina
*Papathanassiou*, Mr Vassilis, ml, Greece
*Papayannopoulou*, Mrs Natalia, fl, Greece
*Pastor*, Mr Manuel, ml, Australia
*Pater*, Frau Margaret, fl, Germany
*Pattel-Gray*, Ms Anne, fl, Australia
*Pattiasina-Toreh*, Rev. Mrs Caroline, fo, Indonesia
*Pattinasarany*, Mrs Jessica, fl, Indonesia
*Peralta*, Mr Carlos, ml, France
*Perkins*, Mrs Anna-Brita, fl, Switzerland
*Perrot*, Ms Agnes, fl, Switzerland
*Philibert*, Mme Janine, fl, France
*Piskunova*, Mrs Olga, fl, USSR
*Pitt*, Miss Sharon, fl, Trinidad
*Pottier*, Mme Françoise, fl, Switzerland
*Rebera*, Mrs Ranjini, fl, Australia
*Richter*, Mme Madeleine, fl, Switzerland
*Richterich*, Ms Anita, fl, Switzerland
*Robinson*, Miss Nancy, fl, Indonesia
*Rollason*, Mr Russell, ml, Australia
*Rzianin*, Mr Sergei, ml, USSR
*Sabanes de Plou*, Sra Dafne, fl, Argentina

*Sainz-Trapaga*, Sra Natividad, fl, Spain
*Santa Ana*, Mme Violaine de, fl, Brazil
*Santoso*, Mr Iman, fl, Indonesia
*Schüller-Leão*, Ms Marilia, fl, Brazil
*Seater*, Rev. Robert, mo, USA
*Siteke*, Monsieur Ubial, ml, Zaire
*Skiller*, Ms Thelma, fl, Australia
*Stephanopoulos*, Mrs Nikki, ml, USA
*Strake-Behrendt*, Dr Gabriele, fl, Germany
*Strecker*, Frau Renate, fl, Germany
*Tatu*, Mme Evelyne, fl, Switzerland
*Taylor-Bouladon*, Ms Valérie, fl, Australia
*Teinaoré*, Monsieur Ralph, ml, French Polynesia
*Ulmer*, Ms Barbara, fl, Australia
*Vickers*, Ms Alison, fl, Australia
*Voskressenski*, Mr Mstislav, ml, USSR
*Walker*, Mrs Elizabeth, fl, Australia
*Ward*, Rev. Geoffrey, mo, Australia
*Webb*, Mr Stephen, ml, Hong Kong
*Wee*, Rev. Dr Paul, mo, Switzerland
*Westphal*, Mme Marthe, fl, France
*Whitmore*, Mr Hal, ml, USA
*Wieser*, Mme Marguerite, fl, Switzerland
*Wik*, Mr Boris, ml, USSR
*Wilhelm*, Herr Clemens, ml, Germany
*Wilson*, Rev. Dr Frederick, mo, USA
*Ziegler*, Ms Harriet, fl, Australia

# 7.10. ASSEMBLY COMMITTEES
# AND SECTION LEADERS

## BUSINESS COMMITTEE

*Held*, Rev. Dr Heinz Joachim, mo, United, Germany, *Moderator*
*Chrysostomos of Myra*, Metropolitan, mo, Orthodox (Eastern), Greece, *Vice-moderator*
*Talbot*, Dr Sylvia, fl, Methodist, Virgin Islands USA, *Vice-moderator*

*Barrow*, H.E. Dame R. Nita, fl, Methodist, Barbados
*Bottoms*, Rev. Ruth, yfo, Baptist, UK
*Bührig*, Dr phil. Marga, fl, Reformed, Switzerland
*Castro*, Rev. Dr Emilio, mo, Methodist, Switzerland
*Crow, Jr*, Rev. Dr Paul, mo, Christian Church (Disciples of Christ), USA
*Daciuk*, Ms Anna, yfl, Orthodox (Eastern), Poland
*Fortes*, Ms Raquel, yfl, Anglican, Brazil
*Francisco*, Rev. Julio, mo, Reformed, Angola
*Gcabashe*, Mrs Virginia, fl, Methodist, South Africa
*Gregorios*, Metropolitan Dr Paulos Mar, mo, Orthodox (Oriental), India
*Hempel*, Bishop Dr Johannes, mo, United, Germany
*Ibrahim*, Metropolitan Gregorios Yohanna, mo, Orthodox (Oriental), Syria
*Jefferson*, Rev. Ruth, fo, Anglican, Canada
*Kaessmann*, Rev. Dr Margot, fo, United, Germany
*Keshishian*, Archbishop Aram, mo, Orthodox (Oriental), Lebanon
*Kirill of Smolensk*, H.E. Archbishop, mo, Orthodox (Eastern), USSR
*Love*, Dr Janice, fl, Methodist, USA
*Makhulu*, Most Rev. W.P. Khotso, mo, Anglican, Botswana
*Malpas*, Mrs Jan, fl, Anglican, Australia
*Motsoeneng*, Mr Tseliso, yml, Reformed, Lesotho
*Nababan*, Ephorus Dr Soritua, mo, Lutheran, Indonesia
*Pasco*, Obispo Maximo Tito, mo, Philippine Independent, Philippines
*Pitakoe*, Mr Luke, ml, United, Solomon Islands
*Raiwaliu*, Mrs Vasiti, fl, Methodist, Fiji
*Rotgans*, Ms Rosalien, fl, Moravian, Surinam
*Schaad*, Pastor Juan Pedro, mo, United, Paraguay
*Tsetsis*, Very Rev. Dr Georges, mo, Orthodox (Eastern), Switzerland
*Voksö*, Mr Per, ml, Lutheran, Norway
*Wilson*, Very Rev. Dr Lois, fo, United, Canada

---

m = male; f = female; o = ordained; l = lay; y = youth

## CREDENTIALS COMMITTEE

*Briggs*, Mr John, ml, Baptist, UK, *Co-moderator*
*Gcabashe*, Mrs Virginia, fl, Methodist, South Africa, *Co-moderator*
*Bobrova*, Mrs Nina, fl, Orthodox (Eastern), USSR, *Vice-moderator*
*Iso Malaipa*, Mr, yml, United, Papua New Guinea, *Vice-moderator*

*Aykazian*, Rev. Fr Viken, mo, Orthodox (Oriental), Switzerland
*Boteler*, Rev. Mary-Gene, fo, Reformed, USA
*Daley*, Rev. Oliver, mo, United, Jamaica
*Deenik-Moolhuizen*, Rev. Jeannette, fo, Reformed, Netherlands
*Kim Hyung Ki*, Mr, ml, Reformed, Korea
*Ruiz Avila*, Obispo Raul, mo, Methodist, Mexico
*Sjoberg*, Bishop Donald, mo, Lutheran, Canada
*Wickramasinghe*, Ms Lydia, yfl, Anglican, Sri Lanka

## FINANCE COMMITTEE

*Abel*, Miss Carol, fl, Anglican, UK, *Co-moderator*
*Voksö*, Mr Per, ml, Lutheran, Norway, *Co-moderator*
*Laham*, Mr Albert, ml, Orthodox (Eastern), Switzerland, *Vice-moderator*
*Le Roux*, Ms Yvette, yfl, Methodist, South Africa, *Vice-moderator*

*Abramides*, Mr Elias, ml, Orthodox (Eastern), Argentina
*Arnold*, Oberkirchenrat Walter, mo, United, Germany
*Bebis*, Prof. Dr George, ml, Orthodox (Eastern), USA
*Burnham*, Rev. Rachel, fo, United, UK
*Bussert*, Rev. Joy, fo, Lutheran, USA
*Engel*, Frau Edeltraud, fl, United, Germany
*Francois*, Mrs Edith, fl, Reformed, Ghana
*Garrett*, Dr Maxine, fl, Moravian, USA
*Habib*, Rev. Dr Samuel, mo, Reformed, Egypt
*Hanna*, Dr Marcelle, fl, Orthodox (Oriental), USA
*Harteveld*, Mr Teunis, ml, Reformed, Netherlands
*Hatendi*, Rt Rev. Dr Ralph, mo, Anglican, Zimbabwe
*Hirata*, Mrs Makiko, fl, United, Japan
*Hye Yeon Yoo*, Ms, yfl, Reformed, Korea
*Isho*, Mrs Susan, yfl, Orthodox (Assyrian), Australia
*Jäggi*, Pfarrer Paul, mo, Reformed, Switzerland
*Jessiman*, Dr Jon, ml, United, Canada
*Karpenko*, Rev. Fr Alexander, mo, Orthodox (Eastern), Switzerland
*Kirkpatrick*, Rev. Clifton, mo, Reformed, USA
*Krusche*, Generalsup. Dr Günter, mo, Germany

*Matumbyo*, Mr Christopher, yml, Anglican, Tanzania
*McGonigle*, Mr George, ml, USA
*Nifon of Ploiesti*, Bishop, mo, Orthodox (Eastern), Romania
*Powell*, Rev. Staccato, mo, Methodist, USA
*Rantakari*, Mrs Birgitta, fl, Lutheran, Zambia
*Rayner*, Most Rev. Dr Keith, mo, Anglican, Australia
*Rodgers*, Deaconess Margaret, fl, Anglican, Australia
*Sandelin*, Mr Holger, yml, Lutheran, Sweden
*Scott*, Dr Beverly, fl, Baptist, USA
*Shava*, Rev. Naison, mo, Lutheran, Zimbabwe
*Tanielu*, Rev. Laau, mo, Reformed, Western Samoa

## MESSAGE COMMITTEE

*Keshishian*, Archbishop Aram, mo, Orthodox (Oriental), Lebanon, *Co-moderator*
*Ketuabanza*, Mme Mfutu, fl, Baptist, Zaire, *Co-moderator*
*Edwards*, Ms Donnalie, yfl, Anglican, Antigua, *Vice-moderator*
*Wood*, Rev. Dr D'Arcy, mo, United, Australia, *Vice-moderator*

*Avramides*, Rev. Stephen, mo, Orthodox (Eastern), Greece
*Bredt*, Rev. Violet, fo, United, Zambia
*Carpenter*, Mrs Jennifer, fl, Methodist, UK
*Havea*, Rev. Dr Sione, mo, Methodist, Tonga
*Huttunen*, Fr Heikki, mo, Orthodox (Eastern), Finland
*Iannuariy*, Archimandrite, mo, Orthodox (Eastern), USSR
*Jones*, Rev. Mac Charles, mo, Baptist, USA
*Kumar*, Miss Rachel, fl, Methodist, India
*Pullam*, Ms Ruth, fl, United, Canada
*Saga*, Mr Stewart, ml, Methodist, Malaysia
*Sauca*, Rev. Prof. Ioan, mo, Orthodox (Eastern), Romania
*Skulason*, Rt Rev. Olafur, mo, Lutheran, Iceland
*Szabó*, Rev. Mrs Marianna, fo, Lutheran, Hungary
*Thompson*, Miss Kristine, yfl, Reformed, USA
*Wilson*, Obispo John, mo, Moravian, Nicaragua

## NOMINATIONS COMMITTEE

*Jefferson*, Rev. Ruth, fo, Anglican, Canada, *Co-moderator*
*Jeremias*, Bishop, mo, Orthodox (Eastern), Poland, *Co-moderator*
*Oliveira*, Reverendo Deão Orlando, mo, Anglican, Brazil, *Vice-moderator*
*Tolentino*, Ms Joy, yfl, Methodist, Philippines, *Vice-moderator*

*Aboud*, Mrs Heather, fl, Orthodox (Eastern), Australia
*Aco*, Sra Graciela, fl, Methodist, Brazil
*Ademola*, Deaconess Isabella, fl, Methodist, Nigeria
*Baah*, Miss Maria, yfl, Methodist, Trinidad
*Bishoy*, Bishop, mo, Orthodox (Oriental), Egypt
*Boyadjian*, Miss Manoushag, fl, Orthodox (Oriental), Cyprus
*Brink*, Rev. Agnete, fo, Lutheran, Denmark
*Cosma*, Mother Filoteia, fl, Orthodox (Eastern), Romania
*Eneme*, Mrs Grace, fl, Reformed, Cameroon
*Epting*, Kirchenrat Dr Karl-Christoph, mo, United, Germany
*Foster*, Rev. Robert, mo, Moravian, Jamaica
*Gam*, Rt Rev. Getake, mo, Lutheran, Papua New Guinea
*Hartmann*, Mme Henriette, fl, Reformed, Switzerland
*Kangrga*, Dr Nedeljko, ml, Orthodox (Eastern), Yugoslavia
*Kitahara*, Ms Yoko, yfl, United, Japan
*Kolowa*, Bishop Sebastian, mo, Lutheran, Tanzania
*Lofton*, Dr Fred, mo, Baptist, USA
*M'Imathiu*, Bishop Lawi, mo, Methodist, Kenya
*Maraki*, Rev. Pakoa, mo, Reformed, Vanuatu
*Mathew*, Mrs Rachel, fl, Mar Thoma, India
*Matsinhe*, Rev. Carlos, mo, Anglican, Mozambique
*Miller*, Mrs Peggy Reiff, fl, Brethren, USA
*Papaderos*, Dr Alexandros, ml, Orthodox (Eastern), Greece
*Rabe Ranjanivo*, Mlle Mialy-Tiana, yfl, Lutheran, Madagascar
*Reber*, Dr Robert, ml, Methodist, USA
*Sergei of Solnechnogorsk*, Archbishop, mo, Orthodox (Eastern), Switzerland
*Tabart*, Dr Jill, fl, United, Australia
*Tapia Gleisner*, Sra Marcela, yfl, Lutheran, Chile
*Tarasar*, Dr Constance, fl, Orthodox (Eastern), USA
*Waspada*, Bishop Dr I Ketut, mo, Reformed, Indonesia

## PROGRAMME POLICY COMMITTEE

*Nababan*, Rt Rev. Dr Soritua, mo, Lutheran, Indonesia, *Co-moderator*
*Ritchie*, Pastora Nélida, fo, Methodist, Argentina, *Co-moderator*
*Daniel of Moldavia and Bukovina*, Metropolitan, mo, Orthodox (Eastern), Romania *Vice-moderator*
*Kinnunen*, Mrs Mari, yfl, Lutheran, Finland, *Vice-moderator*

*Ahn Chu Hye*, Miss, yfl, Methodist, Korea
*Andrea*, Ms Helene, fl, Orthodox (Eastern), Lebanon
*Asuoha*, Mrs Ezinne, fl, Reformed, Nigeria
*Avvakumov*, Rev. Fr Yuri, mo, Orthodox (Eastern), USSR

*Basmajian*, Ms Nancy, fl, Orthodox (Oriental), USA
*Camba*, Bishop Erme, mo, United, Philippines
*Gerritsma*, Drs Nynke, yfl, Reformed, Netherlands
*Gorski*, Bispo William, mo, Lutheran, Chile
*Gregorios*, Metropolitan Dr Paulos Mar, mo, Orthodox (Oriental), India
*Kidu*, Rev. Edea, mo, United, Papua New Guinea
*Kirby*, Ms Ellen, fl, Methodist, USA
*Kishkovsky*, Archpriest Leonid, mo, Orthodox (Eastern), USA
*Klapsis*, Rev. Dr Emmanuel, mo, Orthodox (Eastern), USA
*Koshy*, Prof. George, ml, United, India
*Meade*, Miss Alfreda, fl, Anglican, Montserrat
*Nyirabukara*, Mme Josette, fl, Reformed, Rwanda
*Palmer*, Mr Samuel, ml, Methodist, Sierra Leone
*Ravololoson*, Mme le pasteur Esther, fo, United, Madagascar
*Serapion*, Bishop, mo, Orthodox (Oriental), Egypt
*Sherry*, Rev. Dr Paul, mo, United, USA
*Supit*, Dr Bert, ml, Reformed, Indonesia
*Tveter*, Ms Anne, yfl, Lutheran, Norway
*Urban*, Frau Ursula, fl, United, Germany
*Vogt*, Ms Franziska, yfl, Old Catholic, Switzerland
*Walker-Smith*, Rev. Angelique, fo, Baptist, USA

## PUBLIC ISSUES COMMITTEE

*Love*, Dr Janice, fl, Methodist, USA, *Co-moderator*
*Tóth*, Bishop Dr Károly, mo, Reformed, Hungary, *Co-moderator*
*Okullu*, Rt Rev. Dr J. Henry, mo, Anglican, Kenya, *Vice-moderator*
*Shirras*, Ms Rachel, yfl, Anglican, UK, *Vice-moderator*

*Ayres Mattos*, Bispo Paulo, mo, Methodist, Brazil
*Bakkevig*, Rev. Dr Trond, mo, Lutheran, Norway
*Buevsky*, Dr Alexei, ml, Orthodox (Eastern), USSR
*Daw*, Ms Diana, fl, Baptist, Myanmar
*Edgar*, Pauline, fl, Friends, USA
*Gilbert*, Dr Helga, fl, United, Germany
*Hromádka*, Dr Josef, mo, Reformed, CSFR
*Jacobs*, Mrs Lorraine, fl, Christian Churches (Disciples), New Zealand
*Lee*, Prof. Dr Samuel, ml, Reformed, Korea
*Lynn*, Ms Stephanie, yfl, United, Canada
*Mackenzie*, Ms Vanessa, fl, Anglican, South Africa
*Mitsides*, Dr Andreas, ml, Orthodox (Eastern), Cyprus
*Moussa*, Bishop, mo, Orthodox (Oriental), Egypt
*Pashaian*, Mrs Kariné, fl, Orthodox (Oriental), USSR

*Paul*, Ms Jenny, fl, Anglican, Sudan
*Pheidas*, Prof. Vlasios, ml, Orthodox (Eastern), Greece
*Pitts*, Rev. Tyrone, mo, Baptist, USA
*Richaud*, Mme Vani, fl, Reformed, French Polynesia
*Soone*, Dean Einar, mo, Lutheran, USSR
*Trenaman*, Ms Dianne, yfl, United, Australia
*Turner*, Rev. Eugene, mo, Reformed, USA
*Woldeyes*, Prof. Asrat, ml, Orthodox (Oriental), Ethiopia

## REFERENCE COMMITTEE

*Bartholomeos of Chalcedon*, Metropolitan, mo, Orthodox (Eastern), Turkey, *Co-moderator*
*Raiwalui*, Mrs Vasiti, fl, Methodist, Fiji, *Co-moderator*
*Muwanika*, Ms Harriet, yfl, Anglican, Uganda, *Vice-moderator*
*Raiser*, Prof. Dr Konrad, mo, United, Germany, *Vice-moderator*

*Brandner*, Herr Tobias, yml, Reformed, Switzerland
*Christenson*, Mrs Joyce, fl, Lutheran, Canada
*Dawd-El-Khoury*, Mrs Mahat, fl, Orthodox (Eastern), Syria
*Ebelle-Ekanga*, Mme Nicole-Christine, fl, Reformed, Cameroon
*Farfan Figueroa*, Pastor Erasmo, mo, Pentecostal, Chile
*Gomez*, Rt Rev. Drexel, mo, Anglican, Barbados
*Kao Chun-Ming*, Rev., mo, Reformed, Taiwan
*Katonia*, Citoyen Tusange, yml, Baptist, Zaire
*Lodberg*, Mr Peter, ml, Lutheran, Denmark
*Maeda*, Ms Keiko, fl, Anglican, Japan
*Mya Han*, Most Rev. Andrew, mo, Anglican, Myanmar
*Orlova*, Ms Tatyana, fl, Baptist, USSR
*Page*, Rev. Dr Ruth, fo, Reformed, UK
*Petliuchenko*, Archpriest Viktor, mo, Orthodox (Eastern), USSR
*Popescu*, Mr Cristian, yml, Orthodox (Eastern), Romania
*Rhaburn*, Mrs Violet, fl, Methodist, Panama
*Sahade*, Rev. Fr Ignacio, mo, Orthodox (Eastern), Argentina
*Scouteris*, Prof. Constantine, ml, Orthodox (Eastern), Greece
*Serote*, Bishop Ntwampe, mo, Lutheran, South Africa
*Tate*, Mrs Hazel, fl, Baptist, USA
*Thomas*, Prof. Mary, fl, Orthodox (Oriental), India

## REPORT COMMITTEE

*Azariah*, Mrs Khushnud, fl, United, Pakistan, *Co-moderator*
*Crow, Jr*, Rev. Dr Paul, mo, Disciples, USA, *Co-moderator*

*Attia*, Mr Maged, yml, Orthodox (Oriental), Australia, *Vice-moderator*
*Pogo*, Rt Rev. Ellison, mo, Anglican, Solomon Islands, *Vice-moderator*

*Borovoy*, Protopresbyter Vitaly, mo, Orthodox (Eastern), USSR
*Bösenberg*, Sra Cristina, yfl, United, Argentina
*Brown*, Dr Katheryn Middleton, fl, Methodist, USA
*Correia*, Profesora Evanilza de Barros, fl, Anglican, Brazil
*Efthimiou*, Rev. Dr Milton, mo, Orthodox (Eastern), USA
*Gedisa*, Ms Gabby, fl, Lutheran, Papua New Guinea
*Hannon*, Rt Rev. Brian, mo, Anglican, UK
*Hayes*, Rev. Stephen, mo, Reformed, Canada
*Hirschler*, Landesbischof Horst, mo, United, Germany
*Karickam*, Prof. Abraham, ml, Mar Thoma, India
*Kathindi*, Mrs Nangula, fl, Anglican, Namibia
*Mbise*, Ms Loe Rose, fl, Lutheran, Tanzania
*Misukka*, Ms Marina, yfl, Orthodox (Eastern), Finland
*Pilton*, Ms Linda, yfl, Christian Churches (Disciples), Australia

## SECTION LEADERSHIP

### Section I: Giver of Life — Sustain your Creation!

*Abraham*, Mrs Ruth, fl, Lutheran, Ethiopia, *Co-moderator*
*Kirill of Smolensk*, H.E. Archbishop, mo, Orthodox (Eastern), USSR, *Co-moderator*
*Hebmüller*, Mr Paulo, yml, Lutheran, Brazil, *Vice-moderator*
*Taufatofua*, Rev. Sela, fo, Methodist, Tonga, *Vice-moderator*

*Drafters*
*De Gaay Fortman*, Prof. Dr Bastiaan, ml, Reformed, Netherlands
*Orteza*, Mrs Edna, fl, United, USA

### Section II: Spirit of Truth — Set us Free!

*Gondarra*, Rev. Djiniyini, mo, United, Australia *Co-moderator*
*Kaessmann*, Rev. Dr Margot, fo, United, Germany *Co-moderator*
*Danquah*, Ms Beatrice, yfl, Reformed, Ghana *Vice-moderator*
*Taylor*, Mr Victor, ml, Methodist, USA, *Vice-moderator*

*Drafters*
*Johnston*, Prof. Alexandra, fl, Reformed, Canada
*Totomarovario*, Mme Laurette, fl, Anglican, Madagascar

## Section III: Spirit of Unity — Reconcile your People!

*Ibrahim*, Metropolitan Gregorios Yohanna, mo, Orthodox (Oriental), Syria, *Co-moderator*
*Seim*, Dr Turid Karlsen, fl, Lutheran, Norway, *Co-moderator*
*Kikalao*, Mr Nashon, yml, Lutheran, Tanzania, *Vice-moderator*
*Zacharias Mar Theophilos*, Bishop, mo, Mar Thoma, India, *Vice-moderator*

*Drafters*
*Mayland*, Mrs Jean, fl, Anglican, UK
*Zahirsky*, Mrs Valerie, fl, Orthodox (Eastern), USA

## Section IV: Holy Spirit — Transform and Sanctify Us!

*Dickson*, Rev. Prof. Kwesi, mo, Methodist, Ghana, *Co-moderator*
*Rotgans*, Ms Rosalien, fl, Moravian, Surinam, *Co-moderator*
*Aguilar*, Ms Elizabeth, yfl, United, USA, *Vice-moderator*
*Najarian*, Rev. Fr Haigazoun, mo, Orthodox (Oriental), USA, *Vice-moderator*

*Drafters*
*Jonson*, Rt Rev. Dr Jonas, mo, Lutheran, Sweden
*Kuria*, Rev. Dr Plawson, mo, Reformed, Kenya

# 7.11. THE PRESIDENTS AND MEMBERS
# OF THE CENTRAL COMMITTEE
## (ELECTED IN CANBERRA)

PRESIDIUM

*Aagaard*, Prof. Anna Marie, Evangelical Lutheran Church of Denmark

*Anderson*, Bishop Vinton, African Methodist Episcopal Church, USA

*Boseto*, Bishop Leslie, United Church in Papua New Guinea and the Solomon Islands

*Mendis*, Mrs Priyanka, Church of Ceylon

*Parthenios*, His Beatitude, Greek Orthodox Patriarchate of Alexandria and All Africa, Egypt

*Santana*, Rev. Eunice, Christian Church (Disciples of Christ), Puerto Rico

*Shenouda III*, His Holiness Pope, Coptic Orthodox Church, Egypt

*Tolen*, Dr Aaron, Presbyterian Church of Cameroon

OFFICERS

*Keshishian*, Archbishop Aram, Armenian Apostolic Church (Cilicia), Lebanon, *Moderator*

*Nababan*, Ephorus Dr Soritua, Batak Protestant Christian Church (HKBP), Indonesia, *Vice-moderator*

*Ritchie*, Pastora Nélida, Evangelical Methodist Church of Argentina, *Vice-moderator*

*Castro* Rev. Dr Emilio, Evangelical Methodist Church, Uruguay, *General secretary*

*Abraham*, Mrs Ruth, Ethiopian Evangelical Church Mekane Yesus

*Adams*, Dr Charles, Progressive National Baptist Convention Inc., USA

*Ahn Chu Hye*, Miss, Korean Methodist Church

*Ajalat*, Mr Charles, Greek Orthodox Patriarchate of Antioch and All the East, Syria

*Akhura*, Rev. Levi, African Church of the Holy Spirit, Kenya

*Allsop*, Rev. Ian, Churches of Christ in Australia

*Ambrosius of Joensuu*, Bishop, Orthodox Church of Finland

*Anggui*, Rev. Andreas, Toraja Church, Indonesia

*Arnold*, Oberkirchenrat Walter, Evangelical Church in Germany

*Audi*, Metropolitan Elias, Greek Orthodox Patriarchate of Antioch and All the East, Syria

*Avvakumov*, Rev. Fr Yuri, Russian Orthodox Church

*Ayres Mattos*, Bispo Paulo, Methodist Church in Brazil
*Azariah*, Mrs Khushnud, Church of Pakistan
*Bannister*, Mrs Kathryn, United Methodist Church, USA
*\*Bartholomeos of Chalcedon*, Metropolitan, Ecumenical Patriarchate of Constantinople, Turkey
*Basmajian*, Ms Nancy, Armenian Apostolic Church (Etchmiadzin), USSR
*Bazett*, Barbara, Canadian Yearly Meeting-Society of Friends
*\*Best*, Mrs Marion, United Church of Canada
*Beukenhorst*, Pasteur Martinus, United Protestant Church of Belgium
*Birmelé*, Prof. Dr André, Evangelical Church-Augsburg Confession Alsace/Lorraine, France
*Blei*, Rev. Dr Karel, Netherlands Reformed Church
*Bösenberg*, Sra Cristina, Evangelical Church of the River Plate, Argentina
*Bozabalian*, Archbishop Nerses, Armenian Apostolic Church (Etchmiadzin), USSR
*Bredt*, Rev. Violet, United Church of Zambia
*\*Briggs*, Mr John, Baptist Union of Great Britain
*Browning*, Most Rev. Edmond, Episcopal Church, USA
*Bue*, Bishop Bjørn, Church of Norway
*Buevsky*, Dr Alexei, Russian Orthodox Church
*Carvalho*, Mr Ari, United Methodist Church, USA
*Chiwanga*, Mrs Gladys, Church of the Province of Tanzania
*Chrysanthos of Limassol*, Metropolitan, Church of Cyprus
*Chrysostomos of Peristerion*, Metropolitan, Church of Greece
*Correia*, Prof. Evanilza de Barros, Episcopal Church of Brazil
*Crow, Jr*, Rev. Dr Paul, Christian Church (Disciples of Christ), USA
*Csiha*, Dr Kálmán, Reformed Church of Romania
*\*Daniel of Moldavia and Bukovina*, Metropolitan, Romanian Orthodox Church
*\*Danquah*, Ms Beatrice, Presbyterian Church of Ghana
*David of Suchumi and Abkhazeti*, Metropolitan, Georgian Orthodox Church
*Dometian of Vidin*, Metropolitan, Bulgarian Orthodox Church
*Engel*, Frau Edeltraud, Evangelical Church in Germany
*Farfan Figueroa*, Pastor Erasmo, Pentecostal Mission Church, Chile
*Francisco*, Rev. Julio, Evangelical Congregational Church in Angola
*Ganaba*, Mrs Olga, Russian Orthodox Church
*Garrett*, Dr Maxine, Moravian Church in America (Northern Province)
*\*Gcabashe*, Mrs Virginia, Methodist Church of Southern Africa
*Gerka*, Prof. Dr Milan, Orthodox Church of Czechoslovakia
*Gerny*, Bischof Hans, Old Catholic Church of Switzerland
*Ghose*, Most Rev. John, Church of North India
*Giannopoulos*, Archimandrite Theophilos, Greek Orthodox Patriarchate of Jerusalem

---

*Member of the executive committee.

*\*Gomez*, Rt Rev. Drexel, Church in the Province of the West Indies
*Gondarra*, Rev. Djiniyini, Uniting Church in Australia
*Hannon*, Rt Rev. Brian, Church of Ireland
*Hirata*, Mrs Makiko, United Church of Christ in Japan
*Houmbouy*, M. Béalo, Evangelical Church in New Caledonia and the Loyalty Isles
*Ibrahim*, Metropolitan Gregorios Yohanna, Syrian Orthodox Patriarchate of Antioch and All the East, Syria
*Izard*, Miss Rosemary, Methodist Church, UK
*Jägers*, Mrs Maryon, Church of England
*Jarjour*, Mrs Rosangela, National Evangelical Synod of Syria and Lebanon
*Jones*, Dr Mac Charles, National Baptist Convention of America
*Jung*, Dr Hans-Gernot, Evangelical Church in Germany
*\*Kaessmann*, Rev. Dr Margot, Evangelical Church in Germany
*Kathindi*, Mrs Nangula, Church of the Province of Southern Africa
*Katonia*, Citoyen Tusange, Episcopal Baptist Community, Zaire
*Kidu*, Rev. Edea, United Church in Papua New Guinea and the Solomon Islands
*\*Kirill of Smolensk*, H.E. Archbishop, Russian Orthodox Church
*Kirov*, Mr Dimitre, Bulgarian Orthodox Church
*\*Kishkovsky*, Very Rev. Leonid, Orthodox Church in America
*Konach*, Mr Wsiewolod, Autocephalic Orthodox Church in Poland
*Koshy*, Prof. George, Church of South India
*Krusche*, Generalsup. Dr Günter, Federation of Evangelical Churches, Germany
*Larsson*, Dr Birgitta, Church of Sweden
*Liddell*, Dr Shirley, Christian Methodist Episcopal Church, USA
*Lodberg*, Mr Peter, Evangelical Lutheran Church of Denmark
*Love*, Dr Janice, United Methodist Church, USA
*Malpas*, Mrs Jan, Anglican Church of Australia
*Mandeng*, Rev. Dr David, Presbyterian Church of Cameroon
*Mandysová*, Mrs Nadeje, Evangelical Church of Czech Brethren
*\*Mapanao*, Miss Maryssa, United Church of Christ in the Philippines
*Mbugo*, Mr Andrew, Province of the Episcopal Church of the Sudan
*Mendez*, Rev. Hector, Presbyterian Reformed Church in Cuba
*Miller*, Dr Donald, Church of the Brethren, USA
*Moseme*, Rev. Dr Abiel, Lesotho Evangelical Church
*Moukouyou-Kimbouala*, Monsieur Michel, Evangelical Church of the Congo
*Müller-Stöver*, Dr Irmela, Evangelical Church in Germany
*Mulder*, Dr Edwin, Reformed Church in America
*Mungania*, Rev. John, Methodist Church in Kenya
*Muttiah*, Rev. Dr Thesiganesan, Methodist Church [Sri Lanka]
*Mwondha*, Mrs Faith, Church of Uganda
*Neliubova*, Ms Margarita, Russian Orthodox Church
*Nifon of Ploiesti*, Bishop, Romanian Orthodox Church
*Nontawasee*, Mrs Prakai, Church of Christ in Thailand

*Oettel*, Frau Christine, Federation of Evangelical Churches, Germany
*\*Okullu*, Rt Rev. Dr J. Henry, Church of the Province of Kenya
*Omodunbi*, Bishop Amos, Methodist Church, Nigeria
*Omoyajowo*, Very Rev. Prof. Joseph, Church of Nigeria
*Page*, Rev. Dr Ruth, Church of Scotland
*Park Jong-Wha*, Prof. Dr, Presbyterian Church in the Republic of Korea
*Pasco*, Obispo Maximo Tito, Philippine Independent Church
*Patelos*, Prof. Constantine, Greek Orthodox Patriarchate of Alexandria and All
    Africa, Egypt
*Paulin*, Rev. Rachel, Presbyterian Church of New Zealand
*Pavlovic*, Metropolitan Jovan, Serbian Orthodox Church, Yugoslavia
*Peers*, Most Rev. Michael, Anglican Church of Canada
*Petliuchenko*, Archpriest Viktor, Russian Orthodox Church
*Predele*, Ms Aida, Evangelical Lutheran Church of Latvia
*Rakotomaro*, Pasteur Jean-Baptiste, Malagasy Lutheran Church
*Rani*, Ms V.R. Vidhya, United Evangelical Lutheran Churches in India
*\*Rantakari*, Mrs Birgitta, Evangelical Lutheran Church of Finland
*Rhaburn*, Mrs Violet, Methodist Church in the Caribbean and the Americas
*Rogerson*, Rt Rev. Barry, Church of England
*Romanides*, Prof. John, Church of Greece
*Rusch*, Rev. Dr William, Evangelical Lutheran Church in America
*Rusterholz*, Pfarrer Heinrich, Swiss Protestant Church Federation
*Salvador*, Pastor José da Silveira, Evangelical Presbyterian Church of Portugal
*Sanchez*, Pastor Carlos, Baptist Association of El Salvador
*Scoutas*, Mrs Patricia, Ecumenical Patriarchate of Constantinople, Turkey
*Seddoh*, Mme Nenevi, Evangelical Church of Togo
*Serapion*, Bishop, Coptic Orthodox Church, Egypt
*Sherry*, Rev. Dr Paul, United Church of Christ, USA
*Soedjatmoko*, Mrs Sri Winarti, East Java Christian Church (GKJW), Indonesia
*Sumbayak*, Mr Harrys, Simalungun Protestant Christian Church (GKPS),
    Indonesia
*Supit*, Dr Bert, Christian Evangelical Church in Minahasa (GMIM), Indonesia
*Szabó*, Rev. Mrs Marianna, Lutheran Church in Hungary
*Szarek*, Okr Jan, Evangelical Church of the Augsburg Confession in Poland
*\*Talbert*, Bishop Melvin, United Methodist Church, USA
*Tanielu*, Rev. Laau, Congregational Christian Church in Samoa
*Taufatofua*, Rev. Sela, Methodist Church in Tonga
*Tetelepta*, Dr Hesina, Protestant Church in the Moluccas (GPM), Indonesia
*Thomas*, Prof. Mary, Malankara Orthodox Syrian Church, India
*Thompson*, Ms Kristine, Presbyterian Church (USA)
*Timotheos*, H.G. Archbishop, Ethiopian Orthodox Church
*Tsetsis*, Very Rev. Dr Georges, Ecumenical Patriarchate of Constantinople,
    Turkey
*Turner*, Rev. Dr Eugene, Presbyterian Church (USA)

*Tveter*, Ms Anne, Church of Norway
*Twagirayesu*, Pasteur Michel, Presbyterian Church of Rwanda
*Vásquez*, Sra Denise, Evangelical Lutheran Church in America
*Viczian*, Rev. Dr Janos, Baptist Union of Hungary
*Walker-Smith*, Rev. Angelique, National Baptist Convention USA Inc.
*Weiss*, Rev. Dr Daniel, American Baptist Churches in the USA
*Welch*, Rev. Elizabeth, United Reformed Church in the UK
*Werkström*, Archbishop Bertil, Church of Sweden
*Wessels*, Rev. Martin, Moravian Church in South Africa
*Westra*, Drs Aukje, Reformed Churches in the Netherlands
*Williams*, Mrs Tungane, Cook Islands Christian Church
*Wolde Eyesus*, Dr Markos, Ethiopian Orthodox Church
*\*Zacharias Mar Theophilos*, Bishop, Mar Thoma Syrian Church of Malabar, India
*Zau Yaw*, Rev. M., Myanmar Baptist Convention
*Zita*, Pasteur Amos, Presbyterian Church of Mozambique

# 7.12. MEMBER CHURCHES, ASSOCIATE MEMBER CHURCHES AND ASSOCIATE COUNCILS

## AFRICA

African Christian Church and Schools [Kenya]†
African Church of the Holy Spirit [Kenya]*
African Israel Church, Nineveh [Kenya]
African Protestant Church [Cameroon]*
Angolan Council of Evangelical Churches**
Baptist Community of Western Zaire
Botswana Christian Council**
Christian Council of Ghana**
Christian Council of Tanzania**
Christian Council of Zambia**
Church of Jesus Christ in Madagascar
Church of Jesus Christ on Earth by the Prophet Simon Kimbangu [Zaire]
Church of the Brethren in Nigeria
Church of the Lord Aladura [Nigeria]
Church of the Province of Burundi, Rwanda and Zaire [Burundi]
Church of the Province of Central Africa [Botswana]
Church of the Province of Kenya
Church of the Province of Nigeria
Church of the Province of Southern Africa [South Africa]
Church of the Province of Tanzania
Church of the Province of the Indian Ocean [Seychelles]
Church of the Province of West Africa [Liberia]
Church of Uganda
Community of Disciples of Christ [Zaire]
Community of Light [Zaire]
Council of Churches in Namibia**
Council of Churches in Sierra Leone**
Council of Swaziland Churches**
Dutch Reformed Mission Church of South Africa

---

† Names and locations of churches are given according to information available to the WCC at the time of publication. The name of the country appears in square brackets where it is not obvious from the name of the church. Geographical references are provided only where they are necessary to identify the church or when they indicate the location of headquarters of churches with regional or world membership. The mention of a country in this list does not imply any political judgment on the part of the WCC.

* Associate member church.                                   **Associate council.

Episcopal Baptist Community [Zaire]
Ethiopian Evangelical Church Mekane Yesus
Ethiopian Orthodox Church
Evangelical Church of Cameroon
Evangelical Church of Gabon
Evangelical Church of the Congo
Evangelical Church of Togo
Evangelical Community [Zaire]
Evangelical Congregational Church in Angola
Evangelical Lutheran Church in Southern Africa [South Africa]
Evangelical Lutheran Church in Tanzania
Evangelical Lutheran Church in Zimbabwe
Evangelical Pentecostal Church of Angola*
Evangelical Presbyterian Church [Ghana]
Evangelical Presbyterian Church in South Africa
Gambia Christian Council**
Lesotho Evangelical Church
Liberian Council of Churches**
Lutheran Church in Liberia
Malagasy Lutheran Church
Mennonite Community [Zaire]
Methodist Church, Ghana
Methodist Church in Kenya
Methodist Church in Zimbabwe
Methodist Church, Nigeria
Methodist Church of Southern Africa [South Africa]
Methodist Church Sierra Leone
Moravian Church in Southern Africa [South Africa]
Moravian Church in Tanzania
Nigerian Baptist Convention
Presbyterian Church in Cameroon
Presbyterian Church in the Sudan
Presbyterian Church of Africa [South Africa]
Presbyterian Church of Cameroon
Presbyterian Church of East Africa [Kenya]
Presbyterian Church of Ghana
Presbyterian Church of Mozambique*
Presbyterian Church of Nigeria
Presbyterian Church of Rwanda
Presbyterian Church of Southern Africa [South Africa]
Presbyterian Community [Zaire]
Presbytery of Liberia*
Protestant Church of Algeria*
Protestant Methodist Church in Benin and Togo [Benin]

Protestant Methodist Church, Ivory Coast
Province of the Episcopal Church of the Sudan
Reformed Church in Zimbabwe
Reformed Church of Equatorial Guinea*
Reformed Presbyterian Church of Southern Africa [South Africa]
Sudan Council of Churches**
The South African Council of Churches**
Union of Baptist Churches of Cameroon
United Church of Zambia
United Congregational Church of Southern Africa [South Africa]
United Evangelical Church of Angola*
Zimbabwe Council of Churches**

## ASIA

Anglican Church of Australia
Anglican-Episcopal Church in Japan
Associated Churches of Christ in New Zealand
Australian Council of Churches**
Bangladesh Baptist Sangha
Baptist Union of New Zealand
Batak Christian Community Church [Indonesia]*
Batak Protestant Christian Church [Indonesia]
Bengal-Orissa-Bihar Baptist Convention [India]*
China Christian Council
Christian Church of Central Sulawesi [Indonesia]
Christian Evangelical Church in Minahasa [Indonesia]
Christian Protestant Angkola Church [Indonesia]*
Christian Protestant Church in Indonesia
Church of Bangladesh*
Church of Ceylon [Sri Lanka]
Church of Christ in China, The Hong Kong Council
Church of Christ in Thailand
Church of North India
Church of Pakistan
Church of South India
Church of the Province of Burma [Myanmar]
Church of the Province of New Zealand
Churches of Christ in Australia
Communion of Churches in Indonesia**
Conference of Churches in Aotearoa-New Zealand**
Council of Churches of Malaysia**
East Java Christian Church
Evangelical Christian Church in Halmahera [Indonesia]

Evangelical Christian Church in Irian Jaya [Indonesia]
Evangelical Church of Sangir Talaud [Indonesia]
Evangelical Methodist Church in the Philippines
Hong Kong Christian Council**
Indonesian Christian Church (GKI)
Indonesian Christian Church (HKI)
Japanese Orthodox Church
Javanese Christian Churches
Kalimantan Evangelical Church [Indonesia]
Karo Batak Protestant Church [Indonesia]
Korean Christian Church in Japan*
Korean Methodist Church
Malankara Orthodox Syrian Church [India]
Maori Council of Churches [New Zealand]**
Mar Thoma Syrian Church of Malabar [India]
Methodist Church in India
Methodist Church in Malaysia
Methodist Church in Singapore*
Methodist Church of New Zealand
Methodist Church [Sri Lanka]
Methodist Church, Upper Burma [Myanmar]
Myanmar Baptist Convention
Myanmar Council of Churches**
National Christian Council in Japan**
National Christian Council of Sri Lanka**
National Council of Churches in India**
National Council of Churches in Korea**
National Council of Churches in the Philippines**
National Council of Churches, Singapore**
Nias Protestant Christian Church [Indonesia]
Pasundan Christian Church [Indonesia]
Philippine Episcopal Church
Philippine Independent Church
Presbyterian Church in Taiwan
Presbyterian Church in the Republic of Korea
Presbyterian Church of Korea
Presbyterian Church of New Zealand
Protestant Christian Church in Bali*
Protestant Church in Indonesia
Protestant Church in Sabah [Malaysia]*
Protestant Church in the Moluccas [Indonesia]
Protestant Evangelical Church in Timor [Indonesia]
Samavesam of Telugu Baptist Churches [India]
Simalungun Protestant Christian Church [Indonesia]

Toraja Church [Indonesia]
United Church of Christ in Japan
United Church of Christ in the Philippines
United Evangelical Lutheran Churches in India
United Presbyterian Church of Pakistan
Uniting Church in Australia

## CARIBBEAN

Church in the Province of the West Indies [Barbados]
Ecumenical Council of Cuba**
Jamaica Council of Churches**
Methodist Church in Cuba*
Methodist Church in the Caribbean and the Americas [Antigua]
Moravian Church, Eastern West Indies Province [Antigua]
Moravian Church in Jamaica
Moravian Church in Suriname
Presbyterian Church in Trinidad
Presbyterian Reformed Church in Cuba*
St Vincent Christian Council**
United Church of Jamaica and Grand Cayman
United Protestant Church [Netherlands Antilles]*

## EUROPE

Action of Churches Together in Scotland**
Armenian Apostolic Church
Autocephalic Orthodox Church in Poland
Baptist Union of Denmark
Baptist Union of Great Britain
Baptist Union of Hungary
Bulgarian Orthodox Church
Catholic Diocese of the Old Catholics in Germany
Church in Wales
Church of England
Church of Greece
Church of Ireland
Church of Norway
Church of Scotland
Church of Sweden
Congregational Union of Scotland
Council of Christian Churches in Germany**

Council of Churches for Britain and Ireland**
Council of Churches in the Netherlands**
Cytun — Churches Together in Wales**
Czechoslovak Ecumenical Council of Churches**
Czechoslovak Hussite Church
Ecumenical Council of Churches in Austria**
Ecumenical Council of Churches in Hungary**
Ecumenical Council of Churches in Yugoslavia**
Ecumenical Council of Denmark**
Ecumenical Council of Finland**
Ecumenical Patriarchate of Constantinople
Estonian Evangelical Lutheran Church
European Continental Province of the Moravian Church — Western District [Bad Boll, Germany]
Evangelical Baptist Union of Italy*
Evangelical Christian Baptist Union of the USSR
Evangelical Church in Germany
    Church of Lippe
    Evangelical Church in Baden
    Evangelical Church in Berlin-Brandenburg
    Evangelical Church in Hesse and Nassau
    Evangelical Church in Württemberg
    Evangelical Church of Bremen
    Evangelical Church of Hesse Electorate-Waldeck
    Evangelical Church of the Palatinate
    Evangelical Church of the Rhineland
    Evangelical Church of Westphalia
    Evangelical Lutheran Church in Bavaria[+]

---

[+] This church is directly a member of the World Council of Churches in accordance with the resolution of the general synod of the United Evangelical Lutheran Church of Germany, dated 27 January 1949, which recommended that the member churches of the United Evangelical Lutheran Church should make the following declaration to the Council of the Evangelical Church in Germany concerning their relation to the World Council of Churches:

"The Evangelical Church in Germany has made it clear through its constitution that it is a federation (Bund) of confessionally determined churches. Moreover, the conditions of membership of the World Council of Churches have been determined at the assembly at Amsterdam. Therefore, this Evangelical Lutheran Church declares concerning its membership in the World Council of Churches:

(a) It is represented in the World Council as a church of the Evangelical Lutheran confession.
(b) Representatives which it sends to the World Council are to be identified as Evangelical Lutherans.
(c) Within the limits of the competence of the Evangelical Church in Germany it is represented in the World Council through the intermediary of the Council of the Evangelical Church in Germany."

Evangelical Lutheran Church in Brunswick[+]
Evangelical Lutheran Church in Oldenburg
Evangelical Lutheran Church of Hanover[+]
Evangelical Lutheran Church of Schaumburg-Lippe[+]
Evangelical Reformed Church in Northwestern Germany
North Elbian Evangelical Lutheran Church[+]
Evangelical Church of Czech Brethren [Czechoslovakia]
Evangelical Church of the Augsburg and Helvetic Confessions [Austria]
Evangelical Church of the Augsburg Confession in Poland
Evangelical Church of the Augsburg Confession in Romania
Evangelical Church of the Augsburg Confession of Alsace and Lorraine [France]
Evangelical Lutheran Church [Netherlands]
Evangelical Lutheran Church of Denmark
Evangelical Lutheran Church of Finland
Evangelical Lutheran Church of France
Evangelical Lutheran Church of Iceland
Evangelical Lutheran Church of Latvia
Evangelical Methodist Church of Italy
Evangelical Presbyterian Church of Portugal*
Evangelical Synodal Presbyterial Church of the Augsburg Confession in Romania
Federation of Evangelical Churches [Germany]
    Evangelical Church of Anhalt
    Evangelical Church of the Görlitz Region
    Evangelical Church of the Province of Saxony
    Evangelical Lutheran Church in Thuringia
    Evangelical Lutheran Church of Mecklenburg
    Evangelical Lutheran Church of Saxony
    Pomeranian Evangelical Church
Georgian Orthodox Church
Greek Evangelical Church
Lusitanian Catholic-Apostolic Evangelical Church [Portugal]*
Lutheran Church in Hungary
Mennonite Church [Germany]
Mennonite Church in the Netherlands
Methodist Church [UK]
Methodist Church in Ireland
Mission Covenant Church of Sweden
Moravian Church [Herrnhut, Germany]
Moravian Church in Great Britain and Ireland
Netherlands Reformed Church
Old Catholic Church of Austria
Old Catholic Church of Switzerland
Old Catholic Church of the Netherlands
Old Catholic Mariavite Church in Poland

Orthodox Church of Czechoslovakia
Orthodox Church of Finland
Polish Catholic Church in Poland
Polish Ecumenical Council**
Presbyterian Church of Wales
Reformed Christian Church in Slovakia [Czechoslovakia]
Reformed Christian Church in Yugoslavia
Reformed Church in Hungary
Reformed Church of Alsace and Lorraine [France]
Reformed Church of France
Reformed Church of Romania
Reformed Churches in the Netherlands
Remonstrant Brotherhood [Netherlands]
Romanian Orthodox Church
Russian Orthodox Church
Scottish Episcopal Church
Serbian Orthodox Church [Yugoslavia]
Silesian Evangelical Church of the Augsburg Confession [Czechoslovakia]
Slovak Evangelical Church of the Augsburg Confession [Czechoslovakia]
Slovak Evangelical Church of the Augsburg Confession in Yugoslavia
Spanish Evangelical Church
Spanish Reformed Episcopal Church*
Swedish Ecumenical Council**
Swiss Protestant Church Federation
Union of Welsh Independents
United Free Church of Scotland
United Protestant Church of Belgium
United Reformed Church in the United Kingdom
Waldensian Church


## LATIN AMERICA

Baptist Association of El Salvador*
Baptist Convention of Nicaragua
Bolivian Evangelical Lutheran Church*
Church of God [Argentina]*
Church of the Disciples of Christ [Argentina]*
Episcopal Church of Brazil
Evangelical Church of Lutheran Confession in Brazil
Evangelical Church of the River Plate [Argentina]
Evangelical Lutheran Church in Chile
Evangelical Methodist Church in Bolivia*

Evangelical Methodist Church in Uruguay*
Evangelical Methodist Church of Argentina
Evangelical Methodist Church of Costa Rica*
Free Pentecostal Mission Church of Chile
Latin American Reformed Church [Brazil]
Methodist Church in Brazil
Methodist Church of Chile*
Methodist Church of Mexico
Methodist Church of Peru*
Moravian Church in Nicaragua
National Council of Christian Churches in Brazil**
Pentecostal Church of Chile
Pentecostal Mission Church [Chile]
Salvadorean Lutheran Synod*
United Evangelical Lutheran Church [Argentina]*
United Presbyterian Church of Brazil*


## MIDDLE EAST

Apostolic Catholic Assyrian Church of the East [Iraq]
Armenian Apostolic Church [Lebanon]
Church of Cyprus
Coptic Orthodox Church [Egypt]
Episcopal Church in Jerusalem and the Middle East
Greek Orthodox Patriarchate of Alexandria and All Africa [Egypt]
Greek Orthodox Patriarchate of Antioch and All the East [Syria]
Greek Orthodox Patriarchate of Jerusalem
National Evangelical Synod of Syria and Lebanon [Lebanon]
Syrian Orthodox Patriarchate of Antioch and All the East
Synod of the Evangelical Church of Iran
Synod of the Nile of the Evangelical Church [Egypt]
Union of the Armenian Evangelical Churches in the Near East [Lebanon]


## NORTH AMERICA

African Methodist Episcopal Church [USA]
African Methodist Episcopal Zion Church [USA]
American Baptist Churches in the USA
Anglican Church of Canada
Canadian Council of Churches**

Canadian Yearly Meeting of the Religious Society of Friends
Christian Church (Disciples of Christ) [Canada]
Christian Church (Disciples of Christ) [USA]
Christian Methodist Episcopal Church [USA]
Church of the Brethren [USA]
Episcopal Church [USA]
Estonian Evangelical Lutheran Church [Canada]
Evangelical Lutheran Church in America
Evangelical Lutheran Church in Canada
Evangelical Lutheran Church of Latvia in Exile [Canada]
Hungarian Reformed Church in America
International Council of Community Churches [USA]
International Evangelical Church [USA]
Moravian Church in America (Northern Province)
Moravian Church in America (Southern Province)
National Baptist Convention of America
National Baptist Convention, USA, Inc.
National Council of the Churches of Christ in the USA**
Orthodox Church in America
Polish National Catholic Church [USA]
Presbyterian Church in Canada
Presbyterian Church (USA)
Progressive National Baptist Convention, Inc. [USA]
Reformed Church in America
Religious Society of Friends: Friends General Conference and Friends United
    Meeting [USA]
United Church of Canada
United Church of Christ [USA]
United Methodist Church [USA]


## PACIFIC

Church of Melanesia [Solomon Islands]
General Assembly, Congregational Christian Church in American Samoa
Congregational Christian Church in Samoa
Cook Islands Christian Church
Evangelical Church in New Caledonia and the Loyalty Isles [New Caledonia]
Evangelical Church of French Polynesia
Evangelical Lutheran Church of Papua New Guinea
Kiribati Protestant Church
Methodist Church in Fiji
Methodist Church in Samoa

Methodist Church in Tonga
National Council of Churches of American Samoa**
Papua New Guinea Council of Churches**
Presbyterian Church of Vanuatu
Tonga National Council of Churches**
Tuvalu Christian Church
United Church in Papua New Guinea and the Solomon Islands

# 7.13. CONSTITUTION AND RULES

## *Constitution*

### I. Basis

The World Council of Churches is a fellowship of churches which confess the Lord Jesus Christ as God and Saviour according to the scriptures and therefore seek to fulfill together their common calling to the glory of the one God, Father, Son and Holy Spirit.

### II. Membership

Those churches shall be eligible for membership in the World Council of Churches which express their agreement with the Basis upon which the Council is founded and satisfy such criteria as the Assembly or the Central Committee may prescribe. Election to membership shall be by a two-thirds vote of the member churches represented at the Assembly, each member church having one vote. Any application for membership between meetings of the Assembly may be considered by the Central Committee; if the application is supported by a two-thirds vote of the members of the Committee present and voting, this action shall be communicated to the churches that are members of the World Council of Churches, and unless objection is received from more than one-third of the member churches within six months the applicant shall be declared elected.

### III. Functions and purposes

The World Council of Churches is constituted for the following functions and purposes:

1) to call the churches to the goal of visible unity in one faith and in one eucharistic fellowship expressed in worship and in common life in Christ, and to advance towards that unity in order that the world may believe;
2) to facilitate the common witness of the churches in each place and in all places;
3) to support the churches in their worldwide missionary and evangelistic task;
4) to express the common concern of the churches in the service of human need, the breaking down of barriers between people, and the promotion of one human family in justice and peace;

5) to foster the renewal of the churches in unity, worship, mission and service;
6) to establish and maintain relations with national councils and regional conferences of churches, world confessional bodies and other ecumenical organizations;
7) to carry on the work of the world movements for Faith and Order and Life and Work and of the International Missionary Council and the World Council on Christian Education.

## IV. Authority

The World Council shall offer counsel and provide opportunity for united action in matters of common interest.

It may take action on behalf of constituent churches only in such matters as one or more of them may commit to it and only on behalf of such churches.

The World Council shall not legislate for the churches; nor shall it act for them in any manner except as indicated above or as may hereafter be specified by the constituent churches.

## V. Organization

The World Council shall discharge its functions through: an Assembly, a Central Committee, an Executive Committee, and other subordinate bodies as may be established.

### 1. The Assembly

a) The Assembly shall be the supreme legislative body governing the World Council and shall ordinarily meet at seven-year intervals.
b) The Assembly shall be composed of official representatives of the member churches, known as delegates, elected by the member churches.
c) The Assembly shall have the following functions:
   1) to elect the President or Presidents of the World Council;
   2) to elect not more than 145 members of the Central Committee from among the delegates which the member churches have elected to the Assembly;
   3) to elect not more than 5 members from among the representatives which the associate member churches have elected to the Assembly;

4) to determine the policies of the World Council and to review programmes undertaken to implement policies previously adopted;

5) to delegate to the Central Committee specific functions, except to amend this Constitution and to allocate the membership of the Central Committee granted by this Constitution to the Assembly exclusively.

## 2. *The Central Committee*

a) The Central Committee shall be responsible for implementing the policies adopted by the Assembly and shall exercise the functions of the Assembly itself delegated to it by the Assembly between its meetings, except its power to amend this Constitution and to allocate or alter the allocation of the membership of the Central Committee.

b) The Central Committee shall be composed of the President or Presidents of the World Council and not more than 150 members.

1) Not more than 145 members shall be elected by the Assembly from among the delegates whom the member churches have elected to the Assembly. Such members shall be distributed among the member churches by the Assembly giving due regard to the size of the churches and confessions represented in the Council, the number of churches of each confession which are members of the Council, reasonable geographical and cultural balance, and adequate representation of the major interests of the Council.

2) Not more than 5 members shall be elected by the Assembly from among the representatives whom the associate member churches have elected to the Assembly.

3) A vacancy in the membership of the Central Committee, occurring between meetings of the Assembly, shall be filled by the Central Committee itself after consultation with the church of which the person previously occupying the position was a member.

c) The Central Committee shall have, in addition to the general powers set out in (a) above, the following powers:

1) to elect its Moderator and Vice-Moderator or Vice-Moderators from among the members of the Central Committee;

2) to elect the Executive Committee from among the members of the Central Committee;

3) to elect committees and boards and to approve the election or appointment of working groups and commissions;

4) within the policies adopted by the Assembly, to approve programmes and determine priorities among them and to review and supervise their execution;

5) to adopt the budget of the World Council and secure its financial support;

6) to elect the General Secretary and to elect or appoint or to make provision for the election or appointment of all members of the staff of the World Council;

7) to plan for the meetings of the Assembly, making provision for the conduct of its business, for worship and study, and for common Christian commitment. The Central Committee shall determine the number of delegates to the Assembly and allocate them among the member churches giving due regard to the size of the churches and confessions represented in the Council; the number of churches of each confession which are members of the Council; reasonable geographical and cultural balance; the desired distribution among church officials, parish ministers and lay persons; among men, women and young people; and participation by persons whose special knowledge and experience will be needed;

8) to delegate specific functions to the Executive Committee or to other bodies or persons.

## 3. Rules

The Assembly or the Central Committee may adopt and amend Rules not inconsistent with this Constitution for the conduct of the business of the World Council.

## 4. By-laws

The Assembly or the Central Committee may adopt and amend By-Laws not inconsistent with this Constitution for the functioning of its committees, boards, working groups and commissions.

## 5. Quorum

A quorum for the conduct of any business by the Assembly or the Central Committee shall be one-half of its membership.

# VI. Other ecumenical Christian organizations

1. Such world confessional bodies and such world ecumenical organizations as may be designated by the Central Committee may be invited to send non-voting representatives to the Assembly and to the Central Committee, in such numbers as the Central Committee shall determine.

2. Such national councils and regional conferences of churches, other Christian councils and missionary councils as may be designated by the Central Committee may be invited to send non-voting representatives to the Assembly and to the Central Committee, in such numbers as the Central Committee shall determine.

# VII. Amendments

The Constitution may be amended by a two-thirds vote of the delegates to the Assembly present and voting, provided that the proposed amendment shall have been reviewed by the Central Committee, and notice of it sent to the member churches not less than six months before the meeting of the Assembly. The Central Committee itself, as well as the member churches, shall have the right to propose such amendment.

## *Rules*

# I. Membership of the Council

Members of the Council are those churches which, having constituted the Council or having been admitted to membership, continue in membership. The term "church" as used in this article includes an association, convention or federation of autonomous churches. A group of churches within a country or region may determine to participate in the World Council of Churches as one church. The General Secretary shall maintain the official list of member churches noting any special arrangement accepted by the Assembly or Central Committee.

The following rules shall pertain to membership.

## *1. Application*

A church which wishes to become a member of the World Council of Churches shall apply in writing to the General Secretary.

## 2. *Processing*

The General Secretary shall submit all such applications to the Central Committee (see Art. II of the Constitution) together with such information as he or she considers necessary to enable the Assembly or the Central Committee to make a decision on the application.

## 3. *Criteria*

In addition to expressing agreement with the Basis upon which the Council is founded (Art. I of the Constitution), an applicant must satisfy the following criteria to be eligible for membership:
a) A church must be able to take the decision to apply for membership without obtaining the permission of any other body or person.
b) A church must produce evidence of sustained independent life and organization.
c) A church must recognize the essential interdependence of the churches, particularly those of the same confession, and must practise constructive ecumenical relations with other churches within its country or region.
d) A church must ordinarily have at least 25,000 members.

## 4. *Associate membership*

A church which would be denied membership solely under Rule I.3(d) but which is otherwise eligible may be elected to associate membership in the same manner as member churches are elected. A church applying for associate membership must ordinarily have at least 10,000 members. An associate member church may participate in all activities of the Council; its representatives to the Assembly shall have the right to speak but not to vote. Associate member churches shall be listed separately on the official list maintained by the General Secretary.

## 5. *Consultation*

Before admitting a church to membership or associate membership, the appropriate world confessional body or bodies and national council or regional conference of churches shall be consulted.

## 6. *Resignation*

A church which desires to resign its membership in the Council can do so at any time. A church which has resigned but desires to rejoin the Council must again apply for membership.

## II. Responsibilities of membership

Membership in the World Council of Churches signifies faithfulness to the Basis of the Council, fellowship in the Council, participation in the life and work of the Council and commitment to the ecumenical movement as integral to the mission of the church. Churches which are members of the World Council of Churches are expected to:

1) appoint delegates to the WCC Assembly, the major policy-making body of the Council, and participate in council with other member churches in shaping the ecumenical vision and the ecumenical agenda and to assume responsibility for the costs of such representation;

2) inform the WCC of their primary concerns, priorities, activities and constructive criticisms as they may relate to WCC programmes as well as any matters which they feel need expression of ecumenical solidarity or which merit the attention of the WCC and/or churches around the world;

3) communicate the meaning of ecumenical commitment, to foster and encourage ecumenical relations and action at all levels of their church life and to pursue ecumenical fellowship locally, nationally, regionally and internationally;

4) interpret both the broader ecumenical movement and the WCC, its nature, purpose and programmes throughout their membership as a normal part of their own reporting to their constituency;

5) encourage participation in WCC programmes, activities and meetings, including:

   a) to propose persons who could make a particular contribution to and/or participate in the various committees of the WCC, meetings and consultations, WCC programmes and publications and staff;

   b) to establish links between their own programme offices and the appropriate WCC programme offices; and

   c) to submit materials for and to promote WCC communications resources: books, periodicals and other publications;

6) respond to decisions of the Central Committee which call for study, action or other follow-up by the member churches as well as respond to requests on matters referred by the Central or Executive Committee or the General Secretary for prayer, advice, information or opinion;

7) make an annual contribution to the general budget and programmes of the WCC commensurate with their resources as part of regular and intentional negotiation with the Council as to responsibilities of membership.

## III. Presidium

1. The Assembly shall elect one or more Presidents but the number of Presidents shall not exceed eight.
2. The term of office of a President shall end at the adjournment of the next Assembly following his or her election.
3. A President who has been elected by the Assembly shall be ineligible for immediate re-election when his or her term of office ends.
4. The President or Presidents shall be ex officio members of the Central Committee and of the Executive Committee.
5. Should a vacancy occur in the Presidium between Assemblies, the Central Committee may elect a President to fill the unexpired term.

## IV. The Assembly

*1. Composition of the assembly*

a) *Persons with the right to speak and to vote*

The Assembly shall be composed of official representatives of the member churches, known as delegates, elected by the member churches, with the right to speak and with the sole rights to vote and to propose and second motions and amendments.

1) The Central Committee shall determine the number of delegates to the Assembly well in advance of its meeting.
2) The Central Committee shall determine the percentage of the delegates, not less than 85 per cent, who shall be both nominated and elected by the member churches. Each member church shall be entitled to a minimum of one delegate. The Central Committee shall allocate the other delegates in this part among the member churches giving due regard to the size of the churches and confessions represented in the Council, and the number of churches of each confession which are members of the Council, and reasonable geographical and cultural balance. The Central Committee shall recommend the proper distribution within delegations among church officials, parish ministers and lay persons; and among men, women and young people. The Central Committee may make provision for the election by the member churches of alternate delegates who shall serve only in place of such delegates who are unable to attend meetings of the Assembly.

3) The remaining delegates, not more than 15 per cent, shall be elected by certain member churches upon nomination of the Central Committee as follows:

1. If the Moderator or any Vice-Moderator of the Central Committee is not elected a delegate within the provisions of paragraph 2 above, the Central Committee shall nominate such officer to the member church of which such officer is a member. Paragraphs 5 and 6 below apply to such nominees.

2. The Central Committee shall determine the categories of additional delegates necessary to achieve balance in respect of:
   a) the varied sizes of churches and confessions;
   b) the historical significance, future potential or geographical location and cultural background of particular churches, as well as the special importance of united churches;
   c) the presence of persons whose special knowledge and experience will be necessary to the Assembly;
   d) proportions of women, youth, lay persons and local pastors.

3. The Central Committee shall invite the member churches to propose the names of persons in the categories so determined whom the churches would be willing to elect, if nominated by the Central Committee.

4. The Central Committee shall nominate particular individuals from the list so compiled to the member church of which each individual is a member.

5. If that member church elects the said nominee, he or she shall become an additional delegate of that member church.

6. The member churches shall not elect alternate delegates for such delegates.

Member churches are encouraged to consult regionally in the selection of the delegates described in paragraphs 2 and 3 above, provided that every delegate is elected by the church of which he or she is a member in accordance with its own procedures.

b) *Persons with the right to speak but not to vote*
In addition to the delegates, who alone have the right to vote, the following categories of persons may attend meetings of the Assembly with the right to speak:

1) *Presidents and Officers:* Any President or Presidents of the Council or Moderator or Vice-Moderator or Vice-Moderators of

the Central Committee who have not been elected delegates by their churches.

2) *Members of the retiring Central Committee:* Any members of the retiring Central Committee who have not been elected delegates by their churches.

3) *Representatives of associate member churches:* Each associate member church may elect one representative.

4) *Advisers:* The Central Committee may invite a small number of persons who have a special contribution to make to the deliberations of the Assembly or who have participated in the activities of the World Council. Before an invitation is extended to an adviser who is a member of a member church, that church shall be consulted.

5) *Delegated representatives:* The Central Committee may invite persons officially designated as Delegated Representatives by organizations with which the World Council maintains relationship.

6) *Delegated observers:* The Central Committee may invite persons officially designated as Delegated Observers by non-member churches.

c) *Persons without the right to speak or to vote*
The Central Committee may invite to attend the meetings of the Assembly without the right to speak or to vote:

1) *Observers:* Persons identified with organizations with which the World Council maintains relationship which are not represented by Delegated Representatives or with non-member churches which are not represented by Delegated Observers.

2) *Guests:* Persons named individually.

## 2. Presiding officers and committees

a) At the first business session of the Assembly the Central Committee shall present its proposals for the moderatorship of the Assembly and for the membership of the Business Committee of the Assembly and make any other proposals, including the appointment of other committees, their membership and functions, for the conduct of the business of the Assembly as it sees fit.

b) At the first or second business session, additional nominations for membership of any committee may be made in writing by any six concurring delegates.

c) Election shall be by ballot unless the Assembly shall otherwise determine.


## 3. *Agenda*

The agenda of the Assembly shall be proposed by the Central Committee to the first business session of the Assembly. Any delegate may move to amend the agenda by including an item or items of new business or by proposing any other change, which he or she may have previously proposed to the Central Committee or to the Business Committee after its election. New business or any change may be proposed by the Business Committee under Rule IV.5(b) or by a delegate under Rule XV.7.


## 4. *Nominations Committee of the assembly*

a) At an early session of the Assembly, the Assembly shall elect a Nominations Committee, on which there shall be appropriate confessional, cultural, and geographical representation of the membership of the Assembly and representation of the major interests of the World Council.

b) The Nominations Committee in consultation with the officers of the World Council and the Executive Committee shall make nominations for the following:

   1) the President or Presidents of the World Council of Churches;
   2) not more than 145 members of the Central Committee from among the delegates which the member churches have elected to the Assembly;
   3) not more than 5 members of the Central Committe from among the representatives which the associated member churches have elected to the Assembly;

c) In making nominations, the Nominations Committee shall have regard to the following principles:

   1) the personal qualifications of the individual for the task for which he or she is to be nominated;
   2) fair and adequate confessional representation;
   3) fair and adequate geographical and cultural representation;
   4) fair and adequate representation of the major interests of the World Council.

The Nominations Committee shall satisfy itself as to the general acceptability of the nominations to the churches to which the nominees belong.

Not more than seven persons from any one member church shall be nominated as member of the Central Committee.

The Nominations Committee shall secure adequate representation of lay persons — men, women and young people — so far as the composition of the Assembly makes this possible.

d) The Nominations Committee shall present its nominations to the Assembly. Additional nominations may be made by any six delegates concurring in writing, provided that each such nominee shall be proposed in opposition to a particular nominee of the Nominations Committee.

e) Election shall be by ballot unless the Assembly shall otherwise determine.

### 5. *Business Committee of the assembly*

a) The Business Committee of the Assembly shall consist of the Moderator and Vice-Moderator or Vice-Moderators of the Central Committee, the General Secretary, the Presidents of the Council, the moderators of sections and committees (who may appoint substitutes), and ten delegates who are not members of the outgoing Central Committee, who shall be elected in accordance with Rule IV.2.

b) The Business Committee shall:
1) coordinate the day-to-day business of the Assembly and may make proposals for rearrangement, modification, addition, deletion or substitution of items included on the agenda. Any such proposal shall be presented to the Assembly at the earliest convenient time by a member of the Business Committee with reasons for the proposed change. After opportunity for debate on the proposal, the Moderator shall put the following question to the Assembly: Shall the Assembly approve the proposal of the Business Committee? A majority of the delegates present and voting shall determine the question;
2) consider any item of business or change in the agenda proposed by a delegate under Rule XV.7;
3) determine whether the Assembly sits in general, business or deliberative session as defined in Rule XV;
4) receive information from and review the reports of other committees in order to consider how best the Assembly can act on them.

## 6. *Other committees of the Assembly*

a) Any other committee of the Assembly shall consist of such members and shall have such powers and duties as are proposed by the Central Committee at the first business session or by the Business Committee after its election and accepted by the Assembly.

b) Any such committee shall, unless the Assembly otherwise directs, inform the Business Committee about its work and shall make its report or recommendations to the Assembly.

## V. Central Committee

### 1. *Membership*

a) The Central Committee shall consist of the President or Presidents of the World Council together with not more than 150 members elected by the Assembly (see Constitution, Art. V.2(b)).

b) Any member church, not already represented, may send one representative to the meetings of the Central Committee. Such a representative shall have the right to speak but not to vote.

c) If a regularly elected member of the Central Committee is unable to attend a meeting, the church to which the absent member belongs shall have the right to send a substitute, provided that the substitute is ordinarily resident in the country where the absent member resides. Such a substitute shall have the right to speak and to vote. If a member, or his or her substitute, is absent without excuse for two consecutive meetings, the position shall be declared vacant, and the Central Committee shall fill the vacancy according to the provisions of Article V.2 (b) (3) of the Constitution.

d) Moderators and Vice-Moderators of committees and boards who are not members of the Central Committee may attend meetings of the Central Committee and shall have the right to speak but not to vote.

e) Advisers for the Central Committee may be appointed by the Executive Committee after consultation with the churches of which they are members. They shall have the right to speak but not to vote.

f) Members of the staff of the World Council appointed by the Central Committee as specified under Rule IX.3 shall have the right to attend the sessions of the Central Committee unless on any occasion the Central Committee shall otherwise determine. When present they shall have the right to speak but not to vote.

g) The newly elected Central Committee shall be convened by the General Secretary during or immediately after the meeting of the Assembly.

## 2. Officers

a) The Central Committee shall elect from among its members a Moderator and a Vice-Moderator or Vice-Moderators to serve for such periods as it shall determine.

b) The General Secretary of the World Council of Churches shall be ex officio secretary of the Central Committee.

## 3. Nominations Committee of the Central Committee

a) The Central Committee shall elect a Nominations Committee which shall:

1) nominate persons from among the members of the Central Committee for the offices of Moderator and Vice-Moderator or Vice-Moderators of the Central Committee;

2) nominate a person for the office of President to fill the unexpired term should a vacancy occur in the Presidium between Assemblies;

3) nominate members of the Executive Committee of the Central Committee;

4) nominate members of committees and boards and where appropriate their Moderators;

5) make recommendations regarding the approval of the election of members of commissions and working groups;

6) make recommendations regarding the election of persons proposed for staff positions under Rule IX.3.

In making nominations as provided for by (1) to (4) above the Nominations Committee of the Central Committee shall have regard to principles set out in Rule IV.4. (c) and, in applying principles 2, 3 and 4 to the nomination of members of committees and boards, shall consider the representative character of the combined membership of all such committees. Any member of the Central Committee may make additional nominations, provided that each such nominee shall be proposed in opposition to a particular nominee of the Nominations Committee.

b) Election shall be by ballot unless the Committee shall otherwise determine.

## 4. Meetings

a) The Central Committee shall ordinarily meet once every year. The Executive Committee may call an extraordinary meeting of the Central Committee whenever it deems such a meeting desirable and shall do so upon the request in writing of one-third or more of the members of the Central Committee.

b) The General Secretary shall take all possible steps to ensure that there be adequate representation present from each of the main confessions and from the main geographical areas of the membership of the World Council of Churches and of the major interests of the World Council.

c) The Central Committee shall determine the date and place of its own meetings and of the meetings of the Assembly.

## 5. Functions

In exercising the powers set forth in the Constitution the Central Committee shall have the following specific functions:

a) In the conduct of its business, the Central Committee shall elect the following committeees:
   1) Finance Committee (a standing committee);
   2) Nominations Committee (appointed at each meeting);
   3) Reference Committee or Committees (appointed as needed at each meeting to advise the Central Committee on any other questions arising which call for special consideration or action by the Central Committee, except that recommendations from committees of the programme units may be considered by the Central Committee without prior consideration by a Reference Committee).

b) It shall adopt the budget of the Council.

c) It shall deal with matters referred to it by member churches.

d) It shall organize programme units and specialized units and regional offices or representations as may be necessary to carry out the work of the World Council of Churches. It shall elect a committee for each programme unit, a board for each specialized unit, and approve the election or appointment of a commission or a working group for each sub-unit of the programme units and receive reports from them at each of its meetings. It shall determine the general policy to be followed in the work of each programme unit, each specialized unit, and the Department of Finance and Central Services.

e) It shall report to the Assembly the actions it has taken during its period of office and shall not be discharged until its report has been received.

## VI. Executive Committee

### 1. Membership

a) The Executive Committee shall consist of the President or Presidents of the World Council, the Moderator and Vice-Moderator or Vice-Moderators of the Central Committee and the Moderator of the Finance Committee, all ex officio, and not more than 16 nor less than 14 other members of the Central Committee.

b) If a member of the Executive Committee is unable to attend, he/she has the right — provided that the Moderator agrees — to send a member of the Central Committee as a substitute. Such a substitute shall — as far as possible — be of the same region and church family, and shall have the right to speak and to vote.

c) The Moderator of the Central Committee shall also be the Moderator of the Executive Committee.

d) The General Secretary of the World Council of Churches shall be ex officio the secretary of the Executive Committee.

e) The officers may invite other persons to attend a meeting of the Executive Committee for consultation, always having in mind the need for preserving a due balance of the confessions and of the geographical areas and cultural backgrounds, and of the major interests of the World Council.

### 2. Functions

a) The Executive Committee shall be accountable to the Central Committee, and shall present to the Central Committee at its next meeting a report of its work for approval. The Central Committee shall consider such a report and take such action in regard to it as it thinks fit.

b) Between meetings of the Central Committee, the Executive Committee shall carry out decisions of the Central Committee and implement policies adopted by it. The Executive Committee shall not make decisions on policy except in those matters specifically delegated to the Executive Committee by the Central Committee and in circumstances of special emergency when it may take provisional decisions. The Executive Committee's power to make public statements is limited and defined in Rule X.5.

c) The Central Committee may by specific action provide for the election of staff to those positions specified in Rule IX.3 by the Executive Committee which should report these actions to the next meeting of the Central Committee.

d) The Executive Committee shall supervise the operation of the budget and may, if necessary, impose limitations on expenditures.

3. *Elections*

a) The Central Committee shall elect an Executive Committee at its first meeting after the Assembly.

b) At its first meeting after the Assembly, the Central Committee shall also make a schedule for rotation of all non- ex officio members of the Executive Committee. This rotation shall be made in such a way that no rotation takes place before two years after an Assembly and in the two years before the next Assembly.

c) Outgoing members of the Executive are not eligible for reelection till after the next Assembly.

d) The Central Committee may elect already at its first meeting successors for outgoing members of the Executive Committee.

e) Vacancies on the Executive Committee shall be filled by the next meeting of the Central Committee.

## VII. Programme units, specialized units and departments

1. There shall be three programme units:
— Programme Unit I: Faith and Witness
— Programme Unit II: Justice and Service
— Programme Unit III: Education and Renewal

The Central Committee shall determine the size and composition of the committee for each programme unit (so that at least two-thirds of the members of each programme unit committee are also members of the Central Committee) and elect the members of each committee and its Moderator. Each committee shall propose, for consideration by the Central Committee, by-laws for the conduct of the work of the programme unit, including a statement of the aim and functions of the unit, a description of the sub-units into which the unit will be divided, if any, and the allocation of functions among them, provision for a working group or commission related to each sub-unit, and such other materials as it deems desirable.

2. There shall be two specialized units:
a) Library;
b) Ecumenical Institute, including its Graduate School.

The Central Committee shall determine the size and composition of the board for each specialized unit and elect the members of each board. Each board may propose for consideration by the Central Committee by-laws for the conduct of the work of the specialized unit.

3. There shall be a Department of Finance and Central Services and a Department of Communication. The Central Committee shall determine the size and composition of the committee for the Department of Communication and shall elect the members of it.

## VIII. Finance Committee of Central Committee

1. The Finance Committee of the Central Committee shall consist of not less than nine members, including:

a) a Moderator, who shall be a member of the Executive Committee;

b) five members, who shall be members of the Central Committee, two of whom shall also be members of the Executive Committee;

c) three members, one of whom shall be designated by each programme unit committee from the membership of said Committee. Each programme unit committee may designate an alternate who may attend if his or her principal is unable to be present.

2. The Committee shall have the following responsibilities and duties:

a) To present to the Central Committee:

   1) in respect of the expired calendar year, an account of income and expenditure of all operations of the World Council of Churches and the balance sheet of the World Council of Churches at the end of that year and its recommendation, based on review of the report of the auditors, regarding approval and granting of discharge in respect of the accounts of the World Council of Churches for the completed period;

   2) in respect of the current year, a review of all financial operations;

   3) in respect of the succeeding calendar year, a budget covering all activities of the World Council of Churches and its recommendations regarding the approval of that budget in the light of its judgment as to the adequacy of the provisions made for the expenditure involved in the proposed programme of activities and the adequacy of reasonably foreseeable income to finance the budget; and

   4) in respect of the year next following the succeeding calendar year a provisional budget prepared on a similar basis together with recommendations thereon as in (3) above.

b) To consider and make recommendations to the Central Committee on all financial questions concerning the affairs of the World Council of Churches, such as:

   1) the appointment of the auditor or auditors who shall be appointed annually by the Central Committee and shall be eligible for reappointment;

   2) accounting procedures;

   3) investment policy and procedures;

   4) the basis of calculation of contributions from member churches;

   5) procedures and methods of raising funds.

## IX. Staff

1. The Central Committee shall elect or appoint or provide for the election or appointment of persons of special competence to conduct the continuing operations of the World Council. These persons collectively constitute the staff.

2. The General Secretary shall be elected by the Central Committee. He or she is the chief executive officer of the World Council. As such he or she is the head of the staff. When the position of General Secretary becomes vacant, the Executive Committee shall appoint an acting General Secretary.

3.A. In addition to the General Secretary, the Central Committee shall itself elect one or more Deputy General Secretaries, and one or more Assistant General Secretaries and the Directors of programme sub-units, including the Ecumenical Institute and the Department of Communication.

3.B. The Executive Committee shall elect all other staff in grades 6-10 and shall report its actions to the Central Committee.

4. The Staff Executive Group shall consist of the General Secretary, the Deputy General Secretary or Secretaries, the Assistant General Secretary or Secretaries, the Directors of the sub-units, departments and the Ecumenical Institute and other staff members invited by the General Secretary. Care shall be taken that there is confessional, cultural and geographical balance in this group and that women and junior staff members are adequately represented. Additional places shall be available if needed to achieve balance. The possible need for rotation of the members who do not serve ex officio shall be examined at least annually, and in any event following each meeting of the Central Committee. The General Secretary shall be Moderator of the Staff Executive Group; in his or her absence a Deputy General Secretary shall act as Moderator. The Staff Executive Group shall advise the General Secretary on the implementation of policy established by the Central and Executive Committees and may, with his or her approval, establish regular and ad hoc coordinating groups for particular programme activities under the moderatorship of the General Secretary or of a person appointed by him or her.

5. The normal terms of appointment for the General Secretary and for the Deputy and Assistant General Secretaries shall be five years. Unless some other period is stated in the resolution making the appointment, the first term of office for all other staff appointed by the Executive or Central Committee shall normally be four years from the date of the appointment. All appointments shall be reviewed one year before their expiration.

Retirement shall normally be at sixty-five for both men and women or not later than the end of the year in which a staff member reaches the age of sixty-eight.

## X. Public statements

1. In the performance of its functions, the Council through its Assembly or through its Central Committee may publish statements upon any situation or issue with which the Council or its constituent churches may be confronted.

2. While such statements may have great significance and influence as the expression of the judgment or concern of so widely representative a Christian body, yet their authority will consist only in the weight which they carry by their own truth and wisdom, and the publishing of such statements shall not be held to imply that the World Council as such has, or can have, any constitutional authority over the constituent churches or right to speak for them.

3. Any programme unit or sub-unit may recommend statements to the Assembly or to the Central Committee for its consideration and action.

4. A programme unit or sub-unit may publish any statement which has been approved by the Assembly or the Central Committee. When, in the judgment of a programme unit or sub-unit, a statement should be issued before such approval can be obtained, it may do so provided the statement relates to matters within its own field of concern and action, has received the approval of the Moderator of the Central Committee and the General Secretary, and the programme unit or sub-unit makes clear that neither the World Council of Churches nor any of its member churches is committed by the statement.

5. Between meetings of the Central Committee, when in their judgment the situation requires, a statement may be issued, provided that such statements are not contrary to the established policy of the Council, by:
1) the Executive Committee when meeting apart from the sessions of the Central Committee; or
2) the Moderator and Vice-Moderator or Vice-Moderators of the Central Committee and the General Secretary acting together; or
3) the Moderator of the Central Committee or the General Secretary on his or her own authority respectively.

## XI. Associate councils

1. Any national Christian council, national council of churches or national ecumenical council, established for purposes of ecumenical

fellowship and activity, may be recognized by the Central Committee as an associate council, provided:

a) the applicant council, knowing the Basis upon which the World Council is founded, expresses its desire to cooperate with the World Council towards the achievement of one or more of the functions and purposes of this Council; and

b) the member churches of the World Council in the area have been consulted prior to the action.

2. Each associate council:

a) shall be invited to send a delegated representative to the Assembly;

b) may, at the discretion of the Central Committee, be invited to send an adviser to meetings of the Central Committee; and

c) shall be provided with copies of all general communications sent to all member churches of the World Council of Churches.

3. In addition to communicating directly with its member churches, the World Council shall inform each associate council regarding important ecumenical developments and consult it regarding proposed World Council programmes in its country.

## XII. Regional conferences

1. The World Council recognizes regional conferences of churches as essential partners in the ecumenical enterprise.

2. Such regional conferences as may be designated by the Central Committee:

a) shall be invited to send a delegated representative to the Assembly;

b) shall be invited to send an adviser to meetings of the Central Committee; and

c) shall be provided with copies of all general communications sent to all member churches of the World Council of Churches.

3. In addition to communicating directly with its member churches, the World Council shall inform each of these regional conferences regarding important ecumenical developments and consult it regarding proposed World Council programmes in its region.

## XIII. World confessional bodies

Such world confessional bodies as may be designated by the Central Committee shall be invited to send delegated representatives to the Assembly and advisers to meetings of the Central Committee and the World Council will take steps to develop cooperative working relationships with them.

## XIV. Legal provisions

1. The duration of the Council is unlimited.

2. The legal headquarters of the Council shall be at Grand-Saconnex, Geneva, Switzerland. It is registered in Geneva as an association according to Art. 60ff. of the Swiss Civil Code. Regional offices may be organized in different parts of the world by decision of the Central Committee.

3. The World Council of Churches is legally represented by its Executive Committee or by such persons as may be empowered by the Executive Committee to represent it.

4. The World Council shall be legally bound by the joint signatures of two of the following persons: the President or Presidents, the Moderator and Vice-Moderator or Vice-Moderators of the Central Committee, the General Secretary, the Deputy General Secretaries and the Assistant General Secretary. Any two of the above-named persons shall have power to authorize other persons, chosen by them, to act jointly or singly on behalf of the World Council of Churches in fields circumscribed in the power of attorney.

5. The Council shall obtain the means necessary for the pursuance of its work from the contributions of its member churches and from donations or bequests.

6. The Council shall not pursue commercial functions but it shall have the right to act as an agency of interchurch aid and to publish literature in connection with its aims. It is not entitled to distribute any surplus income by way of profit or bonus among its members.

7. Members of the governing bodies of the Council or of the Assembly shall have no personal liability with regard to the obligations or commitments of the Council. The commitments entered upon by the Council are guaranteed solely by its own assets.

## XV. Rules of debate

### 1. Categories of session

The Assembly shall sit either in general session (see Rule XV.4), in business session (see Rule XV.5), or in deliberative session (see Rule XV.6). The Business Committee shall determine the category of session appropriate to the matters to be considered.

## 2. Presiding officers

The presiding officers shall be proposed by the Central Committee at the first business session and by the Business Committee after its election.

a) In general session one of the Presidents or the Moderator of the Central Committee shall preside.

b) In business session the Moderator or a Vice-Moderator of the Central Committee or some other member of the Central Committee shall preside.

c) In deliberative session one of the Presidents, the Moderator or a Vice-Moderator of the Central Committee or a delegate shall preside.

## 3. Formal responsibilities of the Moderator

The Moderator shall announce the opening, suspension or adjournment of the Assembly, and shall announce at the beginning of every session, and at any point where the category changes, that the Assembly is in general or business or deliberative session.

## 4. General session

The Assembly shall sit in general session for ceremonial occasions, public acts of witness and formal addresses. Only matters proposed by the Central Committee or by the Business Committee after its election shall be considered.

## 5. Business session

The Assembly shall sit in business session when any of the following types of business are to be considered: adoption of the agenda presented by the Central Committee, any proposal for change in the agenda, nominations, elections, proposals with reference to the structure, organization, budget or programme of the World Council of Churches, or any other business requiring action by the Assembly, except as provided in paragraphs 4 and 6 of this Rule.

The Rules of Debate applicable to a business session are:

a) *Moderator*

The Moderator shall seek to achieve the orderly and responsible despatch of business. He or she shall seek so far as possible to give fair and reasonable opportunity for differing views to be expressed. He or she shall ensure good order and the observance of the appropriate Rules of Debate and shall seek to ensure relevance and prevent repetition. To those ends the Moderator may request a speaker to move to another point or cease speaking. The Moderator shall grant the right to speak and determine the order of speakers. His or her decision is final in all matters except as to his or her decision on a point of order under paragraph (u) below or his or her announcement as to the sense of the meeting on an issue, under paragraph (l) below or as to the result of voting under paragraphs (n) and (o) below.

b) *Speaking*

Any person desiring to speak shall stand in his or her place and speak only when granted the right to do so by the Moderator. The speaker shall state his or her name and church, and address his or her remarks to the Moderator. A delegate may speak only to propose or second a motion or amendment, to engage in the debate or to state a point of order or procedure, and any other speaker only to engage in debate or to state a point of procedure. Any speaker may give notice of his or her desire to speak to the Moderator, and the Moderator shall have regard to such notice, but the Moderator remains free to grant the right to speak and determine the order of speakers under paragraph (a) of this Rule.

c) *Proposing a motion*

A delegate who desires to propose any motion arising from business on the agenda shall state it orally and, except in the case of a privileged motion or motion under paragraphs (j) or (k) of this Rule, shall furnish a written copy to the Moderator. A delegate who desires to propose an item of new business shall follow the procedure set out in Rule XV.7.

d) *Seconding a motion*

A motion shall not be considered by the Assembly until it is seconded by a delegate. When a motion has been seconded it may not be withdrawn except with the general consent of the delegates present and voting. If general consent is given for withdrawal any delegate may then require the motion to be put in his or her own name.

e) *Debate*

When a motion has been seconded, the debate upon it shall be opened by the delegate who proposed the motion. That delegate may speak for not more than five minutes. That speech shall be followed by a delegate speaking in opposition to the motion who may speak for not more than five minutes. After that the speakers shall alternate as far as the nature of the business allows between those who favour and those who oppose the motion. Each may speak for not more than five minutes. When the debate is closed, the delegate who proposed the motion may reply, but shall speak for not more than three minutes. No other speaker may speak more than once on the motion.

f) *Amendment*

Any delegate may propose an amendment to a motion in the same manner as a motion. Paragraphs (c), (d) and (e) of this Rule shall apply to an amendment as they apply to a motion. The debate on an amendment shall be limited to the amendment. The proposer of the motion shall be given the opportunity to speak in the debate on an amendment. The Moderator shall rule out of order and not receive an amendment which is substantially the negative of the motion being debated.

g) *Amendment to an amendment*

Any delegate may propose an amendment to an amendment in the same manner as an amendment, but the Moderator shall rule out of order and not receive an amendment to an amendment to an amendment. Paragraphs (c), (d), (e) and (f) of this Rule shall apply to an amendment to an amendment as they apply to an amendment.

h) *Debate and voting on amendments*

The debate and vote shall be first upon the amendment to the amendment then upon the amendment, and finally upon the motion. When an amendment to an amendment or an amendment has been voted upon, an additional amendment to the amendment or an amendment may be proposed, but the Moderator shall rule out of order and not receive an amendment to an amendment or an amendment substantially to the same effect as one already voted upon.

i) *Rights of Moderator to take part in a debate*

The Moderator shall not propose a motion or amendment or participate in debate without handing over his or her duties to another presiding officer and shall not, after that, preside again until that matter of business has been decided.

j) *Privileged motions*

Any delegate who has not previously spoken on a motion or amendment may move at any time, but not so as to interrupt a speaker, one of the following privileged motions, which shall take precedence over pending business, and shall have priority in the order listed, the motion with the highest priority being listed first:

1) *To recess or to adjourn*

   If the Assembly decides to recess or adjourn, the matter pending at recess or adjournment shall be taken up when the Assembly reconvenes, unless there is an "order of the day» at that time, in which event the matter pending at recess or adjournment shall be taken up at the conclusion of the "order of the day» or at such time as the Business Committee proposes.

2) *That the question not be put*

   If the Assembly agrees that the question shall not be put, it shall pass to the next business without taking a vote or decision.

3) *To postpone indefinitely*

   When a matter has been postponed indefinitely, it may not be taken up again at the entire meeting of the Assembly, except with the consent of two-thirds of the delegates present and voting.

4) *To postpone to a time specified*

   When a matter is postponed to a time specified, it becomes the "order of the day» for that time and takes precedence over all other business.

5) *To refer to a committee*

   When a matter is referred to a committee, the committee shall report on it during the meeting of the Assembly unless the Assembly itself directs otherwise.

   Once a privileged motion has been seconded, a vote on it shall be taken immediately without debate.

k) *Motion to close debate*

Any delegate may propose a motion to close debate at any time but not so as to interrupt another speaker. If seconded, a vote shall be taken immediately without debate on the following question: Shall debate on the pending motion (or amendment) be closed? If two-thirds of the delegates present and voting agree, a vote shall be taken immediately without further debate on the pending motion (or amendment). After the vote on a pending amendment to an amendment, or on a pending amendment, the debate shall continue on the amendment or on the main motion as the case may be. A further motion to close debate can be made on any business then pending. If a motion to close debate is proposed and seconded on the main motion, before the vote is taken on that motion, the Assembly shall be informed of the names of delegates wishing to speak and any amendments remaining and the Moderator may ask the members of the Assembly for a show of hands of any wishing to speak.

l) *Sense of the meeting*

The Moderator shall seek to understand the sense of the meeting on a pending matter and may announce it without taking a vote. Any delegate may challenge the Moderator's decision on the sense of the meeting, and the Moderator may then either put the matter to the vote under paragraph (n) below or allow further discussion and again announce the sense of the meeting.

m) *Moderator to put question*

The Moderator shall put each matter not otherwise decided to a vote.

n) *Voting — by show of hands*

At the end of a debate, the Moderator shall read the motion or amendment and shall seek to ensure that delegates understand the matter upon which the vote is to be taken. Voting shall ordinarily be by show of hands. The Moderator shall first ask those in favour to vote; then those opposing; then those who abstain from voting. The Moderator shall then announce the result.

o) *Voting — by count or secret written ballot*

If the Moderator is in doubt, or for any other reason decides to do so, or if any delegate demands it, a vote on the matter shall be taken immediately by count on a show of hands or by standing. The Moderator may appoint tellers to count those voting and abstaining. Any delegate may propose that the Assembly vote on any matter by secret written ballot, and if seconded and a majority of the delegates present and voting agree, a secret written ballot shall be taken. The Moderator shall announce the result of any count or secret written ballot.

p) *Results of voting*

A majority of the delegates present and voting shall determine any matter unless a higher proportion is required by the Constitution or these Rules. If the vote results in a tie, the matter shall be regarded as defeated. The number of those abstaining from voting however numerous shall have no effect on the result of the vote.

q) *Voting by Moderator*

Any Moderator entitled to vote may vote in a secret written ballot or any vote by show of hands or standing, or may vote if the vote results in a tie, but in no case shall he or she vote more than once.

r) *Reconsideration*

Any two delegates who previously voted with the majority on any matter which has been voted upon may request the Business Committee to propose to the Assembly that that matter be reconsidered. The Business Committee may agree with or refuse that request, but if they refuse, those delegates may follow the procedure set out in Rule XV.7, except that a matter shall not be reconsidered unless two-thirds of the delegates present and voting concur in the reconsideration.

s) *Dissent and abstention*

Any delegate voting with the minority or abstaining may have his or her name recorded.

t) *Point of order or procedure*

Any delegate may raise a point of order or procedure and may, if necessary, interrupt another delegate to do so. As a point of order, a delegate may only assert that the procedure being followed is not in accordance with these Rules. As a point of procedure, a speaker may only ask for clarification of the pending matter.

u) *Appeal against Moderator's decision*

Any delegate may appeal the decision of the Moderator concerning a point of order, as defined in paragraph (t). If such an appeal is made the Moderator shall put the following question to the Assembly without further debate: Shall the Assembly concur in the decision of the Moderator? A majority of the delegates present and voting shall determine the appeal.

v)  *Time limits*

The Moderator may, at his or her discretion, allow extra time to any speaker if the Moderator believes that injustice may be done to a member through difficulty of language or translation, or for any other reason, or because of the complexity of the matter under debate.

## 6. Deliberative session

The Assembly shall sit in deliberative session when the matters before it are of such a theological or general policy nature that detailed amendment is impracticable. Reports of sections shall be discussed in deliberative session. Any committee or other body reporting may recommend to the Business Committee that its report be considered in deliberative session.

The Rules of Debate applicable to a deliberative session are the same as those for a business session, except that the following additional rules shall apply:

a)  *Motions permitted:*

In addition to privileged motions or the motion to close debate, under paragraphs 5 (j) and (k), the only motion which may be proposed regarding matters to be considered in a deliberative session are:
1)  to approve the substance of the report and commend it to the churches for study and appropriate action;
2)  to refer to the body reporting with instructions to consider whether a new or different emphasis or emphases shall be incorporated in the report;
3)  to instruct the body reporting to provide, in consultation with the Business Committee, for an open hearing on the report before reporting again.

b)  *Matters concerning ecclesiological self-understanding:*

Where a matter being raised is considered by a member to go against the ecclesiological self-understanding of his or her church, he or she may request that it not be put to the vote. The Moderator will in such a case seek the advice of the Business Committee or the Executive Committee in consultation with this member and other members of the same church or confession present at the session. If there is consensus that the matter does in fact go against the ecclesiological self-understanding of the member, the Moderator will announce that the matter be dealt with in deliberative session without vote. The materials and minutes of the discussion will be sent to the churches for their study and comment.

c) *Speaking*

Any person presenting a report may also speak in the debate for purposes of clarification or explanation if the Moderator allows him or her to do so.

## 7. New business or change in the agenda

When any delegate desires to have an item of business included on, or any change in, the agenda and the Central Committee or Business Committee after its election has after consideration not agreed to its acceptance, he or she may inform the Moderator in writing. The Moderator shall at a convenient time read the item of business or proposed change and a member of the Business Committee shall explain the reasons for its refusal. The delegate may then give the reasons for its acceptance. The Moderator shall then without further debate put the following question to the Assembly: Shall the Assembly accept this item of business/proposal? A majority of the delegates present and voting shall determine the question. If the Assembly votes in favour of the acceptance of the item of business or change, the Business Committee shall make proposals as soon as possible for the inclusion of the item of business or for the change, in the agenda.

## 8. Languages

The working languages in use in the World Council of Churches are English, French, German, Russian and Spanish. The General Secretary shall make reasonable effort to provide interpretation from any one of those languages into the others. A speaker may speak in another language only if he or she provides for interpretation into one of the working languages. The General Secretary shall provide all possible assistance to any speaker requiring an interpreter.

## 9. Suspension of rules

Any delegate may propose that any Rule of Debate may be suspended. If seconded, the rule shall be suspended only by vote of two-thirds of the delegates present and voting.

### 10. Central Committee

The Central Committee shall sit in business session, unless it decides to sit in general or deliberative session, and shall follow the appropriate Rules of Debate for that category of session as are applied in the Assembly, except insofar as the Central Committee may decide otherwise.

## XVI. Amendments

Amendments to these Rules may be moved at any session of the Assembly or at any session of the Central Committee by any member and may be adopted by a two-thirds majority of those present and voting, except that no alteration in Rules I, V and XVI shall come into effect until it has been confirmed by the Assembly. Notice of a proposal to make any such amendment shall be given in writing at least twenty-four hours before the session of the Assembly or Central Committee at which it is to be moved.

# Acknowledgments

The WCC wishes to thank all those who have contributed to the planning and organization of the seventh assembly, for their time, services, cooperation, gifts and financial support:
— the member churches for their financial contributions;
— the Australian churches for their welcome and gifts;
— Aboriginal people for their welcome, participation and contributions, their paintings, the banners and tote bags;
— the members and volunteers of the Australian National Coordinating Committee and the Canberra Churches Assembly Committee;
— the Australian National University, the conference office, the colleges and halls, the Union, the faculties, the Instructional Resources Unit, the Arts Centre, the Buildings and Grounds and many other staff;
— the University of Canberra;
— the National Convention Centre;
— City Uniting Church, Canberra;
— Canberra Presbytery, Uniting Church;
— Federal Government of Australia;
— Australian Capital Territory government;
— ACTION buses;
— Australia Post;
— Telecom Australia;
— John Coburn, designer of the plenary hall backdrop;
— Allan Spira, architect and designer;
— architecture students at the University of Canberra;
— Margaret Gambold and Susan Daily, assembly banners;
— Penelope Donovan, graphic designer;
— Tom Hewitt, exhibition designer;
— Ansett Airlines of Australia;
— Apple Computer Australia Pty Ltd;

— Austrade;
— Banksia Information Technology (Australia) Pty Ltd;
— Bible Society of Australia;
— Blue Chip Electronics Pty Ltd;
— British Airways;
— Canon of Australia;
— Canweb Printing Pty Ltd;
— Coles New World;
— Conference Solutions;
— Copy-Qik;
— Kawai;
— Link Communications;
— Microsoft Pty Ltd;
— MTS Travel Service, USA;
— Netcom (Australia);
— Pirie Printers;
— Qantas Airways Ltd;
— Raptim Travel Agency, Geneva;
— Sanitarium Health Foods;
— Stewardship of Australia;
— Stewart Barlen Pty Ltd, hire services, especially for the worship tent;
— Toshiba (Australia) Pty Ltd;
— United Airlines;
— Wang (Australia).

# *Index*